A Social History of the Media
Fourth Edition

A Social History of the Media

From Gutenberg to Facebook

Fourth Edition

Asa Briggs and Peter Burke
with Espen Ytreberg

polity

First published in 2001 by Polity Press
This edition published in 2020 by Polity Press

Polity Press
65 Bridge Street
Cambridge CB2 1UR, UK

Polity Press
101 Station Landing
Suite 300
Medford, MA 02155, USA

ISBN-13: 978-1-5095-3371-8
ISBN-13: 978-1-5095-3372-5(pb)

A catalogue record for this book is available from the British Library.

Library of Congress Cataloging-in-Publication Data
Names: Briggs, Asa, 1921-2016, author. | Burke, Peter, 1937- author. |
    Ytreberg, Espen, 1964- author.
Title: A social history of the media : from Gutenberg to Facebook / Asa
    Briggs, Peter Burke, Espen Ytreberg.
Description: Fourth edition. | Medford : Polity, 2020. | Includes
    bibliographical references and index. | Summary: "The classic text for
    historians and media scholars, updated throughout and with a new chapter
    on social media and big data"– Provided by publisher.
Identifiers: LCCN 2019040330 (print) | LCCN 2019040331 (ebook) | ISBN
    9781509533718 (hardback) | ISBN 9781509533725 (paperback) | ISBN
    9781509533749 (epub)
Subjects: LCSH: Mass media–History. | Mass media–Social aspects. | Mass
    media–Economic aspects.
Classification: LCC P90 .B695 2020 (print) | LCC P90 (ebook) | DDC
    302.2309–dc23
LC record available at https://lccn.loc.gov/2019040330
LC ebook record available at https://lccn.loc.gov/2019040331

Typeset in 9.5/13 Swift Light by
Servis Filmsetting Limited, Stockport, Cheshire
Printed and bound in Great Britain by TJ International Limited

The publisher has used its best endeavours to ensure that the URLs for external websites referred to in this book are correct and active at the time of going to press. However, the publisher has no responsibility for the websites and can make no guarantee that a site will remain live or that the content is or will remain appropriate.

Every effort has been made to trace all copyright holders, but if any have been overlooked the publisher will be pleased to include any necessary credits in any subsequent reprint or edition.

For further information on Polity, visit our website:
politybooks.com

Contents

Illustrations

Preface to the Fourth Edition

The aim of this book – on a vast and ever-expanding theme – has been to show the relevance of the past to the present by bringing history into media studies and the media into history. Our own choice of medium reflects a qualified optimism in the future of the book, which we believe will continue to exist alongside newer forms of communication as manuscripts did in the age of print. There will, however, be a new division of labour between media, which is already apparent.

So far as our own division of labour is concerned, in earlier editions, Peter Burke was primarily responsible for Chapters 1–3, Asa Briggs for Chapters 5–8, and the two authors, converging in Chapter 4, joined forces both to write and to revise the text, meeting regularly in different locales, from King's Cross Station to Claridge's, as well as keeping in touch by telephone. Historians of the twenty-first century may like to note that the text was originally written partly in longhand and partly on a personal computer by two academics whose resistance to driving cars and using email is in no way incompatible with an interest in technological and social change in the present and the future as well as in the past.

We should like to thank Amleto Lorenzini for first yoking us together in a project on the history of communication, and John Thompson for commissioning the volume. We are indebted to Pat Spencer for her help in getting the first three editions into the hands of the printers, while Peter Burke is grateful to Joad Raymond for his comments on a draft of Chapter 3.

There are significant differences between all editions of this book. This fourth edition, revised after the death of the senior author, Asa Briggs, replaces his Chapter 8 with a major new chapter on twenty-first-century media developments by Espen Ytreberg, who has also comprehensively revised the introduction together with Peter Burke. Subheadings have been introduced to make this a more reader-friendly volume and the chronology has been updated. The ever-expanding bibliography has been replaced by recommendations for further reading, while Asa's chapters have been reduced in length. We hope that our craft is now ready to sail or fly into the third decade of the twenty-first century.

1

Introduction

Although the phrase 'the media' only came into use in English in the
1920s, a concern with the means of communication is very much older.
Rhetoric, the art of oral and written communication, was taken very seriously in ancient Greece and Rome. It was studied in the Middle Ages and
the Renaissance and it was still taken seriously in the eighteenth and nineteenth centuries.

The concept 'public opinion' appeared in the late eighteenth century,
together with the idea of political 'propaganda', which emerged during the
French Revolution. A concern with the so-called 'masses' can be traced from
the early nineteenth century onwards, at a time when daily newspapers
were helping to shape national consciousness by making people aware of
their fellow readers, viewing the same items of news at more or less the
same moment.

Journalism became an academic subject early in the twentieth century. The first school of journalism in the USA was founded in 1908,
at the University of Missouri, and the first in Germany (the Institut für
Zeitungswissenschaften) was founded in Leipzig in 1915. With the rise
of radio and television, universities established departments of communication (or communications). For example, the Annenberg School of
Communications (now 'Communication' in the singular) was established
at the University of Pennsylvania in 1958.

More recently, some ambitious theorists, from the French anthropologist Claude Lévi-Strauss (1908–2009) to the German sociologist Niklas
Luhmann (1927–98), have extended the concept of 'communication' still
more widely. Lévi-Strauss wrote about the exchange of goods and women,
Luhmann about power, money and love as so many 'media of communication'. Readers may already be asking themselves, what does *not* count as
communication? This history will deal primarily with the spread of information, ideas and forms of entertainment in words and images by means
of speech, travel, writing, music, print, telegraphy and telephony, radio,
television and, most recently, digital, social, mobile and locative media (a

term that we shall be using in the plural to refer to these different means of communication).

This introductory chapter first introduces the deeper history of communication preceding these media, before discussing orality, literacy and secondary orality as an overarching set of concepts for synthesizing communication history. It then explains how a wider definition of the medium concept has been used in more recent media-historical work. This chapter contains an up-to-date review of theoretical work on media history, while later chapters concentrate chronologically on the real-historical developments of media in society.

Communication in History, History in Communication

Significantly, it was in the age of radio that scholars began to recognize the importance of oral communication in ancient Greece and in the European Middle Ages, as well as in Africa and elsewhere. The First World War and the rise of communism and fascism encouraged the study of propaganda, neatly defined by the American journalist Walter Lippmann (1889–1974) as 'the manufacture of consent'. A classic study by another American, the political scientist Harold Lasswell (1902–78) bore the title *Propaganda Techniques in the World War* (1927), while another classic, by the Austrian Edward Bernays (1891–1995), was called simply *Propaganda* (1928). After the Second World War, members of the so-called Frankfurt School, notably Max Horkheimer (1895–1973), Theodor Adorno (1903–69) and Leo Lowenthal (1900–93), developed a 'critical theory' of what they called 'mass culture' or the 'culture industry'. The beginning of the television age in the 1950s brought in visual communication as well, and also stimulated the rise of interdisciplinary theories of the media.

Contributions were made from economics, history, literature, art, political science, psychology, sociology and anthropology, and led to the emergence of academic departments of communication and cultural studies. Striking phrases encapsulating new ideas were coined by Harold Innis (1894–1952), who wrote of the 'bias of communication'; by Marshall McLuhan (1911–80), who spoke of the 'global village'; by Jack Goody (1919–2015), who traced the 'domestication of the savage mind'; and by Jürgen Habermas (1929–), the German sociologist, once associated with the Frankfurt School, who identified the 'public sphere', a zone for 'discourse' in which ideas are explored and views expressed. This book argues that, whatever the starting-point, it is necessary for people working in communication and cultural studies – a still growing number – to take history seriously, as well as for historians

– whatever their period and preoccupations – to take serious account of communication, including both communication theory and communications technology.

Some phenomena in the media are older than is generally recognized, as two examples may suggest. Today's television serials follow the model of radio serials, which in turn follow the model of the stories serialized in nineteenth-century magazines (novelists from Dickens to Dostoevsky originally published their work in this way). Again, some of the conventions of twentieth-century popular culture draw directly or indirectly on an even longer visual tradition. St Mark, in the painting by Jacopo Tintoretto (1518–94) known as *St Mark Rescuing a Slave*, is presented diving head first from Heaven to rescue a Christian captive, much like Superman saving the day in comics four hundred years later (Figure 1a/b).

Denunciations of new media follow a similar pattern, whether the object of these denunciations is television or the Internet, and they take us back to debates about the unfortunate effects of romances on their readers and of plays on their audiences as early as the sixteenth century: their authors were accused of stimulating the passions. San Carlo Borromeo (1538–84), archbishop of Milan, described plays as the 'liturgy of the devil'. The first chapter of Jerry Mander's *Four Arguments for the Elimination of Television* (1977) was entitled 'The Belly of the Beast'. In the period marked by digitalization, there have been calls for 'digital detox', implying that there is something toxic about digital media. The role of the press, and of the journalists who earn their living from it, has always been controversial: the unreliability of the 'gazetteers' was already a commonplace in the seventeenth century. The charge of 'muck-raking' is also an old one.

Despite all such continuities, this book will concentrate on changes in the media; in presenting them, an attempt will be made to avoid two dangers – that of asserting that everything has got worse and that of assuming that there has been continuous improvement. Either way, the implication that trends have moved in a single direction must be rejected, although writers trusting in it have often been eloquent and distinguished in their own fields. Thus, the Italian historian Carlo Cipolla, in his study *Literacy and Development in the West* (1969), stressed the contribution of literacy to industrialization and more generally to 'progress' and to 'civilization', suggesting that 'widespread literacy meant . . . a more rational and more receptive approach to life'.

In this respect, Cipolla's work is representative of a mid-twentieth-century faith in 'modernization', a faith that underlay the literacy campaigns organized by UNESCO and by the governments of developing countries such as

Fig. 1a Tintoretto, *St Mark Rescuing a Slave*, 1548.

4

Fig. 1b Superman.

Cuba as well as books such as Daniel Lerner's *The Passing of Traditional Society* (1958), a now dated study of the modernization of the Middle East that paid particular attention to what the author called 'media participation'. We should remember, though, that the term 'modern' (coined, paradoxically enough, in the Middle Ages), has many meanings and a long history.

The problems raised by this kind of approach demand discussion. That is just as much true of the Internet, which has been surrounded both by high hopes of 'democratization' and strong fears about surveillance, distortions of fact and the fragmentation of publics. It is not possible at this point in the Internet's history to conclude whether the widening of access and its transformation 'from below' or surveillance and manipulation from above will be the stronger tendency. Still, the combination of media saturation, speed of distribution and complexity of actors in the time of the Internet makes debates about media as pressing and demanding as in any previous period in media history.

A relatively short history like this must be extremely selective and must privilege certain themes, like the role of the public sphere, the supply and diffusion of information, the growth of communications infrastructures and networks, and the rise of mediated entertainment. It must also concentrate on change rather than continuity, although readers will be reminded from time to time that, as new media were introduced, older ones were not abandoned but coexisted and interacted with the new arrivals. Manuscripts remained important in the age of print, as books and radio did in the age of television. This book holds that media need to be viewed in a wider sense, as presenting a set of relationships that are in perpetual change, including technological change.

What follows is essentially a social and cultural history with the politics, the economics and – not least – the technology put in. It resists technological determinism, the notion that technology acts one-sidedly as a cause of effects in society. We call the book 'a' social history of the media, not 'the' history, because we believe that there is no single correct way to write about the past, which, like the present, has been regarded and will continue to be regarded from different points of view. It is a 'social' history in the sense of attempting to place the media in the context of society as a whole. The media shape society, but society also shapes the media.

We were influenced at the outset by the simple but deservedly famous classic formula of Harold Lasswell, describing communication in terms of who says what to whom in which channel and with what effect. It is, however, necessary to extend Lasswell's formula to include the intentions of the sender (For What Purpose?); the style or rhetoric of communication, which is part of the message (How?); the moment that the message was sent (When?); and the place or places where it was received (Where?). The responses of different groups of people to what they hear, view or read always demand study – and have been studied, as in the classic case of the late twentieth-century US soap opera *Dallas*, which was a global success but was viewed in very different ways in different parts of the world. How big the different groups are – and whether they constitute a 'mass' – is also relevant. The language of the masses emerged in the course of the nineteenth century and reminds us to consider Lasswell's 'whom' in terms of 'how many?'

The immediate intentions, strategies and tactics of communicators need at every point in the story to be related to the context in which they are operating – along with the messages that they are communicating. The long-term effects, especially the unintended and sometimes surprising consequences of the use of one means of communication rather than another, are more difficult to separate, even with the gift of hindsight. Indeed, whether 'effects' is the right term, implying as it does a one-way cause–effect relationship, is itself a subject of controversy. The words 'network' and 'web' were already in use in the nineteenth century.

Media of Communication before Print

This book concentrates on the modern West, from the late fifteenth century onwards. It also deals with some of the vital relationships between the West and other parts of the world, and highlights certain important developments in the latter, particularly in later periods when global interconnectedness became acute. The book's narrative begins with printing (*c.* AD 1450) rather than with the alphabet (*c.* 2000 BC), with writing (*c.* 5000 BC) or with speech, but despite the importance often attributed to Johann Gutenberg (*c.* 1400–68), whom readers of one British newspaper voted 'man of the millennium' (*Sunday Times*, 28 November 1999), there is no clean break or zero point at which the story begins, and it will sometimes be necessary to refer back briefly to the ancient and medieval worlds.

In those days, communications were not immediate, but already reached to all the corners of the known world. The twentieth-century Canadian Harold Innis was one of several scholars who noted the importance of the media in the ancient world. Trained as an economist, he made his reputation with the so-called 'staple theory' of Canadian development, noting the successive dominance of the trade in furs, fish and paper, and the effects of these cycles on Canadian society. 'Each staple in turn left its stamp, and the shift to new staples invariably produced periods of crisis.' The study of paper led him into the history of journalism, and the study of Canada, where communications mattered profoundly for economic and political development, colonial and postcolonial, drew him to the comparative history of empires and their media of communication, from ancient Assyria and Egypt to the present. In his *Empire and Communications* (1950), Innis argued, for instance, that the Assyrian Empire was a pioneer in the construction of highways: it was claimed that a message could be sent from any point to the centre and an answer received within a week.

As a good economic historian, when he wrote of 'media', Innis meant the materials used for communication, contrasting relatively durable substances such as parchment, clay and stone with relatively ephemeral products such as papyrus and paper. He went on to suggest that the use of the heavier materials, as in the case of Assyria, led to a cultural bias towards time and towards religious organizations, while the lighter ones, which may be moved quickly over long distances, led to a bias towards space and political organizations. Some of Innis's earlier history is weak and some of his concepts are ill-defined, but his ideas, as well as his broad comparative approach, remain a stimulus as well as an inspiration to later workers in the field. It is to be hoped that future historians will analyse the consequences of using plastic and wire, some of them devastating, in the way in which Innis approached stone and papyrus.

Another central concept in Innis's pioneering theory was the idea that each medium of communication tended to create a dangerous monopoly of knowledge. Before he decided to become an economist, Innis thought seriously about becoming a Baptist minister. The economist's interest in competition, in this case competition between media, was linked to the radical Protestant's critique of 'priestcraft'. Thus, Innis argued that the intellectual monopoly of medieval monks, based on parchment, was undermined by paper and print, just as the 'monopoly power over writing' exercised by Egyptian priests in the age of hieroglyphs had been subverted by the Greeks and their alphabet.

In the case of ancient Greece, however, Innis emphasized speech more than the alphabet. 'Greek civilization', he wrote, 'was a reflection of the power of the spoken word.' In this respect, he shared the approach of a Toronto colleague, Eric Havelock (1903–88), whose *Preface to Plato* (1963) focused on the oral culture of the early Greeks. The speeches in the Assembly at Athens and the plays recited in the open-air amphitheatres were important elements of ancient Greek civilization. In this, as in other oral cultures, songs and stories came in fluid rather than fixed forms, and creation was collective in the sense that singers and storytellers continually adopted and adapted themes and phrases from one another. So do scholars today, although plagiarism is denounced and our conceptions of intellectual property require that the source of borrowed material be acknowledged, at least in a footnote.

Clarifying the process of creation, the Harvard professor Milman Parry (1902–35) argued that the Iliad and the Odyssey – although they have survived into our own time only because they were written down – were essentially improvised oral poems, and to test his theory he carried out fieldwork in the 1930s in rural Yugoslavia (as it then was). He recorded performances by narrative poets on a wire recorder (the predecessor of the tape recorder) and went on to analyse the recurrent formulae (set phrases such as 'wine-dark sea') and recurrent themes (such as a council of war or the arming of a warrior), prefabricated elements which enabled the singers to improvise their stories for hours at a time.

In Parry's work, developed by his former assistant Albert Lord in *The Singer of Tales* (1960), Yugoslavia – and, by analogy, Homeric Greece – illustrated the positive aspects of oral cultures which had too often been dismissed – as they sometimes still are – as merely 'illiterate'.

That ancient Greek culture was shaped by the dominance of oral communication is a view which is now widely shared by classical scholars. Yet Alexander the Great (356–323 BC) carried Homer's Iliad with him on his expeditions in a precious casket, while a great library of about half a million rolls was founded in the city named after him, Alexandria. It is no accident that it was in association with this vast library of manuscripts, which allowed information and ideas from different individuals, places and times to be juxtaposed and compared, that a school of critics developed, taking advantage of the library's resources to develop practices which would only spread in the age of print (see p. 29).

Images, especially statues, were another important form of communication, indeed of propaganda, in the ancient world, notably in Rome in the age of Augustus. This Roman official art was to influence the iconography of the early Church: the image of Christ 'in Majesty', for example, was an adaptation of the image of the emperor. For Christians, images were both a means of conveying information and a means of persuasion. As the Greek theologian Basil of Caesarea (*c.* 330–79) put it, 'artists do as much for religion with their pictures as orators do by their eloquence'. In similar fashion, Pope Gregory the Great (*c.* 540–604) described images as doing for those who could not read, the great majority, what writing did for those who could. The tactile aspect of images also deserves to be noted. Kissing a painting or a statue was a common way of expressing devotion, and one still to be seen in the Catholic and Orthodox worlds today.

It was the Byzantine Church which stayed close to ancient models. Christ as Pantocrator ('ruler of all') figured in the mosaics decorating the interior of the domes of Byzantine churches. In a part of Europe where literacy was at its lowest, Byzantine culture was one of painted icons of Christ, the Virgin and the saints. As an eighth-century abbot declared: 'The gospels were written in words, but icons are written in gold.' The term 'iconography' would pass into high culture and later, in the twentieth century, into popular culture, where 'icon' refers to a secular celebrity such as – appropriately enough – Madonna, the pop singer.

Byzantine icons could be seen in homes and streets as well as in churches, where they were displayed on the iconostasis, the doors screening the sanctuary from the laity. There was no such separation in the Roman Catholic churches. In both faiths, symbolism was a feature of religious art and the messages it conveyed, but in Byzantium, unlike the West until the Reformation, teaching through visual culture was sometimes under assault, and images were intermittently attacked as idols and destroyed by iconoclasts (image-smashers), a movement which reached its climax in the year 726.

Islam, an oral culture in which the Koran was transmitted by recitation and higher education, depended on face-to-face communication between masters and disciples, banned the use of the human figure in religious art, as did Judaism, so that mosques and synagogues looked very different from churches. Nonetheless, in Persia from the fourteenth century, human figures, along with birds and animals, were prominent in illuminated manuscripts, which went on to flourish in the Ottoman Empire and Mogul India. They were illustrating history or fable. The most famous Western example of such illustration was in needlework, the Bayeux Tapestry (c. 1100), which vividly depicted the Norman Conquest of England in 1066. A strip 232 feet in length presented a visual narrative which has sometimes been compared to a film in respect of its techniques and effects.

In medieval cathedrals, images carved in wood, stone or bronze and figuring in stained-glass windows formed powerful media of communication. In his novel *Notre Dame de Paris* (1831–2), Victor Hugo portrayed the cathedral and the book as two rival media: 'this will kill that'. In fact, the two coexisted and interacted for a long time, like manuscript and print later. 'To the Middle Ages', according to the French art historian Emile Mâle (1862–1954), 'art was didactic.' People learned from images 'all that it was necessary that they should know – the history of the world from the creation, the dogmas of religion, the examples of the saints, the hierarchy of the virtues, the range of the sciences, arts and crafts: all this was taught them by the windows of the church or by the statues in the porch'.

Ritual was another important medieval medium which remained significant in later contexts. The importance of public rituals in Europe, including the rituals of festival, during the thousand years 500–1500 has been explained (perceptively if inadequately) by the low rate of literacy at that time. What could not be recorded needed to be remembered, and what needed to be remembered had to be presented in a memorable way. Elaborate and dramatic rituals such as the coronation of kings and the homage of kneeling vassals to their seated lords demonstrated to the

Fig. 2 Anon tapestry, *Apocalypse*, fourteenth century.

beholders that an important event had occurred. Transfers of land might be accompanied by gifts of symbolic objects such as a piece of turf or a sword. Ritual, with its strong visual component, was a major form of publicity, as it would be once more in the age of televised events such as the coronation of Queen Elizabeth II. The word 'spectacle', commonly used in the seventeenth century, was revived in the twentieth. (See below, pp. 48–50.)

Nonetheless, medieval Europe, like ancient Greece, has been viewed as an essentially oral culture. Preaching was an important means of spreading information. In the words of a pioneering student of the subject, the Cambridge don H. J. Chaytor, what we now call medieval literature was produced for 'a hearing not a reading public'. In his book *From Script to Print* (1945), Chaytor explained that if the reading room of (say) the British Library were to be filled with medieval readers, 'the buzz of whispering and muttering would be intolerable'. Medieval accounts were 'audited' in the literal sense of someone listening to them being read aloud. So were poems of all kinds, monastic or secular. The Icelandic saga, stretching back into a non-Greco-Roman past, takes its name from the fact that it was read aloud – in other words, spoken or 'said'.

From Orality to Literacy and Secondary Orality

The history of the West roughly from the eleventh century onwards is one of gradual and multifarious movements from orality towards literacy, from speech towards writing. The latter began slowly to be employed for a variety of practical purposes by popes and kings, and a trust in writing – as Michael Clanchy showed in *From Memory to Written Record* (1979) – developed still more slowly. In England in 1101, for example, some people preferred to rely on the word of three bishops rather than on a papal document, which they described contemptuously as 'the skins of wethers blackened with ink'. Nevertheless, despite such examples of resistance, the gradual penetration of writing into everyday life in the later Middle Ages had important consequences, including the replacement of traditional customs by written laws, the rise of forgery, the control of administration by clerks (literate clerics) and, as Brian Stock has pointed out in *The Implications of Literacy* (1972), the emergence of heretics who, in justifying their unorthodox opinions by appealing to biblical texts, threatened what Innis called the 'monopoly' of knowledge of the medieval clergy. For these and other reasons, scholars speak of the rise of written culture in the twelfth and thirteenth centuries.

Manuscripts, including illuminated manuscripts, were being produced in increasing numbers in the two centuries before the invention of printing, a new technology introduced in order to satisfy a rising demand for reading matter. And in the two centuries before printing, visual art was also developing what in retrospect came to be regarded as portraiture. The poet Dante (*c.* 1265–1321) and the artist Giotto (1266–1330) were contemporaries. Both were fascinated by fame, as was Petrarch (1304–74) a generation later, and all three achieved it in their own lifetime. So, too, did Boccaccio (1317–75) and Chaucer (*c.* 1340–1400) in England. The latter wrote a remarkable poem, 'The House of Fame', which, through the images of dream, drew on the treasury of his brain to contemplate what fame meant. Petrarch wrote a 'Letter to Posterity' in which he gave personal details, including of his personal appearance, and proudly proclaimed that 'the glorious will be glorious to all eternity'. In later centuries, fame was rearticulated in print, electronic and digital media as stardom and as celebrity. The acknowledgement of prominent persons would be ever more closely tied to the workings of media, their more secular and shorter-term impacts.

With the spread of manuscripts and later print came a broader cultural movement from orality to literacy, which involved not merely the ability to read, but also, following thinkers like Innis, different forms of knowledge, perhaps even of empire and civilization. The potential for a grand overview of history in this tradition was most daringly exploited by Marshall McLuhan, who became both a celebrity and a key thinker on media and history, although academics have often found him speculative and hyperbolic, not without justification. With Innis, McLuhan spearheaded what came to be known as the Toronto School of media theory (the name, like that of the Frankfurt School, is a reminder of the continuing importance of cities in academic communication). In *The Gutenberg Galaxy* (1962), written in experimental form, McLuhan, following in the wake of his Toronto colleagues Innis and Havelock, asserted the centrality of the media, identifying and tracing their specific characteristics irrespective of the people who use them, the organizational structures within which their providers operate and the purposes for which they are used. Referring back to Parry and Lord, McLuhan claimed that the Western world after Gutenberg was transformed not only by literacy but even more with its articulation by print technology. Nationalism, democracy and capitalism could all be explained with reference to print, according to McLuhan, as could the rationalism, individualism and alienation of 'typographic man'.

To support these claims, McLuhan referred to some basic characteristics of print – that it works on a principle of segmenting information and rebuilding it in systematic and linear sequence. Others have discussed the wider implications of such characteristics in more nuanced ways. The anthropologist Jack Goody discussed the social and psychological consequences of literacy. For example, in his book *The Domestication of the Savage Mind* (1977), he emphasized the reorganization or reclassification of information (a form of decontextualization made possible by writing), on the basis of an analysis of written lists in the ancient Middle East. Drawing on his own fieldwork in West Africa, he noted the tendency of oral cultures to acquire what he called (following the sociologist John Barnes) 'structural amnesia' – in other words, forgetting the past, or, more exactly, remembering the past as if it were like the present. The permanence of written records, on the other hand, acts as an obstacle to this kind of amnesia and so encourages an awareness of the difference between past and present. The oral system is more fluid and flexible, the written system more fixed. More recently, the psychologist David Olson, in *The World on Paper* (1994), used the phrase 'the literate mind' to sum up the changes which the practices of reading and writing have made – so he argues – to the ways in which we think about language, the mind and the world, from the rise of subjectivity to the image of the world as a book.

These claims about the consequences of literacy have been challenged, notably by another British anthropologist, Brian Street. In *Literacy in Theory and Practice* (1984), Street criticized not only the concept of the 'Great Divide' but also what he calls the 'autonomous model' of literacy as 'a neutral technology that can be detached from specific social contexts'. In its place he proposed a model of literacies, in the plural, which focused on the social context of practices such as reading and writing and the active role of the ordinary people who make use of literacy. Taking examples from his fieldwork in Iran in the 1970s, he made a contrast between two literacies: the art of reading taught in the Koranic school and the art of keeping accounts taught in the commercial school in the same village.

A similar point might be made about Turkey, where the country's leader Mustafa Kemal Atatürk (1881–1938) ordered a change from Arabic script to the Western alphabet in 1929, declaring that 'our nation will show with its script and with its mind that its place is with the civilized world'. The change vividly illustrates the symbolic importance of the media of communication. It is also related to the question of memory, since Atatürk wanted to modernize his country and, by changing the script, to cut the younger generation off from access to written tradition. However, in the Koranic schools in Turkey, as in Iran, the traditional Arabic script is still taught.

The exchange between Goody and Street, and the experience of Turkey, where an Islamic government is challenged by spokesmen (and soldiers) citing the example of Atatürk, together with more recent debates on virtual reality, pointing back to Plato, where the word 'reality' is at stake, offer vivid and always pertinent illustrations of the need to move across disciplinary boundaries. For example, psychologists may be able to discuss dreams more profoundly than philosophers. Again, in the course of their fieldwork, anthropologists have more opportunities than historians to investigate social context in depth, watching television in a village in Egypt, for instance, or – like the anthropologist Daniel Miller – studying the uses of the Internet in Trinidad. On the other hand, anthropologists have fewer opportunities than historians for observing changes over the long term.

The latest transformation addressed by thinkers on orality and literacy was that from a print-based culture to an electric one, where moving images came to dominate, and, to a lesser extent, to the later era of computers and digital media. Here the most suggestive formulations came from McLuhan's student, the Jesuit priest and scholar Walter Ong (1912–2003), best known for his *Orality and Literacy* (1982). Ong acknowledged his debt to the Toronto School of media theory. He was more interested in context, however, and in the hidden ways that writing and print would continue to shape communication. It was not, of course, the case that electronic and digital technologies hindered print – quite the opposite, as the spread of e-books and digital newspapers illustrates. Ong's point was that, increasingly, writing was used in the planning stages for communication that mimicked orality. The 'talking heads' of radio and television want to seem informal: they mimic the immediacy and communal qualities of oral, interpersonal communication. Something of an illusion is thus involved in this 'secondary orality', since, according to Ong, it requires that 'we plan our happenings carefully to make sure that they are thoroughly spontaneous'. Related things could be said of blogs and Web-based discussion fora (see pp. 330–1), where interactions have a strong flavour of orality but the templates still amount to an extensive setting-up of the communication that goes on. Also, there is an intricate intermeshing of the oral and literate in that we now do so much of our informal and everyday communication by 'texting' what we want to say.

Ong's sceptical take on the relationship between oral and literate modes in more recent times may reflect an urgency about the consequences of basic shifts in the ways we communicate. Following the development of electrical communication, beginning with the telegraph in the nineteenth century (see p. 155), a sense of imminent as well as immediate change developed. Media debates from the second half of the twentieth century to the early twenty-first have encouraged a re-evaluation both of the invention of printing and of all the other technologies that were treated at their beginning as wonders. That changes in the media have had important social and cultural consequences is generally accepted. It is the nature and scope of these consequences that is more controversial. Are they primarily political or psychological? On the political side, do they favour democracy or dictatorship? The 'age of radio' was not only the age of Roosevelt and Churchill, but also that of Hitler, Mussolini and Stalin. On the psychological side, do reading, listening and viewing encourage empathy with others, or do they encourage withdrawal into a private world? Do television and digital media destroy communities, or create new kinds of community in which spatial proximity matters less?

Again, are the consequences of literacy more or less the same in every society, or do they vary according to the social or cultural context? Is it possible to distinguish cultures of the eye, in which what is seen outweighs what is heard, and cultures of the ear, more attuned to soundscapes? Chronologically, is there a 'Great Divide' between oral and literate cultures, or between societies pre and post-television? How do the steam engine and industrialization relate to this division, or the bits and bytes of the 'information age'?

Media in an Expanded Sense

Above, the difficulty in determining what is and is not communication was emphasized, and the same could be said for the concept of 'medium' and 'media'. At its narrowest, a medium can be defined as the technological means by which a message is communicated. A telephone wire system is the medium for a phone call, for instance, and newspaper print is the medium for an op-ed. The fact that a great many messages are carried in many media brings the further realization that media are interrelated. One medium will routinely work on another, at a given moment and over time. That realization can be expanded to seeing media as environments for communication – for instance, the way social media provide an environment for making acquaintances and friends. All these narrower and wider meanings can be rooted in the concept's rich etymological history, and have been variously activated over time.

Thinking about media as an overall whole, rather than as mere carriers of single messages, became more salient with the rise of media-saturated urban environments. The throng of window designs, posters, newsstands, billboards and advertisements in a place like nineteenth-century Paris suggested thinking about the media more inclusively than in terms of each newspaper on the stand or poster on the wall. The challenge was taken up by thinkers such as the German sociologist and philosopher Georg Simmel (1858–1918) and German Marxist critic Walter Benjamin (1892–1940), whose observations of the distinct experiences of European urban environments served as springboards for their analyses of modernity and capitalism. A further step towards speaking in overarching and inclusive terms of the media came in the twentieth century with the establishment of film and broadcasting. These were grouped together with print as 'mass media', and were thought to have strong, uniform and largely detrimental effects on 'the masses'. Later, further media layers would be added in the form of screens and recorded music whose visual and auditive drone permeates public space and provides an ongoing 'ambient media' addition to the urban experience.

The introduction and spread of digital media have further encouraged a thinking about the media in toto, as something that is significantly more than a means of relay for individual messages. The Internet has been described as an 'über-medium' and digital technology as a standard of conversion that is able to transform all previous media by means of digital code. More and more newspaper content is now available in a digital form, where the text, the images and the newspaper's design are all handled and represented digitally. Also, digital newspapers can approach über-medium status by including living images in the form of clips and streaming, as well as interactive discussion fields and dedicated social media communities. Technologically looser conglomerations also exist, on a grand scale and in the mainstream of culture. The *Star Wars* movie franchise, the Olympics sports events and a major entertainment event like the Eurovision Song Contest all comprise a multifarious cluster of technologically distinct media. Varying degrees of coordination will exist between these brands' media components, as signalled in research that investigates the complexities of what is variously called 'intermedia', 'cross-media', 'trans-media', 'cross-platform' or 'media ecologies'.

In tandem with historical developments towards larger-scale and more complex media environments, theorists have begun to speak of 'the media' as a total entity, and as a distinct force in society. Here, too, McLuhan spearheaded developments for the post-war period, with the famous dictum from his most famous publication from 1964, *Understanding Media*: 'The medium is the message.' This was something of a strategic exaggeration, a rhetorical move to highlight the fact that in post-war Western societies, media constituted an omnipresent and pervasive force. McLuhan included electric light in his definition of a medium: it clearly can and does carry information, yet electric light has no 'message' as such. The notion of media as an environment, something subjects are immersed in, was applied in similar ways to the concept of communication. The cultural historian James W. Carey (1934–2006) was both influenced by, and a perceptive critic of, McLuhan. During the 1970s he turned to the relationship between communication and culture, and in 1988 he published his thoughtful book, *Communication as Culture*. There, he opposed a narrow view of communication as the transmission of messages to a cultural view of communication whose key act is the ritual – an immersive occasion that highlights why the concept of 'communication' has etymological affinities with that of 'communion'.

Later instantiations of what has become known as 'medium theory' emphasized the role of digital technology in making technology a force that not only extends man but in some respects extends beyond man's reach. When the German media theorist Friedrich Kittler introduced his book *Gramophone, Film, Typewriter* with the pronouncement 'Media determine our situation', he was making an argument about media-historical ruptures back to the nineteenth century that was at the same time based on a digital and information-theoretical vocabulary of code and hardware. Writing technologies depended on a writing hand and hence had some kind of direct link to a subject expressing itself, argued Kittler. He pinpointed a watershed in the nineteenth century, with the introduction of electric technologies of analogue recording such as the phonograph and photograph. These replaced the continuously creating hand with a mechanical recording and storing of 'slices of life'. Since the introduction of the computer, digital media have taken over more key functions. Computers not only record and store; they also distribute and even perceive, argued Kittler. For instance, software applications guided by algorithms (so-called 'crawlers') search the net for us by courtesy of Google, and identify and then present for us information, for the most part without our knowing how it happens.

Kittler's position, as polemical as that of McLuhan, has provoked charges of technological determinism. A somewhat less problematic position would be to see digital technology as the prime example of an ever deeper entanglement of technology with the social and with human subjects. These discussions of man's relation to the machine are longstanding in the disciplines of history and social studies, and are often conceptualized as an opposition between structure and socially situated agency. On one side, there are those who claim that there are no consequences of computers as such, any more than there are consequences of literacy (including visual literacy and computer literacy). There are only consequences for individuals using these tools. On the other, there are those – as different from each other as Goody and Kittler – who suggest that using a new medium of communication inevitably changes people's views of the world, in the long term if not earlier. One side accuses the other of treating ordinary people as passive, as objects undergoing the impact of literacy or computerization. The reverse accusation is that of treating the media, including the press, as passive, as mirrors of culture and society rather than as agencies transforming culture and society.

In more recent media-theoretical and media-historical work, a number of concepts have been introduced that stem largely from reflections over digital media, but also have a wider application. One such concept is the 'network', which lexically speaking describes connections between the distributed elements of a system with some complexity. Telegraph lines, terrorist sleeper cells, circuited fire alarms in a building and the nerves in a human body are all examples of networks. This concept has been popularized in language about the social media, and stems from the Internet's architecture of computers connected by the technical standards and protocols that form the Internet Protocol Suite (IPS).

The network concept has also come to be used for characterizing the interconnected elements and protocols of broadcasting, of telephony and of the telegraph. In principle, any system of communication via distributed

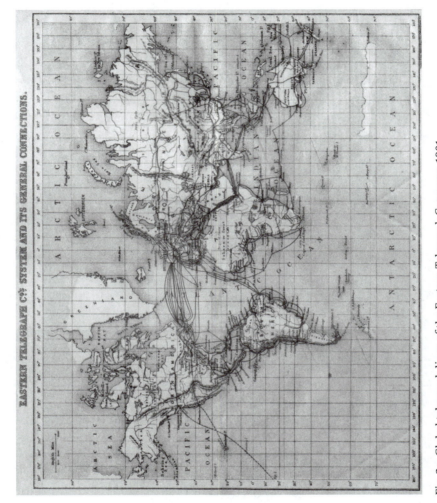

Fig. 3a Global telegraph lines of the Eastern Telegraph Company, 1901.

19

Fig. 3b Network of fibre-optic cables, 2019.

and linked-up elements could be described as a network, all the way back to the chains of fire beacons used for alerts in premodern societies. The 'network society' proposed in the 1990s by the sociologist Manuel Castells (1942–) was dominated by digital networks that enabled simultaneous communication on a global scale. In Castells's account of the 'information age', these media networks, themselves products of an advanced stage in capitalism, enabled similarly networked forms of capitalist organization and production, giving rise to a distinct form of contemporary society.

Somewhat in parallel with the network concept, and sometimes overlapping with it, the concept of infrastructure has risen to prominence in media-theoretical and media-historical research. In an Internet context, infrastructure is typically conceived in terms of material objects – such as fibre-optic cables for data transmission, server storage buildings and (with the mobile Internet) mobile phone towers. This concrete and material meaning is well established and widely used in ordinary language; we speak of roads and waterworks as infrastructure, for instance. A wider definition also comprises the collective work necessary to set up and maintain the Internet's networks, such as hardware and software engineering, and the designing and moderating of content. In this sense, infrastructures are parts of social life and shaped by it, as are networks. The Internet involves not only immaterial communication in the user-friendly and ready-to-hand environments of social media platforms, but also the very real labour of workers setting up and maintaining servers in the cold temperatures required to keep the servers' microchips functioning efficiently.

Infrastructures are a reminder that the apparent placelessness and immateriality of much mediated communication can mislead. Uploading one's files to 'the Cloud' means that information is moved into the care of humans and organizations that are placed in space and time, and act according to protocols that may be as opaque to the uploader as actual clouds are. Infrastructure tends to become invisible to its users, which makes all the more important what the media researchers Lisa Parks and Nicole Starosielski have termed 'critical infrastructure studies', where the power of producers/distributors is emphasized. It is clearly of key importance that the global infrastructure of undersea fibre-optic cables that now connect the Internet in Europe, America and Asia is operated at the time of writing by a commercial company and not an entity that exists to serve the public interest.

A concern with infrastructures of media and communication to some extent leads away from looking at messages (or content, or texts) towards paying greater attention to the material, and to objects and how they are shaped together with subjects and with information. Here, movement and distribution turn out to be key topics, both of which have been explored by historians. Industrialization in the eighteenth and nineteenth centuries would create new infrastructures of communication, both medial and transportational. In 1994, in *The Invention of Communication*, the Belgian sociologist Armand Mattelart (1936–) in effect provided a modern history of media networks and infrastructures before the digital era. He emphasized how the impetus towards change came from the military, from capitalist trade interests, and from a need to make the complex communications of nation-states work more efficiently. Mattelart demonstrated how the communications networks underlying the European nation-states of the seventeenth and eighteenth centuries relied on better roads, bridges and canals – infrastructures that allowed a transport of objects, people and information throughout the nation. The nineteenth century then saw the rise of trains and telegraphs that enabled movement to traverse whole continents. The communications networks that were enabled by these technologies came to be invested with promises of human progress and of bringing the world's peoples together. These networks also effectively put a few countries and urban centres in charge of the networks' standards and protocols, however. It was no accident that in Britain's heyday as a colonial empire, the point of synchronization for a global temporal standard, a 'Greenwich mean time', was located in London.

This temporal standard was an act of control and dominance not only over the globe's cultures, but also over nature. In the widest sense, one might say the media environment is a natural environment. According to the media theorist and historian John Durham Peters, media are 'elemental' in the sense of providing conditions of existence. For him, skies, water and fire are media in the fundamental sense that the existence of humans is sustained by them. Saying this much at the same time means returning the media concept to some of its oldest meanings, which were rooted precisely in the natural world. They still persist, since one may still say today that air is a medium for sound, or that certain nutritious solvents are media for the cultivation of bacteria. Such a very inclusive definition reaches much wider than what is covered in this book. Still, it is worth being aware of what lies beyond: the 'deep' history of the natural world, the precarious future of what is now termed our Anthropocene epoch and also the ways in which these have been, and will be, mediated.

2

Printing in Its Contexts

This chapter and the chapter that follows are concerned with Europe in what historians call the 'early modern' period, running from about 1450 to about 1789 – in other words, from the 'print revolution' to the French and industrial revolutions. The year 1450 is the approximate date for the invention in Europe, probably by Johann Gutenberg of Mainz, of a printing press – perhaps inspired by the wine presses of his native Rhineland – which used movable metal type.

The Spread of Print

In China and Japan, printing had been practised for a long time – from the seventh century, if not before – but the method generally used was what is known as 'block printing', the carved woodblock being used to print a single page of a specific text. This method was appropriate for cultures which used thousands of ideograms rather than an alphabet of 20–30 letters. It was probably for this reason that the Chinese invention of movable type in the eleventh century had few consequences. In the early fifteenth century, however, the Koreans invented a form of movable type with what has been described by the French scholar Henri-Jean Martin (1924–2007) in *The History and Powers of Writing* as 'an almost hallucinatory similarity to Gutenberg's'.

The Western invention may have been stimulated by news of what had happened in the East. What the Irish political scientist Benedict Anderson (1936–2015) called 'print capitalism' certainly existed in East Asia before Gutenberg, especially at the popular level. In China, where full literacy was confined to the elite, ordinary people, including some women, especially in cities, were able to recognize some two thousand ideograms and therefore to understand simple texts (this 'functional literacy', as it is called, may have included 30 per cent of males and 2 per cent of females in the eighteenth century). In order to meet demand from this kind of reader, commercial printers, especially in the province of Fukien, produced songs, stories and simple encyclopaedias, especially from the sixteenth century onwards. Print capitalism took a new form in China in the 1870s, when cylinder presses were introduced to Shanghai from the West. Chinese book production moved from block printing to letterpress in a generation and a half. In Japan, there was an explosion of popular printed matter after 1600, while the eighteenth-century Japanese prints now sought by collectors originated as posters advertising actors, tea-houses, courtesans and even brands of sake.

In Europe, the practice of printing spread via a diaspora of German printers. By 1500, presses had been established in more than 250 places in Europe – 80 of them in Italy, 52 in Germany and 43 in France. Printers had reached Basel by 1466, Rome by 1467, Paris and Pilsen by 1468, Venice by 1469, Leuven, Valencia, Cracow and Buda by 1473, Westminster (distinct from the city of London) by 1476 and Prague by 1477. Between them, these presses produced about 27,000 editions by the year 1500, which means that – assuming an average print run of 500 copies per edition – about thirteen million books were circulating by that date in a Europe of a hundred million people. About two million of these books were produced in Venice alone, while Paris was another important centre of printing, with 181 workshops in 1500.

In contrast, print was slow to penetrate Russia and the Orthodox Christian world more generally, a region (including modern Serbia, Romania and Bulgaria) where the alphabet was usually Cyrillic and literacy was virtually confined to the clergy. In 1564 a White Russian trained in Poland brought a press to Moscow, but his workshop was soon destroyed by a mob. This situation changed in the early eighteenth century, thanks to the efforts of Tsar Peter the Great (ruled 1686–1725), who founded a press at St Petersburg in 1711, followed by the Senate Presses (1719) in Petersburg and Moscow, the Naval Academy Press (1721) and the Academy of Sciences Press (1727). The location of these presses suggests that the Tsar was interested in literacy and education primarily in order to make Russians familiar with modern science and technology, especially military technology. The fact that printing arrived so late in Russia also suggests that print was not an independent agent, and that the print revolution did not depend on technology alone. Printing required favourable social and cultural conditions in order to spread, and Russia's lack of a literate laity was a serious obstacle to the rise of print culture.

In the Muslim world, although block printing of amulets and talismans had been practised for a long time, resistance to print remained strong throughout the early modern period. Indeed, the Muslim countries have been regarded as a barrier to the passage of printing from China to the West. According to an imperial ambassador to Istanbul in the middle of the sixteenth century, the Ottoman Turks thought it a sin to print religious books. In 1515, Sultan Selim I (ruled 1512–20) issued a decree punishing the practice of printing with the death penalty. At the end of the century, Sultan Murad III (ruled 1574–95) allowed the sale of non-religious printed books in Arabic characters, but these were probably imports from Italy. The problem was that print, as British historian Francis Robinson puts it, 'struck right at the heart of person to person transmission of knowledge', which was fundamental in the world of Islam.

Some Europeans were proud of their technical superiority in this respect. Henry Oldenburg (1618–77), the first secretary of the Royal Society of London, and a man professionally concerned with scientific communication, linked the absence of print with despotism, claiming in a letter of 1659:

> Ye Great Turk is an enemy to learning in regard of his subjects, because he finds it his advantage to have such a people on whose ignorance he may impose. Whence it is, that he will endure no printing, being of this opinion, that printing and learning, especially such as is found in universities, are the chief fuel of division among Christians.

The chequered history of printing in the Ottoman Empire reveals the strength of the obstacles to this form of communication, as also to visual representations. The first Turkish press was established only in the eighteenth century, more than 200 years after the first Hebrew press (1494) and more than 150 years after the first Armenian press (1567). A Hungarian convert to Islam (formerly a Protestant clergyman) sent a memorandum to the sultan on the importance of the press, and in 1726 he was given permission to print secular books. However, there was opposition from scribes and religious leaders. The new press printed only a handful of books, and it did not last long. The official Ottoman gazette was not founded until 1831, while the first unofficial newspaper in Turkish (launched by an Englishman) appeared in 1840.

The Effects of Print

The idea that the invention of printing was epoch-making is an old one, whether the new technique was discussed on its own, coupled with the invention of gunpowder, or taken as part of a trio of print, gunpowder and the compass. For the English philosopher Francis Bacon (1561–1626), this was a trio which had 'changed the whole state and face of things throughout the world', although the French essayist Michel de Montaigne (1533–92), writing a generation earlier, had reminded his readers that the Chinese had already enjoyed the benefits of printing for 'a thousand years'. Samuel Hartlib, an East European exile in Britain who supported many schemes of social and cultural reform, wrote in 1641 that 'the art of printing will so spread knowledge that the common people, knowing their own rights and liberties, will not be governed by way of oppression'.

The bicentenary of the invention of printing was celebrated – about ten years too early, according to modern scholars – in 1640 and its tercentenary in 1740, and in the famous outline of world history by the Marquis de Condorcet (1743–94), published in 1795, printing, like writing, was identified as one of the milestones in what the author called 'the progress of the human mind'. The unveiling of the statue of Gutenberg at Mainz in 1837 was accompanied by enthusiastic celebrations. 'Among salvoes of artillery the veil was removed from the statue and a hymn was sung by a thousand voices. Then came orations; then dinners, balls, oratorios, boat races, processions by torchlight . . . Gutenberg! was toasted in many a bumper of Rhenish wine.'

All the same, some commentators wished the new epoch had never arrived. The triumphalist accounts of the new invention were matched by what we might call catastrophist narratives. Scribes, whose business was threatened by the new technology, deplored the arrival of the press from the beginning. For churchmen, the basic problem was that print allowed readers who had a low position in the social and cultural hierarchy to study religious texts for themselves, rather than relying on what the authorities told them. For governments, the consequences of print to which Hartlib referred were no reason for celebration.

The rise of newspapers in the seventeenth century increased anxieties about the effects of print. In England in the 1660s, the chief censor of books, Sir Roger L'Estrange, was still asking the old question 'whether more mischief than advantage were not occasion'd to the Christian world by the invention of typography' (see p. 99). 'O Printing! How thou hast disturbed the peace of Mankind!', wrote the English poet Andrew Marvell (1621–78) in 1672.

Scholars, or more generally anyone in search of knowledge, confronted other problems. The so-called information 'explosion' – a metaphor uncomfortably reminiscent of gunpowder – which followed the invention of printing, called for new methods of information retrieval and information management, just as the Internet does in the twenty-first century. In the early Middle Ages, the problem had been the lack of books, their paucity.

By the sixteenth century, the problem had become one of superfluity. An Italian writer was already complaining in 1550 that there were 'so many books that we do not even have time to read the titles'. Books were a forest in which readers could lose themselves, according to the reformer Jean Calvin (1509–64). They were an ocean in which readers had to navigate, or a flood of printed matter in which it was hard to escape drowning. The problem of 'information overload', as it is now known, goes back a long way. As books multiplied, libraries had to become larger, and as they became larger, it was more difficult to find any given book on the shelves, so catalogues became increasingly necessary. Compilers of catalogues had to decide whether to arrange information by subject or in the alphabetical order of authors, and they had to work hard to keep the catalogues up to date. From the mid-sixteenth century, printed bibliographies offered information about what had been written, but as these compilations increased in size, subject bibliographies were needed. Since so many more books existed than could be read in a lifetime, readers had to be helped to discriminate by means of select bibliographies and, from the later seventeenth century, reviews of new publications in learned journals, but as the numbers of these journals multiplied, it was necessary to look elsewhere for information about them.

The coexistence of triumphalist and catastrophist accounts of printing suggests the need for discrimination in any discussion of its consequences. The Victorian historian Lord Acton (1834–1902) was more precise than his predecessors, emphasizing both what might be called the lateral effects of print – making knowledge accessible to a wider audience – and its vertical or cumulative effects – enabling later generations to build on the intellectual work of earlier ones. Print, according to Acton in his lecture 'On the Study of History' (1895), 'gave assurance that the work of the Renaissance would last, that what was written would be accessible to all, that such an occultation of knowledge and ideas as had depressed the Middle Ages would never recur, that not an idea would be lost'. More recent studies have pointed out that the invention of printing changed the occupational structure of European cities. The printers themselves were a new kind of group, artisans for whom literacy was essential. Proof-correcting was a new occupation, called into existence by print, while a rise in the number of booksellers and librarians naturally followed the explosion in the numbers of books.

More adventurous and more speculative than the historians, Marshall McLuhan emphasized the shift from auditory to visual punctuation, on occasion going so far as to speak of 'the print-made split between head and heart'. Both the strength and the weakness of his approach is summed up in one of the many concepts he did much to launch, that of 'print culture', which suggested links between the new invention and the cultural changes of the period, without always specifying what these links might be. Walter Ong, in *Ramus: Method, and the Decay of Dialogue* (1958) was more cautious, but he too believed in the long-term psychological consequences of print. 'While the invention of printing has been discussed convention-ally in terms of its value for spreading ideas, its even greater contribution is its furthering of the long-developing shift in the relationship between space and discourse.' Ong also emphasized the rise of diagrams and the visual or spatial organization of sixteenth-century academic books with their dichotomized tables of contents, 'which mean everything to the eye and nothing to the ear' because they are impossible to read aloud. The contents of the first edition of Robert Burton's *Anatomy of Melancholy* (1621) were summarized in this way. The same point about information designed for the eye might be made about timetables and astronomical tables (from the sixteenth century onwards) and tables of logarithms (first printed in the seventeenth century).

Such books were too expensive and too technical to appeal to more than a tiny minority of the population, but printed matter also came in cheaper and simpler forms such as 'chapbooks', often illustrated, though the illus-trations were sometimes taken over from earlier books and had little to do with the text. Chapbooks were booklets which were sold by 'chapmen' or pedlars in most parts of early modern Europe, and in some regions in the nineteenth and even twentieth centuries as well. Since the 1960s, histori-ans have been studying French chapbooks – the 'Blue Library' (*Bibliothèque Bleue*), as they are called, referring to the fact that the booklets were bound in the coarse blue paper used for wrapping sugar. The major centre of production was Troyes, in north-east France, but thanks to the pedlar net-work the booklets were widely distributed in the countryside as well as the towns. The most common subjects of these booklets were lives of the saints and romances of chivalry, leading some historians to the conclusion that the literature was escapist, or even a form of tranquillizer, and also that it represented the diffusion downwards to artisans and peasants of cultural models created by and for the clergy and the nobility.

This conclusion is too simple to be accepted without qualification. In the first place, the books were not bought by ordinary people alone. Noblewomen are known to have read them. In the second place, the *Bibliothèque Bleue* did not cover the whole culture of its readers: their oral culture was probably more important for them. Furthermore, we do not know how readers or listeners reacted to the stories; whether, for example, they identified themselves with Charlemagne or with the rebels against him. Nevertheless, despite the problems raised by Blue Library studies, it is clear that in France and other European countries, including Italy, England and the Netherlands, printed matter had become an important part of popular culture by the seventeenth century, if not before.

An Unacknowledged Revolution?

Summing up the work of a generation on the subject, an American historian, Elizabeth Eisenstein, made the claim, in an ambitious study first published in 1979, that printing was 'the unacknowledged revolution' and that its role as an 'agent of change' had been underestimated in traditional accounts of the Renaissance, the Reformation and the scientific revolution. Drawing on the ideas of both McLuhan and Ong, Eisenstein domesticated them by translating them into terms which would be acceptable to her own professional community, that of historians and librarians. While she was cautious in drawing general conclusions, she emphasized two long-term consequences of the invention of printing. In the first place, print standardized and preserved knowledge which had been much more fluid in the age of oral or manuscript circulation. In the second place, the critique of authority was encouraged by print, which made incompatible views of the same subject more widely available.

To illustrate this point, Eisenstein took the example of Montaigne, whose scepticism she linked to his wide reading. 'In explaining why Montaigne perceived greater "conflict and diversity" in the works he consulted than had medieval commentators in an earlier age,' she argued, 'something should be said about the increased number of texts he had at hand.'

Eisenstein's book remains a valuable synthesis, but in the years since its publication the author's claims for revolutionary changes following the invention of printing have come to look somewhat exaggerated. In the first place, the changes she outlined took place in the course of at least three centuries, from Gutenberg's Bible to Diderot's *Encyclopédie* (to be discussed below, see p. 106). Adaptation to the new medium was gradual, therefore, whether in the case of styles of presentation or habits of reading (see p. 68). In other words, as in the case of the industrial revolution – in the eyes of some of its recent historians – what we see is what the British critic Raymond Williams (1921–88) called a 'Long Revolution' (it is an intriguing question, whether a revolution that is not rapid can be regarded as a revolution at all).

A second problem is the problem of agency. To speak of print as the agent of change is surely to place too much emphasis on the medium of communication at the expense of the writers, printers and readers who used the new technology for their own different purposes. It might be more realistic to view print, like new media in later centuries (television, for example), as a catalyst, assisting social changes rather than originating them. In the eighteenth century, the production of trade cards reflected an increase in trade more than the stimulus of ephemeral printing.

A third problem is that Eisenstein viewed print in relative isolation, yet in order to assess the social and cultural consequences of its invention and development, it is necessary to look at the media as a whole, to view all the different means of communication as interdependent, treating them as a package, a repertoire, a system, or what the French call a 'regime', whether authoritarian, democratic, bureaucratic or capitalist. To think in terms of a media system means emphasizing the division of labour between the different means of communication available in a given place and at a given time, without forgetting that different media may compete with or echo one another as well as complement one another.

The system, it must be stressed, was in perpetual change, even if some of the changes became visible only in the perspective of the long term. For example, print technology did not stand still after Gutenberg. The Dutch printer Willem Blaeu (1571–1638) improved the design of the wooden press in the seventeenth century. Large presses were introduced in order to print maps. The Stanhope iron hand press (1804) doubled the normal rate of production, while the German inventor Friedrich Koenig's (1774–1833) steam press (1814) quadrupled the productivity of the Stanhope (see p. 128).

Physical Communication

Changes in the media system also need to be related to changes in the transportation system, the movement of goods and people in space, whether by land or water (river, canal and sea). It was, of course, traditional for information flows to follow trade flows, since merchants operating by sea and land brought news along with their merchandise. Printing itself had spread across Europe via the Rhine, from Gutenberg's Mainz to Frankfurt, Strasbourg and Basel. In the sixteenth, seventeenth and eighteenth centuries, messages on paper followed the silver route from Mexico or Peru to the Old World, or the sugar route from the Caribbean to London. What is new in the sixteenth and seventeenth centuries is the evidence of increasing awareness of the problems of physical communication. The enthusiasm of Renaissance humanists for ancient Rome included an interest in Roman

Fig. 4 John Ogilby, road map from his *Britannia*, 1675.

roads, discussed, for instance, in Andrea Palladio's famous treatise, *Four Books of Architecture* (1570). Guides to the roads of particular countries were also published, notably Henri Estienne's *Guide des chemins de France* (1553) and John Ogilby's *Britannia* (1675; see Figure 4), the first English road atlas, the roads being displayed on what the author called 'imaginary scrolls'. An up-to-date version of these maps in reduced format was produced in 1719 and reached its twenty-second edition in 1785, ample testimony to travellers' need for such a book.

Governments also concerned themselves more with roads, even if major improvements in the European system are difficult to discern before the middle of the eighteenth century. In France, a new official position was created around 1600, that of *Grand Voyer*, in order to oversee the system. One reason for this concern with roads was the increasing need, in an age when

European states were becoming more centralized, to transmit commands more rapidly from the capital to the provinces. The interest in communication on the part of governments was a major reason for the rapid expansion of the postal system in the early modern period, although merchants and other private individuals also took advantage of it.

In early modern Europe, transport by water was usually much cheaper than transport by land. An Italian printer calculated in 1550 that to send a load of books from Rome to Lyons by land would cost eighteen *scudi*, compared with four if sent by sea. Letters were normally carried overland, but a system of transporting letters and newspapers, as well as people, by canal barge developed in the Dutch Republic in the seventeenth century. The average speed of the barges was a little over four miles an hour, slow compared to a courier on horseback. On the other hand, the service was regular, frequent and cheap, and allowed communication not only between Amsterdam and the smaller towns, but also between one small town and another, thus equalizing accessibility to information. It was only in 1837, with the invention of the electric telegraph (see p. 155), that the traditional link between transport and the communication of messages was broken.

Communications, as the American political scientist Karl Deutsch (1912–92) put it, are 'the nerves of government', especially important in large states, above all in far-flung empires. Charles V (Holy Roman emperor; ruled 1519–58), whose dominions included Spain, the Netherlands, Germany and much of Italy as well as Mexico and Peru, tried to solve the problem of communication by travelling incessantly throughout Europe. His abdication speech noted that in the course of four decades as emperor he had made forty journeys: ten to the Low Countries, nine to Germany, seven to Italy, six to Spain, four to France, two to England and two to North Africa. Yet the traditional medieval style of nomadic kingship was no longer sufficient for Charles's needs. The age of the 'paper empire' had arrived, together with a regular system for the transmission of messages: the postal system, so-called because it involved the establishment of posts with men and horses stationed along certain routes or post-roads.

In the sixteenth century, one family dominated the European postal system, that of the Tassis or Taxis (the term 'taxi', now in international currency, is derived from their name). It was this family, postmasters to the Habsburg emperors from 1490 onwards, that developed the system of ordinary couriers, operating according to a fixed timetable (available in print from 1563). Brussels – now the centre of so much else – was the hub of their system. One route went via Augsburg and Innsbruck to Bologna,

Florence, Rome and Naples. Another went to Paris and through France to Toledo and Granada.

The Speed of Communication

Special couriers, changing horses at frequent intervals, were able to travel up to 125 miles a day and so to bring the news of important events relatively rapidly. In 1572, for example, the news of the massacre of Protestants in Paris (known as the Massacre of St Bartholomew) arrived in Madrid in three days. To travel 'posthaste' was a common expression of the period. However, the time normally taken for messages to arrive was considerably longer, since ordinary couriers averaged from six to eight miles per hour. From Rome to Milan, an ordinary courier took 2–3 days, according to the season; from Rome to Vienna, 12–15 days; from Rome to Paris, about 20; and it required 25–30 days for the courier from Rome to reach London or Cracow. Ordinary couriers took about 11 days from Madrid (which was Spain's capital from 1556 onwards) to Paris, and 12–13 days from Madrid to Naples (which was part of the Spanish Empire).

The Spanish Empire in the age of Charles V's son and successor Philip II (ruled 1556–98), although smaller in extent, has been well described by the great French historian Fernand Braudel (1902–85), in his famous study *The Mediterranean and the Mediterranean World in the Age of Philip II* (1949), as 'a colossal enterprise of sea and land transport' requiring 'the daily dispatch of hundreds of orders and reports'. Philip's strategy was the opposite of his father's. It was to remain as far as possible in one place, in or near Madrid, and to sit at his desk for many hours a day, reading and annotating the documents which reached him from all over his dominions. No wonder that his subjects gave him the mocking nickname of 'the king of paper' (*el rey papelero*).

The great problem was the length of time the documents took to reach Philip, or, conversely, the time his orders took to reach their recipients. The obsession of sixteenth-century statesmen and ambassadors with the arrival of the mail was emphasized by Braudel. The delays of the Spanish government were notorious, leading one official to wish that Death would arrive from Spain. The delays cannot (or cannot always), be explained by the indecisiveness of Philip II, however, but rather by the communication problems of an empire which stretched across the Mediterranean from Spain to Sicily, across the Atlantic to Mexico and Peru, and across the Pacific to the Philippines (named after Philip because they became a Spanish possession in his time). At this time, it would normally take a ship one or two weeks, according to the winds, to cross the Mediterranean from north to south, and two or three months from east to west, so that Braudel called the Mediterranean world of the period '60 days long'.

Nevertheless, communication by sea was usually swifter than communication over land. In Mexico, for example, the Spaniards had to construct what they called 'royal roads', like the famous 'silver road' from the mines in Zacatecas to Mexico City. The names of these roads survive in modern California and New Mexico. In Eastern Europe, where the population was less dense and cities smaller and fewer than in the West, communication was correspondingly slower. In the Russian Empire in the age of Catherine the Great (ruled 1762–96), for example, it might take eighteen months for an imperial order sent from St Petersburg to reach Kamchatka in Siberia, and another eighteen months for the reply to be received in the capital. Communication problems help to explain why the empires of early modern Europe, Russia excepted, were seaborne empires. They included the Portuguese, Spanish, Dutch, French and British intercontinental empires, and also the Swedish Empire in Europe, constructed around the Baltic sea.

In order to communicate with his viceroys in Mexico and Peru, Philip II and his successors were dependent on the annual departures and returns of the ships that transported the silver of the New World to the port of Seville and for safety's sake sailed in convoy. The convoy to Mexico, for example, sailed in the summer and began the return voyage from the New World in the autumn. Letters from Spain to Mexico might take as little as four months to arrive, but to Lima they normally took six to nine months and they might take up to two years to reach the Philippines. Communications between England and New England were much more rapid, but letters might be lost or at least delayed. A letter relating the execution of Charles I, written in March 1649, only arrived in New England in June. It was common practice to make copies of letters and to send them by different ships in order to minimize the risk of loss.

Only in the eighteenth century did improvements in communications shrink the Atlantic, at least as far as the British Empire was concerned. Sea traffic between England and North America doubled between the 1680s and the 1730s. In 1702, a system of ships (known as 'packet boats'), carrying letters from London to Barbados or Jamaica, was set up, with monthly sailings, a 100-day schedule and some 8,500 letters carried in each ship. As a result, from the point of view of communications, the Atlantic had been shrunk to the size of the Mediterranean in the age of Philip II.

The ships crossing the Atlantic carried not only letters but also books and newspapers. Since books were heavy physical objects, the majority of copies tended to remain fairly near the place in which they had been manufactured. However, there is evidence of long-distance distribution. In the sixteenth century, for example, romances of chivalry were exported to Mexico and Peru in considerable numbers, despite the disapproval of the clergy. In 1540, a single printer had 446 copies of the popular romance *Amadis de Gaula* in stock in his shop in Mexico City. The same book was one of the favourites in Lima in 1583. In 1600, no fewer than 10,000 copies of another romance, *Pierres y Magalona*, arrived in Mexico City. In Puritan New England, by contrast, there seems to have been more demand for printed sermons. Individuals such as the clergyman Increase Mather (1639–1723) received regular shipments of barrels of books from London. Newssheets were sent to Boston during the English Civil War, and by the early eighteenth century the regular arrival of news encouraged the foundation of local newssheets such as the *Boston Newsletter* (1704). What the Australian historian Geoffrey Blainey describes as the 'tyranny of distance' was gradually being undermined.

Oral Communication

It is sometimes claimed that the invention of the printing press did not alter the fundamentally oral nature of European culture. As this book attempts to show, the claim is exaggerated (and the attempt to characterize European culture in terms of a single medium misguided), but behind the exaggeration lurks an important point. Despite the huge scholarly literature on the importance of oral communication and especially what is often called 'oral literature', the place of the oral medium in the history of early modern Europe – and its relation to changes in visual culture – has received less attention than it deserves.

In the Middle Ages the altar rather than the pulpit was at the centre of Christian churches. Yet preaching was already an accepted priestly duty, and friars preached in the streets and squares of cities as well as in churches. Distinctions were drawn between *sermones dominicales* for Sundays and *sermones festivi* for the many days of festival, and the style of preaching (plain or flowery, serious or entertaining, restrained or histrionic) was consciously adapted to the audience, whether it was urban or rural, clerical or lay. In short, the possibilities of the oral medium were consciously exploited by the masters of what was known in the sixteenth century as 'ecclesiastical rhetoric', and the sociologist Zygmunt Bauman (1925–2017) has gone so far as to describe the pulpits of the Catholic Church as a 'mass medium'. After the Reformation, Sunday preaching became an increasingly important part of religious instruction for Protestants and Catholics alike. Although Martin Luther (1483–1546) hailed the new printing press as 'God's highest gift of grace', he still considered the Church as 'a mouth house and not a pen house'. Some preachers drew crowds, among them the poet John Donne (c. 1572–1631), who was dean of St Paul's in London. The public role of the sermon was acknowledged by Roman Catholics too, especially after the Council of Trent, and there were great Catholic preachers such as Jacques Bossuet (1627–1704) at the court of Louis XIV. The enthusiasm of some members of the public for sermons which lasted two or three hours is attested in the diaries of the time. Governments were well aware of the value of the pulpit for communicating information, especially in rural areas, and also for encouraging obedience. Queen Elizabeth I spoke of the need to 'tune the pulpits', and Charles I agreed, declaring that 'people are governed by the pulpit more than the sword in times of peace', a classic early statement of the idea of cultural hegemony.

Another kind of oral communication was academic. The art of speaking (and gesturing) was considered by rhetoricians to be just as important as the art of writing. The language of gesture, taken seriously in early modern Europe, was taught in schools as part of the discipline of rhetoric, and was the subject of a number of treatises, from *The Art of Gesture* (1616) by the Italian jurist Giovanni Bonifacio to the *Chirologia* (1644) of the English physician John Bulwer, concerned with 'manual rhetoric' – in other words 'the natural language of the hands'. In the grammar schools, great emphasis was placed on speaking Latin, and dialogues and plays were composed by the teachers in order to give the students practice in speaking well. Instruction in universities took place through lectures, formal debates or disputations (testing the logical skills of the students), and formal speeches or declamations (testing their powers of rhetoric). By contrast, the written essay, like the written examination, was virtually unknown in academic circles at this time. Yet another important domain of oral communication was the song, especially the ballad, the song which told a story. The theories of Milman Parry and Albert Lord, discussed in Chapter 1, are highly relevant to the ballads that circulated in early modern Europe. In the case of the famous border ballads of northern England and the Lowlands of Scotland, for instance, as in their equivalents in Scandinavia or Spain, it is not difficult to identify both formulae and themes. 'Blood-red wine', for example, or 'milk-white steed' are epithets as formulaic as Homer's 'wine-dark sea'. Recurrent themes of British ballads include sending a letter, sitting in a bower and galloping on a horse; plants grow out of the graves of tragic lovers and join them at last. The survival, in manuscript or in print, of a given ballad, *The Bonny Earl of Murray*, for example, or *Barbara Allen*, in versions differing in length and in phrasing, suggests that, as in Parry's Yugoslavia, individual minstrels developed their own style of recitation which was probably semi-improvised.

Again, rumour has been described as an 'oral postal service' which operates with remarkable speed. The messages transmitted were not always spontaneous: they were sometimes disseminated for political reasons, and in times of conflict one side would regularly accuse the other of spreading rumours. Three famous examples of rumour and its effects in early modern Europe, whether spontaneous or not, are the movement of iconoclasm of 1566 in northern France and the Netherlands (see p. 94); the English 'Popish Plot' in the 1680s (see p. 99); and the so-called 'Great Fear' in the French countryside in 1789, studied in depth in the 1930s by the French historian of the Revolution, Georges Lefebvre (1874–1959). In this last case, news circulated among French peasants to the effect that brigands were coming to massacre them or to attack their harvests, perhaps at the orders of the British or the aristocracy. Rather than either dismissing these rumours or believing them, Lefebvre studied their chronology and geography with care and used them as evidence of social tensions.

Oral culture in this period should not be thought of purely in terms of survival or of what Ong has called 'oral residue'. New institutions which structured oral communication developed in this period, including such more or less formal discussion groups as academies, scientific societies, salons, clubs and coffee-houses. To judge from the treatises on the subject, the art of conversation was cultivated with particular intensity at this time. Bookshops, too, functioned as social centres, and James Boswell met Samuel Johnson for the first time in the back parlour of a bookshop owned by Tom Davies.

The development of commerce had important consequences for oral communication, notably the rise of exchanges or bourses, including Bruges (1409), Antwerp (1460), Lyons (1462), Amsterdam (1530), London (1554), Hamburg (1558) and Copenhagen (1624). A vivid description of one of them, Amsterdam, was given by the Sephardic Jewish merchant Joseph Penso de la Vega in a dialogue in Spanish entitled *The Confusion of Confusions* (1688), which shows that the habit of speculation in company shares and even the categories of 'bulls' and 'bears' had already become standard practice at this time. So too had the deliberate spreading of rumour in order to force prices up and down. The volatile behaviour of stock exchanges, their liability to mood swings from manic to depressive, most obvious in this period in the rapid rise and collapse of the South Sea Bubble (in other words, speculation in the stock of the South Sea Company of London in 1720), should be explained in part at least in terms of the oral medium. The phenomenon is still to be seen and heard on stock exchanges – and in banks – in our own time.

Centres of oral communication included taverns and public baths and coffee-houses, an innovation in this period. Istanbul was famous in the late sixteenth century for its coffee-houses, some 600 of them. Storytellers performed there, as they still did in Yugoslavia in the 1930s, when Parry and Lord visited the *kafanas*, as they were called, carrying their tape-recorders. There were at least 500 coffee-houses in London in the age of Queen Anne (reigned 1702–14). Discussions of scientific subjects might be heard in Child's coffee-house, or Garraway's, or the Grecian coffee-house, where one might see and hear Sir Isaac Newton (1642–1727). Insurance was discussed at Lloyd's, which was a coffee-house in the late seventeenth century before it developed into an independent institution. In the mid-eighteenth century, Slaughter's coffee-house was the locale for a club of artists which included William Hogarth (1697–1764). In eighteenth-century Paris, the leading cafés included the *Café de Maugis*, a centre for attacks on religion, and *Le Procope*, founded in 1689 (and still open), which was frequented by leading intellectuals of the Enlightenment. The authorities in most cities, concerned with coffee-houses as places which encouraged subversive comments about the government, kept them under surveillance more or less effectively.

Clubs and coffee-houses inspired the creation of imagined communities of oral communication. The best English example is the imaginary Spectator Club, composed of a variety of characters including a country gentleman, a merchant, a clergyman and an army officer, which functioned as a framework for *The Spectator*, edited by Joseph Addison (1672–1719) and Richard Steele (1672–1729) and published 1711–12, discussed below (p. 78). A journal founded in Leipzig in 1698 took the title *The Curious Coffeehouse at Venice*. The Milanese journal *Il Caffè* (1764–6) played an important role in the Italian Enlightenment (see p. 79). In several countries, plays also were set in coffee-houses, culminating in Voltaire's comedy *Le Café, ou l'Écossaise* (1760), in which the customers are shown in the act of making critical remarks about other plays.

Benedict Anderson argued in *Imagined Communities* (1983) that nineteenth-century newspapers contributed to the formation of national consciousness by treating their readers as a national public. In similar fashion, some eighteenth-century newspapers, from the *Bristol Postboy* to the *Hamburgische Patriot*, helped create imagined local communities.

Contexts of Literacy

The importance of the contexts in which writing is learned or utilized was already plain in early modern Europe, where reading and writing were often taught separately. For the commercial context of literacy and the business demand for writing and numeracy, we may turn to Florence in the fourteenth and fifteenth centuries, where specialized abacus-schools taught writing and arithmetic, based on commercial examples, to boys who were going to become merchants or bookkeepers. Like other cities in the Mediterranean world, Florence might be described as a notarial culture, in which written documents had an indispensable function, especially to record transfers of property on the occasion of marriages and deaths. Lay literacy was relatively high in Florence, and the practice of keeping diaries or chronicles was relatively widespread. Examples of this kind of personal document can also be found in other towns, among them Augsburg, Barcelona, Bologna, London, Nuremberg and Paris. They focused on the family or the city rather than the individual and sometimes circulated in manuscript form within an urban neighbourhood.

The religious context of literacy is particularly visible in Protestant Europe in the seventeenth and eighteenth centuries. A classic example is that of Lutheran Sweden, in which the Church conducted annual examinations of every household to see how well each member of the family could read, how well they knew their catechism, and so on. The results were recorded systematically, distinguishing levels of ability such as 'beginning to read', 'reads a little' and so on. The records were preserved with care and remain a uniquely rich source for the study of early modern literacy (see Figure 5). Among other things, they reveal that the widespread ability to read, which extended as far as women and children in rural areas, was the result of a massive campaign between 1670 and 1720. On the whole, however, early modern Europe was a society of restricted literacy in which only a minority of the population (especially males, townspeople and Protestants) could read and fewer still could write. Hence the importance of what has been called 'mediated literacy', in other words, literacy employed for the benefit of the illiterate.

In cities of the period, a not uncommon occupation – as in Mexico City and Istanbul today, or at least until recently – was that of public writer, a man with an 'office' in the street, composing as well as writing letters for people who lacked these skills. In Paris, for example, some of these writers operated in the Cemetery of the Innocents. The English traveller John Evelyn (1620–1706) described them as 'inditing letters for poor maids

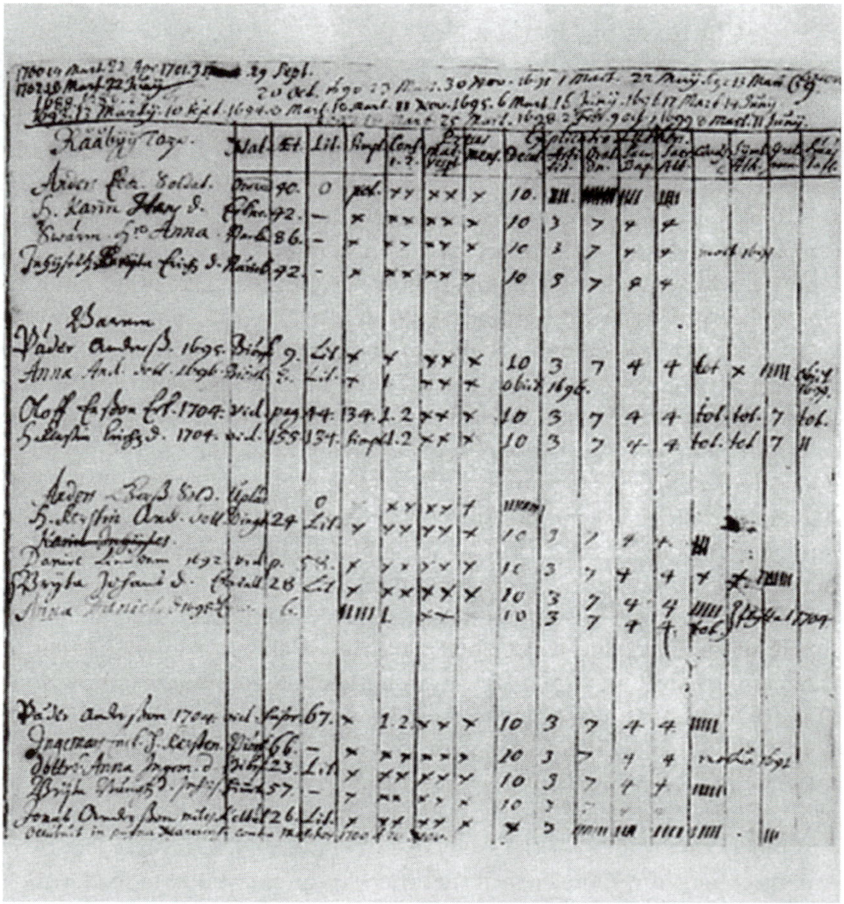

Fig. 5 Register of household literacy examination in Sweden.

and other ignorant people who come to them for advice and write for them into the country, both to their sweethearts, parents and friends, every large grave stone a little elevated serving them for a table'. In eighteenth-century Finland, illiterate peasants needed to communicate with the government in writing to avoid recruitment into the Swedish army. In their case, the local clergyman serving as a scribe was the crucial intermediary.

For a dramatic illustration of mediated literacy and its unintended conse-quences, one might take a case that came before the Tribunal of the Governor of Rome in 1602, involving a love letter written by a certain Giovanantonio to his 16-year-old neighbour Margarita. Unfortunately, Margarita could not read, so she needed to pass the letter to another neighbour to have it read to her, thus increasing the chances of detection by her parents, who did indeed discover the affair and take the case to court.

The consequences of the spread of literacy and its increasing penetration into everyday life were many and various. There was a rise in the number of people in occupations connected with writing – for example, clerks, book-keepers, scriveners, notaries, public writers and postmen. Some of these occupations had a relatively high social status, among them that of private secretary in the service of important people who did not have the time to write their own letters. Literacy, an obstacle to the traditional process of 'structural amnesia' (see p. 13), encouraged a sense of distance between past and present. A sense of historical anachronism, for instance, seems to have become increasingly sharp from the fourteenth and fifteenth centuries onwards.

The political consequences of literacy included the spread of written records – noticeable by the thirteenth century, if not before – and with it great dependence on the processing of 'information'. This term was to figure prominently in future theories of communication – for example, in the late twentieth-century identification of an 'information society' (see p. 317). The information might relate to numbers (what came to be called 'statistics') as well as to facts. Given access to it, the style of government moved closer to the model of administration by paperwork – or 'bureau-cracy', as the German sociologist Max Weber (1864–1920) called it. In his discussion of what he called 'legal-rational authority', Weber emphasized the relationship between the increasing use of writing to formulate and record decisions and a more impersonal kind of administration, character-ized by the imposition of formal rules for the appointment of officials, for their respective spheres of responsibility and for their place within a hierarchy. Weber's arguments have since been extended from politics to the domains of religion, business and the law.

Philip II of Spain, whose problems of communication have already been discussed, was not the only paper king in early modern Europe. Great nobles, who saw their participation in decision-making eroded, frequently complained about what they called the 'rule of the secretaries'. The increas-ing use of writing in the process of administration was a necessary condi-tion for control at a distance, for the rise of the centralized state. Yet the increase in the number of documents to be read and signed was too much even for conscientious monarchs such as Philip II or, in the seventeenth century, Louis XIV of France. Secretaries had to be authorized to forge the king's signature on documents he had not seen, the point being that orders would not be obeyed if they did not appear to come directly from the king. As so often happens, social practices lagged behind technical innovations.

The political uses of literacy for ordinary people should not be forgotten. Rebellions were accompanied by the formulation of grievances in writing, during the German Peasant War of 1525, for example, or in the famous *cahiers* at the beginning of the French Revolution, to mention only two of the most profound upheavals. The signing of petitions by a wide range of people was a practice which entered English politics in the seventeenth century. In 1640, at the beginning of the Civil War, 15,000 citizens of London signed the *Root and Branch Petition*, and later petitions displayed as many as 30,000 signatures. In the nineteenth century, they were claimed to have reached millions.

The medium of writing is not synonymous with handwriting, still less with pen and ink. In the early modern period, painted and chiselled inscriptions were a distinct form of communication. The epitaphs on gravestones and church monuments were chosen with care, and foreign visitors often made a point of reading them, a practice facilitated by the fact that before the eighteenth century most of them were in Latin. A history of communication cannot afford to neglect the linguistic media through which communication took place.

Languages of Communication

The rise of a print society is often associated with the rise of the vernacular languages of Europe, in contrast to a medieval pre-print society in which written communication was predominantly in Latin and oral communication in local dialect. The increasing employment of the vernaculars for literary purposes was accompanied by their standardization and codification, a process aided by print. Martin Luther's translation of the Bible into German is often cited as an example of the new trend, important in itself and also as a model for other translations such as Tyndale's Bible (see p. 92), the Czech Bible of 1579–94 (the Kralice Bible) and the English Bible of 1611 (the *Authorized Version*).

Yet Dante and Chaucer had written their poems in Italian and English, and, concerned as he was with the status of Latin, Petrarch, too, employed Italian for his introspective poetry and his praise of his muse, Laura. Outside Italy, the Frenchman Joachim Du Bellay (1522–60) and the German Martin Opitz (1597–1639) were among the writers who sang the praises of the vernacular as a medium for poetry.

In the field of politics, a date often cited is that of 1539, when King Francis

I of France ordered legal documents to be drawn up in French instead of the traditional Latin. In the academic domain, the German physician Theophrastus von Hohenheim, known as Paracelsus (1493–1541), broke with tradition by lecturing in the vernacular at the University of Basel, although most of his colleagues resisted this innovation and it was only in the eighteenth century that German, English or Italian could regularly be heard in the lecture rooms of universities. At around the same time, French replaced Latin as the main language of international diplomacy.

Nevertheless, as the last two examples suggest, the decline of Latin must not be dated too early. Translations from the vernaculars into Latin were common, especially translations from Italian and French, made for a northern European public. At least 1,200 such translations were made between the late fifteenth and the late eighteenth centuries, reaching their peak in the first half of the seventeenth century. To take only English examples, the essays of Francis Bacon, the philosophy of John Locke, Robert Boyle's *Sceptical Chemist*, Newton's *Optics*, and even Milton's *Paradise Lost* and Gray's *Elegy in a Country Churchyard* were most familiar on the Continent in Latin versions, since the English language was not well known in other countries until the second half of the eighteenth century.

Visual Communication

As for visual communication in a broader sense, Renaissance humanists would have had little to learn from the French critic Roland Barthes (1915–80) about what he called 'the rhetoric of the image' – as Barthes himself, who analysed modern advertisements with the help of Aristotle's *Rhetoric*, would probably have been the first to recognize.

Despite their remarkable innovations in style, what are commonly and somewhat anachronistically called the 'works of art' of the Renaissance should be seen as images or even what the sociolinguists call 'communicative events'. For example, *The Punishment of Corah*, a fresco by the Florentine painter Sandro Botticelli (1445–1510) in the Sistine Chapel in Rome, represents the earth opening to swallow a man who had dared to rebel against the authority of Moses. Commissioned by Pope Sixtus IV at a time, the late fifteenth century, when there was talk of summoning a council of the Church to limit the power of the Pope, the fresco makes a firm statement to the effect that the Pope is the new Moses and that rebellion does not pay. The famous religious paintings of the Renaissance, such as Michelangelo's *Last Judgement* or Tintoretto's *St Mark Rescuing a Slave* (see Figure 1a), were not innovative in this respect, although the new three-dimensionality may have made them more effective as religious communication.

Secular paintings, increasingly identified with individual painters from the years around 1500 onwards, communicated a greater variety of messages to smaller audiences. Whereas a large number of religious paintings were displayed in churches where anyone could see them, most secular paintings of the Renaissance were bought by private individuals to hang in their own houses. Botticelli's *Primavera* ('Spring'), for instance, may be well known today, thanks to exhibitions and reproductions, but in the Renaissance itself the painting was invisible to most people because it hung on the walls of a private villa.

Both religious and secular works were generally made on commission, for particular clients and according to their specifications, which were sometimes extremely precise, as surviving contracts show. Literary works, too, were often created for specific patrons and dedicated to them. It was only in the course of the early modern period (in the sixteenth century in Italy and the Netherlands, in the eighteenth century in France and England) that artists and writers began to work for the market, producing first and selling afterwards rather than the other way round.

The rise of the market was associated with the rise of the mechanically reproduced image, and in particular of the 'print', a general term for printed images, whether the medium employed was a block of wood or a copper or steel plate, whether the image was incised on the plate (an engraving) or eaten away by acid (as in the case of the etching).

The first known woodcut dates from the late fourteenth century, and was probably inspired by the stamping of patterns on textiles. In fact, collections of woodcut images of religious scenes were already being produced a generation before Gutenberg's Bible. The etching developed in the sixteenth and seventeenth centuries (Rembrandt's etchings are particularly famous). The advantage of this method, in which a metal plate is covered with wax on which lines are drawn before the plate is submerged in a bath of acid, is that gradations of tone can be achieved by immersing the plate more than once, adding new lines and making the old ones deeper and so darker. In the eighteenth century, the invention of the mezzotint, with tiny holes of different depths replacing the lines on the plate with still more subtle gradations, made it possible to make realistic reproductions of oil paintings in black and white. In 1796, the lithograph was invented by Aloys Senefelder (1771–1834). Produced by drawing on stone with grease pencils, the new medium allowed cheap coloured images to be created for the first time.

The rise of the print was the most profound change in visual communication in this whole period, since it made images so much more widely available than before. Print-making quickly involved leading artists of the Renaissance, such as Botticelli, who produced a series of woodcut illustrations for Dante's *Divine Comedy*. Prints were reasonably cheap to make and transport, thus enabling the work of their designers to reach relatively large numbers of people fairly quickly. It is likely, for instance, that the most vivid and memorable images of the New World were not conveyed in words by Christopher Columbus or later explorers, but by the woodcuts of Indians wearing feathered headdresses and cooking and eating human flesh. Popular piety was encouraged by woodcuts of saints distributed on their feast days, and similar images of Luther – on occasion, with a halo – helped to spread the ideas of the reformers of the Church in the 1520s. The paintings of Leonardo, Raphael and Michelangelo were reproduced in the form of woodcuts and engravings and so introduced to a wider audience, like the paintings of Rubens in the seventeenth century. Prints also introduced West European images to other cultures. They were used as models by painters of religious images in the Russian Orthodox world from the middle of the seventeenth century onwards, and they also influenced styles of representation as far afield as Persia, India, China, Mexico and Peru.

Popular political consciousness, to be discussed in more detail in the next chapter, was encouraged by the spread of satirical prints, especially in seventeenth- and eighteenth-century England and in revolutionary France (see pp. 101, 103, 109). Some of these images are known to have sold extremely well. For example, a print celebrating the repeal in 1766 of the Stamp Act, to which the American colonies strongly objected, sold 2,000 copies at a shilling each in only four days, and it is said that another 16,000 copies were sold in illegal versions (see Figure 6). In the course of the period, the conventions of representation changed, with the allegorical print, such as the mock-funeral, being replaced by the more direct political caricature of, for instance, Sir Robert Walpole, Charles James Fox or the Prince of Wales, the main target of the artist James Gillray (1756–1815) in the 1780s, before he turned to satirizing the French Revolution.

In the world of scholarship, systematic discussions of the significance of the printed image as a medium of communication parallel the detailed investigations of printed texts. Nineteenth- and twentieth-century bibliographers concerned themselves with the appearance, the dating and the printing history of books, while art historians considered prints in similar fashion. Both groups of scholars were supposed to pay attention to reproduction and to the number of copies in circulation, although they did not always do so. According to Walter Benjamin, the work of art changed its

Fig. 6 *The Repeal, or the Funerary Procession of Miss Americ-Stamp*, 1765.

character following the industrial revolution. 'That which withers in the age of mechanical reproduction is the aura of the work of art.' The machine 'substitutes a plurality of copies for a unique existence' and in so doing produces a shift from the 'cult value' of the image to its 'exhibition value'. It is worth noting that the question whether or not the aura of the image is lost is a difficult hypothesis to test, and it might even be argued that familiarity with a reproduction sharpens rather than sates the desire to see the original.

Benjamin was thinking of nineteenth-century media such as lithography and photography, but William M. Ivins Jr (1881–1961), a curator of prints at the Metropolitan Museum of Art in New York, made a case for the importance of sixteenth-century prints as 'exactly repeatable pictorial statements'. Ivins argued that prints were 'among the most important and powerful tools of modern life and thought'. He pointed out that the ancient Greeks, for instance, had abandoned the practice of illustrating botanical treatises because of the impossibility of producing identical images of the same plant in different manuscript copies of the same work. From the late fifteenth century, on the other hand, herbals were regularly illustrated with woodcuts.

Maps, which began to be printed in 1472, offer another example of the way in which the communication of information by images was facilitated by the repeatability associated with the press. In a more literal sense than that meant by David Olson (see p. 13), they offered readers 'the world on paper' and made it easier than ever before for groups armed with these documents to control parts of the earth, whether their control was primarily military, political, economic or ideological. Generals and governments, merchants and missionaries encouraged the making of manuscript maps of the world beyond Europe. They often hoped to keep this information to themselves, but it was gradually leaked into print and into the public domain.

The transfer of the two-dimensional map to the three-dimensional globe, of which the oldest surviving example (1492) is that of German cartographer Martin Behaim (1459–1507), made it easier to think of the earth as a whole. When maps were collected into atlases, beginning with the *Theatre of the World* by Abraham Ortelius (first published at Antwerp in 1570), they allowed viewers to see the world both as a whole and in detail. Although the ideal of cosmopolitanism goes back as far as the Stoic philosophers in the age of the Roman Empire, the spread of these globes and printed maps must have encouraged global consciousness.

Another development of this period was the narrative strip or picture story, the ancestor of the twentieth-century comic strip. The visual narrative in which the viewer 'reads' the episodes, usually from left to right and from top to bottom, was already known in the Middle Ages, but its importance increased with the rise of the woodcut in the Renaissance. Woodcuts in particularly long strips were produced to record events such as processions through the streets. These strips, the printed equivalents of medieval rolls, gave their viewers the impression of watching the procession pass. The true 'moving pictures' of the early modern period, however, were the processions themselves.

Multimedia Communication

It is likely that the most effective forms of communication at this time were – as they are today – those that appealed simultaneously to the eye and to the ear and combined verbal with nonverbal messages, musical as well as visual, from the drums and trumpets of military parades to the violins accompanying indoor performances. In early modern Europe these forms included rituals, spectacles, masques, plays, ballets and operas.

Rituals were messages, but they were both more and less than a way of communicating information. They were less, because it is unlikely that very much of the information encoded in the action was actually assimilated by a majority of the spectators, because they failed to understand allusions to ancient history or classical mythology, for example, or because they were literally in no position to see what was going on. On the other hand, rituals were more than a means of transmitting information in the sense that they created solidarity, whether between the priest and his congregation, the ruler and his subjects, or the members of a guild or corporation marching together in procession. It should be added that it was commonly believed at this time that rituals were a means to make changes happen in the world. The consecration of the Host transformed it into the body and blood of Christ, while the ceremony of coronation turned a person into a king or queen. The touch of the kings of France and England was supposed to heal the sick, at least those suffering from the skin disease known as scrofula, and sufferers arrived at the royal palaces in their thousands on certain days of the year.

'Ritual' is not always the best term to describe many of these multi-media events. It might be better to follow seventeenth-century usage and to describe some of them at least as spectacles. The main form of public spectacle at this time was the procession (generally religious but sometimes secular, as in the case of royal entries into cities). Mock battles, such as medieval jousts and tournaments, might also be described as a form of outdoor spectacle, and one which continued to be important in this period too, but there was nothing 'mock' about executions, another common form of spectacle at this time. They were staged in public precisely to impress spectators and to communicate the message that it was hopeless to try to resist the authorities and that evildoers would come to a bad end. Another kind of spectacle might be described as the 'theatre' of the everyday life of the ruler, who often took meals in public and might even turn his getting up in the morning and going to bed at night into rituals, as in the famous case of Louis XIV of France. Again, Queen Elizabeth I, who declared that princes were 'set on stages', was skilful in exploiting this situation for political purposes, turning herself into a goddess or a myth, as effectively as Eva Perón in the very different media system of Argentina in the middle of the twentieth century.

These examples suggest that students of the media should try to place in historical perspective the claim of French left-wing politician Roger-Gérard Schwartzenberg that the rise of the 'spectacle state' and the 'star system' in politics was a consequence of the rise of television, or the assertion of French Marxist theorist Guy Debord (1931–94; see below, p. 262) that twentieth-century society is a 'society of the spectacle' in which the 'ruling order discourses endlessly upon itself in an uninterrupted monologue of self-praise'. Television may be responsible for a revival of political theatre, and has certainly given it new forms (by allowing so many people to observe political leaders in close-up), but the public dramatization and personalization of politics, like the official monologue of self-praise, goes back a very long way.

As a case-study of spectacle as communication, the Florentine festival of St John the Baptist in the late fifteenth century is of interest, because it was a celebration of the wealth and power of the city of Florence and especially of its government. Florence was a large city for the period (with about 40,000 inhabitants) as well as a city-state controlling a substantial part of Tuscany. St John the Baptist was the principal patron and protector of the city, and his feast, on 24 June, was a particularly splendid occasion. One of the main festive events was a procession from the cathedral to the river Arno and back, a procession in which monks, friars, secular clergy, choirboys and religious confraternities took part. They walked through streets decorated with rich cloths and filled with spectators, accompanied by music, carrying relics and followed by floats representing religious scenes such as the birth of St John and his baptism of Christ.

The secular part of the celebrations in Florence included an exhibition of luxury goods produced by the craftsmen of the city, notably cloth, jewels and goldsmiths' work, displayed outside the workshops, and also a race (*palio*), not unlike the race that still takes place in Siena twice a year, with colourful costumes for the horses and their riders. The events of the day were organized by the different wards of the city, deputations were received from Tuscan towns subject to Florence, among them Pisa and Arezzo, offering tribute to the saint and so to the city of which he was a patron, and a banquet was held for the *Signoria*, the local equivalent of the mayor and aldermen. All these rituals may be described as an expression of the collective identity of the Florentines.

The idiom of European ritual changed in the sixteenth and seventeenth centuries. Two of these changes deserve particular emphasis – restructuring ritual along ancient Roman lines and the rise of the theatre, which culminated in one of the most famous 'slogans' associated with communications: 'All the world's a stage.' Renaissance humanists, in the process of reviving classical antiquity, classicized ritual, as in the case of the mock naval battle which was waged, in the style of the ancient Romans, in the courtyard of the Palazzo Pitti in Florence, which had been filled with water for the occasion. In a number of other cities, scattered in different countries, a recurring version of classical spectacle was provided by the ritual entry of a prince. Following ancient Roman precedent, he rode in a chariot, passing through triumphal arches and attended by figures personifying Fame, Victory or Justice. Famous examples were the entry of Emperor Charles V into Bologna for his coronation in 1530 and the entry of King Henri II of France into Rouen in 1550. The practice became widely taken up and was not limited to rulers. In London in the seventeenth century, the new Lord Mayor passed through triumphal arches of this kind in his inauguration ritual – the annual Lord Mayor's Show.

How intelligible were these spectacles? To help spectators understand what was happening at the time of the performance, an interpreter might be introduced, like St George in the Lord Mayor's Show in London in 1609. Alternatively, written notices might be attached to particular figures, a procedure mocked by the playwright Ben Jonson (1572–1637), who preferred a learned to a popular audience, with his satirical examples 'This is a dog', or 'This is a hare'. The spectacles were also frequently described in printed and illustrated books which might be available on the day itself, or shortly afterwards, precisely in order that the spectators, or some of them, would know what to expect and how to understand what they were seeing, or discover the meaning of what they had just seen.

Returning to Harold Lasswell, it is worth asking, 'Who was saying what to whom through these rituals?' In the case of state visits to cities, the obvious answer is that the city was demonstrating its loyalty to the prince. This answer is not incorrect but it is incomplete. Communication was a two-way process, a form of dialogue, and princes demonstrated their good will towards their subjects as well as received their applause. Furthermore, the rituals were sometimes performed for the benefit of foreign princes, to whom the expression of loyalty was inappropriate. Bologna was part of the states of the Church when it welcomed Charles V in 1529, and Venice was an independent republic when King Henri III of France made a formal entry into it in 1574. Finally, it is possible to find occasions when cities used rituals to send another kind of message to the prince, not so much a panegyric as a petition. When Charles V entered Bruges in 1515, the pageants drew attention to the economic decline of the city, which was being displaced as a centre of commerce by the port of Antwerp. One of the scenes shown to Charles was a wheel of fortune, with Bruges sitting at the bottom. The message was clear. It was an appeal to the prince to restore the lost prosperity of the city.

Major festivals were the traditional time for the performance of plays, religious plays on the feast of Corpus Christi, for example, or secular plays during carnival. These performances usually took place either in the street, at the royal court, or in private houses. A major new development, from the later sixteenth century onwards, was the rise of the public theatre in London, Madrid, Paris and elsewhere. Plays began to be performed by professional actors in inns or in purpose-built playhouses, such as the *Hôtel de Bourgogne* in Paris (1548) or the *Globe* (1598) in London, open to all on payment of a reasonably low fee. Admission cost a penny in Shakespeare's London, a price which apprentices as well as merchants and gentlemen could afford. The commercial opera began a little later, in Venice, where the first public theatre was opened in 1637.

The rise of the commercial theatre at much the same time in different countries suggests that – apart from the imitation of new foreign models – a crucial factor in its development was the rise in the population of cities above a threshold of 100,000 people or so. With a potential audience of this size, professional actors were able to settle down in one place instead of wandering the country in search of new spectators. They could now perform the same play to different people night after night, or, more often, perform the same two or three plays over a few weeks.

Multimedia events are not the only examples from this period of the interaction between different means of communication. Another is that of so-called iconotexts, images that depend for their interpretation on texts incorporated in them – like speech scrolls coming from the mouths of the characters or captions over or under the image. For example, the prints of William Hogarth, such as *Gin Lane*, *The Harlot's Progress* or *The Industrious Apprentice*, depend for their elucidation on textual material tucked away in corners of the image. Hogarth was also commissioned to produce paintings illustrating scenes from an extremely successful musical of his day, John Gay's *The Beggar's Opera*.

The Survival of the Manuscript

Another kind of interaction may be illustrated by the function of manuscripts in early modern Europe. That they continued to be used for private communications, such as family or commercial letters, is obvious enough, but it is less obvious that the manuscript letter was influenced by print in this period, via the many treatises on the art of letter-writing published in large numbers in Italy and elsewhere from the sixteenth century onwards. These printed treatises offered useful models for letters of congratulation or condolence, love letters, apologies, or letters requesting money.

What requires more extended examination here is the survival into the early modern period of the manuscript as a major channel for the public circulation of messages. To be more precise, manuscripts were still used to transmit messages in a semi-public manner. In Russia as late as 1700, secular literature was still circulating in manuscript form as well as orally because the few existing presses were located in monasteries and used for the production of religious books. Even in Western Europe, which was full of presses, as we have seen, circulation in manuscript continued to perform some useful functions.

In the sixteenth and seventeenth centuries, men of high status (and women even more so) were often unhappy with the idea of publishing books, on the grounds that the books would be sold to the general public and so make the authors look like tradespeople. As a result of this prejudice, poets and other writers preferred to circulate their work in manuscript copies to their friends and acquaintances. It was in this form that the poems of Sir Philip Sidney (1554–86), for example, the sonnet sequence *Astrophel and Stella*, circulated in Elizabethan England. Again, the love lyrics of John Donne, written in the 1590s, were not published until 1633, two years after the author's death. Donne was probably unwilling to publish poems on love because he had entered the Church and become a deservedly famous preacher (see p. 36).

This form of manuscript circulation differed from printed circulation in a number of ways. It was a means of social bonding between the individuals involved, often a group of friends. The calligraphy of the manuscripts sometimes made them into works of art in their own right. The texts were less fixed and more malleable than printed ones because transcribers often felt free to add to or subtract from the verses they copied, or to change names in order to adapt what was written to their own situation. Manuscript was what we would now call an 'interactive' medium.

A second and still more important reason for manuscript circulation was to evade religious, moral and political censorship. In other words, to adopt a term widely current a few years ago, manuscript was the *samizdat* of the early modern period, the equivalent of the 'publish-it-yourself' typescripts and xeroxes criticizing communist regimes that circulated unofficially in the USSR, Poland and elsewhere before 1989. For example, the *Letter to the Grand Duchess* by Galileo Galilei (1564–1642), a discussion of the delicate issue of the relationship between religion and the study of the natural world, circulated widely in manuscript before it was finally published in 1636.

In France towards the end of the reign of Louis XIV, a great variety of manuscripts satirizing the king, his family and his ministers were in circulation.

Books attacking Christianity also circulated in this underground fashion. In some cases, printed books were copied for clandestine distribution in a region in which their publication was banned. In early eighteenth-century Paris, for example, the trade in manuscript copies of unorthodox books was highly organized, with professional copyists working for entrepreneurs who sold their wares near cafés. More than 100 unorthodox texts circulated in this way in the first half of the eighteenth century.

In between the two kinds of manuscript discussed above came the manuscript newsletters, letters sent in multiple copies to a limited number of subscribers, especially from 1550 to 1640, in other words in the generation or two before the rise of newspapers. The flexibility of the manuscript form permitted variations in the news sent to individual subscribers, according to their interests and needs. This personalized news service was available only to wealthy people, but it allowed the circulation of information which governments might have preferred to remain secret. Hence there was still a market for manuscript newsletters after 1650 despite the rise of the printed newssheet (see p. 96). In France, for example, the Comte de Lionne was the centre of a manuscript news network in Paris around the year 1671. His employees followed the French armies abroad and sent reports back to him which he put into wider circulation.

Another example of the interaction between manuscript and print takes us back to the letter. The editors of printed journals of different kinds, from the *Transactions of the Royal Society* to *The Spectator*, often solicited and received correspondence from their readers. Some of these letters were printed, while others influenced the topics chosen for discussion and the opinions expressed in the journal.

For a final example of the interfaces between media, we may turn to the relation between orality and print. Printed texts often reproduced what Ong has called 'oral residue', turns of phrase or grammatical constructions more appropriate to speech than to writing, to the ear than to the eye. Books in dialogue form, popular throughout the early modern period, from Castiglione's *Courtier* (1528) to Diderot's *Rameau's Nephew* (written in the 1760s, though not published until 1830), were fuelled by oral exchanges in courts, academies or salons. Preachers were often inspired by texts, from the Bible to the sermon outlines which were already available in print in the fifteenth century, so that clergymen did not need to lie awake on Saturday night thinking what to say to their congregations the next day. Preachers also sent their own texts to the printer, or, if they did not do so, others acted for them, taking down their words in shorthand and transcribing them afterwards.

The uses of printed books in this period also reveal the interaction between speech and print. For example, one of the most famous devotional books of the sixteenth century was the *Spiritual Exercises* (1548), written by the founder of the Jesuit order, Ignatius Loyola (1491–1556), a guide to meditation and to the examination of conscience. Published in Latin, the *Exercises* were not intended to be read by the Catholic laity. The text was an instruction manual for a priest or spiritual director, who would pass the message on to the laity by word of mouth. In similar fashion, the drill manuals which began to appear in print in the seventeenth and eighteenth centuries were intended for officers or sergeants rather than the rank and file.

In early seventeenth-century England, printed ballads were sometimes used as aids to oral performance, the equivalent of today's *karaoke*. The texts were pasted onto the walls of taverns so that people who did not know or could not remember the words of a particular ballad could sing along with the rest. There was still such a lively oral culture, however, that many people exercised more creativity, composing ballads of their own about their neighbours or enemies. These homemade ballads might adapt verses from a printed text – in a manner similar to the writers of the manuscripts discussed above – and they were often sung to tunes which broadside ballads had made familiar.

The art of conversation was influenced, if not transformed, by the spread in print of books on the subject, beginning in sixteenth-century Italy with Baldassare Castiglione's *Courtier* (1528), Giovanni Della Casa's *Galateo* (1558) and Stefano Guazzo's *Civil Conversation* (1574), and continuing through a series of French, Spanish and German treatises and the reflections on the subject by Swift, Fielding and Lord Chesterfield. These treatises offered instruction to men and women of different ages and social groups, advising them when to speak or keep silent, to whom, about what and in what style. The number of editions through which they passed, together with the underlinings and annotations in some surviving copies, suggest that this advice was taken seriously. In other words, print was contributing to what the authors of the treatises would have called the refinement of speech, and also to its increasing uniformity, a process which was also encouraged by the publication of grammars of different European languages. Indeed, language is one of the domains which best illustrates Eisenstein's point about the connections between printing and standardization.

The interactions between orality and print may be studied in more detail by analysing some Italian examples of what English scholars generally call chapbooks (see p. 28). An examination of some of these booklets, published in Italy in the late fifteenth and early sixteenth centuries, reveals the continuing importance of romances of chivalry – as in France more than a century later. An account-book recording the expenses of a printing shop near Florence between 1476 and 1486 reveals that nearly 500 copies of one romance of chivalry were sold wholesale to a man described as Bernardino 'who sings on a bench'. It therefore seems plausible to suggest that what Bernardino did was what is still done in remote parts of Brazil and elsewhere in the Third World – to recite the poem and then to sell printed copies of it. The performance was a form of marketing. It drew an audience of potential readers, and gave them a chance to test the quality of the product. Buying the text allowed listeners to repeat the performance to their families and friends. If they were illiterate, they could always ask someone else to read or recite the poem to them.

Many other texts published in Florence or Venice at this time open or close with formulae suggesting that a singer is performing in public, with the openings often calling on God to help and on bystanders to pay attention. 'Pay attention to me, for I can recite a new poem in rhyme.' Or: 'If you pay attention I will make you enjoy yourselves.' Or again: 'Lords and good people I can tell you many stories which I know by heart.' The closing formulae express the hope that the listeners have enjoyed the story, presumably passing the hat around for money at the same time. 'This story is told in your honour.' 'Think about my needs, prudent listener.' 'Elegant beautiful and gracious ladies, I thank you for the attention you have given my poor eloquence.' Such openings and closings recall passages, usually in verse, at the beginning and end of stage plays (and later of operas), where the playwright (or composer) directly addresses the audience.

In these texts it is not difficult to identify formulae and themes of the kind discussed by Milman Parry and Albert Lord (see p. 8). They include some of the very themes used by the twentieth-century Yugoslav poets, such as the holding of a council or the sending of a letter (reminding us of the importance of writing in a semi-oral culture). Examples of the formulae include 'with sweet speech', 'threw him to the ground', 'like a cat', 'appeared to be a dragon' and so on. The texts also offer frequent examples of the redundancy typical of oral performance: 'Crying and weeping with sorrow' (*Lagrimando e piangendo con dolore*) for instance, or 'That day was one of great heat and it was burning hot' (*Era quel dì gran caldo e grande ardore*). Redundancy of this kind should not be interpreted as a weakness on the part of the poet. It was a device that made it easier for the audience to follow the story.

In short, oral and printed media coexisted and interacted in fifteenth- and sixteenth-century Italy, as they did on the Anglo-Scottish borders in the eighteenth century. In his famous study of oral poetry, Lord argued that literacy and print necessarily destroy traditional oral culture. He went so far as to speak of the 'death' of oral tradition. These Italian examples, on the other hand, suggest that oral culture and print culture were able to coexist for a considerable period. It is of course thanks to this kind of coexistence that the traditional ballads of Scotland, England and Scandinavia, which were written down and printed from the sixteenth century onwards, have survived.

Censorship

As the remarks in the last section about clandestine communication by manuscript have already suggested, censorship of the media was a major preoccupation of the authorities in European states and churches, Protestant and Catholic alike, in the early modern period, whether they were principally concerned with heresy, sedition or immorality.

In a society in which only a minority were literate, repression could not be confined to books alone. Plays, for instance, were often subject to censorship. In London, they had to be licensed by the Master of the Revels before they could be performed. Texts were carefully scrutinized for references to important people, at home and abroad, as well as for comments on topical religious or political issues. The censor's problem was that although the text of the play might be submitted in advance, it was difficult to prevent actors from improvising subversive remarks in the course of performance. It was for this reason that some plays running in London, such as Thomas Middleton's notorious *A Game at Chess* (1625), which satirized the court of Spain, were brought to an abrupt end by order of the Bishop or the Privy Council.

A reforming archbishop of Bologna spoke of drawing up an index of prohibited images. It never happened, perhaps because it was too difficult to organize such an enterprise, but specific images were not infrequently criticized, destroyed or expurgated by repainting. In the case of Michelangelo's *Last Judgement*, for instance, the naked bodies were ordered to be furnished with fig-leaves. The painter Paolo Veronese (1528–88) was summoned before the Venetian Inquisition because his painting of the Last Supper included what the inquisitors called 'buffoons, drunkards, Germans, dwarves and similar vulgarities'. Some Protestants smashed images, considering them idolatrous, while Catholics buried the images they were coming to view as unseemly – naked St Sebastians, for example, or representations of St Martin as a soldier and of St Eloy as a goldsmith.

The most famous and widespread censorship system of the period was that of the Catholic Church, with its 'Index of Prohibited Books'. This was a printed catalogue – perhaps better described as an 'anti-catalogue' – of printed books that the faithful were forbidden to read. There were many local indexes too, beginning with the one published in 1544 by the Sorbonne (the Faculty of Theology of the University of Paris), but the important ones were those issued by papal authority and binding on the whole Church, from the mid-sixteenth century to the mid-twentieth century.

The index might be said to have been invented as a Counter-Reformation antidote to Protestantism and printing. It was an attempt to fight print with print. The model index, issued in 1564, began with a set of general rules forbidding three main types of book: the heretical, the immoral and the magical. Then came an alphabetical list of authors and titles, the authors divided into first class (all their writings being prohibited) and second class (in which case the ban extended only to specific works). Most of the books on the Church's list were devoted to Protestant theology in Latin, but some literary works which later became classics can also be found on it, among them the satires written by the humanist Erasmus and the *Gargantua and Pantagruel* of Rabelais (not for the obscenity which worried some eighteenth- and nineteenth-century readers, but for the author's criticisms of the Church). Machiavelli's *Prince* was also prohibited, as were Petrarch's sonnets against the papacy, Boccaccio's *Decameron* and Dante's treatise *On Monarchy* (thanks to its exaltation of the emperor over the Pope) .

There was disagreement among censors as to how far to go. A hard line was taken by the Italian Jesuit Antonio Possevino (1534–1611), who attacked romances of chivalry as 'stratagems of Satan' (perhaps for their emphasis on love, perhaps for their magic). On the other hand, another Italian Jesuit, Roberto Bellarmino (1542–1621), defended the great trio of Tuscan writers, Dante, Petrarch and Boccaccio, on the grounds that they were all good Catholics.

Two examples of censorship at work may show more clearly what the inquisitors were looking for. When Montaigne visited Italy, he submitted his recently published *Essays* to a papal censor who suggested a few alterations – references to fortune should be changed to providence, for instance, while references to heretical poets should be deleted altogether. A Calvinist pastor expurgated the *Essays* before their publication in Geneva was permitted, removing a favourable reference to the Roman emperor Julian 'the Apostate', who was converted from Christianity to paganism.

The second example is that of Boccaccio's *Decameron*, which had long been a target for clerical critics. Its condemnation was discussed at the

Council of Trent, which met in the middle of the sixteenth century to discuss the reform of the Church. The Duke of Florence sent an ambassador to the Council to beg for the reprieve of the book, since his own prestige depended on the cultural capital represented by the local writers Dante, Petrarch and Boccaccio. Thanks to this diplomatic lobbying, the book's condemnation was commuted to expurgation. The Inquisition was always hypersensitive to its own reputation, and in the expurgated edition, one story (dealing with the hypocrisy of an inquisitor) completely disappeared. Elsewhere in the text the names of saints and clerics were removed, at the price of making some stories virtually unintelligible. As in the case of Rabelais, what worried the inquisitors was not the frequent obscenity of Boccaccio's stories, but their anti-clericalism.

The campaign of repression had its absurd side, but it may have been a reasonable success in its own terms. From the point of view of the orthodox, books were dangerous. The example of Menocchio, the Italian miller who was encouraged by books to think for himself (see p. 71), suggests they had a point. It is difficult to measure the effectiveness of the repression, but the Inquisition records themselves reveal the continuing importance of the trade in contraband books, such as the copies of Erasmus and Machiavelli which were still being smuggled into Venice in the 1570s and 1580s.

Protestant censorship was less effective than Catholic censorship, not because the Protestants were more tolerant but because they were more divided, fragmented into different churches such as the Lutheran and the Calvinist, with different administrative structures. In Calvinist Geneva, manuscripts were submitted by the printer in advance of publication, to be read by experts in theology, law, medicine and so on, before written permission to print was given. To ensure that the orders were obeyed, the printing houses were regularly inspected, and forbidden books were confiscated and might be burned by the public executioner. Secular censorship in France, England, the Dutch Republic, the Habsburg Empire and elsewhere was organized on similar lines.

In England, printing was restricted to London, Oxford and Cambridge and was controlled through the Stationers' Company, founded in 1557. It registered new publications and, before they were published, the manuscripts of books were also inspected. According to the English *Licensing Act* of 1662, law books had to be inspected by the Lord Chancellor, history books by a secretary of state, and most other kinds of book by the Archbishop of Canterbury and the Bishop of London or their deputies. The system was brought to an end in 1695 when the *Licensing Act* was allowed to lapse.

The efficacy of the censorship system should not be overestimated. One of its unintended consequences was to awaken interest in banned titles which some readers might not otherwise have known about. Another reaction to formal censorship was to organize or reorganize clandestine communication.

Clandestine Communication

A considerable variety of messages was communicated underground, from the secrets of governments to commercial or technical secrets, and from unorthodox religious ideas to pornography.

'Pornography' – a term that was not coined until the nineteenth century – is not easy to define. If it is used to refer to texts which are not only intended to arouse lust but also to sell for this very reason, the term is applicable to a number of early modern works. The *120 Days of Sodom*, by the Marquis de Sade (1740–1814) was among the most notorious examples, but far from the first. A century earlier, the anonymous *Venus in the Cloister* (1683) had been equally infamous. In the early sixteenth century, images of different sexual postures drawn by Giulio Romano (1499–1546) and engraved by Marcantonio Raimondi (d. 1534), with accompanying verses by Pietro Aretino, circulated in Rome before they were discovered and suppressed.

It is not easy to draw the line between public and private in this domain. The communication of secrets by word of mouth, however safe it might have seemed, might be vulnerable to eavesdropping, in one case at least in the literal sense of the term. In 1478, some Venetians made a hole in the roof of the Doge's Palace in order to discover the latest news from Istanbul, news which was of obvious commercial value. It is no wonder that secrecy within a given group was sometimes maintained by the use of a private language, as in the case of the jargon of professional beggars and thieves.

Occult and alchemical works, as well as heretical or subversive ones, often circulated in manuscript copies. In other cases, what was transcribed was a confidential letter or report, such as an account of a foreign country presented to the Venetian Senate by an ambassador on his return from a mission abroad. Unofficial copies of these reports were sold openly in Rome in the seventeenth century, and one at least travelled as far as the Bodleian Library in Oxford. Again, in eighteenth-century Paris, police reports sometimes circulated among members of the public. To prevent leaks of this kind, codes and ciphers of various kinds were often used by merchants, by governments and even by scientists.

Governments made considerable use of cipher, and the ciphers, thanks to the aid of leading mathematicians, code-makers and code-breakers, became more and more sophisticated in the early modern period. Private individuals also used ciphers, and the diarist Samuel Pepys was not alone in using foreign languages to conceal some of the activities he recorded from possible readers, including his wife.

Raids on printers suspected of trading in forbidden books were not uncommon, but presses were sometimes set up in private houses and moved around the country in order to avoid detection. In Elizabethan England, for example, pamphlets attacking the episcopate were originally printed in a country house in Surrey, and later in Northampton and Warwick. The *Lettres Provinciales* (1657), a famous attack on the Jesuits by the polymath Blaise Pascal (1623–62), were printed in secret. Again, a critique of serfdom, censorship and autocracy, the *Journey from Petersburg to Moscow* (1790), was published by the author, Aleksandr Nikolaevich Radishchev (1749–1802), on a private press on his estate in the country. He was immediately imprisoned and later exiled to Siberia.

The authors of such publications usually wrapped themselves in a cloak of anonymity, referring to themselves only by pseudonyms. The attacks on the Elizabethan bishops were signed 'Martin Marprelate'; Pascal's attacks on the Jesuits were signed 'Louis de Montalte'. The printers likewise disguised their identities, while the place of publication, if it was mentioned at all, was generally false, often imaginary and sometimes extremely imaginative. As two early seventeenth-century Italian cardinals complained, 'to deceive the Catholics more easily', Protestant propaganda arrived with the names of Catholic cities on the title page, and some printers even imitated the typography of the Catholic printers of Paris, Lyons or Antwerp. A favourite imaginary place of publication was 'Freetown' or its equivalent in other languages (Villefranche, Vrijstadt, Eleutheropolis). Another, for some reason, was Cologne, where for 150 years books were attributed to a non-existent printer, Pierre de Marteau, presumably so-called because he hammered his victims. The printer of the Marprelate pamphlets claimed to work 'overseas, in Europe, within two furlongs of a bouncing priest'. Some late eighteenth-century French pornographic works claimed to be published 'at the press of the odalisques' in Istanbul or even at the Vatican itself.

Another possibility in the early modern period – as for so many East European writers in the age of the Cold War – was actually to print abroad rather than simply claim to do so. A famous seventeenth-century example is that of the antipapal *History of the Council of Trent*, written by the Venetian friar Paolo Sarpi (1552–1623). The book was first published in London, in Italian, in 1619. The manuscript was brought in secret from Venice to London via the British Embassy in instalments described in the correspondence by the code name of 'songs'.

Printed books were also frequently smuggled across frontiers. By the early 1550s there were regular clandestine routes from Switzerland to Venice along which heretical books travelled. Again, in the early seventeenth century, prohibited books, usually unbound, were being smuggled into Spain, the large bibles hidden in bolts of cloth and the small catechisms disguised as packs of playing cards. Books which were critical of King Louis XIV and his court were published in French in Amsterdam, and then smuggled into France.

Finally, it was of course possible to publish in the normal way but to communicate messages on two levels, the manifest and the latent. In the early modern period, Aesop, the ancient Greek writer of fables about animals, often provided a cover, as he did in Poland in the twentieth century under the Communist regime. The 'method of Aesop' could easily be applied to the human world. One of the most famous examples is that of the *Fables* of Jean de Lafontaine (1621–95). They are now treated as stories for children, but the fact that Lafontaine refused to serve Louis XIV, remaining loyal to a patron who had fallen into political disgrace, suggests that the figure of the tyrannical lion, for instance, should be read in a political manner.

Alternatively, a message about a topical subject might be disguised as a history of similar events in the past. For example, the deposition of King Richard II by Henry of Bolingbroke (the future King Henry IV) had considerable political resonance towards the end of the reign of Queen Elizabeth, with the Earl of Essex cast in the role of Henry. No wonder, then, that in 1599, when Sir John Hayward published a history of the *Life and Reign of King Henry IV*, the queen asked Francis Bacon whether there was treason in the book. Again, when the Earl of Essex rebelled against the queen, his followers gave money to actors to play Shakespeare's *Richard II*. Elizabeth was said to have remarked at the time: 'I am Richard II, know you not that?' Similar allegorical techniques were in use in late seventeenth-century England during the so-called 'Exclusion Crisis' (discussed on p. 101).

A relatively recent example of this allegorical method is the play *The Crucible* (1953) by Arthur Miller (1915–2005). The play presented a critique of the 'witch-hunting' of communists by US Senator Joe McCarthy (1908–57), in the form of a trial for witchcraft in New England in the seventeenth century.

Print in Consumer Society

Printing might be dangerous, but it was also profitable. Some printers (though not all) were mercenaries, working for Catholics and Protestant

alike during the Wars of Religion (see p. 92). Indeed, one important consequence of the invention of printing was the close involvement of entrepreneurs in the process of spreading knowledge. Bestsellers go back to the
early days of printing. *The Imitation of Christ*, a devotional work attributed
to the fourteenth-century Netherlander Thomas à Kempis (1379–1471) had
appeared in no fewer than 99 editions by 1500. The Scriptures, too, sold
well at this time, especially the New Testament and the Psalms, although
the Catholic Church prohibited vernacular bibles in the later sixteenth
century on the grounds that they encouraged heresy. Print runs of books
were normally small by later standards, averaging from 500 to 1,000 copies,
but as many as three or four million copies of almanacs were printed in
seventeenth-century England.

In order to sell more books, printers, whose range of products might
involve far more than what is now known as 'literature', published catalogues and engaged in other forms of advertising. In Italy, the first known
catalogue of books with prices goes back to 1541. In the sixteenth century,
the Frankfurt Book Fair made particular titles known internationally, as it
still does today. Pages at the front or back of books advertised other works
sold by the same printer or bookseller (later distinctions between printer,
publisher and bookseller were not yet drawn in this period).

Advertising in print also developed in the seventeenth century. In London
around 1650, a newspaper would carry about six advertisements on the
average; 100 years later, it would carry about fifty. Among the goods and
services advertised were plays, race meetings, quack doctors and 'Holman's
Ink Powder', perhaps the first brand name, for a product that was patented
in 1688.

News was itself a commodity and it was indeed viewed as such at the
time, at least by satirists such as Ben Jonson in his play *The Staple of News*
(1626), imagining an attempt to monopolize the trade. As the sociologist
Colin Campbell has argued, eighteenth-century novels, like television serials today, allowed readers the vicarious enjoyment of expensive consumer
goods and also encouraged them to buy, thus acting as midwives in what
has been called 'the birth of consumer society' (see below, p. 67).

The rise of the idea of intellectual property was a response both to the
spread of printing and the emergence of consumer society. Yet some sense
of literary ownership goes back to the fifteenth century, if not before, for
there were humanists who accused one another of theft or plagiarism
while themselves claiming to practise creative imitation. Thus, the second
part of *Don Quixote*, published in 1614, was not written by Miguel Cervantes
(1547–1616) but by a certain 'Avellaneda'. This was a slightly unusual form

of plagiarism, since it involved stealing a character rather than a text, or stealing someone else's name for one's own work in order to cash in on his reputation. All the same, the original author resented it. In order to drive out the work of his competitor, Cervantes had to produce a second part of his own.

In this way, market forces encouraged the idea of individual authorship, an idea reinforced by new practices such as printing the portrait of the author as a frontispiece to the work, or introducing an edition of someone's collected works by a biography of the author. By 1711, the first issue of *The Spectator* could poke gentle fun at the reader unable to enjoy a book 'till he knows whether the writer of it be a black or a fair man, of a mild or choleric disposition, married or a bachelor'.

During the eighteenth century, legal regulation reinforced the idea of literary or intellectual property. In Britain, for example, an Act was passed in 1709 which granted authors or their assignees the sole right to print their work for fourteen years. William Hogarth, who suffered from piracies of his popular series of engravings of *The Harlot's Progress* (1732), campaigned with success for a new *Copyright Act* (1735), which gave graphic artists like himself similar rights to those enjoyed by authors. An earlier 1709 *Act*, dealing with books, was clarified in the courts in cases such as *Millar v. Taylor* (1769) and *Donaldson v. Beckett* (1774), by which time the term 'copyright' was in general use. Further changes were made in the nineteenth century, but there was no acceptable international copyright before the Bern Convention of 1887.

For a close-up view of the developing market in the media, an imperfect market, it may be illuminating to examine in chronological sequence three of the main centres of the book trade in early modern Europe: sixteenth-century Venice, seventeenth-century Amsterdam and eighteenth-century London.

In the fifteenth century, more books were printed in Venice than in any other city in Europe (about 4,500 editions, equivalent to something like two million copies, or 20 per cent of the European market). The Venetian book industry had a capitalist organization, with a small group in control and the financial backing of merchants whose economic interests ranged much more widely than books.

In the sixteenth century it has been estimated that about 500 Venetian printers and publishers produced from 15,000 to 17,500 titles and possibly eighteen million copies. The most famous of these printers, Aldo Manuzio (c. 1450–1515), made his reputation – and possibly his fortune – by publishing editions of the Greek and Latin classics in a small format which allowed scholars and students to carry them about with ease (a correspondent praised his 'handy' volumes which could even be read when walking). There was cut-throat competition between printers, who regularly ignored one another's privileges and published the same books as their rivals, claiming that their editions were more correct or included new material, even if this was not the case. The large number of printers and publishers in Venice was one of the attractions of the city for men of letters, since it allowed them to make a living independent of patrons, even if it did not make them rich.

Some of these men of letters were nicknamed the *poligrafi* because they wrote so much and on such a wide variety of topics in order to survive. They were what would be known in eighteenth-century English as 'hacks', in other words, writers who were for hire, like hackney carriages. Their works included verse as well as prose and original compositions as well as translations, adaptations and plagiarisms from other writers. A genre in which they specialized was that of works offering practical information, including conduct books; a treatise explaining how to write letters on different topics; and a guide to Venice for foreign visitors that was still being reprinted in the seventeenth century. Some of these writers served particular printers (notably Gabriel Giolito, who published some 850 books in his long career) as editors and proof-readers as well as authors. In a sense, the *poligrafi* were on the frontier between two worlds. They were essentially compilers working in the medieval tradition, recycling the work of others, but, living as they did in the age of print, they were treated as individual authors with their names on the title page. Consequently, they were criticized by their rivals for plagiarism, an accusation from which medieval writers had been free.

The economic and political position of Venice was skilfully exploited by the printers. For example, they drew on the skills of different groups of immigrants in the city in order to print books in Spanish, Croat, demotic Greek, Old Church Slavonic, Hebrew, Arabic and Armenian. They also looked beyond Europe, as the city of Venice did more generally. Among their specialities were accounts of the discovery of distant new lands. In the sixteenth century, Venice was second only to Paris in publishing books about the Americas, including various editions of the letters of Christopher Columbus (1451–1506) and Hernán Cortés (1485–1547).

The distinctive Venetian contribution to the book trade, associated with the city's tradition of tolerance for other cultures and other religions and the practical live-and-let-live attitude of its merchants, was undermined by the spread of the Counter-Reformation. The Inquisition was established in Venice in 1547; books were burned on Piazza San Marco and near the Rialto in 1548; a Venetian *Index of Prohibited Books* was produced in 1549 (fifteen years before the Index binding on the whole Church); and a ban on printing in Hebrew was issued in 1554. Booksellers began to be interrogated on charges of smuggling heretical or otherwise pernicious books from abroad. Some printers migrated to other cities such as Turin, Rome and Naples. Others, such as Gabriel Giolito, shifted their investments towards the publication of devotional books in Italian for a geographically more limited market. In the seventeenth century the Dutch republic replaced Venice as an island of relative tolerance of religious diversity and also as a major centre of information. The export of printed matter in Latin, French, English and German made an important contribution to the prosperity of this new nation. One of the leading printers in the republic, the Elzevir family, followed the example of Aldo Manuzio in publishing editions of the classics in small format. Elzevir also launched what may have been the first series of books ever to have an academic editor, Caspar Barlaeus, who was in charge of a range of compendia of information about the organization and resources of different states of the world, from France to India.

Barlaeus may be described as a Dutch equivalent of the *poligrafi*. Other hack writers included French Calvinist pastors who came to the Dutch Republic after Louis XIV had forced them to choose, in 1685, between conversion to Catholicism or emigration. There were too many pastors for the needs of the French Protestant churches in exile, so some of these well-educated men turned to writing for a living. Pierre Bayle (1647–1706), for example, who had left France for Rotterdam, edited a literary journal, the *News of the Republic of Letters*, which appeared monthly from 1684 onwards, as well as compiling his famous *Historical and Critical Dictionary* (1696).

The centre of Dutch publishing, as of much else in European industry and finance, was the city of Amsterdam. In the early seventeenth century Amsterdam was already Europe's major centre of newspapers, a new literary genre which probably illustrates the commercialization of information better than any other. The papers, which appeared once, twice or three times a week in Latin, French and English as well as in Dutch, included the first newspapers printed in English and French, the *Corrant out of Italy, Germany etc.*, and the *Courant d'Italie*, both of which began publication in 1620. From 1662 onwards, a weekly paper in French, the *Gazette d'Amsterdam*, offered not only information about European affairs but also criticisms of the Catholic Church and of the policies of the French government. By the second half of the seventeenth century Amsterdam had become the most important centre of book production in Europe, as Venice had once been. More than 270 booksellers and printers were active there in the 25 years between 1675 and 1699. A substantial proportion of them were, like the professional writers, Protestant refugees from France.

As in Venice, maps and accounts of voyages to exotic places formed an important part of the printers' repertoire. The most important printing establishment in Amsterdam, that of the Dutch cartographer Joan Blaeu (c. 1598–1673), son of Willem Blaeu (see p. 30) – an enterprise so large that it was one of the sights of the city for foreign visitors – belonged to a firm that specialized in atlases, with nine presses for type and six more for engravings. The Blaeu family advertised in a newspaper in 1634 that they were about to produce a world atlas in four languages: Latin, Dutch, French and German. The two-volume atlas duly appeared in 1635 and contained 207 maps. A few years later, a rival Amsterdam publisher published a still more comprehensive atlas, only to be overtaken in his turn by the second version of the Blaeu atlas, in six volumes this time, published in 1655.

As in Venice, and once again drawing on the skills of different groups of immigrants, books were printed in Amsterdam in a variety of languages, including Russian, Yiddish, Armenian and Georgian. In 1678 an English visitor to the city found a Dutch printing-house producing bibles in English and commented that 'you may buy books cheaper at Amsterdam in all languages than at the places where they are first printed'. French books were acquired by German readers through the mediation of Dutch entrepreneurs. Protestant printers produced Latin missals (with 'Cologne' on the title page) to sell in the Catholic world. The printers did not worry too much about infringing the rights of their competitors. During the eighteenth century the primacy of Amsterdam passed to London. London booksellers, like those of Venice and Amsterdam before them, were already notorious by the late seventeenth century for the theft of their rivals' literary property, a practice known as 'counterfeiting' or as 'piracy' (in the twentieth century the term was to be extended to unofficial radio stations).

As a protection against piracy, dealers in books began to form alliances and to share their expenses. Pooling their resources allowed them to finance large and expensive works that required considerable investment, such as atlases and encyclopaedias. Works of this kind were not infrequently published by subscription, often with a printed list of subscribers prefacing the book. In the course of the century, however, booksellers meeting in private devised schemes of sharing costs and risks that enabled them to dispense with subscriptions. A few authors benefited from their booksellers' deals. Thus, Dr Johnson (1709–84), whose hatred of patronage was notorious, received £1,575 in advance for his *Dictionary* from a group of five booksellers, including Thomas Longman and Andrew Millar. Millar gave the philosopher-historian David Hume (1711–76) an advance of £1,400 for the third volume of his *History of Britain*, and William Robertson (1721–93) an advance of £3,400 for his *History of Charles V*. The poet Alexander Pope (1688–1744), who managed his own business affairs with skill, had received a still higher sum, £5,300, for his translation of Homer's *Iliad*. Millar's successors, William Strahan, a printer, and Thomas Cadell, a bookseller, offered £6,000 for the copyright of Captain Cook's discoveries.

We should not be too hasty in idealizing the situation of writers in eighteenth-century London. A group of them, known collectively as 'Grub Street' after the place in London where some of them lived, were struggling to make ends meet, like earlier groups in Amsterdam and Venice. As in Amsterdam, this group included a number of French Protestant émigrés who were particularly active in journalism. Even for the more successful, the new freedom had its price. Johnson would probably have preferred to write his own books rather than compile a dictionary, and Pope to work on his own poems rather than translate Homer's. Hume wrote history because it sold better than philosophy, and if he were able to return to earth and consult the catalogue of the British Library, it is unlikely that he would be pleased to find himself listed as 'David Hume, historian'. All the same, some eighteenth-century men of letters enjoyed a greater degree of independence than their sixteenth-century predecessors, the *poligrafi*, had done.

The wider context for these developments in publishing is what some historians came to call 'the birth of a consumer society' in the eighteenth century, a phenomenon particularly visible in England but extending to other parts of Europe and even beyond. English examples of the commercialization of leisure at this period included horse-racing at Newmarket; concerts in London (from the 1670s onwards) and some provincial cities; operas at the Royal Academy of Music (founded in 1718) and its rivals; exhibitions of paintings at the Royal Academy of Art (founded in 1768); lectures on science in coffee-houses; and balls and masquerades in newly constructed public assembly rooms in London, Bath and elsewhere. Like the plays presented in the *Globe* and other public theatres from the late sixteenth century onwards, these events were open to anyone who could afford the price of a ticket.

Five Kinds of Reading

The commercialization of leisure included reading. In considering the practice of reading books and newspapers, or indeed viewing prints, we move from supply to demand. At first sight, the idea of a history of reading may appear odd, since reading is an activity that most of us take for granted. In what sense can it be said to change over time? And suppose that it did so, given that the movement of the eye produces no traces on the page, how can historians possibly say anything reliable about the changes? The last generation of historians have been addressing themselves to these problems. Arguing from the evidence of the physical format of books, from marginal notes written in books and from descriptions or pictures of readers, they have concluded that styles of reading did indeed alter between 1500 and 1800. Five kinds of reading deserve separate attention here: critical reading, dangerous reading, creative reading, extensive reading and private reading.

1. Traditional accounts of the effects of print, as we have seen (p. 27), emphasize the rise of critical reading, thanks to increasing opportunities for comparing the diverse opinions propounded in different books on the same subject. The change in habits must not be exaggerated, since reading was not always critical. There is ample evidence of respect or even reverence for books in early modern times. Satirists made fun of people who believed everything they saw in print. The Bible, not yet subjected to critical scrutiny by scholars, with the exception of a few unorthodox individuals such as the Jewish philosopher Baruch Spinoza (1632–77), was a particular object of reverence. San Carlo Borromeo, archbishop of Milan, was said to read Scripture on his knees. The Bible was sometimes used as a form of medicine and placed under the pillow of the sufferer. Its pages might be opened at random and the passages coming into view treated as heavenly guidance directed towards the problems of the reader.

2. The dangers of private reading were frequently discussed. Whether or not it acted as a tranquillizer (see p. 28), contemporaries sometimes viewed the activity as dangerous, especially when practised by subordinate groups such as women and 'the common people'. Parallels with twentieth-century debates about 'mass culture' and the dangers of television are clear enough, and they were pointed out more than a generation ago by the sociologist Leo Lowenthal (1900–93). Today, the rise of the Internet has initiated another debate of this kind.

If we define the issues more broadly, these debates may be placed in a still longer perspective. The decline after 1520 of images of the Blessed Virgin reading, images that had been relatively common in the late Middle Ages, appears to have been an early response to what might be called the demonization of reading by the Catholic Church. In late sixteenth-century Venice, for instance, a silk-worker was denounced to the Inquisition because 'he reads all the time' and a swordsmith because he 'stays up all night reading'. In similar fashion, both then and later, secular authorities considered unsupervised reading to be subversive. The reading of newspapers in particular was seen as encouraging ordinary people to criticize the government.

The dangers of reading fiction, especially for women, were regularly discussed by male writers from the early sixteenth century onwards. As in the case of plays, novels were feared for their power to arouse dangerous emotions such as love. Some men thought that women should not learn to read at all in case they received love-letters, although, as we have already seen (pp. 40–1), illiteracy was not an impregnable defence. Others thought that women might be permitted to read, but only the Bible or devotional books. A few brave people argued that upper-class women might or even should read the classics.

Several sources suggest that, in practice, more kinds of women read more kinds of book than the critics allowed. In Spain, for instance, St Teresa of Ávila (1512–82) described her youthful enthusiasm for romances of chivalry. Some of the evidence comes not from autobiographies but from portraits, in which women are sometimes represented with books of poetry in their hands. The evidence of fiction points in the same direction. The heroine of an Italian story by the priest Matteo Bandello (*c.* 1485–1561) is described as reading Boccaccio's *Decameron* and Ariosto's *Orlando Furioso* in bed. In the France of Louis XIV, the most important novelists were women, notably Madame de Lafayette (1634–93), writing primarily for other women. In Britain, the number of female writers of fiction grew in the eighteenth century.

Opportunities for women to read increased in the eighteenth century when novels and some historical writings, including histories of women published in Britain and Germany, were deliberately aimed at the female market. A commentator in 1726 described books as 'closet companions', and a number of eighteenth-century paintings of women show them with books in their hands (see Figure 7). By this time, some women were also reading newspapers. A 23-year-old French girl working as a cook, interrogated in 1791, claimed to read four newspapers regularly.

3. The extent of creative reading requires a different kind of examination. The meaning of texts has been a major topic of debate within literary studies since the 1990s. From a historian's perspective, it has long been clear that texts can be read and often have been read in ways quite contrary to the author's intentions. *Utopia*, by Thomas More (1478–1535), for instance, has been treated not only as a satire on the England of his day, but also as a blueprint for an ideal society, a 'utopia' in the modern sense of the term. *The Book of the Courtier*, by Baldassare Castiglione (1478–1529), an open

Fig. 7 Marguerite Gérard and Jean-Honoré Fragonard, *The Reader*.

dialogue in which appropriate behaviour in different social situations is debated inconclusively, was presented by sixteenth-century printers and treated by some readers (as we know from their marginal annotations) as an unproblematic guide to good conduct. The ironies of Daniel Defoe (1660–1731) and Jonathan Swift (1667–1745) escaped some literal-minded readers, who believed that Defoe's *Shortest Way with the Dissenters* was really recommending the persecution of Nonconformists and that Swift's *Modest Proposal* was arguing in favour of cannibalism.

The sixteenth-century Italian miller Menocchio, rescued from obscurity by the Italian historian Carlo Ginzburg (1939–), offers a fascinating example of unorthodox reading in more than one sense of that term. Menocchio, interrogated by the Inquisition on a heresy charge, was asked about the books he had read, which included the Bible, Boccaccio's *Decameron*, the imaginary *Travels* of a certain Sir John Mandeville (a well-known book in the fifteenth and sixteenth centuries) and possibly the Koran as well. What Menocchio read was less surprising to the inquisitors than the way he read it, the interpretations that he gave to the texts. From Boccaccio's story of the three rings, for example, he derived the conclusion that, if he had been born a Muslim, he should have remained one.

4. Menocchio offers a good example of an 'intensive reader', rereading a few texts and brooding over them, a style of reading apparently as typical of the first centuries of print as it was of the manuscript age which had preceded it. However, it has been argued that the later eighteenth century witnessed a 'reading revolution' in the sense of a shift towards the practices of skimming, browsing and chapter-hopping in the course of consulting books for information on a particular topic. In the period before 1750, there were fewer books, and print was often treated as sacred. The period after 1750, on the other hand, has been described as a period of 'extensive' reading, marked by the proliferation and the consequent desacralization of books. Dr Johnson, with his contempt for people who 'read books through', offers a vivid example of the new kind of reader.

The shift must not be exaggerated, because it is perfectly possible to practise the intensive and extensive styles alternately according to need. On one side, there is evidence of reading for reference in the late Middle Ages, especially in academic circles. On the other, there are the examples of the absorbed readers of the later eighteenth century, buried in one of the tear-jerking romances popular at that time, from the *New Héloise* of Jean-Jacques Rousseau (1712–78) to *The Sorrows of Werther* by Johann Wolfgang von Goethe (1749–1832). What is likely to have occurred is a shift in the relative importance of the two styles of reading, linked to the trend towards privatization. The format of books changed in ways which facilitated skimming or browsing. Texts were increasingly divided into chapters and, within chapters, into paragraphs. Printed notes in the margin summarized the message of each section. Detailed tables of contents and indexes organized in alphabetical order helped hurried readers to find particular items of information.

5. The privatization of reading has often been viewed as part of the rise of individualism and also of empathy or 'psychic mobility', as the media sociologist Daniel Lerner called it in his book *The Passing of Traditional Society* (1958). The basic idea behind the phrases is well captured in the images, relatively common from the eighteenth century onwards, of a man or woman alone, reading a book, sitting or sprawled on the floor and oblivious to the outer world. The long-term trend towards 'privatization' from the fourteenth century to the twentieth is reflected in the format of books. Fifteenth-century books were often folios in large print which needed to be read on stands or lecterns. In the sixteenth and seventeenth centuries, small books became popular, the octavo, for instance, or the still smaller 12-mo or 16-mo format, which the famous Venetian printer Aldo Manuzio used for his editions of the classics.

In his brief life of Thomas Hobbes (1588–1679), the biographer John Aubrey (1626–97) told the story that when the philosopher was employed as a page to the Earl of Devonshire, he bought himself 'books of an Amsterdam print that he might carry in his pocket (particularly Caesar's *Commentaries*) which he did read in the lobby or anti-chamber, whilst his Lord was making his visits'. This passage gives us the reader's view of the uses of the Elzevir classics in small format which were discussed above (p. 65). Books of poetry in particular were often printed in this format, which encouraged reading in bed, especially in the eighteenth century, when bedrooms in upper- or middle-class houses were gradually becoming private places.

Nevertheless, to view the history of reading in terms of a transition from public to private is as much of an oversimplification as viewing it in terms of a simple shift from the intensive to the extensive mode. Silent reading had sometimes been practised in the Middle Ages. Conversely, reading aloud in public persisted in the early modern period, as it was to do in working-class circles in the nineteenth century. The German Reformation offers some vivid examples of reading as a public activity (see p. 86).

It may be possible to make a distinction between reading habits according to social class – the middle classes tended to read in private, while the working classes listened in public. It is also necessary to make distinctions by situation. For example, the medieval practice of reading aloud at meals, whether in monastic refectories or royal courts, persisted into the sixteenth and seventeenth centuries. Reading aloud at home in the family circle persisted into the nineteenth century, at least as an ideal, as many images attest. It is likely that the texts of the Bibliothèque Bleue, discussed above (p. 28), which circulated in regions where literacy rates were low, were read aloud during the *veillées*, occasions when neighbours met to spend the evening working and listening. The rise of newspapers also encouraged reading aloud at breakfast or at work, while the fact that so many people were reading the same news at more or less the same time helped to create a community of readers.

The uses of reading in early modern Europe were as varied as they are today, although these uses were not described in quite the same way then as now. The main categories were information and moral instruction, and it was only very slowly that a third kind of book, oriented solely towards entertainment, was admitted to be a legitimate use of readers' time.

The increasing importance, between 1450 and 1800, of reading to acquire information is revealed by the proliferation of what we call 'reference books' of various kinds – dictionaries, encyclopaedias, chronological tables, gazetteers and a range of 'how-to-do-it' books on subjects as varied as agriculture, good manners, cooking and calligraphy. The importance of moral instruction is revealed by the number of sermons that appeared in print as well as by treatises on the virtues requisite for particular roles in society (noble, wife, tradesman and so on).

On the other hand, the history of the words 'entertainment' and 'entertaining' tells us something about the obstacles to the emergence of this category of book or pamphlet. In the early seventeenth century, entertainment was associated with the hospitality shown to visitors. It was only around 1650 that the term acquired the additional meaning of something interesting or amusing, and only in the early eighteenth century that performances, such as plays, could be described as 'entertainments'. (For the later history of the media as entertainment, see Chapter 6.)

Books that we might describe as entertaining, from jest-books to romances, were already in print as early as the fifteenth century, but they were often provided with a moralizing framework or packaging, presumably in order to weaken the resistance to these kinds of text on the part of clerics, fathers of families and other 'gatekeepers'. Pamphlets and single-sheet broadsides retailing the exploits of criminals (a new sixteenth-century genre which may have been designed to appeal to a new group of readers) were presented in a similar fashion, emphasizing the punishment and if possible the 'hearty repentance' of the criminal.

However, this moralizing approach was undercut by a rhetoric of sensationalism, with title pages, like modern headlines, referring to 'terrible', 'wonderful' or 'dreadful' events, 'bloody' atrocities, 'strange and inhuman murders', and so on. Over the long term, and especially in the eighteenth century, the literature of entertainment broke out of its moralizing framework, to become part of the commercialization of leisure, alongside concerts, horse races and circuses.

The Print Revolution Revisited

After this survey of the early modern media it may be illuminating to return to the discussion of the print revolution. There is an obvious parallel between the controversy over the logic of writing and that regarding the logic of print, as there is between debates over the consequences of printing and the consequences of literacy, down to such details as the rise of the fixed text and the problems of trusting a new medium. Critics of the revolution thesis often argue that print is not an agent, but a technology employed by individuals or groups for different purposes in different locales. For this reason, they recommend the study of the uses of print in different social or cultural contexts. The defenders of the revolution thesis, on the other hand, see print, like writing, as an aid to decontextualization. We seem to have returned to the conflict between an autonomous model and a contextual model, a problem discussed above (p. 14). Should we speak of print culture in the singular, or of cultures of print in the plural?

It is not necessary, of course, to take up an extreme position in this controversy. It is more rewarding to ask what insights each group of scholars has to offer, and to consider whether, by making the appropriate distinctions and qualifications, it may be possible to combine their interpretations. One might begin by rejecting the stronger formulations on both sides, both the determinism implicit in the revolutionary position and the voluntarism of the contextualists. It is probably more useful to speak, as Innis did (see p. 2), of a built-in bias to be found in each medium of communication. From the geographical point of view, it is prudent to think in terms of similar effects of print in different places, rather than effects which were either identical everywhere or completely different in each locale. From the chronological point of view, it is helpful to distinguish between the immediate and the long-term consequences of the introduction of print. The contextualists deal more satisfactorily with the short term, with the intentions, tactics and strategies of individuals. The revolutionaries, on the other hand, grapple more closely with the long-term and with the unintended consequences of change.

In early modern Europe, as in other places and periods, cultural change was often additive rather than substitutive, especially in the early stages of innovation. As was suggested already, the old media of oral and manuscript communication coexisted and interacted with the new medium of print, just as print, now an old medium, coexists with television and the Internet in the early twenty-first century.

At this point we may return to the arguments about permanence and fixity discussed earlier (p. 14), adding the necessary qualifications. It is true that writing encouraged the fixing of texts long before print was known. It is also true that many printed works were treated by contemporaries as ephemeral. Divergences between copies of early printed books are quite common, because proofs were corrected in the workshop during the process of production. Print, especially in the hands of 'pirates' (see p. 66), often put inaccurate texts into circulation. For these reasons, scholars such as David McKitterick and Adrian Johns have emphasized the instability of print. However, these qualifications do not overturn the moderate argument that the work of printers made texts more stable than the work of scribes had done.

A similar answer may be given to the larger question of the stability of knowledge. Print facilitated the accumulation of knowledge by making discoveries more widely known as well as by making it more difficult for information to be lost. On the other hand, as was pointed out above (p. 28), print destabilized knowledge, or what had been thought to be knowledge, by making readers more conscious of the existence of conflicting stories and interpretations. As in the case of texts, therefore, the fixity of knowledge encouraged by print was relative rather than absolute. The changes which took place, however important, were changes in degree rather than in kind.

One of these changes was a relatively new concept of writing which we now call 'literature', together with the concept of an 'author', linked to the idea of a correct or authorized version of a 'text'. As it was remarked earlier, oral culture is fluid, and oral creation a cooperative enterprise. In manuscript culture, there was already a tendency to fixity, but this was countered by the inaccuracy and also, as we have seen (p. 52), by the creativity of scribes. What we call plagiarism, like the intellectual property it threatens (see pp. 62–3), is essentially a product of the print revolution.

Another important consequence of the invention of printing was to involve entrepreneurs more closely in the process of spreading knowledge. The use of the new medium encouraged increasing awareness of the importance of publicity, whether economic ('advertising', see p. 62), or political (what we call 'propaganda', a term which came into use at the end of the eighteenth century).

Propaganda

Early modern rulers, or their advisers, were quick to see the uses of the new medium of print for spreading their reputation and justifying their policies. The reputation of Louis XIV, for example, his 'glory' as he called it, owed more than a little to print. Several hundred engraved portraits of the king were put into circulation during his reign. Official poets sang the praises of Louis – and other monarchs of his day – in print, and official historians published accounts of his marvellous deeds for contemporaries and posterity alike. The major court festivals, expensive but ephemeral events, were fixed in the memory by printed and illustrated descriptions.

Another form of mechanical reproduction was the bronze medal. Following classical precedents, the medal was revived in fifteenth-century Italy and was soon adopted by rulers as a means of spreading a favourable image of themselves and their policies. The number of copies struck was relatively low, perhaps no more than 100, but these copies would be distributed to foreign ambassadors or foreign heads of state in order to make an impression where it mattered most. Persuasion by medals became increasingly important in the seventeenth century. Earlier rulers had contented themselves with 30 or 40 different medals, but 300-odd medals were struck to commemorate the major events of the reign of Louis XIV. They could be viewed in cabinets, but the volumes which displayed engravings of the medals together with explanatory and glorificatory comments reached a much wider public.

Among the events that were captured in this way were some which never happened. According to the American historian Daniel Boorstin, in *The Image* (1962), the creation of 'pseudo-events' was the result of what he calls the 'Graphic Revolution' of the nineteenth and twentieth centuries, the age of photography and television. Yet examples of such events are not difficult to find in the age of woodcuts and engravings. The last dying speeches of criminals who were executed at Newgate in London in the eighteenth century, complete with illustrations, were sold on the day of the execution, and, in cases in which the criminal was reprieved at the last moment, he was in a position to read about his own death. An engraving of Louis XIV being shown around the Royal Academy of Sciences in Paris was published in 1671 at a time when the king had not yet visited the newly founded academy.

Print Was Everywhere

Reliable or unreliable, printed matter became an increasingly important part of everyday life. This pervasiveness deserves to be emphasized. The spread of books, pamphlets and journals was only part of a story which also included the rise of two genres normally associated only with the nineteenth and twentieth centuries – the poster and the official form. Official notices multiplied on street corners and on church doors. In Florence in 1558, for example, the new *Index of Prohibited Books* was displayed on the church doors of the city. In London from *c.* 1660 onwards, plays currently being performed were advertised on placards posted in the street. A Swiss visitor to London in 1782 was struck by the prevalence of shop names rather than signs. Street names were increasingly written on walls. For the inhabitants of Europe's major cities, illiteracy was becoming more and more of a disadvantage. A Western visitor to Tokyo today may be in a good position to appreciate the anxiety of someone who is aware that many messages are displayed in the street (possibly important ones), but is completely unable to decode them.

As for printed forms, they were already being used in the early modern period for leases, tax declarations, receipts and censuses. In sixteenth-century Venice, for instance, all the census-takers had to do was to fill in the appropriate boxes, classifying households as nobles, citizens or artisans, and counting the numbers of servants and gondolas. The Church as well as the state made use of forms. Parish priests filled in forms in order to certify that female orphans who were about to marry were good Catholics. By the seventeenth century, cardinals were using printed forms in Conclave to vote for a new pope, with blank spaces in which they wrote, in Latin, both their own name and the name of the candidate they were supporting.

Journals and Newspapers

It was thanks, above all, to the daily newspaper, a piece of ephemera that was to become increasingly valuable for social historians, that print became part of daily life in the eighteenth century, at least in some parts of Europe (when Goethe visited the city of Caltanissetta in Sicily in 1787, he discovered that the inhabitants had not yet heard of the death of Frederick the Great the year before). In England alone, it has been estimated that fifteen million newspapers were sold during the year 1792. And the daily or weekly or bi-weekly paper was supplemented by monthly or quarterly publications, by what came to be called 'periodicals' and 'magazines'. There were also scholarly journals like *The Transactions of the Royal Society of London* (1665–) or the *News of the Republic of Letters* (1684–), which spread information about new discoveries, the deaths of scholars and, not least, about new books. The book review was an invention of the late seventeenth century. In this way, one form of print advertised and reinforced another.

Other journals, like the French periodical the *Mercure Galant*, founded in 1672, were aimed at a less scholarly public. Written (mainly, at least) by a man, the playwright Jean Donneau de Visé (1638–1710), but aimed at female readers in particular, the journal, which was illustrated, took the form of a letter written by a lady in Paris to a lady in the country. The letter naturally gave news of the court and the city, recent plays and the latest fashions in clothes and interior decoration, but *Mercure Galant* also carried short stories, mostly concerned with love. Readers were invited to send in verses and solve puzzles, and the names and addresses of those who succeeded were printed in the journal along with the winners of poetry-writing competitions. *The Mercure Galant* also included accounts, generally flattering, of the actions of Louis XIV and the victories won by his armies, a form of propaganda for which the editor received a substantial pension from the government.

By contrast, the English periodical *The Spectator*, which began publication in 1711, two years after *The Tatler*, prided itself on its independence. The point of the journal's title was to emphasize its detachment from party politics and the desire of the editors to watch the fray rather than to join it. Its declared aim was to bring philosophy out of academic institutions 'to dwell in clubs and assemblies, at tea-tables and in coffee-houses'. Its coverage ranged from deep moral and aesthetic questions to the latest fashion in gloves. Like Donneau de Visé, its editors (Joseph Addison and Richard Steele, hiding behind the mask of 'Mr Spectator' and the 'Spectator Club') encouraged their readers to participate in the journal, placing an advertisement in the first issue advising 'those who have a mind to correspond with me' to direct their letters to the printer. Many people did so, and some letters were published. In similar fashion, a few years before Addison and Steele, the London bookseller John Dunton (1659–1733) had founded a journal, *The Athenian Mercury*, 'resolving all the most nice [precise] and curious questions proposed by the ingenious'. In its six-year existence, the journal offered answers to about 6,000 questions from its readers. The idea of an interactive medium, so often discussed today, clearly has its roots in the past. The success of the Addison–Steele formula may be measured partly by the number of collected editions of *The Spectator* which continued to appear in book form for the rest of the century, partly by its translation into foreign languages, and, above all, by the many 'moral weeklies' which imitated its style and approach, in England, France, Holland, Germany, Italy, Spain and elsewhere.

The effects of the rise of newspapers and other journals have been discussed from that day to this. From the start they had their critics, some complaining that they were bringing into the open what should have been kept secret, others accusing them of triviality. Yet they had their admirers too. Thus the Milanese journal, *Il Caffè* claimed that they broadened the mind and more exactly that they turned Romans and Florentines into Europeans. The rise of new kinds of reference book such as the 'newspaper dictionary' (*Zeitungslexikon*) or the 'gazetteer' (originally a dictionary of the names of places mentioned in gazettes) suggests that such papers widened their readers' horizons, not least by making people conscious of what they did not know.

Two concrete examples of the way in which they may have helped to shape the attitudes of their readers concern suicide and scepticism. In *Sleepless Souls* (1990), Michael MacDonald and Terence Murphy argued that 'the style and tone of newspaper stories about suicides promoted an increasingly secular and sympathetic attitude towards self-killing' in eighteenth-century England. The impression was being created through the frequency of the reports that suicide was a commonplace event. Suicide notes were printed in the papers, allowing readers to see the event from the actor's point of view, and these printed letters in turn influenced the style of the notes left by later suicides.

Newspapers may also be said to have encouraged scepticism. The discrepancies between reports of the same events in different newspapers, which offer a more extreme case of the discrepancies between books noted by Eisenstein (see p. 29), generated a distrust of print. Even if people read only one paper, they could hardly fail to be impressed by the regularity with which later reports of an event contradicted the statements made in earlier issues. By the late seventeenth century, discussions of the trustworthiness of historical writing commonly cite the gazettes as a paradigm case of unreliable accounts of events. For those who had participated in them – or simply witnessed them – the accounts of these events printed in the papers often seemed blatantly untrue, at least in detail.

Those were the negative consequences. On the positive side, newspapers contributed to the rise of public opinion – to be discussed in the following chapter.

3

The Media and the Public Sphere in Early Modern Europe

'Public opinion' is a term that is first recorded in French around 1750, in English in 1781 and in German in 1793. Its development was redefined as the rise of the 'public sphere', thanks to an influential book by the German sociologist Jürgen Habermas (1929–), *The Structural Transformation of the Public Sphere*, first published in 1962. To be more exact, the phrase has spread thanks to the translation of Habermas's abstract term *Öffentlichkeit* (literally, 'publicity' in the general sense of 'making public') into a more concrete and explicitly spatial term, a transformation that itself tells us something about the process of communication between cultures.

The Rise of the Public Sphere

As in the case of Elizabeth Eisenstein on the print revolution (see p. 29), what Habermas has given us is not so much a new argument as the reformulation of a traditional one. Instead of speaking about public opinion, which may seem to assume consensus, he examines an arena in which debate took place and offers an argument about argument. Habermas claims that the eighteenth century (a long eighteenth century, beginning in the 1690s) was a crucial period in the rise of rational and critical argument, presented within a liberal bourgeois 'public sphere' that – at least in principle – was open to everyone's participation. Habermas's study is especially important for its view of the media as a system (including newspapers, coffee-houses, clubs and salons) in which the different elements worked together: he emphasizes the structural transformation of this sphere in the later eighteenth century in England and France, its 'non-instrumentality' (in other words, its freedom from manipulation), and its contribution to the rise of rational and critical attitudes to what would be known – after the French Revolution – as the 'old regime'.

The views of Habermas on public debate have themselves led to a public debate, in which he has been criticized for offering a 'utopian' account of that century, for failing to notice the manipulation, even in the eighteenth century, of the public by the media, for placing too little stress on people who were in practice excluded from the discussion (ordinary men and women) and for placing too much stress on what he calls the 'model case' of Britain in the late eighteenth century at the expense of other places and periods.

It has also been argued that there was more than one public sphere in early modern Europe, including that of the royal courts, where political information was available in abundance and avidly discussed. Rulers such as Louis XIV (as we have seen earlier in this book) were well aware of the need to have themselves presented in a favourable light to this court public via a wide range of media from poems and plays to paintings, engravings, tapestries and medals.

We might add that it is more illuminating to think not of the presence or absence of the public sphere in particular cultures, but of its presence in a greater or lesser degree. Even in authoritarian regimes such as the USSR, an unofficial public sphere could be found, though it was located not in public places but in the kitchens of dissidents. It may also be useful to distinguish between a permanent or 'structural' public sphere and a temporary or 'conjunctural' one that appears at a time of revolt or revolution but fades away afterwards.

Politics in Florence

As in the case of the print revolution, there is no single landmark date at which to begin the story of the public sphere, no clean break with what had gone before. In the late Middle Ages, in the Italian city-states, especially Florence in the thirteenth, fourteenth and fifteenth centuries, constant reference was made to 'the people' (*il popolo*, the members of trade and craft guilds). A relatively high proportion of the population participated in Florentine political life, 4,000–5,000 adult males in a city of fewer than 100,000 people. Important political offices were filled by drawing names out of a bag and might be held for as little as two months. Florentine political culture, like that of classical Athens (see p. 8), was essentially oral and visual. The squares of the city, especially Piazza della Signoria, where the town hall stood, framed a kind of public sphere in which speeches were given and politics discussed. Fluent speech was highly appreciated in this culture because it was crucial to what the Italians of the time called the *vita civile*, the politically active life of a citizen.

Urban chroniclers sometimes recorded the political posters displayed and the graffiti written on the walls, and the public relations of the city were conducted not only orally, by sending ambassadors to other states, but also in writing. The Florentine chancery, in which official letters were written in the name of the government, was staffed by humanists – students of the culture of classical antiquity who were able to write letters in an elegant and persuasive Latin. The Duke of Milan, a leading enemy of the Florentine republic, was said to have remarked that he feared the pen of the humanist chancellor, Coluccio Salutati (1331–1406), more than he feared a troop of horsemen. On a smaller scale than Florence or Venice, some cities in the Netherlands, Germany and Switzerland, such as Antwerp, Nuremberg and Basel, developed a similar civic culture.

Five Clusters of Events

What follows is an attempt to test the Habermas thesis by examining some public discussions of both religion and politics in Europe from the Reformation to the French Revolution. Hence, this chapter offers a narrative of change in the media focusing on five events or clusters of events to which labels have been attached – the Reformation, the Wars of Religion, the English Civil War, the Glorious Revolution of 1688 and the French Revolution of 1789. We shall see how the different media contributed to these events, and conversely, how the events contributed to the evolution and modification of the media system.

A study of early newsbooks, Joad Raymond's *The Invention of the Newspaper* (1996), warned readers against the traditional linear account 'of an expansion of political franchise being reflected in increasingly wide access to news; of the breakdown of censorship and the evolution of political liberty; in short, of the movement from an ancient regime to a democratic one'. By contrast, the story to be told in these pages might be described as a zigzag narrative, moving from region to region and noting particular moments in which access to information became narrower rather than wider. All the same, certain long-term changes are visible between the 1520s and the 1790s.

The Reformation

If the Italian city-state was the milieu in which the Renaissance developed, the German city-state or 'free city', such as Nuremberg or Strasbourg (not yet incorporated into France), was the milieu of the Reformation, the first serious ideological conflict in which printed matter played a major role. The public sphere of the Reformation was on a much larger scale, both geographically and socially, than that of the Renaissance.

The Reformation, at least in its first generation, was a social movement, a collective enterprise, even if its conscious aim was to reform the old Church rather than, as actually happened, to found new ones. Martin Luther, a friar turned heretic, was a professor (at Wittenberg University in eastern Germany) who deeply resented what he saw as the Italian dominance of the Church, the 'magic' within it and its commercialization. In favour of more direct involvement of the laity in religious activities, Luther encouraged reading of the Bible in the vernacular – this involved new translations – and using a vernacular liturgy. He justified this involvement by what he called the 'priesthood of all believers', the idea that everyone had direct access to God without the need for clerical mediation.

Habermas has stressed what he calls the 'privatizing' effects of the Reformation, a withdrawal of believers into the interior realm, a withdrawal which was supported by Luther's belief that obedience to the ruler was the duty of a good Christian (it should be pointed out that Luther did not live in a free, self-governing city, but was a subject of the Elector of Saxony). As far as the long-term consequences of the Reformation are concerned, Habermas may well be right. In the early years of the movement, however, the vigorous debates which took place, first in Germany and then in other parts of Europe, about the functions and powers of the Pope and the Church and the nature of religion, made an important contribution to the rise of critical thought and of public opinion.

The Sorcerer's Apprentice

These events followed a recurrent pattern which may be described as a 'sorcerer's apprentice' model of political change in early modern Europe. Again and again, disputes within elites led to their appealing for support to a wider group, often described as 'the people'. In order to reach this wider group, the elites could not rely on face-to-face communication and so they turned to public debates and to pamphlets. The appeal to the people was often successful. Indeed, it was sometimes more successful than those initiating it expected or even wanted. On a number of occasions, frightened by what they had started, the elite tried to damp down debate, only to discover that they were too late and that the forest fire was out of control.

Although the term 'public opinion' was not yet in use in the early sixteenth century, the views of the people mattered to governments at this time for practical reasons, whether they tried to suppress these views, mould them or – much more rarely – to follow them (as in a few towns in

Germany in the 1520s, in which citizens were asked by the council to vote whether the city should remain Catholic or turn Protestant).

The involvement of the people in the Reformation was both a cause and a consequence of the involvement of the media. The invention of printing undermined what has been described, with some exaggeration, as the information monopoly of the medieval Church (see p. 12), and some people were aware of this point at the time. The English Protestant John Foxe, for instance, claimed that 'either the pope must abolish knowledge and printing, or printing must at length root him out'. As we have seen, the popes seem to have agreed with Foxe, and it was for this very reason that the *Index of Prohibited Books* was established (see p. 57).

Books and Pamphlets

After the Protestant churches – Lutheran, Calvinist and Zwinglian – had become established, they were able to pass on their traditions through the education of children. Plays, paintings and prints were now rejected in favour of the word, whether written or spoken, Bible or sermon.

In the first generation, on the other hand (a fairly short period, essentially the 1520s and 1530s), the Protestants relied on what might be called a 'media offensive', not only to communicate their own messages but also to weaken the Catholic Church by ridiculing it, drawing on the traditional repertoire of popular humour in order to destroy their enemy through laughter. This was a period when, in contrast to their later behaviour, Protestant zealots were often satirical, irreverent and subversive.

A major aim of the reformers was to communicate with all Christians. Where the great humanist Erasmus (*c.* 1466–1536), who also wanted to reform the Church, wrote in Latin so that he would be read in academic circles all over Europe, Luther usually followed the opposite strategy. He wrote in the vernacular so that his message could be understood by ordinary people, at the price of restricting it in the first instance to the German-speaking world.

Thanks to the new medium of print, Luther could not be silenced in the way that earlier heretics such as the Czech reformer Jan Hus (1369–1415), whose ideas resemble Luther's in a number of respects, had been silenced by being burnt at the stake. Hence it is sometimes said, or written, that without the book there would have been no Reformation.

Print converted a rebellion that might have been suppressed into a permanent revolution. It would indeed have helped the Catholic Church very little if Luther had been burnt as a heretic once his writings were available in large numbers at a fairly low price. Within a few days of its publication in 1520 by the printer Melchior Lotter of Wittenberg, who was a friend of the author, 4,000 copies of Luther's address 'To the Christian Nobility of the German Nation' (*An der christlichen Adel Deutscher Nation*) had already been sold.

In the long run, Luther's translation of the Bible was even more important than his pamphlets for the development of Protestantism. He was not altogether pleased with the printed text of his *New Testament* of 1522, which included some errors, but any printed version in the vernacular allowed far more people to read the Bible than before. A single printer in Wittenberg, Hans Lufft, sold 100,000 copies of the Bible in the 40 years from 1534 to 1574. Luther's *Small Catechism* (1529) probably reached an even wider public.

This achievement should not be taken too lightly. There was no standard vernacular German language at this time, partly because there was little popular printed literature – and one reason for there being little popular printed literature was that there was no standard vernacular language. Somehow or other, Luther managed to break out of this vicious circle, writing not in his own Saxon dialect, but in a kind of lowest common denominator of dialects, modelled on the style of the imperial chancery and more or less intelligible from east to west, from Saxony to the Rhineland. In this way, the potential readership of Luther's writings was multiplied, making their printing a commercial proposition, while over the longer term Luther's translation of the Bible helped standardize written German. It was not print alone or Luther alone but their combination which made this achievement possible.

Some printers in Strasbourg and elsewhere were prepared to print both Luther's writings and those of his Catholic opponents (see p. 42), but others, like Lufft and Lotter, printers who were committed to the ideas which Luther and his followers helped put into circulation, confined themselves to Protestant works. They were not alone. A letter to the Swiss reformer Ulrich Zwingli (1484–1531) mentions a pedlar who sold Luther's writings, and nothing else, from door to door. Despite its small size, the university city of Wittenberg, where Luther lived and taught, was the communications centre of Lutheranism. One reason for the spread of Luther's ideas in north-east Germany – in contrast to the south-west, where the ideas of Zwingli prevailed – was the ease with which preachers and printed matter from Wittenberg could reach this region.

In both places, pamphlets addressing ordinary people in the vernacular were of crucial importance to the success of the Reformation. More than 80 per cent of the books in German published in the year 1523 – to be exact,

418 titles out of 498 – dealt with the reform of the Church. In 1525, 25,000 copies of the *Twelve Articles* of the rebel peasants were printed. Between 1520 and 1529 as many as 296 polemical pamphlets appeared in the city of Strasbourg alone. By 1550, about 10,000 pamphlets in German had been printed. These pamphlets have been described, with some exaggeration, as a 'mass medium'. The exaggeration lies in the fact that only a minority of the German-speaking population were able to read, and only a minority of that minority could afford to buy pamphlets. However, the texts were often read in public and their message was heard by many more people than were able to read it.

Other Media

Print was not the only medium to spread the ideas of the reformers. The part played by music in the Reformation was an important one, with Luther himself a writer of vernacular hymns, the most notable of which, still sung, was 'A Mighty Fortress Is Our Lord (*Ein feste Burg ist unser Gott*). The participation of the congregation in religious services in the vernacular was very different from the traditional practice of 'hearing Mass' in Latin. Johann Sebastian Bach (1685–1750), member of a distinguished musical family and renowned in his own lifetime as an organist, wrote no fewer than 300 sacred cantatas, enriching the tradition of Protestant music (he did also compose a Mass in B Minor).

There was also an important role in the movement for both oral and visual propaganda. Since only a minority of the population could read, let alone write, it follows that oral communication must have continued to predominate in the so-called age of the printing press. It took many different forms in different settings, ranging from sermons and lectures in churches and universities to rumour and gossip in the marketplace and the tavern. Preaching was of particular importance in the early years of the Reformation.

Judicial archives, recording attempts to repress heresy, have much to tell us about the reception of the new ideas via different media. For example, they reveal the frequency of the singing of printed ballads dealing with topical religious and political events, yet another example of the interaction between media discussed earlier (see p. 55). Many of these records shine a searchlight on the tavern in particular, revealing it as an important centre for the exchange of ideas and rumours. This communicative function of inns may well have been a traditional one, but it is not often recorded in the Middle Ages. In the divided Germany of the 1520s, however, a number of individuals are caught in the beam of the searchlight, in the act of criticizing the clergy, discussing pamphlets or raising doubts about Catholic doctrines such as transubstantiation or the Immaculate Conception.

The records reveal both the importance of public discussions of heretical ideas and the role of the book or pamphlet in provoking such discussions. The heresy trials thus support the so-called 'two-step' theory of communication, developed from a study of the American presidential election of 1940. According to this theory, put forward by Elihu Katz and Paul Lazarsfeld in *Personal Influence* (1955), voters who changed their mind were not directly influenced by the messages which reached them from newspapers and the radio. What they felt was the 'personal influence' of local 'opinion leaders'. These leaders follow events in the media (in our case, the Protestant pamphlets) with more attention than their fellows, but then influence their followers primarily through face-to-face contact.

Images too were enlisted in the religious struggle. Luther, unlike Calvin, did not disapprove of them – he displayed a picture of the Virgin Mary in his study. What he opposed was what he called 'superstition' or 'idolatry' – in today's language, the veneration of the signifier at the expense of what it signified. In Lutheran churches in Germany and Scandinavia, some religious paintings continued to be displayed, mainly paintings of Christ, with the *Resurrection* as a particularly popular subject.

Images in print were a still more important means for the diffusion of Protestant ideas, as Luther himself was well aware when he appealed to the 'simple folk', as he called them. His friend the artist Lucas Cranach (1472–1553) produced not only paintings of Luther and his wife but also many polemical prints, like the *famous Passional Christi und Antichristi*, which contrasted the simple life of Christ with the magnificence and pride of his 'Vicar', the Pope. One pair of woodcuts shows, on the one hand, Christ fleeing from the Jews because they are trying to make him their king, while, on the other, the Pope defends with the sword his claim to temporal rule over the states of the Church (an obvious reference to the belligerent Pope Julius II, who had died in 1513). Christ was crowned with thorns, the Pope with the triple crown or tiara. Christ washed the feet of his disciples, but the Pope presents his foot for Christians to kiss. Christ travelled on foot while the Pope is carried in a litter (see Figure 8).

Many paintings of Luther were produced in the workshop of the Cranach family in Wittenberg, doubtless to hang in private houses as a symbol of loyalty to the Reformation. Some of these images, notably a woodcut made in 1523, present the reformer as a kind of saint, complete with a halo and a dove hovering over his head to signify his inspiration by the Holy Ghost (see

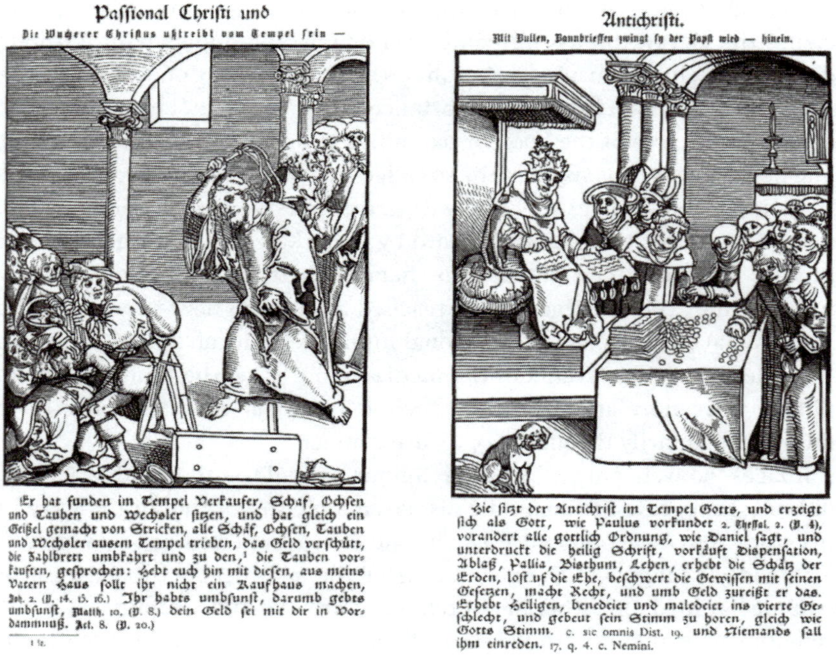

Paſſional Chriſti und

Die Wucherer Chriſtus uſtreibt vom Tempel fein —

Er hat funden im Tempel Verkaufer, Schaf, Ochſen und Tauben und Wechsler fiszen, und hat gleich ein Geißel gemacht von Stricken, alle Schaf, Ochsen, Tauben und Wechsler ausem Tempel trieben, das Geld verſchürt, die Zahlbrett umbfahrt und zu den,[1] die Tauben vor-kauffen, geſprochen: Hebt euch hin mit diesen, aus meins Vatern Haus ſolle ihr nicht ein Kaufhaus machen, Joh. 2. (V. 14. 15. 16.) Ihr habts umbſunst, darumb gebts umbſunst, Matth. 10. (V. 8.) dein Geld sei mit dir in Vor-dammnuß. Act. 8. (V. 20.)

Antichriſti.

Mit Bullen, Bannbrieffen zwingt ſy der Papſt wied — hinein.

Wie fiszt der Antichriſt im Tempel Gotts, und erzeigt ſich als Gott, wie Paulus vorkünder 2. Theſſal. 2. (V. 4), vorandert alle gottlich Ordnung, wie Daniel ſagt, und unterdruckt die heilig Schrift, vorkäuft Dispensation, Ablaß, Pallia, Biethum, Lehen, erhebt die Schätz der Erden, loſt uf die Ehe, beſchwert die Gewiſſen mit ſeinen Geſetzen, macht Recht, und umb Geld zureißt er das. Erhebt Heiligen, benedeiet und maledeiet ins vierte Ge-ſchlecht, und gebeut ſein Stimm zu hören, gleich wie Gottes Stimm. c. ſic omnia Diſt. 19. und Niemands ſoll ihm einreden. 17. q. 4. c. Nemini.

Fig. 8 Lucas Cranach, woodcuts of *Passional Christi and Antichristi*, 1521. British Library.

Figure 9). Such a use of conventions facilitated communication with ordinary people with traditional mentalities. The price of the facility, however – a price that has been paid many times in the history of communication – was that it diluted the Protestant message by adopting the very practices which it was supposed to replace.

Like images, ritual was a means as well as an object of debate at this time. Catholic rituals were parodied by a Protestant procession in Saxony in the 1520s carrying horses' bones as mock relics, in protest against the recent canonization of a local saint, Benno of Saxony. In the early years of the Reformation, the Protestants also resorted to street theatre to turn the people against the Church. For example, in 1521 the Swiss printer Pamphilus Gengenbach of Basel (*c*. 1480–1524) staged an attack on the profits the clergy made from the doctrine of Purgatory. The play was called 'The Eaters of the Dead' (*Die Totenfresser*), and it showed a bishop, a monk and other clerics sitting around a table carving up a corpse. Again, in 1528 the Swiss painter Nikolas Manuel of Bern (*c*. 1484–1530) staged a play enti-

Fig. 9 Woodcut of Martin Luther, *c.* 1523.

tled 'The Seller of Indulgences' (*Der Ablasskrämer*), in which he mocked the Catholic commercialization of religion, just as Luther had done before him.

The Conservative Dilemma

The fact that the 'Roman Catholics', as they came to be called by Lutherans, Calvinists and Anglicans, did not respond to the Protestant challenge in the same media, at least not on the same scale or for the same wide public, divided different parts of Europe. The Catholics did not produce as many pamphlets to defend the Church as the Protestants did to attack it, although they issued papal bulls and, after various sessions of the Council of Trent, summoned by Pope Paul III in 1545, published a formal *Catechism* in 1566. They did not produce their own translations of the Bible because the Church thought that such translations were dangerous. When they did produce religious plays, these were generally directed at an elite audience such as the parents of the noble pupils at Jesuit colleges in France, Italy and Central Europe, rather than a popular one.

This point illustrates a general feature of communication which might be called the conservative dilemma, common to authoritarian regimes – at least in societies of restricted literacy – whenever they are under attack. In the sixteenth-century case, if the Church did not reply to Luther, people might be led to think that the heretic was in the right. On the other hand, if the Church did reply, this might encourage the laity, in the manner discussed above (p. 83), to compare the two sides, think for themselves, and choose between alternatives instead of doing as they were told. For defenders of old regimes, who rely on habits of obedience, the right response at the level of message might therefore be the wrong response at the level of medium.

For their part, the Catholics continued to put a good deal of effort into the production of religious images, particularly after iconoclastic Protestants had destroyed them both inside and outside churches, in the process trans-forming the appearance of 'holy places'. Catholics now paid more attention to the rhetoric of the image, making sacred paintings and statues a more dramatic and, so they believed, an even more effective means of persuasion than they had been before the Counter-Reformation and the Council of Trent, which was not dissolved until 1563. The new images often referred to the doctrines that the Protestants had attacked. Scenes showing the repent-ance of St Peter or St Mary Magdalen, for example, were selected specifically because they were considered to justify the sacrament of confession. Saints, too, were given back their haloes, some of which (despite Luther's halo) had been swept away.

The development of the opposed – but, in retrospect, complementary – institutions of propaganda and censorship may have been inevitable conse-quences of the invention of printing, but they were the immediate result of the religious disputes of the sixteenth century. Propaganda and censorship were religious before they became political. Just as printing helped guar-antee the survival of the Protestant Reformation, making it impossible to suppress the ideas of Luther in the way that the ideas of medieval heretics had been suppressed, so in turn the Reformation was an economic boon for printers, whether in the form of bestselling pamphlets or, in the longer term, vernacular bibles.

Significance of the Reformation

In short, contrary to Habermas's thesis, it may be argued that the German Reformation contributed to the rise of a 'public sphere', at least for a time, especially during the 1520s. The writers of pamphlets used self-conscious strategies of persuasion, they tried to appeal to a wide public and they encouraged criticism of the Church.

There are some important similarities between what happened in the German-speaking world in the early sixteenth century and what is happening in the Muslim world of our own day. Once again, we see the rise of a public sphere that is largely religious and linked to the emergence of new media (print in the sixteenth century, audio and video cassettes, and websites today). In both cases the access of ordinary people to new media undermined the authority of a learned elite – the priesthood in the German case and the *ulama* in the world of Islam. The laity began to make their own interpretation of sacred books – the Bible in one case and the Koran in the other. No wonder then that specialists on Islamic culture, such as Dale Eickelman, describe the new trends by using the metaphor of Muslim 'Protestantism'.

As for the secular authorities, they too discovered that the new medium was a powerful force that might serve political ends. The conflict between the Emperor Charles V and his rival King Francis I of France was conducted through pamphlets as well as on battlefields from the mid-1520s onwards, and the timing of this paper campaign suggests that both rulers had learned a lesson from Luther.

After the 1520s, the surviving evidence of public discussion declines as the Lutherans turned into a Church that limited or suppressed popular debate. The emphasis shifted from the priesthood of all believers to the importance of a learned ministry that would tell the people what to believe and what the Bible meant. We find similar developments in other parts of Europe later in the century.

The Wars of Religion

From the point of view of the media, the battle between Catholics and Protestants is often presented as a war between a culture of the image and a culture of the book. This view is too simple. In the Catholic world, the standardization of religious practice associated with the Counter-Reformation fitted in with the needs of printers as with those of image-makers. There was an increasing demand for missals, breviaries and, above all, catechisms, and some printers, Christophe Plantin of Antwerp, for instance, enriched themselves by supplying these standardized products. Some of the laity read lives of the saints and other devotional works.

Nonetheless, there was a relative contrast between a Protestant book culture and a Catholic image culture. For example, long before the Counter-Reformation, at a time when it was dangerous to print Protestant literature in France, Italy or in the England of Henry VIII, the city of Antwerp was the home of a flourishing export business, printing bibles and pamphlets in French, Italian and English. On one occasion, on the instructions of the Bishop of London, who seems not to have mastered the economics of printing, a Catholic English merchant in Antwerp, Augustine Packington, bought up the whole edition of William Tyndale's *New Testament* (originally published in Worms in 1526), in order to burn it.

According to a contemporary source, Edward Hall's *Chronicle*:

> Augustine Packington came to William Tyndale and said, 'William, I know thou art a poor man, and hast a heap of new Testaments and books by thee for the which thou hast both endangered thy friends and beggared thyself, and I have now gotten thee a merchant which with ready money shall dispatch thee of all that thou hast, if you think it so profitable for your self.' 'Who is the merchant?' said Tyndale. 'The Bishop of London', said Packington. 'Oh that is because he will burn them', said Tyndale. 'Yea, Mary', quoth Packington. 'I am the gladder', said Tyndale, 'for these two benefits shall come thereof: I shall get money of him for these books to bring myself out of debt, and the whole world shall cry out upon the burning of God's word. And the overplus of the money that shall remain to me, shall make me more studious to correct the said New Testament, and so newly to imprint the same once again, and I trust the second will much better like you than ever did the first'. And so forward went the bargain, the Bishop had the books, Packington the thanks, and Tyndale had the money.

Iconoclasm

In the sixteenth century, Calvinists in particular encouraged a wave of iconoclasm that spread over much of Europe, directed primarily against statues (though stained glass also suffered). Sometimes the statues were smashed, sometimes merely removed. The movement was under way in the German-speaking world in the 1520s, supported by the radical reformer Andreas von Karlstadt in Wittenberg and Ulrich Zwingli in Zürich, spreading to Geneva and to parts of England and France in the 1530s. It reached its climax in France and the Netherlands in the summer of 1566, when image-smashing can be documented in twenty-five places between 10 August and 29 September of that year. A map of iconoclasm (see Figure 10) suggests that in many places it was a reaction to news or rumours of image-breaking elsewhere. It is tempting to interpret this organized movement (the first on a large scale since the Byzantine Empire in the eighth century) as a reaction to the increase in the proliferation of images and especially in the communicative power of statues in the late Middle Ages and the Renaissance.

While Lutherans were not iconoclastic, so that Karlstadt was only able to remove the images from Wittenberg churches when Luther was away, communication through images was specifically prohibited in Calvinist areas. In a Calvinist 'temple', as in a mosque, the visual field of the worshipper was dominated by painted texts such as of the *Ten Commandments*. It was the Calvinists who took the lead in two conflicts in the later sixteenth century: the religious wars in France from the early 1560s to the mid-1590s, and the revolt of the Netherlands from the 1560s to 1609. These conflicts are important in the context of this book because of the role played in them by the media and because the mixture of religious and political debates that they encouraged suggests that we may speak of a public sphere in these two neighbouring countries as early as the 1570s and 1580s.

The French Wars of Religion

The French Wars of Religion were media wars as well as conflicts with swords and guns, conflicts in which pamphleteering, image-making, image-breaking and oral communication were all important. Already in 1534, French Protestants had turned to the press in order to publicize their ideas. Broadsheets or placards attacking the Catholic Mass were printed in Switzerland, smuggled into France and displayed in public places and even, briefly, on the door of the king's bedchamber. In the 1570s, the conflict turned into a triangular one when the powerful Guise family accused the government of being too tolerant of Protestants and organized a Catholic League with Spanish support. The League conducted what we would call a media campaign in which verses posted on walls, satirical images, fiery sermons and incendiary pamphlets all played a part.

That something can be said today about this campaign is largely due to the activities of the Paris lawyer Pierre L'Estoile (*c.* 1546–1611), who made it his business to record rumours and sermons, and to paste otherwise ephemeral placards and engravings into his journal. It is thanks to L'Estoile that we know that the French civil wars were in part wars of images, many of them produced in one street in Paris: rue Montorgueil near Les Halles. On one side, a satirical 'Map of Popery' was in circulation, while the other side preferred the image of 'The Pot Knocked Over' (*La Marmite renversée*), a large pot spilling out Protestants and atheists into the flames. When Henri

The dates

8 Aug	Steenvoorde
3 Aug	La Chapelle d'Armentières, Bailleul
4 Aug	Poperinge
5 Aug	Ypres, Estaires
6 Aug	Roubaix
8 Aug	Oudenaarde
20 Aug	Antwerp
22 Aug	Ghent, Veere, Breda's-Hertogenbosch
	Amsterdam
22 Aug	Tournai, Mechelen
24 Aug	Valenciennes, Utrecht
25 Aug	The Hague, Delft
25 Aug	Leiden, Hulst, Cateau Cambresis
8 Sept	Leeuwarden
23 Sept	Maastricht

Key

——— Provisional boundaries

············ Present frontiers of France, Belgium and Luxembourg

BRUSSELS Capitals

• Important town

GHENT Town where images were smashed

Scale
0   100 km

Fig. 10 The seventeen provinces and principal cities for iconoclasm in 1566.

III (ruled 1575–89) had his enemies Henri Duc de Guise and his brother Cardinal Guise assassinated, woodcuts immediately appeared commemorating their 'cruel deaths'.

Printed words played an even more important part in the struggle. Like Germany in the 1520s, France in the later sixteenth century was in an age of pamphlets, with more than thirty a year produced between 1559 and 1572. After the Massacre of St Bartholomew, in which many Protestants were murdered, the pamphlets became more violent in their attacks on individuals, such as the 'whore' or 'tiger' Queen Catherine de' Medici (1519–89). They also turned from religion to politics. Hence the conclusion of the historian Donald Kelley that in 1572 'modern political propaganda came of age'.

Reaching a peak in the period 1588–94, and then declining in numbers when peace was re-established, pamphlets returned on a still grander scale during the political crisis of 1614–17 when a group of nobles rebelled against the king. More than 1,200 political pamphlets were produced in that short period. Cardinal Richelieu, who ruled France in partnership with King Louis XIII between 1630 and 1643, may well have learned about the political importance of the media from that crisis. At all events, he inspired the foundation of an official newspaper, the *Gazette*, in 1631, and on occasion sent items of news to the editor for inclusion in it.

The Revolt of the Netherlands

The public role of the media was, if anything, still greater in the Netherlands than it was in France, beginning with the revolt against Philip II of Spain or, as the Dutch now call it, the Eighty Years' War, from 1568 to 1648. More than 7,000 pamphlets from this period still survive in Dutch libraries. The print runs of pamphlets were commonly from 1,000 to 1,250, but they were quickly reprinted in response to demand. It was the pamphlets, for example, that spread the so-called 'Black Legend' of Spanish despotism, obscurantism and fanaticism. The writers in the service of the rebel leader, William the Silent (1533–84), presented Philip II as a tyrant who had failed to respect the traditional liberties and privileges of the cities of the Netherlands.

Printed verses glorifying the rebels and denouncing Philip II as 'Herod' or 'Pharaoh' and the Spaniards as the descendants of 'unbelieving Jews' were also in circulation, probably more widely than the pamphlets, since they were sung and heard even more often than they were read. Printed images also made a contribution to the rebels' campaign. For example, a woodcut of the execution of the counts of Egmont and Hoorne in 1568 by order of

Philip II soon circulated in the Netherlands, the captions telling the viewers what to think of the events illustrated.

The Dutch pamphlets were not produced continuously but clustered in response to major historical events, notably in the periods 1578–85, 1598–1606, 1618, and 1647–8. A sudden increase in production around 1607 has also been noted, in other words, a few years before the outpouring of pamphlets in the French crisis of 1614–17 mentioned above. The political pamphlet was becoming a part of Dutch political life. There was even a debate about debate, with one dialogue, for instance, discussing whether or not everyone 'may express his opinion on affairs of state'.

It was surely no accident that it was in the Dutch Republic, and especially in Amsterdam, that the newspaper (first recorded in Germany in 1609) became a popular institution (see p. 65). Unlike the pamphlet, the newspaper appeared at regular intervals, usually once or twice a week, and the issues were normally numbered so that readers would know whether or not they had missed one. In the unusually literate, urban society of the seventeenth-century Dutch Republic, the temporary public sphere was becoming a permanent one. In contrast to its Dutch equivalent, the English pamphlet before 1640 was moral rather than political, but the situation was to change very quickly on the outbreak of the Civil War.

The English Civil War

The English Civil War, otherwise known as the English Revolution, was also conducted in the media: in speeches and sermons, in texts and images, and in ritualized actions such as processions and image-breaking. Once again we find a 'sorcerer's apprentice' situation in which the elites were divided and both sides appealed to the people for support, with consequences which they were unable either to foresee or to control.

In important respects, the English Civil War was a religious war, waged between the supporters of a Church of England that was close in liturgy, if not in doctrine, to the Catholic Church and, on the other side, the so-called 'Puritans', who believed in simpler forms of worship (tables instead of altars, the prohibition of religious images, ritual reduced to a minimum, and so on). However, in the course of the wars the conflicts within the party of Puritans or 'Roundheads' (so-called because they wore their hair short) became ever more acute. Presbyterians, Baptists, Ranters, Fifth Monarchists and others attempted to convert readers and listeners to their own form of Christianity. Returning to the media, the clergy lost control of the sermon at this time and had to compete with lay preachers, some of them artisans, like the ex-tinker John Bunyan (1628–88), author of *The Pilgrim's Progress*, and some of them women, including the Baptist preacher Mrs Attaway.

In London at least, this was an age of politics by placard, by petition and by demonstration. For example, in 1640 the so-called 'Root and Branch' petition against the bishops was signed by some 15,000 people, while more than 1,000 took the petition to Parliament. In 1642 Parliament received the *Petition of the Gentlewomen, Tradesmen's Wives and many others of the Female Sex.* Artisans and apprentices were involved in politics on an almost daily basis. No wonder then that some recent historians of the period speak of the rise of 'mass politics', despite the problematic nature of the term 'mass'.

The middle years of the seventeenth century were great years for pamphlets and newspapers in which royalists and parliamentarians pressed their respective views. Between 1640 and 1663 a bookseller, George Thomason, an English equivalent of L'Estoile in Paris, was able to collect nearly 15,000 pamphlets and more than 7,000 newspapers, a collection now kept in the British Library and known as the *Thomason Tracts*.

The outbreak of the Civil War also coincided with what has been called 'the outbreak of the English newsbook' in 1641. *Mercurius Aulicus* was a leading newspaper on the Royalist side, *Mercurius Britannicus* a leading newspaper of the Parliamentarians, each producing its own version of events, and followed by *Mercurius Melancholicus, Mercurius AntiMelancholicus, Mercurius Morbicus, Mercurius Phreneticus, Mercurius Pragmaticus, Mercurius Anti-Pragmaticus* and many others.

This explosion of printed matter was the context for the famous debate about the freedom of the press in which the Puritan poet John Milton took part, publishing his *Areopagitica* (1644), an attack on the Long Parliament's *Press Ordinance* and a defence of 'the freedom of unlicensed printing', criticizing censorship of all kinds on a variety of general grounds, not least that independent men should be free to choose. He associated censorship with Catholicism, noting that the popes had 'extended their dominion over men's eyes' by inventing 'the new Purgatory of an Index'.

Topical messages were not confined to pamphlets and newspapers. Political graffiti on London walls and other public places provide vivid illustrations of the extension of the public sphere at this time. Pictorial propaganda was prominent too. About 150 political prints have survived from the year 1641 alone, some of them attacking Charles I's ministers, the Earl of Strafford and Archbishop Laud. The scene of Laud in a cage offers a clue to the style of the street theatre that flourished in London at the time, as it had done in German cities during the Reformation (see

p. 88), while the trial of Charles I, followed by his public execution on a scaffold outside the Banqueting House in Whitehall in 1649, was a high political drama which compensated in part for the closing of the theatres in 1642. The continuing importance of oral communication is revealed in the so-called Putney Debates in 1647, when a draft constitution known as the 'Agreement of the People' was discussed in an Army Council in which all ranks were represented. The claims of property were challenged and the extension of the franchise demanded.

Print was also important in the appeal to the people and the consequent extension of the public sphere. In 1641, no fewer than 20,000 copies of the *Grand Remonstrance* of the Parliament against the regime of Charles I were in circulation. Reports of debates in the House of Commons, printed for the first time, enlarged the audience for the speeches of MPs. The rise of printed petitions made a contribution to democratic culture, since they were a means for ordinary people to participate more actively in politics than before by lobbying Members of Parliament.

The great question, here as elsewhere in this study, is the extent to which the media and their messages changed people's attitudes and mentalities. Some scholars have emphasized the trivialization of political issues in the newssheets, but the other side of the coin was the entry of national politics into everyday life.

One pious London artisan, Nehemiah Wallington, referred in his journal to more than 300 pamphlets. Another contemporary declared that *Mercurius Aulicus* did Parliament 'more hurt than 2,000 of the king's soldiers', a remark not unlike the comment on Salutati's letters (see p. 82). Looking back from the standpoint of a later generation and extending the metaphor, a writer in 1682 declared that he knew 'not any one thing that more hurt the late King than the paper bullets of the Press'. One writer literally used his pamphlet as a missile, hurling it at the royal coach in 1641. When the German general Erich von Ludendorff (1865–1937) announced during the First World War that 'words have become battles', he was uttering a commonplace, even if developments in propaganda techniques gave his remark a new point.

The precise effect of this explosion of news and comment remains a matter of controversy. Historians still debate whether English political culture was essentially local or national at this time, while noting that newspapers kept the provinces informed about national events and encouraged discussion and the drafting of local petitions in order to influence politics in London. Illustrating the claim by Deutsch in *The Nerves of Government* (1963) that a community is 'a network of communication channels', the spread of news forged closer links between the political centre and the regions, and in this way helped construct a national political culture.

As in the Germany of the 1520s, a public political sphere and even a popular public sphere came into existence in Britain, and especially in London, in the eventful twenty years between the summoning of the Long Parliament in 1641 and the Restoration of Charles II in 1660. In the words of Nigel Smith, 'Never before in English history had written and printed literature played such a predominant role in public affairs, and never before had it been felt by contemporaries to be of such importance.'

From the Restoration to the 'Glorious Revolution'

The Restoration of Charles II in 1660 presented its makers with the problem, common to such situations, of returning from a relatively open system to a closed one. The licensing of books was reintroduced, while the proliferation of competing newssheets was replaced by the monopoly exercised by the *London Gazette*, an official newspaper on the French model (a more recent example would be *Pravda* in the age of Stalin or Brezhnev). In 1663, Sir Roger L'Estrange, whose disapproval of print has already been quoted (p. 26), was appointed to enforce government regulations, his title of 'Surveyor' of the press being a euphemism for 'censor'.

L'Estrange was well aware of what has been described above (p. 89) as the conservative dilemma, the problem faced by the Catholic Church in the age of Luther: whether to ignore the public criticisms put forward by the radicals or to fight them with their own weapons. He once wrote that 'a public mercury [a newspaper] should never have my vote, because I think it makes the multitude too familiar with the actions and counsels of their superiors'. Nevertheless, he edited no fewer than three newssheets: first *The Intelligencer*, printed, in its own words, 'for the satisfaction and information of the people'; then *The News*; and finally, from 1681 to 1687, *The Observator*. As he wrote in *The Observator* in April 1681, 'Tis the Press that has made 'um mad, and the Press must set 'um right again.' In this way governments were being forced to contribute through journalism to the spread of a popular political consciousness which the elites generally deplored, and to the rise of journalists ('newsmen', as they were known in seventeenth-century England) as a new force in political affairs, later described as a 'fourth estate' (see p. 130).

The workings of the media regime of the Restoration period are illuminated by a major communications event of 1678, the so-called 'Popish Plot' to assassinate Charles II so that his Catholic brother James, Duke of York, could rule in his place. On 6 September 1678, Titus Oates, an ex-convert to Catholicism and an ex-trainee Jesuit, went to a magistrate, Sir Edmund Berry Godfrey, to tell him about the plot, and repeated his story to the Council on 28 September. Godfrey was found dead, apparently murdered, soon afterwards. When his funeral procession took place on 31 October, the House of Commons resolved that there had been a 'damnable and hellish plot contrived and carried on by the popish recusants for the assassinating and murdering [of] the king'. At the trial of the plotters Oates gave evidence, but failed to carry conviction, and from this time onwards he began to lose credibility, just as Senator Joe McCarthy, with his stories of Communist plots, suddenly lost credibility with American public opinion in the 1950s. Oates was eventually convicted for perjury.

The best-known study of the Popish Plot, written by the historian John Kenyon, is marked by a robust common sense and vividly illustrates both the strengths and weaknesses of such an approach. Concerned to eluci-date what actually happened or failed to happen, Kenyon concentrates on showing that there never was any plot, dismissing contemporary beliefs as irrational, as 'panic', 'hysteria', 'paranoiac fear of Catholicism', or even 'mass hypnotism'. The Popish Plot surely requires, however, to be studied in the manner in which the French historian Georges Lefebvre studied the Great Fear of 1789 (see p. 37), in which the role of the media of communica-tion is taken into account. As in so many political crises, stereotypes played an important role – the treacherous Catholic, the subtle Jesuit and so on. Popular memories of the Gunpowder Plot of Guy Fawkes and also of the Great Fire of London in 1666 (for which the Catholics had been blamed) were reactivated.

The official *Gazette* did not mention the plot at all, and since there were no unofficial newspapers in existence at the time, the news of events cir-culated indirectly, either by private letters or by word of mouth – in other words, rumour. The crisis thus illustrates with particular clarity the argu-ment of Tamotsu Shibutani in his *Improvised News* (1966) that rumour flour-ishes when the supply of information is inadequate to meet the demand for it. In this case there was a rumour of mysterious 'night riders' in Yorkshire, Wiltshire, Gloucestershire and elsewhere, followed by reports of a French invasion. Printed images also spread awareness of 'The Horrid Popish Plot', notably a series of engravings on playing-cards representing scenes such as 'The conspirators signing the resolve for killing the king'.

Moreover, after the plot had been finally shown to have been a mere invention, its themes continued to be exploited by the Whig party, who were hostile to Catholics and wanted to limit the powers of the monarch.

There was a direct link, therefore, with the so-called 'Exclusion Crisis' (1679–81), the point being to exclude Charles's Catholic brother James from the succession to the throne (James was next in line, since Charles had no legitimate male heir). The Whigs drew up petitions, published ballads and prints, and organized a number of processions, notably in London in 1679, 1680 and 1681, in which an effigy of the Pope was consigned to the flames. The bill for these political demonstrations was paid by the Green Ribbon Club, a Whig organization.

On these occasions, a professional writer, Elkanah Settle, was hired to design pageants of pope, cardinals, friars, inquisitors and nuns, and a bell-man was employed to cry out, 'Remember Justice Godfrey'. Labels were placed on the figures to make sure that everyone understood the message. Images of the processions were also engraved and printed. An important contribution to the Whig cause (for which he was executed in 1681) was made by the engraver Stephen Colledge, who represented the king as a two-faced puppet-master or 'raree-showman'.

On the other side, the Tories complained – in print – of the abuses of the press, comparing the 'seditious libels' of their opponents with those of 1641. It has been calculated that between five and ten million copies of pamphlets were in circulation between 1679 and 1681, arguing the case for and against exclusion.

More traditional media were not forgotten either. For example, the poet John Dryden (1631–1700) wrote or collaborated on the play *The Duke of Guise* in order to show what he called the 'parallel' between 1583 in France and 1683 in England, with the Whig leader, the first Earl of Shaftesbury (1621–83), in the place of the duke and the Dissenters in place of the Catholic League. In other words, the parallel was a copy in reverse, with ultra-Protestants in England playing the role of ultra-Catholics in France. The play won the approval of Charles II, who asked Dryden to translate a recent history of Guise's Catholic League. Dedicating his translation to the king, Dryden suggested that a comparison of the events of 1584 in France and 1684 in England showed that 'the features are alike in all'.

In spite of everything, James Duke of York succeeded his brother Charles in 1685 and was crowned James II. Yet he was driven out three years later when the Protestant William of Orange (1650–1702), married to James's sister Mary, invaded England from Holland. The place of the media in these revolutionary events was an important one. At the outset, William's *Declaration of the Reasons for the Invasion* was printed and began to be distributed in England before the invasion even took place.

The fact that we still refer to the events of 1688 as the 'Glorious Revolution' testifies to the power of an image which was consciously fabricated at that time. For example, the Lord Mayor's Show of 1689, entitled 'London's Great Jubilee', presented William III as a conquering Protestant hero. The text was written by a professional poet, Matthew Taubman (who had previously written against the Whigs), and the message was supplemented by ballads, processions, prints, medals, playing-cards and sermons. Particularly influential was the sermon preached by Bishop Gilbert Burnet (1643–1715) at St James's in December 1688, which was circulated in print soon afterwards.

A Proliferation of Print

Long-distance communication continued to be difficult. In North America, news of the events of 1688 took time to arrive. The landing of William of Orange and the flight of James II occurred in November and December, 'at the wrong time of year for speedy reports to reach New England'. Thus, William's arrival in England was not known in Boston until early April 1689. In Carolina, William was proclaimed king even later than in New England because the news of his accession had taken longer to arrive.

While the importance of the English Revolution of the mid-seventeenth century in the history of the media is well known, less attention has been paid by historians to this sequence of events. They have noted, however, the lapse of the Licensing Act in 1695, which ended not only the censorship system but also the control of printing through the Stationers' Company, a control which had lasted since the Company had been granted a Royal Charter in 1557; and the Stamp Act of 1712 which, through levying stamp duty, attempted to curb the nascent power of the newspaper press.

There had been a spate of political memoirs and printed sermons in the years between, notably the sermon preached against the Whig government in 1710 by the High Tory divine Henry Sacheverell (c. 1674–1724), which sold 40,000 copies in the space of a few days. Sacheverell's sermon illustrates the way in which a performance in one medium might be echoed or mirrored in another, while the fact that the text sold ten times as many copies as Luther's *Address to the German Nobility* (see p. 85) provides a measure of the increasing importance of printed matter in European culture.

Most significant of all was the rise of an unofficial periodical press, including newspapers such as the *Post Man*, the *Post Boy* – both founded in 1695 – *The Flying Post* and *The Protestant Mercury*. These papers were longer than the official *London Gazette* and appeared more frequently, three times a week instead of twice. They were also considerably more informative. Circulation figures appear to have been quite high: 6,000 copies of the

Gazette at the beginning of the eighteenth century, 4,000 copies of the *Post Man*, 3,000 copies of the *Post Boy*.

It was such unofficial newspapers that gave permanence to the earlier temporary public sphere, turning politics into a feature of the daily life of a considerable proportion of the population, especially in London. Newspapers were often read aloud and discussed in coffee-houses, a political forum in which craftsmen as well as gentlemen, and women as well as men, had a voice. Other kinds of information were also becoming more public. The Stock Exchange and the newspapers spread economic information. Science, too, entered the public sphere, thanks to public lectures as well as to the *Transactions of the Royal Society* (see p. 78), which carried news of recent experiments and discoveries, even if the Society's meetings remained at most semi-public, open only to the members of the club.

It was this British culture that produced the radical politician John Wilkes (1725–97), whose extraordinary career as a defender of liberty and a hammer of the political establishment depended on popular support that was mobilized through the media, not only in newspapers – notably the *North Briton* – but in political prints, handbills and processions, while Wilkes's distinctive features were reproduced on medals, buttons, jugs, snuff boxes and teapots.

For a long time, festivals have carried political messages, as we have seen (see p. 49). What was new in this period was the rise of what the nineteenth century would call a 'demonstration' – an event, not always festive, organized in support of a particular policy.

Another novelty was what we might call the institutionalization of the political print, which now appeared regularly, and not only in times of crisis. Prints encouraged critical thought about politics by satirizing both sides (the Whigs commissioned attacks on the Tories, and vice versa). Not even the royal family was spared. The Duke of Cumberland was represented as a butcher for his brutality in suppressing the Jacobite rebellion of 1745, while the Prince Regent, later George IV, was to be a regular target of visual criticism in the early nineteenth century.

Seventeenth-Century France

On the Continent of Europe, with the exception of the Dutch Republic, the development of a permanent public sphere lagged behind Britain. The European media had plenty of news to report in the 1640s, a decade of crisis. In Portugal, the scene of a struggle for independence from Spain, the Lisbon *Gazeta* gave news of the war from 1641 to 1647. In France, pamphlets once again had a major political role, widely employed in the attack on the government and on the first minister Cardinal Mazarin (1602–61) during the civil war (1648–52) known as the 'Fronde'. Some 5,000 'mazarinades' were produced at this time, selling at a half or a quarter of a *sou* each, the total surpassing the productions of 1614–17, as the pamphlets of that period had surpassed those of the Wars of Religion. Issues of the official *Gazette* were much longer than usual between 1648 and 1650 because there was so much more news to report, and unofficial newspapers such as the *Courrier bordelais* were in circulation.

After 1650, however, and still more obviously after Louis XIV began his personal rule (1660–1715), the public sphere contracted again. This was an age of great writers, among them the playwrights Jean Racine (1639–99) and Jean-Baptiste Poquelin, better known as Molière (1622–73), the poet Jean de Lafontaine and the preacher Jacques Bossuet. In the visual arts, there was the painter Charles Lebrun, the sculptors Antoine Coysevox and Pierre Puget, and the architects Jules Hardouin-Mansart and Claude Perrault. In music, including ballet and opera, there was Jean-Baptiste Lully, followed by Jean-Philippe Rameau.

Thanks in large part to the initiative of Jean-Baptiste Colbert (1619–83), best known for his economic policies but also active as a kind of minister of culture between 1661 and 1683, the talents of these major figures, together with those of many minor ones, were harnessed to the glorification of Louis and his regime. Colbert was even more media-conscious than Richelieu and he supervised a team of artists and writers who fabricated the image of Louis. Tapestries and medals, as well as poetry and prose, painting and sculpture, theatre and ballet, proclaimed the achievements of the 'Sun King', while the palace of Versailles was built to impress foreign courts, the French nobility and posterity with his power. The media, especially printed books, were controlled by censors, and public criticism of the regime was minimal, though satires on Louis circulated by word of mouth, in manuscript or in printed texts smuggled into the country from the Dutch Republic.

This controlled situation changed, however, in the course of the eighteenth century. By the end of Louis' long reign, when the cost of his long wars was apparent (the War of the League of Augsburg, 1688–97, and the War of the Spanish Succession, 1701–14) in men as well as money, critical voices began to be heard. The critics included the Dauphin's son's tutor, François Fénelon (1651–1715), who thought that Louis overburdened his people with taxes. However, he was joined by many anonymous critics, using such media as songs and graffiti. Once again, it seems that the attempts to glorify Louis had backfired by making his subjects more aware of royal policies than before and so more disposed than before to comment unfavourably on the regime.

Enlightenments

The eighteenth-century French Enlightenment, which preceded the French Revolution, changed attitudes towards past, present and future and formed part of a European movement of education, criticism and reform, which had other centres in Scotland and Switzerland and affected North and South America as well.

The metaphor of 'light' was taken seriously in the definition of the movement by its participants. The light was that of 'Reason', a keyword of the time, set against faith and superstition, tradition and prejudice. Another keyword of the period was 'critical'. Yet another was 'modern': in the so-called 'battle' between Ancients and Moderns, supporters of the latter group argued that it was possible to equal or even surpass the achievements of the leading figures of ancient Greek and Roman culture such as Homer, Virgil and Cicero. In his emphasis on rational and critical thought in the eighteenth century, as in his emphasis on modernity or the idea of 'the public', Habermas was repeating or translating into twentieth-century terms what 'enlightened' people had already been saying about themselves. Urging reform rather than revolution, they viewed their role as educational, in the widest sense of the word 'education'. The media were their requisite instruments.

In this movement, a central part was played by French thinkers, the so-called *philosophes*, among them Voltaire (1694–1778), Rousseau (1712–78), Diderot (1713–84) and D'Alembert (1717–83). Calling themselves 'men of letters', they have sometimes been described as the first intellectuals, independent of patrons, or even the first intelligentsia, in the sense of being systematically critical of the regime under which they were living. They tried to spread their message widely, inside and outside France, and to women as well as men – though they did not try to reach the 'people'.

Voltaire in particular was contemptuous of what he called the 'mob' (*canaille*). All the same, by the end of his life, Voltaire, like Rousseau, had become a 'star', overwhelmed by 'fan-mail' and by visitors to his home. It is often thought that the idea of 'celebrity' is a new one, but there is a good case for arguing, that, thanks to the media of the time, what the French historian Antoine Lilti calls 'the invention of celebrity' goes back to the eighteenth century.

These men of letters thought and wrote within a system in which censorship was still in place, although administered more mildly than it had been in the age of Louis XIV. Journals, for example, were not allowed to deal with political subjects. These official restrictions made the oral culture of coffee-houses politically important, like the culture of the salons, in which aristocratic ladies organized intellectual conversations. Private correspondence, not least with sovereigns such as Frederick of Prussia (ruled 1740–86) and Catherine of Russia (ruled 1762–96), was another way in which the philosophes spread their ideas.

Artistic genres such as plays, paintings or historical studies were sometimes the vehicle of political messages that might pass unnoticed by the censors. *The Marriage of Figaro*, for example, by the French playwright Pierre-Augustin Beaumarchais (1732–99), had its première in 1784 after difficulties with the censors, who suspected that the play was a satire on the regime. The political sentiments of Beaumarchais were toned down in the Italian libretto of the opera with the same name by Wolfgang Amadeus Mozart (1756–91). First performed in 1786, it was one of his operatic masterpieces.

The famous *Encyclopédie*, published between 1751 and 1765, was another important vehicle for politics. D'Alembert, Diderot, Voltaire and Rousseau were among the many contributors to volumes which were intended as a means to awaken political consciousness as well as to acquire information. The publication of the *Encyclopédie* was a major event in the history of communication. Only the wealthy could afford to buy it, but cheaper editions followed and many more people could consult the work in libraries open to the public.

Publishers in Britain, beyond the reach of French censorship, were concerned to spread 'enlightened' ideas. Thus, the economic works and social analyses of the Scots Adam Smith (1723–90) and Adam Ferguson (1723–1816) were promoted either in their original, relatively expensive quarto editions, or in cheaper octavo editions, produced either by the original publishers or by 'pirates' who reprinted texts without permission, especially in Dublin, and often exported them to America. Thanks to the rise of translation, the works of Voltaire and Rousseau could be read in England and those of Edward Gibbon and Adam Smith on the Continent (Smith's *Wealth of Nations*, first published in 1776, had appeared in French, German and Danish by 1779).

Meanwhile, clandestine publications inside France itself, which booksellers described as *livres philosophiques*, included pornographic as well as heretical and politically subversive works. The American historian Robert Darnton has suggested that pornography was linked to Enlightenment and

Reform via a process of desacralization. The attack on the sexual conduct of the wife of Louis XVI, Marie Antoinette, entitled *Les Amours de Carlot et de Toinette*, may have encouraged not only reform but revolution as well. The ways in which royal families are presented in the media may have far-reaching political consequences.

The eighteenth century was a time of what has been called an 'explosion' of printed matter in Britain, France, Germany and elsewhere. In England, for instance, there was a rise of small cheap books or 'pocket-books' in the 1770s, while the rate of growth of new titles increased by nearly 3.5 per cent a year between 1780 and 1800. The marketing of books became increasingly sophisticated. The publisher John Newbery (1713–67), for instance, offered a ball for boys or a pincushion for girls at twopence extra if they bought one of his children's books, while James Lackington claimed to have half a million volumes in his 'Temple of the Muses' in Finsbury Square in London and to be 'the cheapest bookseller in the world'.

The expansion of the book trade both depended on and contributed to the rise of literacy. According to the historian Carlo Cipolla, by the year 1700, 'the Netherlands and England were possibly the two most literate countries in Europe'. The annual production of works of fiction in Britain, which had averaged only about seven in the years between 1700 and 1740, rose at least threefold between 1740 and 1770 and more than doubled again between 1770 and 1800. By then, the novel form, highly adaptable, attracted women writers as well as large numbers of women readers.

The ideas of the Enlightenment were able to spread further and faster than those of the Renaissance and the Reformation, thanks to the rise of periodicals. English periodicals had provided a model for a wide range of journals, known in Germany as 'moral weeklies', often adopting similar titles such as the French *Spectateur*, the German *Zuschauer* and the Danish *Tilskuer*. Many people who never read these works derived some idea of their contents from book reviews, an increasingly important element in eighteenth-century periodicals.

As in the case of earlier movements, the involvement of the 'people' in the French Revolution of 1789 was both cause and consequence of involvement of the media.

A similar point might be made about the American Revolution of 1776. The cause of American independence was advanced not only by pamphlets but also by newspapers. There were already 42 different newspapers in the American colonies in 1775 and some of them, such as the *New York Journal*, the *Philadelphia Evening Post* and the *Massachusetts Spy*, advanced the revolutionary cause by describing atrocities committed by the British army. Over the long term they created a national political culture through the news they reported (as in England during the Civil War) and assisted the emergence of a new imagined community, defined against the British. A French visitor to America, after noting the frequent reprinting of Thomas Paine's pamphlet *Common Sense* in the periodical press, claimed that 'Without newspapers, the American Revolution would never have succeeded'. Other European travellers commented on the number of journals in existence in the United States. By 1800 there were 178 weeklies and 24 dailies.

The French Revolution

The relationship of the Revolution to the Enlightenment has often been debated. By the late eighteenth century, the French government recognized public opinion as an entity which needed to be addressed, and in so doing helped the opposition to overthrow the old regime. In this way, the Revolution might be described as a continuation of the Enlightenment by other means. The appeal to reason, personified as a goddess, and to the 'rights of man', treated as universal, followed Enlightenment traditions. The *philosophes* were venerated, and the body of Voltaire was taken in solemn procession to be interred in the Pantheon in 1791.

Nevertheless, the revolutionary programme was more radical. It was to change the system, not to reform it. The reorganization of the calendar, making 1792 into 'Year 1', was an important symbolic act, a declaration of independence from the past. Historians used to see the Revolution as primarily a response to the constitutional, economic and social problems of the 1780s. More emphasis is now placed on the invention of a new political culture and the 'construction' of a new community of citizens, in which a place was created, alongside the two privileged orders, or 'estates', of the clergy and the nobility, for the 'third estate' (lawyers, merchants, artisans and peasants). In this work of invention and construction, a crucial role was once again played by the media.

Printed matter played an important part in the French Revolution, which began with calls for a free press. The Comte de Mirabeau (1749–81) adapted Milton's *Areopagitica* (1788), Marie-Joseph Chénier set out a forceful *Denunciation of the Inquisitors of Thought* (1789) and Jacques-Pierre Brissot produced a *Memoir on the need to free the press* (1789). Brissot was thinking especially of newspapers, for, by the time his memoir appeared, events were moving too fast for books or even pamphlets. There was an explosion of new publications, with at least 250 newspapers founded in the last six months of 1789. Different papers aimed at different target audiences, including peasants (to whom *La Feuille villageoise* was addressed). The Revolution was good for the press, since there was plenty of exciting news to report and no lack of readers either. The cook who confessed in 1791 to reading four newspapers (above) may not have been so unusual in her time. And in its turn, the press was good for the Revolution. It has been suggested by Jeremy Popkin, for example, that the periodical press was 'indispensable to give legitimacy to the new law-making of the Revolution by making that process public'.

All the same, the power of the press should not be exaggerated. In 1789, most French people could not read. Hence the contribution of all the parts of the system of communication needs to be considered, as in the case of earlier movements such as the Reformation.

Oral communication was particularly important. The Revolution was a time of intense debate, of speeches in the National Assembly and in the political clubs newly formed in Paris and other cities. The debates were conducted in a new 'revolutionary rhetoric', appealing to the passions rather than to reason and relying on the 'magic' of words such as *liberté, fraternité, nation, patrie, peuple* and *citoyen*. Outside the assemblies and clubs, rumour was even more important than usual at this time when another rapid succession of dramatic events took place. The notorious 'Great Fear' of 1789, discussed above (p. 37), was simply the most important of the many rumours of the Revolution.

Visual communication, including iconoclasm, was also central to the Revolution. The destruction of religious images expressed a perception of the Church as part of the old regime. There was also secular iconoclasm or 'vandalism', as it was called at the time, as in the case of the destruction of the statues of Louis XIV (still to be seen on two of the main squares of Paris until 1792). On the positive side, a new language of images was created in order to serve the new regime. The painter Jacques-Louis David (1748–1825), for example, was active on behalf of the Revolution, both in and out of his studio. His painting of the assassinated Marat was a contribution to the martyrology of the Revolution. More than 6,000 prints were produced in the revolutionary period to extend the political debate to the illiterate. A woodcut of the fall of the Bastille, for instance, symbolized the fall of the old regime. Even fans and plates carried political messages, such as 'Long live the Third Estate' (*Vive le tiers état*) or 'Union and Liberty' (Figure 11). So, once again, did playing-cards.

The Revolution may be described as a long-running political theatre, often 'black', with the public executions of Louis XVI, Marie Antoinette and later of leading revolutionaries such as Georges Danton (1759–94) and

Fig. 11 Political plate, French Revolution.

Maximilien Robespierre (1758–94) as the most dramatic scenes. There were also public festivals, both in Paris (especially the large open space of the Champ-de-Mars) and in the provinces. They included the Festival of the Federation, of the Sovereignty of the people, of the Supreme Being, and of Reason. The painter David was the designer and choreographer of several of them. Their huge scale was reminiscent to twentieth-century eyes of the Mayday parades of the USSR or the Nazi Nuremberg Rallies filmed by Leni Riefenstahl. They were expressions of a process of secularization, if only in the sense of what the French historian Mona Ozouf calls a 'transfer of sacrality' from the Church to the state.

The conscious mobilization of the media in order to change attitudes may be described as propaganda (see pp. 1–2). Originally a religious term, coined to describe the propagation of Christianity, the word 'propaganda' acquired a pejorative meaning in the late eighteenth century, when Protestants used it to describe the techniques of the Catholic Church. During the French Revolution, the term was adapted to politics. The revolutionary journalist Camille Desmoulins (1760–94), for instance, compared 'the propagation of patriotism' with that of Christianity, while the royalists in exile denounced the 'propaganda' of the Revolution. The new word referred to a new phenomenon. Although the uses of images and texts to shape attitudes goes back a long way in human history, the self-consciousness and the scale of the revolutionary media campaign was something new.

According to Habermas, 'the Revolution in France created overnight ... what in Great Britain had taken more than a century of steady evolution; the institutions ... for critical public debate of political matters'. The limitations of this French 'public sphere' have since been pointed out, notably its virtual exclusion of women. Nevertheless, the French media played a necessary role both in the destruction of traditions and in the attempt to create a new political culture without either Church or king. It is no accident that the phrase *opinion publique*, like the term 'propaganda', came into regular use at this time.

After Revolution

As in the case of England after the Restoration of Charles II, France under Napoleon (ruled 1799–1815) experienced a kind of return to a pre-revolutionary situation. Yet things could never be quite the same again as long as people remembered what had happened. The power of the media resided in the capacity to reactivate memories of the revolutionary past. The long-standing analogy between the press and the army was reactivated by Napoleon, who declared that 'four hostile newspapers are more to be feared than 100,000 bayonets'.

To return to a debate that echoes throughout this study, it would be absurd to deny the creative role of individuals such as Diderot or Robespierre in the politics and in the communication system of the Enlightenment and the Revolution, or to overlook the place within that system of speeches, images and festivals as well as printed matter. Nonetheless, in thinking about the way in which printed matter encouraged political consciousness, while a more acute political consciousness led in turn to a rise in the consumption of printed matter, it is difficult to avoid a phrase like 'the logic of print', just as it is difficult, when speaking of a later period, to avoid a phrase like 'the logic of technology'.

In France, revolution (and empire later) gave a stimulus to science, including the science of communication, beginning with roads. Engineers were honoured and their education promoted. So, too, was invention. Between 1792 and 1798 a new invention project was proposed each year. The pioneer of the telegraph was Claude Chappe (1763–1805), who presented a memorandum to the Legislative Assembly in 1792, urging it to support a semaphore system of conveying messages which would receive a quick response from tower to tower. The first semaphore line between Paris and Lille was built for communicating with the Army in the north, and one of Napoleon's first initiatives was the rapid building of a line between Lyons and Milan.

In contrast to France, the British government turned down offers from Francis Reynolds, 'the father of English telegraphy', in 1816 to provide 'an expeditious method of conveying intelligence'. With the rise of industry, however, private investors sponsored both railways and electric telegraphy. Technology could never be separated from economics, and the concept of an 'industrial revolution' preceded that of a 'communications revolution', long, continuous and unfinished.

Conclusion

This chapter has tried to work with, and also in some ways against, the idea of the rise of the public sphere associated with Jürgen Habermas, who, replying to his critics, has claimed that pushing the idea of the public sphere back into the sixteenth and seventeenth centuries involves 'changing the very concept of the public sphere to such a degree that it becomes something else'. For our part, we have emphasized the structural weaknesses of this sphere in old regimes and distinguished two kinds of public sphere, temporary and permanent, or structural and conjunctural. It might also be illuminating to think in terms of a 'semi-public' sphere in order to discuss the activities of groups, in the early modern world or indeed today, who meet in private houses in more or less formal clubs, salons or other forms of association, and discuss, among other topics, public issues. All the same, in Western Europe from the Reformation onwards, the fragmentation of religious as well as political authority had made it impossible for governments fully to control printing.

We have moved from the German Reformation in the 1520s to the French Revolution of 1789 and have noted a sequence of situations in which elites who were engaged in bitter conflict appealed to the people and in which the media, especially the printed media, helped raise political consciousness. In each situation, a crisis led to a lively but relatively short-lived debate which might be described as the establishment of a temporary or conjunctural public sphere.

Some at least of the characters in this long-running story were aware of their predecessors and attempted to build on their achievements. For example, the English Civil War was viewed at the time as a kind of replay of the late sixteenth-century French Wars of Religion. The 'Exclusion crisis' was also perceived in terms of the French religious wars, with Shaftesbury in the place of Guise (see p. 101). The seventeenth-century English Grand Remonstrance became a model for the American Declaration of Independence. Milton's *Areopagitica*, as adapted by Mirabeau, was used in the French campaign for freedom of the press, while the guillotining of Louis XVI by the revolutionaries in 1793 followed the precedent of the execution of Charles I of England in 1649.

Many key precedents were recorded in print, with pamphlets ensuring that rebellions were remembered and thereby assisting in the construction of what came to be regarded as a tradition of revolution, which, along with the English responses to it, is described in our next chapter. In the long run, an expanded newspaper and periodical press turned the process of criticizing authority into a cumulative one. As was suggested at the beginning of this chapter, this was a zigzag progress. It moved from one region in Europe to another, often with one step backwards after two steps forward.

The process also needs to be traced within a changing global geography. The word 'discoveries' came into use as the oceans of the world were opened up and triangular trade (including trade in slaves) linked Africa and America with France and England. Nonetheless, there was still little sense of there being 'one world'. The economic thrust that carried Europeans into Asia as well as Africa had limited consequences for China and Japan, where print was controlled more closely by the state than in Western Europe, delaying the development of a public sphere for centuries. Even today, the extent to which China has a public sphere remains a matter for debate (see p. 346).

4

Technologies and Revolutions

In boasting that he could offer all that the world wanted – 'power' – the British manufacturer Matthew Boulton (1728–1809) was dependent on the steam engine patents of James Watt (1736–1819), who joined him in the most famous of all partnerships between inventor and businessman. Before the 1760s the number of patents taken out in a year in Britain rarely exceeded a dozen: in 1769 the figure was thirty-six, and in 1783, when the American War of Independence came to an end, it reached sixty-four. Many were concerned with power-driven communications. Watt's patents included those for engines which could not only pump water but also power machines. He also introduced one of the first instruments of technical control, the governor, which provided the greater regularity and smoothness essential in a prime-mover.

The Industrial Revolution

The first steam engine patent held by Boulton and Watt was extended by Act of Parliament in 1775 for twenty-five years with much-debated economic effects. By the time it expired in 1800, the French Revolution itself had gone through as many phases as the steam engine since the fall of the Bastille in 1789, turning some of its European supporters, including the English poet William Wordsworth (1770–1850) into enemies. In 1795, following the execution of Louis XVI and Marie Antoinette and a 'Reign of Terror' during which revolutionaries fought one another, a Directory of five members was appointed, which was overthrown by coup d'état in 1799. Napoleon, then a young general, was made First Consul, a title borrowed from ancient Rome, and after winning dazzling victories he crowned himself Emperor, another ancient title, in 1804. It was in post-Napoleonic France that the term 'industrial revolution' was first coined, in 1827, by a political economist, Adolphe Blanqui. 'While the French Revolution tried out its great experiments on a volcano,' he wrote, 'England tried out hers on the plains of industry.' In the twentieth century, after the term 'industrial revolution' had been popularized by Arnold Toynbee the elder (1852–83) in his posthumously published *Lectures on the Industrial Revolution* in 1884, the two 'revolutions' were frequently to be placed side by side in history textbooks, one said to be based on technologies, the other on ideas. Indeed, they came to be considered as a dual revolution, changing communications and expectations.

For the committed revolutionary Karl Marx (1818–83), and many others who were in no sense political revolutionaries, it all started with the steam engine. In dealing in scholarly perspective with the advent of steam power, which was used before Watt by Thomas Newcomen (1663–1729) and others back in the seventeenth century, David Landes (1924–2013), a distinguished American historian of the long process of industrialization, concentrated in an important new book of 1969, *The Unbound Prometheus*, on three of the features of the industrial revolution: the substitution of mechanical devices for human skills; the replacement of human and animal strength by inanimate power; and a marked improvement in the getting and working of raw materials. He saw that there was nothing final, however, in the association of these developments with steam, as contemporaries themselves had recognized. Instead, a long and continuing process of industrialization had begun in the late seventeenth and eighteenth centuries during which further human skills were acquired, new forms of inanimate power were developed – including, after electricity, nuclear and solar power – and substitute materials were produced through the advances of chemistry and, in the twentieth century, materials science.

Landes used the term Industrial Revolution with capital letters in his first chapter, 'The Industrial Revolution in Britain', having queried in his introduction its more general use to label rapid and significant technological changes in other places and at other times. Other historians, having traced the history of the term and approached economic history quantitatively, have rejected it, preferring the phrase 'early industrialization'. The economics were examined fully in H. Rosenberg and L. E. Bridwell's *How the West Grew Rich* (1986). The two authors went back through seven centuries of expansion of European trade, comparing European expertise, expressed in the emergence and evolution of diverse economic institutions, with that of China where, until the creation of a People's Republic, there was no industrial revolution.

Invention

As a historian of technology, Rosenberg was well aware of the role of invention. It had been significant in early Chinese history, as the historian of science Joseph Needham (1900–95) showed, far earlier than in Europe; and in modern history, where distinctions were drawn between discovery and invention, in all West European countries, as in the United States, invention was seen as a source of wealth. For three centuries it was extolled in the media, as they themselves developed. For the most part, but seldom without argument, they concentrated on innovation as a means of increasing wealth, not on the psychological and social problems that went with it.

One of the bodies fostering invention in eighteenth-century Britain was the Society for the Encouragement of Arts, Manufactures and Commerce, founded in 1754, which set out to divide inventions into categories, of which those relating to transportation were particularly prominent. 'Inland navigation', 'longitude at sea', 'wheels, carriages and roads' figured as early as 1760 on its lists. While he was resident in England before the War of Independence, the American Benjamin Franklin (1706–90), who was chairman of one of the Society's committees dealing with America and the West Indies, himself extended the lists, inventing, besides much else, bifocal spectacles and a metal stove. He also experimented with electricity before Watt produced his steam engine. In the course of the nineteenth century, it became a matter of national pride to be the first to secure an invention. Many inventions were arrived at independently and more or less simultaneously in different places. Not surprisingly, therefore, litigation concerning patent rights was a frequent occurrence. Legal disputes concerning priority were struggles for power as well as for money, the question of how much depending both on how difficult it was to claim priority and how vulnerable it was to challenge. The law, frequently invoked, varied from country to country, and was subject to criticism and change. In Britain, a Patent Law Amendment Act of 1852 simplified application procedures and reduced fees. The story of patents as a whole is illuminating. One well-known and much-quoted philosopher, Alfred Whitehead (1861–1947) claimed in his *Science and the Modern World* (1925) that the greatest invention of the nineteenth century was the invention of the 'method of invention' itself.

The rhetoric surrounding inventions and patents was everywhere abundant, much of it talk of conquering Nature, an alien concept in many countries outside Europe, including, for quite different reasons, China and Australia. Increasing attention has been paid again, as it was by critics at the time, to the losses as well as to the gains of industrialization, a subject of central importance for nineteenth-century social critics – pollution, messy landscapes, exploited and unhealthy children, the threat to community. When Arnold Toynbee popularized the term 'industrial revolution' in Britain, it was the calamitous consequences of the revolution that he stressed.

Nevertheless, for Erasmus Darwin (1731–1802), the grandfather of the great biologist Charles Darwin, living on the edge of Britain's Black Country and writing in the opening year of the first French Revolution, there could be romance in industrial landscapes, 'in smoke . . . curling in spiral wreaths' over the summits of mountains, as there was in transportation, the main key to the future. Darwin, a medical doctor, was a member of the Lunar Society, a West Midlands circle of friends formally constituted as a society in 1780. Boulton and Watt also belonged to it. The members were conscious of their distance from London, although the time taken to reach it by so-called 'flying carriages' fell sharply (in good weather) after the building of turnpike roads. For one member in particular, the potter Josiah Wedgwood (1730–99), canals mattered even more (in a pre-railway age) than roads. His products were fragile and his customers widely scattered.

During the early 1790s, with steam power in its infancy, pioneering engineers like the blind John Metcalf (1717–1810) and the brilliant Scot, Thomas Telford (1757–1834), did much to strengthen the foundations of roads and increase their carrying capacity. John McAdam (1756–1830) looked to their surfaces. Already road mileage had increased five times between 1750 and 1790. Bridges were important in the countryside as well as in cities, and England was the first country to forge them out of iron. The famous cast-iron bridge over the River Severn at Coalbrookdale in Shropshire was opened in 1779: its bicentenary was treated as if it were the first showplace of the industrial revolution, a national treasure in a unique industrial heritage.

Thomas Paine (1737–1809), author of the best-selling *Rights of Man* (1791–2), designed a bridge in Yorkshire in 1791. After visiting cotton factories in Lancashire, steel furnaces in Sheffield and kilns in the Potteries, he wrote to Thomas Jefferson (1743–1826) telling him that all these 'useful projects' might easily be carried out in America, where Paine himself had lived from 1774 to 1787.

From Canals to Railways

Whatever social commentators might feel and say about steam-driven industry or transportation, there was little opposition to the form of transportation that most interested the members of the Lunar Society – not road traffic or steam locomotion, but traffic by canal which was already transforming the economic life of the English Midlands as it was of the North. The first canal phase of transportation history reached its peak in Britain in 1790–3 when cheap capital encouraged a canal 'mania' and fifty-three canal and navigation bills were authorized by Parliament. Such enthusiasm anticipated the railway mania of the 1840s. Indeed, speculation in shares was to figure as prominently as investment in the later history of most of the media, including the history of the Internet (see p. 344). So, too, was the pressure to legislate. How or whether to use the law to regulate communications processes were fundamental questions in the late eighteenth and early nineteenth centuries as they were in the late twentieth century and remain so today. Parliamentary authorization of canal and railway projects was mandatory.

In continental Europe, with miles of navigable rivers, canals were a familiar feature of the landscape before they became so in Britain, and a canal era began there, especially in the Dutch Republic, at the end of the seventeenth century, a time when there were formidable obstacles to road transport. In 1810 in France, the completion of the St Quentin Canal linked the North Sea and the river systems of the Scheldt and Lys with the English Channel via the Somme, and with Paris and Le Havre via the Oise and the Seine. By then Napoleon was emperor, and Britain was engaged in protracted wars against him. It was from Napoleon that the US government secured in 1803 (through the 'Louisiana Purchase') a doubling of its territory and control of a waterway which, by the end of the nineteenth century, was to become part of a continental navigation network that included 4,000 miles of canals. There had been only 100 miles in 1800, but between 1817 and 1825 the Erie Canal, a vital link in the network, was built by the state of New York, opening up the first American West. Beyond it was a moving frontier with the Pacific Ocean miles ahead. No one knew how many miles away it was or what obstacles lay between, although, in a grand expedition, Meriweather Lewis and William Clark set off to find out, blessed by Jefferson, now third President of the United States and the first to govern from Washington. He had been American Minister in Paris before the French Revolution began.

It is not surprising that the title Albro Martin gave to his study of American railroads (a word Americans preferred to 'railways') was *Railroads Triumphant* (1992), for it was the railways that began the effective opening up of a continent. In his book, Martin described how the railroad idea took hold in America with remarkable speed, but how poorly built, if cheaply, the first American railroads were until after the Civil War. The great age of railroad-building was to follow between 1868 and the end of the century. There were around 35,000 miles of track in 1865; by the mid-1870s there were nearly 200,000.

The most exciting moment in the story of American railroads was the

hammering of a golden spike into the ground on the spot where two locomotives met on 10 May 1869, one arriving from the east, the other from the
west. This symbolic ceremony marking the completion of the first trans-
continental railroad was commemorated in a photograph by A. J. Russell,
which was widely circulated around the United States as a wood-engraving
a month after the event. The news had been circulated immediately by
telegraph, which, like the photograph, was a nineteenth-century invention:
a wire attached to the golden spike made it possible for distant crowds to
hear every stroke of the hammer. There were spontaneous celebrations
in San Francisco and Chicago. Church bells rang, and the mayors of San
Francisco and New York exchanged telegrams.

The construction of iron tracks and of high-pressure steam engines powerful enough to move locomotives along them owed nothing to Watt, who
had feared high-pressure steam and had regarded high-pressure engines as
dangerous toys. It was an American and a British engineer who had proved
that locomotives would be capable of propelling carriages. In America,
Oliver Evans (1775–1819), the son of a farmer, started work on a high-pressure engine in the first decade of the nineteenth century, as did the British
mining engineer and inventor Richard Trevithick (1771–1833), who tried
out a locomotive on rails at a Cornish ironworks in 1804. Trevithick had
built a model engine in 1798, and in 1803 he had constructed a working
steam carriage that made several journeys through the streets of London.
Erratic and unbusinesslike, he ceased to make locomotives in 1808, leaving
the way open for a firm of engineers and machine toolmakers in Leeds:
Fenton, Murray and Wood. Leeds had an early company track at Middleton,
carrying freight only, as Cornish railways carried coal, tin and copper until
the 1850s and 1860s.

It was not until the third decade of the century that the English civil
engineer George Stephenson (1781–1848), who knew Trevithick and who
had worked in collieries in England's northeast, produced the most famous
of all locomotives, the Rocket, which in 1829 won a competitive trial at
Rainhill on a newly constructed railway between Liverpool and Manchester.
Four years before that, Stephenson had been entrusted by a colliery owner
and contractor, Edward Pease, with the design and construction of a twenty-
five-mile railway track between Stockton and Darlington, hauling wagons,
as the necessary Act of Parliament put it, by men, horses or 'otherwise'. The
first railway ticket was sold on 27 September 1825. Great public interest was
aroused, and it was in this context that Stephenson was called upon to join
the port of Liverpool, bringing raw cotton from across the Atlantic, to the
mills of Manchester and the textile towns around it. He was given charge

not only of the building of the railway, but of the locomotive power to be used on it.

The railway 'line', as it was now called, was difficult to build. No fewer than sixty-three bridges, including a great viaduct with nine arches, had to be erected: it rose above the water of an early canal. A tunnel also had to be constructed on another part of the line, and there was a quagmire to cross. Stephenson and the 'navvies' working on the line accomplished immense civil engineering feats before a competition was held (with a prize) for the best locomotive engine. The Rainhill trials of 1829 were to be recalled in a quite different context in 1936, when two television systems, one electrical, were pitted against each other (below). Five locomotives took part. They included the Rocket, built by George and Robert Stephenson, the Novelty and Perseverance. Rocket and Novelty reached a speed of about thirty miles an hour, presenting what a newspaper called 'one of the most sublime spectacles of mechanical ingenuity and human daring the world ever beheld'.

The opening of the economically and politically influential line by the Duke of Wellington, who had defeated Napoleon at Waterloo, was attended by disaster as well as by triumph – the death by accident of a politically important statesman, William Huskisson, unlike Wellington a supporter of economic change. It is not known whether Wellington would have approved of the fact that the name of Stephenson's first locomotive had been Blücher, the Prussian general who took part in the battle of Waterloo. Names, then as now, could carry either messages or memories. Novelty carried a message, Blücher a memory, as the airship Hindenberg was to carry a memory in the 1930s.

It was then that an American cultural critic, Lewis Mumford (1895–1990), coined an unforgettable name for the dependence of railways on coal and iron, 'carboniferous capitalism'. Linking technology and economics, he treated iron as a necessary part of an historical equation. Even before the railway, Watt's own achievements would not have been possible had it not been for the skills of John Wilkinson (1728–1808), a great ironmaster whose patent of 1774 for boring military cannon could be adapted to boring steam engine cylinders of unprecedented accuracy. Wilkinson was a great publicist too. He built iron boats, the first of them appositely called *The Trial*, and iron bridges, and in 1788, in the year before the French Revolution began, manufactured forty miles of cast-iron pipes for the water supply of Paris. He asked to be buried in an iron coffin. Huskisson would not have asked for that.

In the early nineteenth century the 'iron horse' became as much a sign as the white horse in pre-Roman Britain. It outsped all other horses as it made its way along the iron ways. Speed was not the least exciting feature of British railways, and there are many striking individual accounts, like that of the actress Fanny Kemble, of the first experience of travelling fast. Nevertheless, until the end of the First World War, horses did not disappear from the industrial or military scene and units of horse power were still used in relation to steam (as they were to be later to the internal combustion engine). With speed went mobility.

Cartoons as well as pamphlets and novels carried the message. A character in George Eliot's novel *The Mill on the Floss* (1860), with no intimations of electricity or of internal combustion engines, summed it up: 'the world goes on at a smarter pace than it did when I was a young fellow . . . It's this steam you see.'

Gas

'Gas' also figured prominently in nineteenth-century attempts to identify the pros and cons of carboniferous capitalism. Coal gas burns with a yellow luminous flame, and in 1805 the Scottish engineer William Murdock (1754–1839) applied gas lighting to a workshop in Birmingham. It made its way into the streets later – and onto the stage. The London and Westminster Gas Company, soon to become the Gas Light and Coke Company, was set up in 1813. Westminster Bridge, memorialized in a sonnet by Wordsworth, was the first bridge to be lit by gas. The provinces followed, Bristol leading the way. In the United States Baltimore was the first city to turn to gas in 1816. In the theatre, gas lighting was first used in the exterior, the foyer and the staircases. From 1817, however, Drury Lane, Covent Garden and the Lyceum were lit throughout by gas, not all observers approving of the change. Gaslight came to be associated with the mid-Victorian imagination. The film *Fanny by Gaslight* caught the mood. In the country as a whole, gasworks with huge gasometers changed the urban landscape more than factory chimneys did. Gaslight in the home made reading easier, and there were unforeseen consequences. In newly gas-lit Heidelberg, the German chemist Robert Bunsen conceived of what came to be called 'Bunsen burners', using them in his new laboratory of 1852.

Pope Pius IX (1857–1939) and, in England, John Henry (Cardinal) Newman (1801–1890) were as unimpressed by the rhetoric of gas as they were by the rhetoric of steam; they thought that it was morally wrong to equate either gas or steam with civilization. By contrast, electricity for long had more than a touch of the divine: it was a 'vital' force. From the 1840s onwards, electricity challenged gas as it came to challenge steam. Electric arc lights were in use at the Paris Opera in the 1840s and were first used throughout a theatre at the Paris Hippodrome in 1878. The first American theatre to use electricity was the California in San Francisco in 1879. The light bulb in the home came later (see p. 140). Ironically, it was almost contemporaneous with the gas mantle.

The terms 'industrial revolution', 'transportation revolution' and 'communications revolution' were all part of the same complex. They seemed to have their own logic, particularly after electricity provided a more mysterious source of power than steam (the word 'electronics' was introduced years later, in the twentieth century).

Bacon's Dream

Some of these changes had been imagined centuries earlier. The English philosopher and statesman Francis Bacon (1561–1626) had forecast 'the opening of the door of Nature'. His vision of a Solomon's House in his *New Atlantis*, written before 1620, incorporated a 'College of Inventors' which would include 'engine houses', where 'engines and instruments for all sort of motions were prepared', two galleries for 'Inventors Past', and 'spaces or bases for Inventors to come'. Within the House 'we imitate flights of birds . . . have ships and boats for going under water and brooking of seas . . . and curious clocks', even some 'perpetual motions'.

His words were not forgotten. In the mid-nineteenth century, when parts of the Western world were becoming a Solomon's House, the great German organic chemist Justus von Liebig (1803–73) wrote that Bacon's 'name glows like a shining star'; and Charles Darwin (1809–82), asserted that he worked on 'true Baconian principles'. In an essay about Bacon published in 1837, the year Victoria came to the throne, the British historian Thomas Babington Macaulay (1800–59) extolled the benefits for the human race that had been achieved under the influence of discovery. As Bacon had predicted, Nature had been harnessed, a better word than tamed, bridges had been built, and distance had been conquered. Considered over time, Baconian philosophy had been 'a philosophy which never rests'. Its law was 'progress'.

Critics of Industrialization

There were always critics of Macaulay, and for the most part these were critics also of industrialization. The Scottish essayist Thomas Carlyle (1795–1881), writing in 1829 in the *Edinburgh Review*, a periodical in which Macaulay also wrote, complained bitterly that he was living through a 'Mechanical Age', not an 'Heroical, Devotional, Philosophical or Moral' one. The increase in wealth had changed 'the old relations' and increased 'the distance between the rich and the poor'. 'Nothing is left to be accomplished by the old, natural methods'. 'Men are grown mechanical in head and in heart, as well as in hand.' John Ruskin (1819–1901), lover of nature and critic of art and the societies that produced it, condemned the 'force of mechanism and the fury of avaricious commerce' in his own society. Developing his own political economy, he based it on the conviction that 'there is no wealth but life'.

Ruskin looked backwards and forwards to 'the economy of heaven'. He came to the conclusion that worship of Mammon condemned the working man of the nineteenth century to an inhuman existence of mindless routine. In 1865 he exclaimed that, having felt 'the force of mechanism and the fury of avaricious commerce', he had given himself up, as he would in a 'besieged city', to seeking 'the best modes of getting bread and butter for its multitudes'. Marx, a Jew born in Trier in the Rhineland, was another critic of industrial society. Looking backwards to societies different from his own and forwards to a new or classless society, Marx set out not only to understand society but to change it. Exiled from Germany in 1848, he spent a short time in the revolutionary Paris of 1848, experiencing its third revolution since 1789, before taking up residence in London in 1849 and, with occasional trips abroad, staying there for the rest of his life. In his writings, which he considered to be scientific not prophetic, he brought together French perceptions of politics and English approaches to economics, both at the core of the two revolutions, political and economic, which form the central theme of this chapter. In examining the contemporary society that Marx was seeking to analyse and explain, it is necessary to take account of demography as well as of political economy. Just how population growth affected economic growth has been a matter of argument, sophisticated and popular, before and after the English clergyman and economist Thomas Malthus (1766–1834) maintained in his *Essay on Population* (1798) that natural population growth would inevitably outrun resources and precipitate crises – famine, epidemics and war. While acknowledging, as enthusiasts for the French Revolution did, that in 'late years' there had been 'great and unlooked-for discoveries . . . in natural philosophy' and an 'increasing diffusion of general knowledge from the extension of the art of printing [and] the ardent and unshackled spirit of enquiry that prevails throughout the lettered and even unlettered world', he refused to draw the conclusion reached by the Marquis de Condorcet (see p. 26) that these changes implied that France or the world would witness the 'perfectibility of man'.

The Dismal Science

Malthus's pessimism was largely responsible for political economy being called 'the dismal science'. Marx drew his inspiration from a very different English economist, David Ricardo (1772–1823), but he fully appreciated how so-called neo-Malthusians at the end of the nineteenth century advocated birth control to limit the size of families. Meanwhile, the demography behind industrialization had involved major changes in the patterns of family life. The end of the 'domestic system' at work broke up families, and factories became dependent both on child and female labour. Marx made a careful study of the English Factory Acts which marked a degree of political control over the economic system and were monitored and enforced by inspectors, new arrivals on the economic scene.

A twentieth-century British economist, deeply interested in economic history, John Richard Hicks (1904–89), wrote in a great footnote on the last page of his *Value and Capital* (1939) that he could not 'repress the thought that perhaps the whole industrial revolution of the last two hundred years [which had by then transformed the United States and Japan] has been nothing else but a vast secular boom, largely induced by the unparalleled rise in population'; he went on: 'If this is so, it would help to explain why, as the wisest hold, it has been such a disappointing epoch in human history.'

During the eighteenth and early nineteenth centuries, when Malthus was writing, England and Ireland had led the way in population growth. In 1801, one-fifth of the British population lived in towns and cities of more than 10,000 inhabitants, and more than one in every twelve persons was a Londoner. By 1851 the urban proportion had nearly doubled. Decennial censuses, first introduced in 1801 (and in the United States in 1800), recorded the details. In early nineteenth-century Britain, Manchester, along with adjacent Salford, grew from 94,000 to 311,000 in 1841, and in 1861 to 400,000; in 1851, one-fifth of the inhabitants were born outside the city. Manchester with Salford was a shock city, which socially aware contemporaries from France and Germany, in particular, had to visit if they wanted to know what was happening to the world.

In no other European country was there a similar urban transformation, and the verb 'urbanize' was not used until the second half of the century. Nor was the word 'urbanization'. In a much-quoted study of nineteenth-century cities, *The Growth of Cities in the Nineteenth Century: A Study in Statistics* (1899), the American economist Adna F. Weber (1870–1968) did not use the word, although he concluded that the concentration of population in cities was commonly recognized as 'the most remarkable social phenomenon of the present century'.

The cultural implications of population growth were everywhere and at all times far-reaching. Newspapers remain the best basic source for exploring individual towns and cities and what came to be called the urban way of life. Some of the journalists writing for them set out to penetrate all the secret places in the growing agglomerations of people in which they themselves lived. This was the achievement of Henry Mayhew, for instance, whose four volumes on *London Labour and the London Poor* had been heralded by newspaper articles in the *Morning Chronicle* in 1849. It was also the achievement of the American ex-reporter Robert Ezra Park (1864–1944), who became a professor of sociology at the University of Chicago and formed a team of researchers to study it. Park believed that the city was the microcosm of all social evolution and that Chicago was a perfect setting for the study of cities.

Whatever the economic, spatial and cultural differences between cities – and they were underplayed by Mumford in his *Culture of Cities* (1938) – in all of them the 'massing' together of people was as controversial as their massing in factories. For some observers, it meant that people 'had their faculties sharpened and improved by constant communication': for others, it meant a severing of face-to-face relationships which they felt it essential to preserve.

Democracy

In *Democracy in America* (1835), the French aristocrat Alexis de Tocqueville (1805–59) asked fundamental questions not only about public order or about centralization, but also about democracy. What had the world to fear or to hope in its inevitable advance? He saw most hope in 'the power of association', which curbed overpowerful government. It was in evidence too in Britain, where, during the nineteenth century, large numbers of voluntary organizations were created – some went back in time – some calling themselves 'philosophical', others 'statistical'. Religion was often a motivating force as they turned their attention to housing, health or education. The role of 'volunteeering' in Britain, often against the odds, was to increase in the twentieth century after a 'welfare state' had been brought into existence by legislation. At the end of the nineteenth century, French observers had reckoned that a large majority of British adults belonged to an average of five or six voluntary organizations, which included trade unions and friendly societies, striving for mutual self-help and placing their hopes in cooperation not competition. On the other side of the Atlantic, Arthur M. Schlesinger (1917–2007), one of the first American historians to study cities, called his country 'a nation of joiners'. Almost a century later, an American political scientist and sociologist, Robert Putnam, fearing that for various reasons this was no longer true, gave warnings about the likely consequences not only for American society, but also for democracy. It was wrong to think of democracy, hailed by successive American governments, just as a matter of elections. It demanded a social infrastructure as much as the economy demanded an economic infrastructure. And the strengths of the 'nonprofit sector' in that economy, which was to grow over time, depended on the strength of private foundations prepared to support voluntary action. They were given tax privileges. There was a sharp contrast in this respect between the United States and France.

Class

Marx approached the questions that interested Tocqueville – and many American sociologists of the city – in a radically different way, and there were later Marxists who either extended or qualified his approach. His answers were set out briefly and eloquently in the *Communist Manifesto* of 1848, which Marx coauthored with his friend Friedrich Engels (1820–95). It was written in German in six weeks and began with the sentence 'The history of all hitherto existing society is the history of class struggles.' In feudal society, the classes concerned were the aristocracy and the bourgeoisie. With the coming of the steam engine and the advance of industrialization and urbanization, they were the bourgeoisie and the proletariat. This was unfamiliar language in Britain, although the terms 'middle' and 'lower' classes had been in use in Britain at least since the late eighteenth century, with the former being used first, and the latter giving way with industrialization to the phrase 'working classes'. It was clear to a number of contemporaries that there was a process of class formation at work in the industrial north.

The journalist William Cooke Taylor (1800–49) wrote in 1842 that, because the rise of a new manufacturing population coincided with the French Revolution with which Parliament was preoccupied, it had 'crept into unnoticed existence'. The 'population' was not new in its formation alone: it was new in its 'habits of thought and action'. Bound by common sentiments and routines, it was distinguishable from 'the poor', the general term employed for centuries, most recently and conspicuously by Malthus. By 1872, when the French Revolution had faded into history in Britain, although not, of course, in France, the Tory *Quarterly Review* could publish an article called 'The Proletariat on a False Scent', conceding that the word Marx had used was 'a useful addition to the vocabulary of serious discussion'. Nevertheless, the words 'classes' and 'masses' continued to be used in Britain rather than proletariat and bourgeoisie.

For Englishmen, it was apparent from the outset that the word 'class' was as difficult to define as the word 'gentleman'. Moreover, it was equally apparent that there were so many different elements both in the working class, however defined, and in the middle class that it was necessary to use both terms in the plural. Within each there were differences of outlook as well as of function and status. Capitalist employees were only one section of the middle classes, factory workers only one section of the working classes. Marx and Engels saluted the triumph of the bourgeoisie more eloquently than the bourgeoisie itself. The *Communist Manifesto* was free, therefore, from any of the doubts about progress which were expressed by British critics of nineteenth-century society. The *Manifesto* dwelt eloquently on the 'accomplished wonders of industrialization', but foretold that scientifically inevitable revolution would come not through technology itself, but through class struggle between the capitalists who owned and controlled steam engines and machinery and the exploited industrial proletariat who worked them. Marx pursued his analysis further in his magnum opus *Das Kapital*, the first volume of which appeared in 1867. He welcomed the main industrial changes since the French Revolution and explained that 'Nature builds no machines, no locomotives, railways, electric telegraphs ... etc. These are products of human industry: natural material transformed into instruments of the human will'. The human will was a necessary motivating force in Marx's approach to history as he drew a distinction between the economic substructure and the cultural superstructure; and in the twentieth century the Italian Marxist Antonio Gramsci (1891–1937) explored the relationship between the two in the light of the rise of the media. He also introduced the word 'hegemony', which brought in the role of controlling cultural power as well as the role of the masses. No such distinction was drawn by the French sociologist Auguste Comte (1798–1857), pioneer and systematizer of sociology, whose influence extended to South America; and when, in France, psychological and social scholarship began to focus on the crowd, it was less concerned with the faces of human beings who made up urban crowds than in the crowd itself as a phenomenon. Linking up with eighteenth-century and earlier talk of the mob, the idea of a 'mass society' made its way into general parlance, complemented in a cultural context in the twentieth century by the words 'elites' and 'mass society'. Sigmund Freud's study of what he called *Massenpsychologie* (misleadingly translated as 'Group Psychology') appeared in 1921, while the Spanish philosopher-essayist José Ortega y Gasset's *Revolt of the Masses* dates from 1930. For the Englishman James Bryce (1838–1927) writing about politics (and what came to be called 'the mass media') in 1900, 'the mutual action and reaction of the makers or leaders of opinion upon the mass, and of the mass upon them' was 'the most curious part of the whole process by which the formation of opinion is produced'.

The Steam Press

Although Marx's reference to 'electric telegraphs' brought in the first electrical invention that was to begin the process of reshaping what came to be called the 'media' (see pp. 1–2), it was on steam and on the relationship between steam and print that he still focused as he asked: 'What became of Fama, rumour, fame, when Printing House Square, the home of the London newspaper, *The Times*, spread news abroad as well as at home?' The newspaper, originally called in 1785 *The Daily Universal Register*, was given its familiar name three years later by its proprietor John Walter I (1739–1812), who had served his apprenticeship with a bookseller who was also a publisher. In 1814, a huge steam printing press, made out of iron and patented in England by Friedrich Koenig (1774–1833), had been installed by his son, John Walter II, in the headquarters of *The Times* in Printing House Square: it not only saved labour, but made possible the production of 1,000 impressions an hour. The newspaper could now go to press later and contain the most recent news.

The idea of using a rolling cylinder in printing was not new, but Koenig's cylinder was; and, as *The Times* of 29 November 1814 put it, without referring to steam, the copy of that first day was 'the practical result of the greatest improvement connected with printing since the discovery of the art itself'. Koenig was referred to as 'an artist'. He was not the first such person to be employed by Walter, however, and after he left the service of *The Times*, having extolled British patent law, there were further substantial technical changes in Printing House Square in 1828 when a four-cylinder steam press was installed. By then it was common to describe newspapers as 'social engines', with the stress not on steam, but on their power over opinion. Marx did not observe (or know?) that *The Times* as a working organization established its ascendancy by its refusal to employ trade-union labour in an industry where 'combinations' or 'unions' of compositors and printers – skilled trades – had been strong since 1785. Before turning to Koenig, who himself had earlier turned to a book publisher, Walter had subsidized a British inventor to develop a press 'by which manual labour should be rendered nearly unnecessary'.

In the subsequent history of the press, printers, now distinct from publishers and booksellers, depended on compositors who were able and knowledgeable enough to fight for their own interests. Both Marx and Engels, who lived for most of his life in industrial Manchester, where he read the Chartist press, including Feargus O'Connor's *Northern Star*, fully appreciated the power of the print media, and wrote for newspapers, among them – ironically in retrospect – the *New York Tribune*. They were both zealous communicators. As well as letters to each other, which fill several volumes, they collaborated on pamphlets and books, ranging from the *Communist Manifesto* to *Das Kapital*, the last two volumes of which were edited by Engels after Marx's death.

There is no evidence that Marx ever entered a great printing press, but those observers who did were usually deeply impressed by what they saw. One of them, who described a visit in 1839 to the great Clowes establishment on the south side of the Thames, wrote a long article in the *Quarterly Review*, graphically recalling arriving early on a December morning just before the gaslights were extinguished. Great steam presses, type and stereotype foundry and paper warehouse were on the right, apartments for compositors, readers, etc. were in front. There were five compositors' halls and in one of them sixty compositors' frames, 'about the height of the music stands in an orchestra'. There were brown slippers under each frame – for the compositors stood as they worked – and a stool, the private property of the compositor. So, too, were pictures, songs, tracts and caricatures they pasted to the wall near their frames. They had access at their own expense to all the main newspapers of the day, and before the 'great statesmen' of the time had read them, the compositors had 'criticised, applauded or condemned' their leading articles.

The writer in the *Quarterly*, who went on to describe 'printers' devils', 'readers', 'gathering boys' and the steam-driven presses, concluded that it was impossible to contemplate a team of sixty compositors, 'literary labourers steadily working together in one room, without immediately acknowledging the important service they are rendering to the civilized world'. 'As railroads have produced traffic, so has printing produced learned men.' Gutenberg, 'we all know', was said to have been the father of printing, and when a statue of him was recently erected there were cries of 'Gut! Guten! Gutenberg' and he was toasted in 'many a bumper of Rhenish wine'. The writer ended by praising the authority of *The Times*, printed by steam, but used the verb 'electrified' to describe the reactions to the Koenig triumph of 28 November 1814. 'It is impossible for the mind to contemplate for a single moment the moral force of the British Press without reflecting, and without acknowledging that, under providence, it is the only engine that can now save the glorious institution of the British empire.' His words echoed Charles Babbage (1792–1871), pioneer of the computer, who in 1832 had published his *On the Economy of Machinery and Manufactures*, welcoming the fact that the 'labour of a hundred artificers is now performed by the operations of a single machine'. Babbage's mechanical computer, which he described as an 'engine', failed to secure government financial backing, but it was placed on public display at a gallery of scientific instruments at King's College in the Strand in 1843.

The media were not associated with what came to be called 'mass culture' until the last decades of the nineteenth century. In particular – and deliberately – *The Times*, best known of British newspapers, was never a mass journal. As late as the 1850s it could be treated as a 'Fourth Estate', a phrase attributed to Macaulay and Carlyle (who in turn attributed it to Edmund Burke), although they were referring to the Press Gallery, where Dickens had once sat, rather than to the press as a whole. The phrase was applied to the whole of the press by F. Knight Hunt, a journalist, in 1850, and the term became accepted not only in Britain, but in several European countries and even in the United States. Indeed, in the twentieth century, the American periodical *Broadcasting* was to print proudly on its cover the words 'The Fifth Estate'.

Long before that – indeed, before the British reduction of the stamp duties on the press in 1836, their abolition in 1855 and the repeal of the paper duties in 1861 – the penny press had appeared in New York, the first successful newspaper being the *New York Sun* (1833), which was started by a struggling job-printer. When he disposed of it in 1838, it was selling 34,000 copies, many of them at street corners. Much of the information it contained related to ordinary people – and the police. A totally fictional account of life on the moon, the 'Moon Hoax', was part of the entertainment it provided. Three years later, Horace Greeley (1811–72), coiner of the phrase 'Go west, young man, go west', launched his *New York Tribune*, the 'Great Moral Organ' which he hoped would be self-sufficient in its supply of news. There were then twelve daily newspapers in the city. While the *Tribune* included articles sent from Europe by Marx (many of them written by Engels, see below), it deliberately excluded some domestic news, refusing to print details of crimes, reports of trials, and theatre plays. The *New York Times* (1851), 'a sane and sensible newspaper', founded by a young reporter from Greeley's staff, Henry Raymond (1820–69), followed a professedly balanced line, in the twentieth century explicitly separating 'news' and 'views'. 'We do not believe that everything in society is either exactly right or exactly wrong; what is good we desire to preserve and improve; what is evil to exterminate and reform.'

Books and Periodicals

The world of Marx and Engels was a world mediated mainly through books and other forms of print, including travel books, spanning space, newspapers, chronicling time, and catechisms posing and answering questions. During their lifetimes, which preceded the first Communist (Bolshevik) revolution in the world, that in Russia in 1917, the number of books on political economy, most of them setting out a different version from theirs, greatly increased, but in all European countries they were still outnumbered by books on religion, dismissed by Marx and Engels as 'opium for the people'. Yet even in an age of events, including the revolutionary Paris Commune of 1870, which was hailed by Marx and exalted in retrospect by Lenin (1870–1924) and the Bolsheviks, newspapers did not supplant pamphlets, periodicals and books.

In the book world, the most creative literary form in nineteenth-century prose was the novel (French, *roman*), a word that had now established itself in England since the eighteenth century, when, as we have seen, many novels had already been published. The subject range and psychological depth of what came to be thought of as 'great novels', some constituting a 'canon', was acknowledged by contemporary reviewers, who themselves acquired an established place in what was coming to be thought of as a literary world. There were links across frontiers, borrowings, translations and mutations, so that it is not possible even for a history of English literature to focus solely on Scott, Dickens, Thackeray, Eliot, Trollope, Melville, James and Hardy. Goethe, Balzac, Stendhal, Manzoni, Baudelaire, Hugo, Zola, Turgeniev and Mallarmé are also part of the cast. In a short social history of communications they can be little more than names, but to put them in place, structural features of the changing book trade and, in particular, changing relationships between readers, publishers, booksellers and critics must be identified. So, too, must 'tendencies', a word in use at the time, in intellectual and cultural history, from Romanticism to Naturalism.

In this particular study the changing role of newspapers at one end of the spectrum and schoolbooks at the other must be focused upon. There were continuities, but also changes. The gap between authors and journalists widened, as did the gap between publishers and booksellers. Printers, despite the contemporary interest in the art, craft and organization of printing, were less influential in the book trade than they had been in the seventeenth and eighteenth centuries. During the early years of the nineteenth century romantic novelists, drawn to autobiography, as romantic poets were, would be as conscious of their special relationship with posterity as of their relationship with their readers. By contrast, the reputation of journalists, most of them then writing anonymously, was insecure. 'It seems epidemic among Parliament men in general', wrote the poet Samuel Taylor Coleridge (1772–1834) in 1816, 'to affect to look down upon and to despise newspapers to which they owe 999/1000 of their influence and character – and at least three-fifths of their knowledge and phraseology.'

The Scottish politician Henry Brougham (1778–1868) who was never short of words, wrote many articles for the early numbers of the *Edinburgh Review*, the first (1802) of Britain's great quarterlies. It and the Tory *Quarterly Review* (1809), with long histories ahead of them, discussed new books and pamphlets at length, and critically. They were to be supplemented later in the century by weeklies, fortnightlies and monthlies. Brougham was also interested in new educational institutions, including mechanics' institutes and University College London. Along with the English publisher Charles Knight (1791–1873), the most eloquent and best-informed advocate of cheap literature, he was one of the founders of the Society for the Diffusion of Useful Knowledge, nicknamed 'the Steam Intellect Society', brought into existence in 1826.

Six years later Knight launched his *Penny Magazine*, addressing his readers as 'the many persons whose time and whose means are equally limited'. He offered them pictures (and diagrams) as well as words. His portraits were as varied as his reproductions of works of art, including sculptures. At its peak, the *Penny Magazine* had a circulation of 200,000. This fluctuated dramatically before its demise in 1845. The three volumes of Knight's autobiography, Passages of a Working Life, which appeared in 1864, explained why.

A new generation of popular magazines figured prominently in an article on 'Cheap Literature', which appeared in 1859, an *annus mirabilis* in what was only just beginning to be conceived of as 'English literature'. Periodicals were defining it. At one end of what was now a spectrum was *Reynolds Miscellany*, founded in 1846 by a Chartist, G. M. W. Reynolds (1814–79), described as the most popular writer of his day, who combined melodrama, mystery and radical politics. It lasted until 1860. At the other end of the spectrum was George Eliot's first major novel, *Adam Bede*, along with Tennyson's *Idylls of the King*, Edward Fitzgerald's *Omar Khayyam*, John Stuart Mill's *Essay on Liberty* and Charles Darwin's *Origin of Species*. A year later, a highly successful publisher of fiction, George Smith, launched his shilling *Cornhill Magazine* with a remarkable group of contributors. No fewer than 120,000 people bought the first issue.

London's major publishers, some of them called leviathans by their contemporaries, were not interested in a mass market for their books, most of which sold fewer than 1,000 copies and have not survived even as titles, except in library catalogues, although as early as the first decade of the nineteenth century the house of Archibald Constable in Scotland, first publisher (along with Longman in London) of the *Edinburgh Review*, had contemplated a series of books that 'must and shall sell not by the thousands or tens of thousands, but by hundreds of thousands – ay by millions'. Constable went bankrupt, almost destroying at the same time the great novelist Walter Scott (1771–1832). Scott's *Waverley* (1814) the first of what came to be called the Waverley novels, was published anonymously in three volumes. In the first year, 5,000 copies were sold.

Nevertheless, there was an increasing number of cheap editions, many of them in series, and a widening of access to books in libraries. In Britain the first Public Libraries Act, overlooked by many historians, was passed in 1850, and two years later the first free public library to be set up under the Act was opened in Manchester. Local authorities were now empowered to levy a small local tax (rate) to set up libraries, but they were slow to do so. They lacked adequate middle-class as well as working-class support. A more important sign of the power of books was the success of Charles Edward Mudie's Circulating Library of London, first opened modestly in Bloomsbury in 1842, but reopened in palatial stuccoed premises in grand style in 1860. The novelist Anthony Trollope (1815–82) called it 'Mudie's Great Flare Up'. Charles Knight and George Cruikshank, the cartoonist, were two of the dignitaries present at the reopening. Five years earlier, Mudie had ordered no fewer than 2,500 copies of volumes three and four of Macaulay's *History of England* and a year earlier 1,000 copies of Tennyson's *Idylls of the King*. It was fiction, however, that was his greatest strength.

It was largely the power of Mudie's, which extended to censorship of the content of fiction, that dictated for a very large part of the century that novels should be in three volumes ('three-deckers'). Reliance on the profits from three-volume novels was undermined when cheaper editions began to be produced soon after they were first published. Mudie's, which did not want to be left with expensive stock, explained that its profits were in jeopardy and turned to one-volume novels in the 1890s, spelling the end of one of the most familiar and entrenched of publishing phenomena. The

Publisher's Circular admitted in February 1895 that the three-volume novel was 'doomed'.

Outside Britain, equivalents of the intellectual quarterlies included the *Revue des Deux Mondes* (1829) in France, the *Russkii Vestnik* ('The Russian Messenger', 1856) and the *Frankfurter Zeitung* (1856) in a still fragmented Germay. As in Britain, public libraries and reading-rooms made books and newspapers accessible to readers who could not afford to buy them. In France in the early nineteenth century, for instance, when new novels cost 12–15 francs, something like two week's wages for a skilled craftsman, *cabinets de lecture* sprang up in Paris and then in the provinces, like video libraries more recently. Similar reading-rooms were established in German-speaking parts of Europe.

There was no Publisher's Association in Britain until 1896, but there had been a Society of Authors, founded by Walter Besant (1836–1901), with Tennyson as its first president. Authors and publishers alike were deeply concerned with copyright not only in Britain but in the United States and other European countries as well. The first International Congress of Publishers was held in Paris in 1896, the second in Brussels in 1897, the third in London in 1898 and the fourth in Leipzig, centre of a great book fair, in 1901.

The sales of books mattered more to some publishers than to others. Three volumes, however, had become a standard size – the volumes were not all of the same length – and this was more than large numbers of potential readers, far short of Constable's 'millions', could afford. Much depended, therefore, on library take-ups, remainders and, later in the century, cheap editions, themselves now standard. It also depended, of course, on levels of literacy. In 1850 these were relatively high in Britain, twenty years before the first National Education Act, although they were higher in Scotland (80 per cent) than in England (60–70 per cent). At that time Sweden had the highest literacy rate in Europe (90 per cent), and the Russian Empire the lowest (5–10 per cent). France had 55–60 per cent and Spain 25 per cent. In these circumstances, the composition of oral poetry and the practice of reading aloud in public naturally remained important in both Eastern Europe and the Latin countries.

The number of novels published in these countries did not reflect levels of popular literacy. Nor did it reflect the extent to which educated people were capable of reading the languages of other countries. Italian, for example, was the educated Englishman's second 'modern' language, coming after French but before German. Translation was one measure of communication. The novels of Jules Verne (1828–1905), finding fantasy in technologies, were translated into twenty languages. In 1883, with his tale *Five Weeks in a Balloon*, the first air technology, he began the publication of what became one hundred volumes of *Extraordinary Journeys in Known and Unknown Worlds*. His *From the Earth to the Moon* appeared in 1865, and *Around the World in Eighty Days* in 1873.

Working, sometimes uneasily, with Charles Dickens (1812–70), the novelist Wilkie Collins (1824–89), like Dickens, reached his public in serialized novels. Dickens's *Pickwick Papers* (1836–7), in twenty illustrated numbers, had set him off on that route. Breaking up the unity of the text introduced a greater element of expectation and suspense into fiction. Some of Dickens's serialized numbers were written only a day or two before publication, and Dickens revised them, lopping and cropping if necessary, while they were at the printers. Their appeal was enhanced by his public readings, another new feature at the time (though a reversion to ancient Roman and medieval practices). His plots were influenced by his love of the stage, including melodrama, one of the delights of the 'unknown reading public', and by his early experiences as a journalist. Through his novels, he served, in a memorable phrase of the English journalist Walter Bagehot, as a 'special correspondent for posterity', a very different kind of posterity from that to which the romantic poets continued to appeal.

The serial form in British radio and television goes back before Dickens, as does the conversion of novels, including those of Dickens himself, into broadcast plays, and serialization was not an exclusively English invention: it was pursued in continental Europe, particularly in France and Spain, where it had its own history. The French word *feuilleton* was used to describe episodes of a novel published in a subsection of a newspaper consisting of such items as theatre announcements and reviews, culinary recipes and political articles disguised as literature. Honoré de Balzac (1799–1850), author of *La Comédie humaine* and a wide range of other novels, much admired by Marx and Engels, serialized novels in *La Presse*. Eugène Sue, admired and copied by Reynolds, combined fact and fiction in his *Mystères de Paris* (1843), quickly translated into English. It had first appeared in serial form. At the other end of Europe, Dostoevsky's *Crime and Punishment* was first published in *The Russian Messenger* in 1866.

Exhibitions

It was during that first French Revolution that attempts were made to give glamour to the task of displaying objects as well as celebrating abstract ideas; and in 1797 and 1798 François de Neufchâteau, Minister for the

Interior under the Directory, organized exhibitions in Paris which proved attractive not only to the public but to French manufacturers competing against the English. 'The French have surprised Europe with the rapidity of their military exploits, and must advance with the same ardour on the paths of commerce and of peace . . . This is not merely an episode in the struggle against English industry, but also the first stone in a mighty edifice which time alone can complete.' After acquiring power, Napoleon approved of such competition, as did the royal and republican regimes that succeeded him; between 1797 and 1849 no fewer than ten exhibitions were held, their scale and scope increasing substantially. More than 4,500 exhibitors displayed their skills at the exhibition of 1849.

It was the French who first suggested in 1834 that their exhibitions should become international, but in this instance it was the English who first took up the idea. After much manoeuvring and with the powerful support of Prince Albert, the 'Great Exhibition of the Industry of All Nations' opened in the newly built Crystal Palace in London's Hyde Park in May 1851. This was three years after the third and most dramatic revolution in France, followed by revolutions in many other countries in Europe. The word 'revolution' was not used much in London in 1851, however, except when Englishmen prided themselves that in 1848 they had avoided one. They were proud too that they were welcoming to London in orderly fashion multitudes from countries that had so recently undergone one. By the time that France had its first great international exhibition four years later, in 1855, Napoleon III had become Emperor.

Prince Albert's concern was very different from Napoleon III's, as was his experience. In 1845, four years after marrying Queen Victoria, he had been made President of the Society for the Encouragement of Arts, Manufactures and Commerce, which set the tone for the Great Exhibition, stressing that it was not a bazaar, where articles were bought and sold, but a celebration of what had so far been achieved in science and industry throughout the world. It was an occasion to take stock. Albert did not use the word 'technology' and he exaggerated the part that science had hitherto played in the process of industrialization. Perhaps the Queen more than Albert appreciated the romance in the Exhibition, not least in the Crystal Palace itself. Its designer, Joseph Paxton (1803–65), not an architect or an engineer, but a gardener's son who became head gardener to a duke, was hailed as a symbol of self-help, and his building in glass and iron, which incorporated two elm trees covered in by the huge roof, 'seemed more like the radiation of the thoughts of some delightful fairy tale of the poet or painter', wrote a visitor to the royal opening sitting opposite the throne.

The Exhibition, which attracted six million visitors, set out to inform and to educate – for example, teaching about the marvels of the newest medium of communication: telegraphy. Exhibitions might be ephemeral vistas, the title of a book on them published in 1988, but a great provincial art exhibition held in Manchester in 1857 attracted more than a million visitors and inspired projects for provincial and national permanent collections. 'Permanent' is as significant an adjective as 'ephemeral'. Napoleon III realized this, and under him science was accorded a place in constructive projects for the future as it had been in the thought of Henri Saint-Simon (1760–1825) and the projects of his followers who were actively at work. The Suez Canal, opened with pomp and ceremony in 1869, was the dream of a Frenchman, de Lesseps, who believed, like Saint-Simon, that, between them, industry and communications could transform history.

In the late nineteenth century two particularly important exhibitions were held in the United States – the Centennial Exhibition of 1876 in Philadelphia and the Columbian, held in Chicago in 1893. At the second of these the great American entrepreneur of entertainment, P. T. Barnum (1810–91), was consulted. Make the Exhibition 'bigger and better than any that have preceded it', was his advice. 'Make it the greatest show on earth – greater than my own Great Moral Show if you can.' The organizers did, but the Exhibition was much more than a show. A Parliament of Religions was staged, and there was an 'ethnographic' display of 'tribes' of 'primitive people' along Chicago's new Midway.

The Paris World Fair of 1900 incorporated some of the features of Chicago, 1893, including a great Ferris Wheel, which could hoist more than 2,000 people into the air, using as an axle the largest piece of steel ever forged, and, a show in itself, an electrically powered moving pavement. The Exposition had new features of its own. It used electric light extensively to create an environment conjuring up fantasy with water cascades, glass and mirrors: 'an opium smoker might have conceived this fairy palace after reading the Arabian Nights'. Moreover, when the days of fantasy were over, there was a legacy in the shape of two buildings – the Grand Palais and the Petit Palais, which would be used for further exhibitions into the twenty-first century, including many that were restricted to works of 'high art' or to particular artists. In similar fashion, an earlier 1889 Paris Exhibition, held in the year of the centenary of the Revolution, left behind it the Eiffel Tower, designed by Gustave Eiffel, partly as a by-product of the work that Eiffel had carried out earlier on the Statue of Liberty. As more than a landmark it was to figure not only in the history of electricity, but in the history of radio, a technological turn that Thomas Edison (1849–1931), most famous and versatile of all inventors, did not foresee. Despite Prince Albert's insistence that the Great Exhibition of 1851 was not a bazaar, there were revealing connections between 'high art' and commerce in the exhibition sequence, just as there were between exhibitions and museums and picture galleries. To understand the making of 'mass culture', associated first with the United States, it is interesting to compare the catalogues of the 1900 Exhibition in Paris with a 1900 catalogue *A Consumers' Guide*, distributed by the American mail-order business, Sears Roebuck. Goods on offer were divided into eighteen departments, beginning with drugs and ending with baby carriages. Sears Roebuck had started by selling watches, moving his headquarters to Chicago in 1887. By 1900 it was necessary to possess a watch in order to live as well as to move. Switzerland did not lose its international watch market, but the United States and later Japan were to develop well-advertised markets of their own.

In Chicago, three of the sponsors of the Columbian Exhibition of 1893 were prominent in local business: George Pullman, Philip Armour and Marshall Field. Pullman wanted to make railway carriages comfortable, even opulent; Armour made a fortune out of meat-canning and packing; Marshall Field's retail business was as famous as Macy's in New York, which offered goods 'suitable for the millionaire at prices in reach of the millions'. Leaving aside these connections, what was happening on both sides of the Atlantic constituted the beginning of a consumer revolution which had its origins, as we have seen, in the eighteenth century, but only now began to affect the lives of millions. Paris, not Chicago, was the mid-nineteenth-century birthplace of the department store, but by 1900 there were notable department stores in Liverpool (which in 1877 had its own great art gallery, the Walker), London, New York, Chicago, Helsinki and Tokyo. The store was, indeed, a big city phenomenon everywhere, a place in which to spend time as well as money. Patterns of spending mattered increasingly. It was an American sociologist, Thorstein Veblen (1857–1927), who introduced the idea of 'conspicuous consumption'. This was a process, like the introduction of 'scientific management' into work, which involved psychology as much as economics or technology.

Electricity

The Austrian economist Joseph A. Schumpeter (1883–1950) was to publish an important book, *Capitalism, Socialism and Democracy*, in 1943. Before 1914, however, he had already produced the model of an economic system propelled by pushes in technology driven by innovative entrepreneurs.

Schumpeter associated enterprise with electrification, writing at a time when a united Germany was undergoing what was sometimes called its own industrial revolution, a very different industrial revolution from that of Britain in the late eighteenth and early nineteenth centuries, a revolution which directly involved the state in the development process.

There were many strands in the nineteenth-century story of the evolution of modern communication, with myth being invoked as much as science. Thus, Marx wrote of Vulcan, the stoker of furnaces. Icarus, who tried to fly, figures, as does Prometheus, who stole fire. It was Marx, however, who in the age of steam wrote without allusion or metaphor that 'modern industry never looks upon and treats the existing form of a process as final'. He was right, as the *Punch* cartoon of 1881 (see Figure 12) demonstrates.

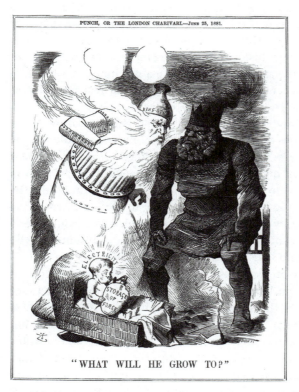

PUNCH, OR THE LONDON CHARIVARI.—June 25, 1881.

"WHAT WILL HE GROW TO?"

Fig. 12 King Steam and King Coal watch anxiously the Infant Electricity. A *Punch* cartoon of 1881 pitting two technologies, old and new, in symbolic opposition. They were to coexist. Electronics was a twentieth-century development.

The infant Electricity carrying a bundle described as 'storage of force' is being looked at uneasily by King Steam and King Coal, concerned about the child's future. King Gas might have been placed alongside them.

Electrification, a protracted process, was to be described by Reyner Banham, a twentieth-century British critic, as 'the greatest environmental revolution in history since the domestication of fire'. Electricity, always difficult to explain, belonged to nature before it entered history. 'Atmospheric electricity' preceded electrical power. As early as 1750 Benjamin Franklin conceived the idea of a lightning conductor to protect buildings from 'mischief by thunder and lightning'. It was not until the last decades of the eighteenth century, however, that Alessandro Volta, Professor at the University of Pavia, deeply engaged in experiments with electricity, introduced the term 'electrical current'. In the subsequently protracted history of international experiment, which left many well-known scientists still uncertain in the 1880s about what electricity was, the study of electro-chemistry was followed by that of electro-magnetism. The story of the electric telegraph, mentioned by Marx, is part of the longer history of signalling rather than the history of electricity: by contrast, the story of the dynamo, a machine for converting mechanical into electrical energy, is a basic element in the history of electricity itself, linking two branches of what came to be called physics.

The English scientist Joseph Swan (1828–1914) and Thomas Edison (1847–1931) in the United States were the two men mainly responsible for the invention of a workable electric light bulb, a new stage in the development of electrical power. Swan demonstrated his tubular electric light bulb in Newcastle in 1878; it was to be put quickly into use in the Craigside, the imposing house where the pioneer businessman Sir William Armstrong lived, and also in the Savoy Theatre in London, founded by Doyly Carte to put on Gilbert and Sullivan operettas. Edison 'inventor of inventors', who was involved in his Menlo Park Laboratory in New Jersey in an extremely wide range of innovative projects, described more fully in the next chapter, displayed his incandescent lamp in 1879. Hundreds of visitors came to see his illuminated home. In the same year he obtained British Patent 4576 a few months before Swan. A bitter patent war might have ensued, but instead the Swan and Edison Companies merged. It now became possible to take electricity into the home as well as into the streets, where lamps had already been in use in Paris, for example, in the Gare du Nord. In order to demonstrate electricity, however, it was necessary to produce more than light bulbs. An expensive new infrastructure was necessary. Electric generation and public power stations were required. The former might be exclusive to one business: the latter were public. In Britain, the North-

Eastern Electricity Supply Company launched in Newcastle led the way. In the United States, Edison found it difficult to raise funds to build stations. Having taken out a patent for a Jumbo dynamo, he had built a central power station in Pearl Street on Lower Manhattan in New York in the area of the city that included Wall Street, the financial capital of the United States, the American counterpart of Lombard Street in London, but when the Pearl Street station threw the switch to begin power generation on 4 September 1882, there was more of a sense of triumph in the offices of the *New York Times* than on the Stock Exchange. As one journalist remarked, 'it seemed almost like writing by daylight'. Edison Jumbo dynamos had been employed in Holborn Viaduct London earlier than in New York. The station made it possible for electric street lights to replace gaslights and for the General Post Office to get its first electric lights also.

Not surprisingly, transport was one of the first forms of communication to be affected by electrification. In 1880, when the *SS Columbia*, a steel ship, left the United States for a voyage round Cape Horn to California, it was the first electrically lit ship in history, and when it reached San Francisco all its 115 incandescent lamps were still aglow. Germany, quick to take up the new source of power, introduced into the streets of Berlin, its capital, its first electric tram. Berlin was a growing city, very different in economic and social structure, in appearance and culture, from the Berlin of the 1840s. Baltimore in the United States followed in 1885, as did Blackpool, a new type of mass holiday resort, in England. By 1900, there were sixty-one British cities and towns that owned electrical tramways, Manchester the largest. In London the electrification of the London Underground Railway was completed by 1900.

Making trams and installing tramlines became a highly competitive business in the United States, the two main competitors being General Electric, an amalgamated company which handled lamp manufacture and the making of dynamos, and Westinghouse, which won the large contract for illuminating the Columbian Exhibition in Chicago in 1893. Westinghouse employed alternating current, favoured by the Croatian-born prophet of electricity, Nikola Tesla (1856–1943), rather than direct current, and won crucial contracts for controlling the immense natural hydro-electric power of the Niagara Falls.

During the 1890s electricity began to be the subject of a growing literature, technical and imaginative, expert and popular, so that in its first number in 1890 the periodical *Electricity and Electrical Engineering* could observe that Electrical power was destined 'to completely revolutionise all existing conditions of industry . . . and all aspects of everyday life'.

The same message had been proclaimed a year earlier when the British Prime Minister, the Conservative Marquis of Salisbury, addressed the first annual dinner of the Institute of Electrical Engineers, which had initially been called Telegraph Engineers. He predicted that the relative ease (he did not refer to the cost) with which electrical power could be distributed would overturn the centralized system of factory production based on the steam engine. 'In the house of the artisan', he went on, 'you [will] turn on power as you now turn on gas.' You did not need to know how it worked. It had been possible to teach about steam before scientists developed theories of energy. It was still impossible to do this with electricity. You could try, however, to put it in perspective. 'It is by the use of steam and electricity that the material world of the nineteenth century is distinguished from the older worlds that have gone before', wrote Sydney Walker in the *Electrical Engineer* in 1895. 'And even now, while steam is young, as the universe judges time, the handwriting is on the wall – its days are numbered. And may it not be also in the future that even the young giant we serve, whose infantile needs are so prodigious, will have to give place to another agent as yet unknown?'

Walker was concerned with social communications more than with transportation. In similar fashion, popular science magazines, revelling in forecasts of the future, usually concentrated on communication. Thus, *Science Siftings* reported in 1894 that Edison was working on a new invention 'to render communication between the ends of the earth possible without telegraph, telephone or any of the many appliances known to modern society'.

After visiting the Paris Exposition of 1900, Henry Adams (1838–1918), historian, world traveller and, not least, member of a distinguished American family, wrote from Paris about the dawn of a new century in which 'what we used to call electricity is its god'. For him, the Exposition had been a source of both 'education' and 'amusement'. The period from 1870 to 1900 is closed, he concluded, 'the period from 1900 to 1930 is in full swing'. 'I go down to the Champ de Mars and sit by the hour over the great dynamos, watching them run as noiselessly and smoothly as the planets.'

5

New Processes and Patterns

This chapter examines one-by-one the story of the various new communications devices which prepared the way for what has been called, with only a touch of exaggeration, 'the media revolution of the twentieth century'. Railways, briefly dealt with in Chapter 4, come first because they set the pattern for much else to follow in technology, economics, politics and management, and, not least, in the world of the imagination. It was no accident that, in 2000, in the corridors outside the office headquarters of Novell, a late twentieth-century hi-tech company in Silicon Valley, there were paintings of great American locomotives.

Railways

In *Macmillan's Magazine* (May–October 1861), a British writer wrote of the opening up of the world not only to travellers and migrants, but also to tourists; and it was tourists, even more than migrants, who first realized most clearly that the world was small, not huge. 'We are now infinitely more familiar than our forefathers were' with the 'idea of the limited dimensions of the Earth, a tiny ball, axled eight thousand miles.' There were also psychological dimensions: 'A well-known use of travel', it was said, 'consists in the self-reliance, and the general inventiveness which it develops.' Fascination with foreign places could be shared at a distance. Travel books and novels relating to foreign countries had a wide circulation – both before and after improvements in physical transportation. It was another British writer who claimed in January 1878 in the *Quarterly Review* that 'our railways may be said to mark the furthest point which the advance of European civilization has reached . . . They have done more than anything achieved by former generations to modify the influence of time and space.'

Locomotives contributed both music and poetry. The American poet Walt Whitman (1819–92) called the railroad the realization of Columbus's dreams, 'the marriage of climates, continents and oceans', and described the 'fierce-throated' locomotive as the 'Type of the modern! . . . [the] pulse of the [American] continent!' As railway journeys, short and long, multiplied, on every continent the ancient metaphor of the journey took new forms. Travellers contributed as much to the imagery as locomotive drivers and signalmen. One widely circulated European engraving showed a spiritual railway to heaven: 'From Earth to Heaven the line extends / To life eternal where it ends.'

It was in Europe, not in the land of the Pilgrim Fathers, that there developed a 'railway literature'. Many publishers, great and small, old and new, were involved. One of the most successful was W. H. Routledge, who in 1849 introduced a shilling series of reprinted fiction, the longest and largest such series, called 'The Railway Library' (imitated by Louis Hachette in Paris when he launched his own series, La Bibliothèque des chemins de fer, in 1853). It was in 1851 that W. H. Smith secured a monopoly of station bookstalls, selling 'yellow backs' on the London and North-Western Railway, with other lines to follow. Cheap German Tauschnitz editions of 'the best in literature', well known to travellers, were not on sale in Britain, but were easily obtainable at railway stations in Switzerland, Italy and Spain as well as Germany.

Widely used guidebooks, particularly those of Karl Baedecker (1801–59) and the Murray guidebooks, were carried around by the world's first 'tourists'. Many of their other requirements, including care of baggage, were met by Thomas Cook (1808–92), a British travel entrepreneur who arranged local, national and international excursions. Bradshaw's complete list of British railway times first appeared in 1839, to be followed by European and American supplements; and on both sides of the Channel and of the Atlantic 'missing the train' became a metaphor, like being 'on track'. Even a minute now mattered in the scheme of things.

At the time, one British novelist, W. M. Thackeray (1811–63), wrote that 'we who lived before railways and survive out of the ancient world are like Father Noah and his family out of the Ark'. Another novelist, however, Charles Dickens, was ambivalent in his reactions. He described railways as 'the power that forced itself upon its iron way', 'defiant of old paths and roads, piercing through the heart of every obstacle'; in one of his finest novels, *Dombey and Son* (1848), in writing of railways, he chose to employ metaphors of death as well as of progress. This novel stands out in the literature of communications as J. M. W. Turner's painting *Rain, Steam and Speed* (1844, painted in his seventieth year) stands out in the realm of art. Later in the century, French Impressionists, among them Claude Monet (1840–1926), added memorably to the range of paintings of locomotives and railway stations (in Monet's case, the Gare Saint-Lazare, Paris) in quite a different manner. One Paris station, the Quai d'Orsay, was to become an art museum in the twentieth century.

From the start, disasters became one of the staples of periodicals and newspapers (as they were to be of radio and television). They were further commemorated in poems and depicted in engravings, some of them melodramatic, many religious, like road shrines in the twenty-first century. In Roman Catholic countries like Mexico, popular *ex voto* art portrayed people saved from railway disasters just in time by angelic or divine intervention. Railways were slow to develop there and in Latin America as a whole. The size and geography of countries like Argentina and Brazil constituted a great obstacle. In Argentina, there were only 20,000 miles of track in 1914, nearly three-quarters of which was concentrated in the pampas, carrying pastoral and agricultural traffic. Chile's first railway was built as early as 1851, but it was decades later that a railway link was made across the Andes: the Transandine Railway was opened to traffic in 1910. In Africa, too, development was slow, although the city of Nairobi in Kenya was to begin its life as a camp for the Uganda Railway.

Whatever the country, whatever the date, so many obstacles stood in the way, financial as well as engineering. The development of railways was seldom straightforward. In the earliest years, before railway shares became a part of settled mid-Victorian portfolios, eager buyers of shares in the Britain of the 1840s learned bitter lessons about the difference between investment and speculation. There were years of mania and there were years of crisis. Risk was never easy to ascertain. The career of George Hudson (1800–71), the 'railway king', with his headquarters in York, collapsed in ruins in 1849: Dickens called him 'The Great Humbug'.

There were usually far more railway plans than railway lines or railway stations, as there were in the United States late in the century, for, whatever the economics, not all engineering problems could be foreseen. There was an obvious case for regulation in the public interest as more and more lines were built, but what counted as the public interest was not always easy to determine.

Even engineers disagreed. There was a battle in Britain, as in Australia, about the width of gauges: as late as 1865 there were no fewer than thirty places in Britain where passengers had to change trains for this reason. The Great Western Railway, with a broad gauge, favoured by Isambard Kingdom Brunel (1806–59), builder of much besides railways, did not fully accept what became the standard gauge until 1892, more than thirty years after Brunel's death. When he laid the South Devon Railway, he wanted to introduce atmospheric power, but it quickly had to be abandoned. By

1892, many records had been broken on the Great Western Railway, one of a small bevy of companies that survived into the twentieth century. Daniel Gooch's Actaeon did the journey from London's Paddington station to Exeter non-stop in 1844, an achievement comparable to that of the most famous twentieth-century British locomotive, the Flying Scotsman, belonging to the London and North-Eastern Railway, which, in 1934, recorded 100 miles per hour on the line from London to Edinburgh.

From the start there had been an incentive for business amalgamation, as there was to be in twentieth-century communications media, but in 1844 there were no fewer than 104 separate companies. As total mileage tripled between 1850 and 1900, when there were almost 19,000 miles of track, four main railway groups emerged, each with its own territory, its own organization and its own records. Slow to adopt electricity or, before it, diesel, they built their own locomotives and their own distinctive carriages with separate compartments and limited corridors. Continental trains, retaining a third class after this had disappeared in Britain, looked and felt different.

Every country, like every railway company, has its own history, with its own landmark dates. By 1845, there were nine countries in Europe that had railways (with Britain having exported a large proportion of the coal, the iron and the locomotives); in 1855, there were fourteen. Outside Europe, where Britain often secured railway business through Thomas Brassey (1805–70), the greatest of the nineteenth-century contractors, there were railways in five continents by 1855. Brassey and his partners often took their labour with them. Thus, when they were constructing railways in Australia in the early 1860s, they organized the transport of 2,000 experienced 'navvies' from England and Scotland. The word 'navvies' (navigators) was inherited from the canal age, and, like the skilled engineers on whose plans they depended, the navvies often faced more damaging risks than the risks faced by railway investors. Lives were at stake, not money.

Across the oceans, the story of Indian railways – the creation of British engineers – is unique. Work on the first two lines did not begin until 1850, and it was not until 1853 that the first locomotive in India, the *Lord Falkland*, pulled a train from Bombay to Thana, a distance of fewer than twenty-five miles. Yet as early as 1844, at the height of the British railway mania, one of the world's railway visionaries, Rowland McDonald Stephenson, had prepared a scheme for linking by rail Bombay, Calcutta, Madras and Delhi; in his simple words, free from rhetoric:

> The first consideration is as a military measure for the better security with less outlay, of the entire territory [then controlled by the East India Company], the second is a commercial point of view, in which the chief object is to provide the means of convey-

ance from the interior to the nearest shipping ports of the rich and varied productions of the country, and to transmit back manufactured goods of Great Britain, salt, etc. in exchange.

This line of argument appealed to the Marquis of Dalhousie, the Governor-General of India, who wrote a landmark minute on railways for the East India Company a few days after the line from Bombay to Thana was opened. 'The commercial and social advantages which India would derive from their establishment' were, he 'truly believed', 'beyond all present calculation.' Bombay's magnificent railway station (1888) was a great popular rendezvous.

What neither Dalhousie nor the railway engineers had ever fully anticipated was the popularity of railways with Indians. As early as 1855, an English-language newspaper, *Friend of India*, could observe in the socially stratified language of the period that 'the fondness for travelling by rail' had become 'almost a national passion among the lower orders'; thereby, it went on, it was 'producing a social change in the habits of general society far more deep and extensive than any that has been created by the political revolutions of the last twenty centuries'. By 1900, India had more than 25,000 miles of track, some of the most costly to build in the world, as against Britain's 18,000, France's 22,500, Germany's 30,000, Russia's 23,000, Canada's 17,500 and the United States' huge network of 260,000 miles. Most of the American lines were built after the Civil War in a period of hectic and highly competitive construction, when great fortunes were assembled by railway tycoons. By comparison with the American Cornelius Vanderbilt (1794–1877), whose wealth was built on railroads and shipping, England's George Hudson was a minor character. China resisted railways, and there were only 250 miles in 1900. The first railway project there in 1865 had been dropped after objections were made to destroying ancestors' graves in the laying of the tracks.

The railway maps of Britain and the United States looked very different in 1900 from what they had looked like half a century before, as did their town and city maps. In Britain, London was at the point of national convergence – no railway 'main line' passed across it – and in the provinces, apart from new railway towns like Crewe and Swindon, where locomotives were manufactured, it was, for the most part, existing communities that were linked together. The same was true in Europe, although there were new transborder junctions, where passengers waited while passports or other travel documents were examined. In the United States, entirely new communities, which grew more quickly than any older communities, were brought into existence. The scale of enterprise there was continental rather than national. Chicago remained the great railway city, with trains moving east and west. The 912-mile journey to New York was cut to twenty-four hours, and more and more miles were added west of the Mississippi. On both sides of the Atlantic, railways physically and socially divided towns and cities. There were always two sides of the track.

Steamships

The story of steamships fascinated contemporaries as much as the story of railways. It was appropriate, therefore, that a British historian of shipping, A. Fraser MacDonald, chose, as the title of his 1893 book on the subject, *Our Ocean Railways*. The story was tied up with that of migration. Between 1776 and 1940, no fewer than thirty million emigrants from Europe reached what for most of them was their favourite destination, the United States. Some were political refugees, some were driven away from their homelands by hunger, some were ambitious young seekers after fortune. There was always a push and a pull. In the late nineteenth century there were greatly increased numbers of migrants from Eastern and Southern Europe. The Statue of Liberty (1886), at the entrance to New York, was designed by a Frenchman, Frédéric Auguste Bartholdi (1834–1904), to mark the centenary of the American Declaration of Independence, with a substantial contribution to the cost of its pedestal having been collected from readers of a popular and aptly named American newspaper, *The World*. The immigrants went on to publish a multitude of newspapers in their own languages. The contributions they made to the culture of late nineteenth-century America – journalistic, literary, musical – were immense.

   The wearing journey that these people had made across the Atlantic had been greatly speeded up by steam power, which Americans had long developed for their own domestic water transport, taking advantage of their many lakes and rivers. Already, before Independence, in 1763 William Henry of Pennsylvania had constructed a steam engine in advance of James Watt, having visited England three years earlier. In 1785, two years after Independence, John Fitch, a Connecticut mechanic, tried out a boat with paddle wheels which he patented within the following two years. In 1787, James Rumsey is said to have propelled a steamboat up the Potomac River, with George Washington on board, and in 1802 Robert Fulton (1765–1815) successfully sailed a steamboat on the Seine in France, where he was living from 1797 to 1804. Back in the United States, he used a Watt engine when, in 1807, he constructed the *Clermont*, 'a monster moving on the waters, defying wind and tide, and breathing flames and smoke': it carried passengers on pleasure trips along the Hudson River. Eight years later in Britain, a steamboat called *James Watt* was operating between London and Leith. When Britain went to war with the United States in 1812, the Americans built a 'steam vessel of war', *Fulton the First*, launched in 1814.

The zenith of the life of America's great Mississippi River, 2,350 miles long, came with the steamboat. The writer Mark Twain (1835–1910), who had much to say about the present and the future of communications, was a pilot on a Mississippi boat before the American Civil War. The riverboats used high-pressure engines and, to the excitement and sometimes the alarm of the passengers, raced against each other. The Atlantic Ocean was crossed for the first time in 1819 by an American ship employing steam, the *Savannah*, but it steamed for only about eight-five hours of a twenty-seven-day passage to St Petersburg. It was not until 1839 that a chartered British ship, *Sirius*, completed a transatlantic voyage from Cork in Ireland to New York entirely by steam – something of a publicity stunt – in eighteen days and ten hours. A few hours later, Brunel's *Great Western*, 'a floating palace' dubbed the Great Western Railway of the Sea, specially constructed for the dangerous journey, arrived in New York from Bristol after fifteen days and fifteen hours, the fastest journey across the Atlantic yet made. It was Brunel's *Great Eastern*, however, deemed a Leviathan, twice as long as any ship at the time and six times larger overall than any previous ship, that received the most lavish publicity. Ominously, its engine had blown up on a trial run in 1838, the first of a series of accidents, and, as for the ship itself, despite her leading part in the laying of Atlantic cables, she never lived up to her publicity and was turned into scrap in 1889.

In 1839, Samuel Cunard (1787–1865), born in Canada, had established his first company, the British and North American Packet Company, with a fleet of four plain sister ships, designed to carry mail rather than cargo. Among the early passengers who travelled on them was Charles Dickens, who took the *Britannia* to Boston in January 1842. He explained in his *American Notes* that he was not impressed: the bunk beds on which he and his wife slept reminded him of coffins. Such a comment could not have been made fifty years later except by 'steerage' passengers. Cunard's *Mauretania*, launched on the Tyne in 1907, had third-class foyers as well as dining saloons that were elegant and commodious. On this, as on all other great pre-1914 liners, there were three classes. From embarking to disembarking, travelling by liner meant belonging to a hierarchical system.

Technology had changed as much as styles. The first ship to incorporate a screw propeller rather than a paddle wheel had been the *John Bowes* in 1852, and compound engines were being brought into use by the end of the decade. One further technical advance, the introduction of a workable steam turbine, not a new gadget, was necessary to increase the speed of great ocean liners, 'queens of the sea'. The man who invented it, Charles Parsons (1854–1931) was an aristocrat: his father was the Third Earl of Rosse, President of the Royal Society, who kept a yacht at Cowes in the Isle of Wight and had himself invented a reflecting telescope. Parsons built his first condensing turbine engine in 1892, and a vessel incorporating it, the *Turbinia*, carried out trials on the Tyne in 1894. Three years later, the year of Queen Victoria's Diamond Jubilee, it 'crashed the party' at the Grand Naval Review at Spithead. The Cunard Line would not buy his patent, however, and it needed an Admiralty subsidy in 1902 before Cunard could build turbine-operated ocean liners capable of reaching a speed of 24–25 knots.

By then, speed had become something of a fetish. These were years of intense Anglo-German naval rivalry, expressed in decoration as much as in technology, which began with the accession of Wilhelm II, Queen Victoria's nephew, to the imperial German throne. It was a rivalry that extended to luxury liners as well as to warships. In 1907, Cunard's *Lusitania*, named after the ancient Roman Portugal and launched in 1907, regained the cross-Atlantic speed record, which had been held for ten years by the German passenger liner, the *Kaiser Wilhelm der Grosse*. Until 1915, one year after the beginning of war between Britain and Germany, the record was then held by the *Mauretania*. In the *Kaiser Wilhelm der Grosse*, built by the Vulcan company at Stettin on the Baltic, imperial eagles gazed down on passengers from a stained-glass dome. Another German ship, the *Deutschland*, also built by Vulcan for the Hamburg-Amerika line, had more than twice as many first-class beds as steerage beds. There was Japanese silk on the walls of the main saloon, and paintings of German rivers and of the Hudson River in New York State.

The First World War broke the pattern of competition – and quickly. Indeed, before the war the *Mauretania* had been provided with gun mountings, and was immediately converted into a troop ship. The *Lusitania*, with regal suites looking back to Versailles and Wedgwood, continued to carry civilians after 1914, but when it left New York on 1 May 1915 for its 202nd journey across the Atlantic, carrying more than 1,200 passengers (and three stowaways), it was torpedoed ten miles from Ireland from a submarine, and sunk. The death toll was 1,201. This was in many ways a more tragic ending than the sinking of the *Titanic*, on which W. T. Stead (see p. 219) was a passenger, and the news of which was sent out by Marconi operators, one of whom, David Sarnoff, had a remarkable future ahead of him (see p. 179).

The *Titanic* was a White Star Line ship that, through its sinking, has passed into history in fiction and in film.

Submarines had themselves figured prominently in pre-1914 fiction, but, although it had a long history behind it, the US Navy did not buy its first submarine until 1900. Just a century earlier, Robert Fulton had tried out a submarine, the *Nautilus*, on the River Seine. In 1898 the American Simon Lake had designed a submarine, the *Argonaut*, which navigated extensively in the open sea. The first US diesel engine submarine began sailing in 1912. By then, barrels of crude oil, a fossil fuel, were crossing the Atlantic from wharves in Philadelphia. Antwerp was the principal European port for the Red Star Line that controlled the trade.

Oil was far more expensive than coal in nineteenth-century Western Europe and America, although it was relatively cheap in southern Russia, and the opening up of new oil fields in Borneo (1898) and Texas (1901) began to change the picture. In the process, a slow one, world geography – and with it world economics and politics – were transformed. It was a landmark date when the Hamburg-Amerika line adopted petroleum in place of coal on its great liners. By then J. D. Rockefeller (1839–1937) was making a fortune out of oil and had founded the University of Chicago.

As early as 1885 a new kind of ship was devised on Tyneside to carry oil. The *Marquis Scielune* was divided from bow to stern by a bulkhead and incorporated eight tanks with holes at the side to prevent explosions and shafts to load and unload the oil. The tanker, for that was what it was, operated between Batoum in the Black Sea and Italian ports on the Adriatic. That was before the demand for petroleum grew in dramatic fashion after 1918, due primarily to the unprecedented increase in the number of automobiles first in the United States and then in every continent. Henry Ford (1863–1947), as influential a figure in his lifetime as Watt or Boulton were in theirs, introduced to the roads his famous Model T in 1908. Standardized, reduced in price and competitively sold automobiles were to become not a luxury, but a mass product over the next century (see p. 207).

Looking back over the story of ships, it is important to note that, as in the case of other technologies, steamships had not immediately replaced sailing ships. Trade winds still blew. Many ships used both sail and steam, and in the cargo traffic between Britain and Asia sail was for long the main source of power. Tea-clippers, dependent on wind and weather, required vast amounts of canvas and rigging, but when the weather was good they could travel from England to Australia via the Cape of Good Hope in little more than two months. The most splendid of them was the *Cutty Sark*, built in 1869, the year that the Suez Canal was opened, but it was also one of the last of its kind. The peak year in sailing-boat construction was 1864. In 1842 the Peninsula and Oriental shipping line (the P&O), founded in 1822, established a regular route around the Cape, a route which had itself changed geopolitics, a noun not yet coined. Australia had been considered an 'empty continent' when the fleet of Admiral Phillips arrived off Botany Bay in January 1788.

This was the land that James Cook, great sea captain, had called New South Wales when he had travelled along its coast twenty years earlier. What became the neighbouring state of Victoria, scene of a gold rush, was founded later, in 1851, and Brunel's *Great Britain*, carrying immigrants, not convicts, made no fewer than thirty-four round voyages from Liverpool to Melbourne, its capital, between 1852 and 1876. Even after 1869, steam did not completely supplant sail. Built on Glasgow's Clydeside, *Great Britain* was made not of iron but of steel, and it was the first ship to be fitted with electric light.

During the 1880s there was ample evidence of a dramatic new burst of invention on the oceans – with steam power giving way to electricity and with 'the media' at the centre of the activity. In 1887, ships passing through the Suez Canal were for the first time furnished with electric headlights to allow travel by night. This cut a long journey by sixteen hours.

The concept of time was transformed, as was the concept of distance, even more drastically in the late nineteenth century than it had been in the late eighteenth and earlier nineteenth centuries when the world was divided into standardized time zones. As late as 1878, there were about eighty different railroad times in the United States, and it was not until 1884 that the representatives of twenty-five countries, convened at the Prime Meridian Conference in Washington, DC, established Greenwich, England, as the zero meridian. Already, Britain, Sweden, Canada and the United States had adopted it. France, objecting to the choice of a British meridian, did not adopt it until 1919, although its government fully accepted the idea of standard time and in 1891 made Paris time, which was nine minutes and twenty-one seconds ahead of Greenwich, the legal time of France. At an international conference on time held in Paris in 1912, the French pressed for accurate time signals to be transmitted around the world. On this occasion France, where the great novelist Marcel Proust was exploring the mysteries of private time, was chosen as the site, and the first signals were transmitted from the Eiffel Tower at ten o'clock in the morning on 1 July 1913.

Postal Communication

Ships, like railways, carried not only people and goods, but also letters – an indispensable mode of communication, local, national and international, without which the development of 'business' would have been impossible. The speeding up of the mail during the last decades of the coaching age had long preceded the introduction of railways and of the world's first adhesive, perforated postage stamp. The first such stamp (1840) was in black, bearing the young Queen Victoria's head. Remarkably soon it was to become a 'collectible'. It was an important nineteenth-century invention, but the word 'stamp' itself was not new, nor, of course, particularly in the United States, was the idea of a stamp tax. Nonetheless, the introduction of the stamp made it possible for letters to travel pre-paid at a cheap and uniform rate over the whole country, wherever the destination. A by-product of the expansion of the mail was the ready-gummed envelope and, a little later, the postcard. The first Post Office postcards, 'open post sheets', were introduced in Austria in 1869, and in Germany and Britain in 1870.

Postcards raised interesting issues, such as privacy, that were relevant to other media of communication: 'Why write private information on an open piece of cardboard that might be read by half a dozen persons before it reached its destination?' It did not much matter whether they read it or not, particularly after picture postcards were introduced during the following decade, with France, Germany and Switzerland leading the way, for what was written on them became increasingly standardized. In 1900, the English journalist G. R. Sims described in *The Referee* how, at the top of a mountain in Switzerland, a favourite tourist country, 'directly we arrived at the summit, everybody made a rush for the hotel and fought for the postcards. Five minutes afterwards, everybody was writing for dear life. I believe that the entire party had come up, not for the sake of the experience or the scenery, but to write postcards and to write them on the summit.'

Hartley Coleridge, son of the poet, hailed the penny post as an invention beneficial to all. This, however, was an idealized version of what had happened. Illiteracy rates in England, though falling between 1840 and 1870, were still high, and intermediaries had to be employed by many of the poor both to write outgoing and to read incoming letters. The radical leader Richard Cobden (1804–65), caught up in popular campaigning, welcomed the penny post not only on political grounds – it made it possible to mobilize opinion in favour of free trade – but on moral grounds too. There was now a new spur to become literate. Meanwhile, the penny post had been of great value politically to the Anti-Corn Law League, which was led by Cobden and John Bright.

It is of interest chronologically that the British postal system developed before the national educational system was devised. Rowland Hill (1795–1879), creator of the system and a passionate advocate of popular education, called the Post Office a 'powerful engine of civilization', and for his brother Matthew, writing in 1862, 'the amount of [Post Office] correspondence will measure with some approach towards accuracy the height which a public has reached in true civilization. When we find that the town of Manchester equals in its number of letters the empire of all the Russians both in Europe and in Asia we obtain a means of estimating the relative degrees of British and Russian civilization.' Other commentators drew the same conclusion when making comparisons with the pre-Victorian past.

A Victorian backbench Conservative MP, Henniker Heaton, extended the argument at the time of Queen Victoria's diamond jubilee, when all the technical and social achievements of the nineteenth century were under review, particularly in the press. An enthusiastic spokesman for an imperial penny post, Heaton claimed, mainly with private letters in mind, that when Victoria had come to the throne, 'the masses were almost as restricted to oral communication and local commerce as their ancestors were under the Stuarts, or as the Turks are under Abdul Hamid'. Different parts of the country were each absorbed in their own interests, knowing no more of other communities than 'one Russian village knows of another a hundred miles away. The gentry and professional men in the rural districts, and the citizens of the great towns, maintained sufficient intercommunication; but while the more elevated points were then ringed with light, darkness reigned below.'

The contrasting images of darkness and light, familiar in the eighteenth-century Enlightenment (see pp. 105), now belonged to an 'age of electricity' with the language of the 'masses', which Heaton used, to a limited extent replacing the language of 'class', a word associated with early industrialization. Nonetheless, it was not the masses but the middle classes that benefited most from the new flat rate of postage, and the continued speeding up of the post was achieved in response to business demands. The painting by W. P. Frith (1819–1909) of the peak hour at London's much publicized General Post Office in St Martin's Le Grand was of the same genre as his painting of Paddington railway station. Nearly half of London's 161 million letters in 1863 came from within the city and were delivered within its inner area twelve times a day. Collection times were announced on post boxes that, like stamps, often bore the Queen's head.

When Heaton urged the introduction of an imperial penny post in 1890, he found other arguments besides business benefit. It would not only stimulate trade, he maintained, but would unite separated 'kith and kin' as twenty-first-century email was often able to do. In geopolitical terms, it would symbolize both 'imperial unity' and 'Anglo-Saxon brotherhood'. There were Americans, notably Elihu Burritt (1810–79), 'the learned blacksmith', who, like Heaton, wanted a cheap universal post in the interest of universal brotherhood. It was New Zealand, however, a country with large numbers of British immigrants, not the United States, where immigrants arrived from all over the world, that was the first country to introduce cheap and standard international postal rates in 1901, the year Queen Victoria died.

The United States had no postage stamps before 1853, the year when the rail link between New York and Chicago was being completed, but from the start it had cheap postal rates, and the number of items carried doubled to 7.4 billion between 1886 and 1901. One of the direct consequences was a growth in mail-order retail business, although some of the products purchased were carried by private firms, the best known of which was Wells Fargo. Standardization of consumer products was to go along with standardization of time and place. The American Post Office, staffed through patronage, did not carry the authority of Europe's post offices, which were required by government, or took it upon themselves, to determine national policies relating to telegraphs, telephones and later what came to be called 'telecommunications' as well as postal services. While European post offices introduced parcel post, and in some countries, postal orders and banking accounts, the most that American postmaster-generals could do, under pressure, was to extend their powers by focusing on free delivery.

Even then, it was not until 1895 that RFD (Rural Free Delivery) was provided for groups of farmers who had petitioned their Congressmen, a move described by Daniel Boorstin as 'the least heralded and in some ways the most important communication revolution in American history'. Long before that time, a general postal union, the Union Postale Universelle, had been founded in 1874 with Britain as a founder member: one British company, De La Rue, was then producing stamps for many different countries in the world, and one of the rules of the Union was standardization of the colours of stamps. By then, black had virtually gone. The Victorian penny lilac had sold in millions.

Telegraphy

Nine years earlier, in 1865, an International Telegraphic Convention had been signed in Paris by representatives of twenty countries who formed a new International Telegraph Union. Britain was not invited to participate at this time because its telegraph service, like the mail-order service in the United States, was then in the hands of private companies. Physical transportation was still in a primitive or transitional state in some countries. One of the delegations represented at the signing – that from Turkey – had to travel part of the way to Paris on horseback. In 1868 the headquarters of the Union were set up in Bern in Switzerland. The first International Radiotelegraph Convention was held in Berlin in 1906, and a quarter of a century later, in 1932 at a conference in Madrid, dealing with radio wavebands, a new name was adopted: The International Telecommunications Union. In 1947, following two further conferences in Atlantic City, it became a specialized agency of the United Nations.

Telegraphy was the first great electrical breakthrough in communications, described in 1889 by Britain's Prime Minister, the Marquis of Salisbury, enthusiastic about science, as 'a strange and fascinating discovery', which had had a direct influence on the 'moral and intellectual nature and action of mankind'. It had 'assembled all mankind upon one great plane, whence they can see everything that is done and hear everything that is said and judge of every policy that is pursued at the very moment when these events take place'. Whether 'all mankind' was placed in that position was not apparent, but it was obvious enough that politicians now had at their disposal a powerful new instrument. They praised it, however, in general terms. Thus, on leaving India in 1856, Dalhousie had composed a final minute for the East India Company referring to 'Uniform Post' and 'Electric Telegraph' along with railways as the 'three great engines of social improvement which the sagacity and science of recent times had previously given to the Western Nations'.

Dalhousie was speaking for many people in power. Railways – carrying people, goods, newspapers and books – and telegraphs – the first nineteenth-century electrical invention to carry 'messages', public and private – were directly related to each other in his and their minds. If, in retrospect, railways, followed by bicycles, automobiles and aeroplanes, seem to belong to the history of transportation, and telegraphs, followed by telephony, radio and television, seem to belong to the history of the media, any such separation is artificial. There was continuity. Telegraphy was closely associated with the development of railways – instantaneous signalling methods were necessary for safety reasons on single tracks – although there were some telegraph wires that followed not railways but canals.

In Australia, the telegraph was judged more important than the railway. In 1830, the total population, held back by 'the tyranny of distance' (above), numbered no more than 70,000, and was dependent on the postal service, 'a people's service', costly but never questioned. Until the gold rush of the 1850s, official communication over short distances was by semaphore. The opening of the first telegraph line between Melbourne and Port Melbourne on 8 March 1854 preceded by six months the opening of the first railway line between the two places: for several years this was the only profitable railway line in Australia. The subsequent story of the telegraph has been told in gripping fashion by Ann Moyal in her *Clear Across Australia: A History of Telecommunications* (1984).

The coming of long-distance links by cable was obviously of enormous importance to both Australia and New Zealand. They were forged slowly as cable links by land and sea gradually crossed Europe and Asia, arriving in the Australian port of Darwin via the Indonesian archipelago in 1872. Even then, they had to make their way across central Australia, where lonely telegraph operators might live more than 100 miles from their nearest neighbours. At first the service was expensive, but by the 1880s costs had fallen significantly. It was only with telephony that private benefits began fully to accrue.

The laying of submarine ocean cables of telegraph wire below the 3,000 miles of the Atlantic, a huge but difficult achievement, envisaged by the American pioneer of telegraphy Cyrus West Field (1819–92), would have been impossible without the improvement and expansion of ocean steam transport. There had to be Anglo-American cooperation too. Two attempts in 1857 and 1858 failed, a third seemed to have succeeded. Charles Bright, British chief engineer, who travelled from Plymouth with Field on the British battleship *Agamemnon*, was given a knighthood at the age of 26, while Field became a hero in the United States. Yet the cable did not succeed in transmitting telegraphic messages, and it was not until 1866, after yet another cable was laid, this time from Brunel's *Great Eastern*, that success was achieved.

For Dickens, the telegraph, domestic or transatlantic, was 'of all our modern wonders the most wonderful', and most people agreed with him. Like canals, railways and ocean highways, it linked national and international markets, including stock exchanges and commodity markets (cotton, corn and fish, for example). It also speeded up the transmission of information, public and private, local, regional, national and imperial, and this in the long run stood out as its most significant outcome. Distance was conquered as information relating to family, business, government affairs, the weather, and natural and manmade disasters was transmitted, much of it in the form of news.

The main inventions in telegraphy, as in many other fields, had been arrived at independently and in different countries in a cumulative process which did not have one single inventor. Nor was one single scientist associated with the underlying theory of electromagnetism, although, from France, André Marie Ampère (1775–1836), who extended the work of the Dane Hans Christian Oersted (1775–1851), gave his name to the ampere, the unit in the current-carrying element in the electro-circuit. In Britain, James Clerk Maxwell (1831–79) formulated in 1864 the basic mathematical equations relating to what came to be called the electro-magnetic field. The word 'field' subsequently became a keyword.

In Britain the first successful, if unlikely, partners in telegraphy had been William Fothergill Cooke and Charles Wheatstone, and it was with them that the invention of the electric telegraph was to be particularly associated. Their joint patent of 1837 bore the magnificent description 'Improvements in Giving Signals and Sounding Alarms in Distant Places by means of Electric Currents transmitted through Metallic Circuits'. Cooke himself used less formidable language when he claimed that the telegraph would enable the railway line to become a 'highway'. In 1837, still fresh, the image of the highway appealed immediately to the *Railway Times*. This was the image to be used by President Clinton in the 1990s (see p. 277), but already in 1858 the *Scientific American* had prematurely described the cable as 'an instantaneous highway of thought between the Old and New Worlds'. It had 'electrified' the whole of the United States.

In the United States it was Samuel Morse (1791–1872), artist by training, son of a Yale-educated minister, who was to be called on his eightieth birthday 'the Father of the Telegraph', who devised a dots and dashes code, which could be read at forty words a minute and came to be used universally in telegraphic transmission. As a young man, he had introduced the daguerreotype photograph (see p. 184) to the United States, and five years later had sent his first telegraphic message, receiving less credit for his achievement in the States than abroad, where, for example, at a London banquet in his honour in 1856, Cooke called Morse's system 'one of the simplest in the world': in that, he added, lay its 'permanence and certainty'. Napoleon III made Morse a Chevalier de la Légion d'Honneur, and Prussia, Austria, Spain, Italy, Denmark and Turkey bestowed medals on him. The medals Morse received, including one that was diamond-encrusted, were more lavish than the basic instruments used by Morse operators – a key, a relay and sounder, a register and a battery. Meanwhile, far away in a different continent, William O'Shaughnessy (1809–89), an assistant surgeon in the Indian Army, was carrying out experiments in Calcutta hanging iron wire on trees.

There were international contacts from the start of telegraphy. Cooke had listened to Professor Muncke lecturing on telegraphy at Heidelberg University and had seen a demonstration of a needle telegraph devised by a Russian diplomat, Baron Pavel Schilling. Morse had addressed the Académie des Sciences in Paris in 1838 and, having been forestalled by Cooke and Wheatstone's telegraph patents in London, had patented his own device in Paris in 1838. This was two years before he patented it in the United States, where a new Patent Law had been passed in 1836 and a new Patent Office established. A young Canadian of Irish extraction, Samuel Walker McGowan (1829–87), who introduced telegraphy to Australia, had worked with Morse and his colleague Ezra Cornell (1807–74), inventor of the first telegraph insulators, and founder of Western Union (see p. 161). The first long-distance message sent in 1872, after Australia had been connected to Europe and Asia via Darwin, was not international but 'Advance Australia', although the message ended with the hope that the 'submarine cable connection would long speak words of peace'.

The first telegraphic message in Britain had passed between Cooke and Wheatstone – the latter a physicist who was also interested in music and invented a concertina. He had originally worked independently, and the two men initially viewed each other with some suspicion. Using a needle system, Cooke telegraphed Wheatstone from Camden Town station one week after the formal opening of the London and Birmingham Railway in 1837, and Wheatstone replied at once from a dingy room, lit only by a candle, at Euston station, having experienced what he called in his own words 'a tumultuous sensation' such as he had never felt before: 'All alone in the still room, I felt all the magnitude of the invention pronounced to be practicable beyond cavil or dispute.' Such recollections of first sensations and of first conversations were to become part of the folklore of the media. The telephone, radio, television and the Internet were to provide others. Morse's first message was 'What hath God wrought?'

In India it took fourteen years for O'Shaughnessy's experiments to produce operational results. The first telegraph line between Calcutta and Bombay was not to be completed until 1854. It had military uses, and in a military context, always significant in the history of telecommunications, telegraphy affected both planning and operations on land as well as at sea, just as semaphore telegraphy had done during the revolutionary and Napoleonic Wars. It was organized through 'chains of command' and 'general' and 'special' orders. The first time it was used significantly on an operational scale was during the Crimean War when a 340-mile cable was laid across the Black Sea. Its value was demonstrated even more strikingly during the American Civil War when more than 15,000 miles of telegraph line were in use and more than 1,000 operators worked the system.

By then, the Reuter Telegram Company, founded in London in 1851 by Baron Julius Reuter, who had arrived there from Germany, and known simply as Reuters, had in 1859 supplied news of Napoleon III's battles in Italy and the text of the Emperor's twenty short despatches that he sent each day to the front. There was no American news agency until 1846, when Associated Press (AP), known at first as the Associated Press of Illinois, was launched, but in France the Agence Havas had been founded in Paris in 1835. In 1889 Reuters started a 'Special India and China Service', and thereafter, for almost a century, India, in the words of Reuters' historian, Donald Read, was 'destined to play a central part in the Reuter Empire within the British Empire'.

As early as 1846 there were more than 1,000 miles of American line, including a stretch of 450 miles between New York and Buffalo. A telegraphic link between New York and San Francisco was completed in 1859. By the end of the Civil War, which greatly stimulated telegraphic business – and the business of Western Union, in particular – there were 37,000 miles of line.

Apart from assisting in the construction of the first telegraph line, government in Washington played little part in this story, which was left to unregulated private enterprise – with market forces clashing, often dramatically, in the early years of what has been called 'reckless expansion'. According to A. D. Chandler, American business historian and author of an indispensable book, *The Visible Hand* (1977), the competitive telegraphic companies then formed were the first modern business enterprises to appear in the United States. Yet out of competition between many firms came oligopoly, with few firms competing imperfectly, and out of oligopoly attempts at monopoly.

Regulating Communications

As telegraphic business expanded, key questions were continually raised in many countries about the respective roles of private and public enterprise, and of state and market. 'Is not telegraphic communication as much a function of Government as the conveyance of letters?' the *Quarterly Review* asked in London in 1854, when no fewer than 120 provincial newspapers, then at the height of their influence, were receiving columns of parliamentary news by telegraph. Comparisons were drawn with other countries in which the system was state-controlled, such as Switzerland, where, for every 100,000 people, there were 6.6 telegraph offices, as against 5.6 in Britain.

In the United States the state had been involved at first when Morse secured public funds to build an experimental Washington to Baltimore overhead line: its role thereafter was very different, however, from its role in Europe. The American Post Office might state firmly that 'an instrument so powerful for good and evil' could not 'with safety be left in the hands of private individuals uncontrolled by law', but politicians responsible for running it knew that they were never likely to be provided with adequate investment to run it. At first private investment was inadequate too, but the subsequent decision to hand over the telegraph to business was crucial in the history of United States communication. As a result of it, a massive corporate enterprise, Western Union, which acquired that name in 1854, was to take shape. Its then chairman, William Orton (1826–78), under whom it secured a near monopoly of telegraphic traffic, emphasized that 'the telegraph lives upon commerce. It is the nervous system of the commercial system'.

In France, state control of communications had been deemed essential from the start, with a French Minister of the Interior emphasizing equally strongly in 1847 that telegraphy should be an instrument of policy, not of commerce. The 3,000 miles of semaphore lines in the 1840s were all operated by the Ministry of War. A law of 1837 had laid down that there should be a continuing government monopoly in distance communications, and, whatever the subsequent constitutional regime in France, this approach persisted. Very similar attitudes towards *l'espace nationale* were to characterize twentieth-century French policy in relation to radio and telecommunications.

In the pre-1848 European regimes, telegraphy had arrived before the revolutions, and it was inevitable that in the Habsburg Empire its leading statesman Klemens Wenzel von Metternich (1773–1859), given his anti-liberal policies, would urge that the telegraph should be a government monopoly, closed to the public. As was the case too in Prussia, and it remained so after the 1848 revolutions which overthrew Metternich. In Russia, which, like Britain, avoided revolution in 1848, Nicholas I had connected St Petersburg to Warsaw and on to the German border by semaphore, and had opened a branch line from St Petersburg to Moscow, with towers, each manned by six men, five to six miles apart. Nicholas banned the circulation of any information concerning electrical telegraphy on the grounds that it would be subversive, even though Baron Schilling had devised a system using a battery-powered galvanometer and a binary code.

Before and after 1848, one country – Belgium – where the telegraphy lines, like the railways, were state built, seemed to be setting an example.

Its lines were said in 1869 to have been 'excellently planned and cheaply constructed', so that as a consequence the tariffs charged, always a matter of concern in Britain and the United States, were comparatively low. At that date, the stock market accounted for half the traffic and 'family affairs' for 13 per cent. By contrast, the press accounted for only 4 per cent and government for 2 per cent.

Inside the British Post Office, one ambitious official, Frank Scudamore, who had already created a Post Office Savings Bank, was strongly of the opinion that the Post Office should take over the telegraph companies, and by the 1868 Telegraph Act, passed under a Conservative government but supported by the Liberal politician W. E. Gladstone (1809–98) – then in opposition, but soon to become Prime Minister – it duly purchased them, along with the telegraphic business of the railway companies, the first of which had been the Electric Telegraph Company, founded in 1846. The 1868 measure was fiercely but unsuccessfully opposed by the railway and telegraph companies, closely linked through interlocking directorships, an interesting early example of concentration of media control.

The railway companies were a major interest in Parliament also, straddling both sides of the House and showing their power as early as the 1840s, when a younger Gladstone, then a Conservative President of the Board of Trade, was forced to withdraw a clause in his 1844 Railway Regulation Bill, giving government authority to buy up (i.e. nationalize) railways that had started operating after the Bill became law. The Railway Regulation Act, as finally passed, prescribed that all future railway companies should provide third-class accommodation on at least one train a day travelling in each direction. These so-called 'parliamentary trains' (a hybrid too) were to survive deep into the twentieth century.

In 1868 a financial deal was reached with the telegraph companies before the Post Office, supported by the press, took them over. Critics had warned in vain of the likely 'stagnation and dreary routine inseparable from official regulations' that would follow nationalization, but the government pledged that telegraphs were now to be treated like postal services and that a uniform rate would be introduced for a twenty-word telegraphic message irrespective of distance. In 1844 there had been no such railway regulation concerning rates after the nationalization clause had been withdrawn.

The Post Office monopoly was to run into financial problems in the nineteenth century, although the number of messages transmitted rose from 6.5 million just after the Act had been passed to 26.5 million just ten years later, a huge increase in comparison with other European countries and, indeed, with the United States. Yet more than comparative statistics were involved, for, as Post Office losses on unremunerative traffic, described by critics as a 'subsidy', increased with the number of messages transmitted, there was bound to be parliamentary and public criticism which raised other media issues also. The press, which enjoyed the benefit of what to the Post Office were unremunerative rates, could defend them on the grounds that they stimulated public interest in the news. It, too, constituted an interest, but of a different kind.

After the move to public ownership, many of the directors of the old private telegraph companies, with compensation money in their pockets, acquired holdings in telegraph companies dealing in overseas business, and a large new merger, the Eastern Telegraph Company, was founded in 1872, which for almost a quarter of a century paid dividends of between 6.5 and 10 per cent. It was one of several concerns which, at the end of the century, buttressed British dominance in the international cable business. There was an acknowledged imperial interest in this, for, as an official committee put it in 1902, it was 'desirable that every important colony or naval base should possess one cable to this country which touches on British territory or on the territory of some friendly neutral'. Commercial incentives were said to come second. 'After this there should be as many alternative cables as possible', and these 'should be allowed to follow the normal routes suggested by commercial considerations.' Not surprisingly, suspicion of British financial interests, there from the start, grew in continental Europe towards the end of the nineteenth century, and Paris journalists pondered in 1894 as to whether 'the security of other nations' could be upheld if Britain controlled 'all sources of information'. Americans went on to ask the same question.

The giant Western Union, which was favoured by advantageous leasing and franchising arrangements and which benefited from its alliances with railroad interests, claimed that monopoly was natural. Between 1870 and 1890 its corporate profits in real terms rose even in years when major sectors of the American economy were depressed, and the number of its offices increased from 3,972 to 19,382. The largest of these were in New York, where no fewer than 444 telegraphers were employed in a huge operations room. Thomas Edison began his long career as an operator in Western Union's Boston office in 1868. By 1890, 80 per cent of the country's message traffic was in Western Union hands, and critics of monopoly, although always in evidence, could be dismissed airily with the maxim that it was 'the result of an inevitable law that the business shall be mainly conducted under one great organization'. Morse himself, who made little money out of his achievements, had wished from the start that a telegraphic network

Fig. 13 Thomas Edison at work. Both his laboratory and his study were workplaces. 'Inventor of inventors', he had more inventive ideas than anyone before or since. He secured his patent for the phonograph in 1878 two months after applying: the Patent Office had known nothing like it before.

would make 'one great whole like the Post Office'. During the last decades of the century there was a further argument for monopoly: it alone would make possible the pursuit of necessary innovative research. Yet in 1894 a Sherman Anti-Trust Act was passed which had no counterparts in Britain, Germany or France.

There was no shortage of research during the second half of the nineteenth century, including research on automatic telegraphs, machines that could read messages without the need for skilled operators. A Wheatstone patent of 1858 offered a direct replacement for a telegrapher – an automatic reader that could transmit messages in Morse from a pre-punched tape at very high speed. The device, which achieved its purpose, was of particular value in the newspaper business.

With the development of Duplex, a single telegraph line could be used for the transmission of two messages, in opposite directions; and when in 1874 Quadruplex was devised by Edison, this doubled the capacity yet again. This was impressive technological progress, but the effects on manpower – and womanpower – could be catastrophic. Unskilled workers could now operate telegraphy at only a quarter of the salary of skilled Morse code operators. The Western Union was in full control, however, and in 1879 it totally broke a great national telegraphic strike by the Brotherhood of Telegraphers of the United States and Canada. The ultimate challenge to the telegraphic business was to come not from workers within it but from the advance of telephony outside it.

The Telephone

The story of the telephone, which became an instrument both of private and public communications, began long before March 1876, when Alexander Graham Bell (1847–1922), an American inventor born in Scotland, patented his 'telephone', a word first used in 1796 for a purely acoustic method of communication. In 1837 the American C. G. Page had discovered that rapid changes in the magnetization of iron produced a musical note, 'galvanic music', and some of the experimenters who followed in his wake used a diaphragm to increase the output of sound. Notable amongst them was Philip Reiss, a teacher in Frankfurt who claimed that he had transmitted 'intelligible speech'. The German scientist who had the biggest influence on Bell was Hermann von Helmholtz (1821–94), whom Lord Salisbury found time to visit in 1878 when he was taking part in the Congress of Berlin concerned with European diplomacy.

If the words of Reiss had been received, it must have been accidentally for short periods. Only Bell could claim correctly that he had made the telephone work. He demonstrated it at the great Centennial Exhibition in Philadelphia in 1876, and his first telephone call to his partner Thomas Watson, totally different from him in background, temperament and education, is another message that has passed, perhaps mistakenly, into folklore: 'Mr Watson come here, I want you.' There was an element of undoubtedly royal telephone folklore in Britain too. Queen Victoria, who had Bell presented to her in 1876, listened attentively to Kate Field singing 'Comin' Through the Rye' on what she described as 'the most extraordinary' model telephone, which Bell had brought with him.

In 1876, it has been suggested, 'there was no need for the telephone. Society did very well without it.' But this comment, which could never have been made about the telegraph, is misleading. Received at first with incredulity, in the twentieth century the telephone was to become a 'necessity' for many people both in the office and the home, and later, indeed, with the mobile phone, in the street. The *Scientific American* had already suggested comprehensively in 1880 that it would usher in 'a new organization of society – a state of things in which any individual, however secluded, will have at his call every other individual in the community, to the saving of no end of social and business complications, of needless goings to and fro'.

It was an Australian Professor of Engineering at Melbourne University who stated in an address of 1897 that 'if a prediction of coming achievement had been made to any intelligent person in 1837 . . . of all modern inventions, the telephone would have aroused the greatest scepticism'; and it was Sir William Thompson, the eminent Scots scientist, later Lord Kelvin (1824–1907), prominent in the story of the laying of the transatlantic cable, who, after trying out Bell's telephone in Philadelphia, where he was a judge at the Centennial Exhibition, described it as 'the most wonderful thing he had seen in America'. Thompson, one of the first people in Britain to install electric lighting in his home, brought back to Britain two Bell telephones which he and Sir William Preece (1834–1913), a key figure in Post Office history, who became its Chief Engineer (see pp. 175), displayed in 1877 to members of the British Association for the Advancement of Science. In the same year, an American woman journalist, hired by Bell, presented a *Matinée téléphonique* to coincide with the opening of Parliament. In Australia, news of the invention reached Sydney and Melbourne in the same year via the printed word – articles in the *English Mechanic and World of Science* and in the *Scientific American*. Immediately, Australians set about trying to produce home-made telephones.

Bell, who had worked earlier on the problems involved in teaching the deaf to speak, had conceived of the idea of transmitting speech by electric waves in 1865, and in 1874 he fashioned a phonautograph, a word coined by another experimenter, which was modelled on the structure of the human ear. His 1876 device was patented on his birthday in March 1876. It had been applied for on 14 February, the same day as another American inventor, Elisha Gray, had also applied for a telephone patent. Litigation, won by Bell, was to follow, with the victory being controversial at the time and remaining so afterwards.

Big business came into the story as well, converging with technology. Having failed to interest Orton, Chairman of Western Union, Bell set up a private company in 1877, which three years later was converted into a public company, National Bell. Quickly realizing that he had made a serious mistake, Orton turned hopefully for technical advice to Edison, who produced a successful carbon transmitter, which led Bell to consider litigation, but, instead, an out-of-court deal, not the last of its kind, was reached in November 1879, from which Gray benefited modestly too. The terms were that Western Union would become the sole manufacturer of telephones and their components and that the operation of the telephone system would be left to a new National Bell Company, which could make use of all the relevant Western Union patents.

The deal worked for several reasons. One was that National Bell attracted as its general manager an outstanding individual – Theodore Vail (1845–1920), a cousin of one of Morse's assistants, who had managed the American railroad postal network before joining National Bell. Under his effective leadership, the company was to grow in strength, successfully defending all Bell's patent rights which were subjected to no fewer than 600 challenges before they expired in 1893. While they lasted, National Bell enjoyed the same kind of business advantage that Boulton and Watt had enjoyed a century before. Bell, now a rich man, lived until 1922, keenly interested in every aspect of telephone development – and in much else in the field of telecommunications.

From the start, indeed, Bell had proved himself to be more than an inventor: he offered the world a 'vision', as Vail was to do: that of a 'universal network reaching into homes, offices and workplaces'. This he admitted, 'might sound utopian', but with the construction of exchanges and switchboards it soon proved not to be. The exchange principle led rapidly to the creation of networks covering whole countries and, in the twentieth century, whole continents. The first switchboard was installed in New Haven in 1878, and the first exchange in London was opened in Coleman Street in 1879. It was a doctor in Lowell, a city once again figuring in the history of communications, who suggested a numbering system in 1880, but dialling did not arrive until 1896 (in Milwaukee).

Mechanized switching, with which the name of A. B. Strowger, a Kansas City undertaker, is usually linked, was introduced in La Porte, Indiana, in 1892: for the first time, subscribers could make a call without the aid of an operator. Nevertheless, the introduction of mechanized exchanges was slow, even in the United States; and in Britain, outside the City of London, where a Strowger exchange was installed in 1897, only Epsom, Surrey, near the famous racecourse where the Derby was staged, had a similar system installed in May 1914. Later in that eventful year, in the wake of a flurry of telegrams, telephones speeded up military mobilization. Railways played their part also: 'Build no more fortresses', the German general, Helmuth

Fig. 14 Telephone operators, Seattle, Washington, USA, 1952.

von Moltke, had ordered; 'build railways.' Telegraphs and telephones went with them.

During its very early years, many people had foreseen a different future for telephones, associating them as much with entertainment for a scattered audience as with point-to-point, one-to-one communication between individuals, and for this reason alone the telephone must figure larger than the telegraph in the pre-history of broadcasting. Nonetheless, the same association had been made earlier between entertainment and the telegraph: in 1848, *Punch* had reported, as a pseudo-news item, songs being sent by telegram from Boston to New York. In 1876 *Nature* forecast that 'by paying a subscription to an enterprising individual who will no doubt come forward to work this vein we can have from him a waltz, a quadrille or a gallop just as we desire'.

In the next year the *Springfield Republican* predicted that by means of the telephone 'all the music of a prima donna could be distributed over the country while she was singing, thus popularizing good music to an extent as yet unknown'; and far away from Springfield, in Switzerland, an engineer relayed a Donizetti opera in 1879.

It was further away still, in Hungary, that the most enterprising and most sustained project for using telephones for entertainment was devised by a Hungarian inventor, Theodore Puskás (1844–93). He had worked for the Edison Company, had exhibited at the Paris Electricity Exhibition of 1881 and had secured exclusive rights to develop the telephone in Hungary in the same year. Puskas was assisted by his brilliant friend Nikola Tesla (1856–1943), another popular pioneer of electricity and of the use, in particular, of alternating current, the form of power favoured by the huge Westinghouse Company, which in 1922 created KDKA, the landmark American radio station (see p. 174). Tesla was frequently drawn into argument about the merits of electrical systems, whereas another pioneer of electricity, the American journalist Park Benjamin, without going into differences, relied on rhetoric in his book *The Age of Electricity* (1887) when he described the multiple uses of electricity as 'simply legion'. One of them was directly bound up with what became broadcasting. 'It will talk in our voices hundreds of miles away [it was far from doing that then]. It will record the votes which changed the destiny of a great nation or set down the music of the last popular melody.'

This was what Puskás was seeking to do when he inaugurated (and his brother continued) a *Telefon Hirmondó* service in Budapest in 1893, which offered subscribers what was in effect, though not yet in name, the world's first broadcasting system. Providing his subscribers with long flexible wires and two smooth round earpieces in their homes, he offered a daily schedule of items to which they could listen, including news bulletins and summaries of the newspapers, stock exchange reports, 'lectures', sports news and 'visits to the opera'. There was also a weekly children's programme, along with 'linguistic lectures' in English, Italian and French.

The word *Hirmondó* had its roots in the past. It was often translated as 'telephone journal' or telephone newspaper' and sometimes as 'news announcer', and recalled the older terms 'town crier' or 'herald' as well as the name of the first newspaper published in Hungarian, *Magyar Hirmondó* (1780). News, however, was only one feature in what one of the first English writers on the work of the 'station', Arthur Mee, who became editor of *The Children's Newspaper* in 1908, called – railway-fashion – a 'timetable'. The magazine *Invention* called it a 'programme'. Mee's own vision was global: 'If as it is said to be not unlikely in the near future that the principle of sight is applied to the telephone as well as that of sound, earth will be in truth a paradise, and distance will lose its enchantment by being abolished altogether.' *Telefon Hirmondó* had no more subscribers in 1914 than it had in 1897 (estimates varied between 6,000 and 20,000), but it survived the outbreak of the First World War. In 1930, when it was broadcasting radio programmes, the most precise estimate was 9,107.

The Hungarian service was far more ambitious and successful than a parallel Electrophone Company in Britain, which in 1884 offered, for an annual subscription, connections to theatres, concerts and, not least, church services: the sermons were to be delivered by 'the most eminent divines'. And a United States venture, the Telephone Herald in Newark, New Jersey, which had begun seven years after the London company, folded in 1904. Various 'theatrephone' schemes in Paris, dating back to the 1880s, also collapsed before 1914, despite the interest of Marcel Proust, who foresaw many of the future uses of the telephone, which some commentators thought of largely as a 'toy'. Bell was right in forecasting that the 'serious uses' of the telephone would prevail and that it would serve primarily as a two-way conversational medium. Bell's foresight was usually ahead of the current technology, but over time 'phoning' would prove as easy and as natural as talking face-to-face, while dialling 'Time' would prove as reliable, or more reliable, than consulting a watch. As early as 1893 Budapest had its own version of an electrical time-keeping system, first developed by a Berlin Normalzeit Company. Six times a day, a number of clocks connected on a single circuit around the city were electrically synchronized by the time signal of *Telefon Hirmondo*.

Different though the telephone system, with its subscriber base, was from the telegraph system that for decades coexisted with it, the British government, backed by the courts, decided in 1880 that, within the terms of the Telegraph Act of 1868 (see p. 162), the telephone was a telegraph. The decision followed a merger between the British Bell and British Edison companies, which encouraged the Post Office, supported by strong telegraph interests, to acquire control of all telephone activity in Britain. It was to be operated largely through a licensing system, with licensee companies being required to pay a royalty on their business, but the Post Office maintained some exchanges of its own, for example, at Newcastle-upon-Tyne, and there were also a number of municipal telephone companies, for example, Hull, to be the longest surviving of them. The National Telephone Company, the biggest of the licensees, acquired a near monopoly, however, before being taken over completely by the Post Office in 1912. By then, a national 'trunk' system had been developed and international traffic had increased. Across the Atlantic, the first long-distance line, completed in 1880, was between Boston and Lowell, and by 1892 there were open lines between New York and Chicago, to be followed by lines between New York and San Francisco. Two American inventions, the wave filter and the loading coil, made such communication increasingly economical: the substitution of amplifiers or repeaters of an electronic type for electro-mechanical repeaters is said to have heralded a new era.

By comparison with the United States (and Canada), progress in extending telephone use in Britain, which led the world in the manufacture of cables, and in other European countries had been slow. Indeed, in Britain there was no sense, as *The Times* put it in 1902, that the telephone was 'an affair of the million'. It was, rather, a 'convenience for the well-to-do and a trade appliance for persons who can well afford to pay for it'. 'An overwhelming majority of the population do not use it and are not likely to use it at all except perhaps to the extent of an occasional message from a public station.' A year earlier, the Chancellor of the Exchequer had claimed that 'telephonic communication is not desired by the rural mind', while in Canada, the United States and Australia it was in the rural areas that the telephone was most in demand.

By 1900 the United States was far ahead of all European countries in telephone distribution, with one telephone for every 60 people. Sweden came first among European countries, with one for every 215. France had one for every 1,216 and Russia one for every 6,958. In 1904 there were 6.5 telephones per 100 persons in Manhattan and the Bronx, and only 1.4 per 100 in London. The main American drive, well expressed in the title of a 1914 article in *McClure's Magazine*, 'Telephones for the Millions', came from the American Telephone and Telegraph Company (AT&T), which had been brought into existence in New York in 1885 as a long-distance network subsidiary of National Bell, located from the start in Boston. In an imaginative move (in two senses) in 1899, AT&T became the parent company, with New York as its corporate headquarters. Another electrical equipment manufacturing company, Western Electric, had already been assimilated in a cumulative process starting in 1881.

Vail's ambitions were being realized, and, after a long spell outside AT&T,

during which he made a fortune, he took over the presidency of the company in 1907, and two years later engineered the buy-out of Western Union,
the major telegraphic company (see pp. 166–7). He also tightened control
over the finance of the licensing companies. Yet whatever he claimed about
the importance of control and regulation, there were strong American
objections, local and national – and inside and outside government – to
AT&T's monopoly. 'We do not ask the government to fight our battles,'
the National Association of Independent Telephone Exchanges, founded
in 1897, declared in 1910, 'but we do ask for protection against outrageous
methods of warfare, which are illegal and detrimental to the public welfare.'
In what became a struggle of Social Darwinian proportions, Vail had one
particular advantage: he believed in research while most of the independent companies did not, and a generation after the expiry of the original Bell
patents, the Bell Telephone Laboratories, to be known worldwide, were to be
formally set up in 1925.

In relation to the question of monopoly, a compromise between what
appeared to be radically different approaches to thorny issues, practical as
much as theoretical, had been reached in 1913 and was reaffirmed after
the First World War in the 1921 Graham Act. AT&T disgorged Western
Union, made its distance toll lines available to independents and agreed to
obtain prior approval from the Interstate Commerce Commission for the
opening up of new telephone systems. The Graham Act, acknowledging this
agreement, exempted AT&T from the provisions of anti-trust legislation.
Nevertheless, AT&T continued to face hostility from opponents of monopoly, and in 1926 was forced in a further compromise to abandon broadcasting stations. From 1934 onwards, it was subjected to regular questioning in
the Federal Communications Commission (see pp. 234–5), yet on the eve of
the Second World War it controlled 83 per cent of all US telephones and 98
per cent of long-distance toll wires. It also had a total monopoly of overseas
radio telephony. It was the largest company in history.

Outside the United States, different countries reached out slowly towards
an ideal of 'universal service' as they had done in the evolution of their
postal systems, relying mainly on their Post Offices to dictate telecommunications policy, as it had come to be described. The technological and
financial challenges in providing a universal telephone service involved the
integration of new technologies, including radio broadcasting, into official
systems. The United States relied on private enterprise, with AT&T running the operating companies, and Western Electric manufacturing most
of the equipment (and sharing the costs of Bell Telephone Laboratories), but
Sweden, a far smaller country, provided an alternative model.

More was involved, however, than system building. There were always cultural ramifications. Telephone culture developed in its most expansive form in the United States, making farm life less isolated, and changing not only marketing methods, but medical practice, politics and the reporting of news. Social habits were changed too, not least those of women, soon happy 'to chat on the phone'; in the morning, when husband and children had left home, was the favourite time. There was, indeed, an emerging 'telephone language and culture'. Not everything said or written about the telephone was positive, particularly in England. The appearance of the countryside and historic towns, it was complained, was being ruined by wires. The intrusion of the telephone into the home was often under attack, as television intrusion was to be decades later. Chatting on the phone was no substitute for conversation. Swearing on the phone raised ethical issues. Should it be treated as an offence? 'Telephone crime' was linked with other forms of crime, anticipating articles almost a century later dealing with the Internet: 'The Telegraph and Telephone Companies [and here they were treated as associated, not as competing, agencies] are allies of the criminal fraternity.' Not surprisingly, other critics thought of them as 'allies of the police'. There was agreement, however, that telephones were the 'allies of the press' and of banking and stock exchange interests. As early as April 1877, New York stockbrokers were already using the new medium, and in London as early as 1880 *The Times* set up a telephone link with the House of Commons, in order to include the reporting of late-night debates in the next day's editions. By 1900, the daily mass journalism of the United States had come to depend more on telephonic than on telegraphic communication.

In France, however, there was a different emphasis. The French word for 'exchange' was 'central', a word which suggested a very non-American (and non-British) way of looking at what came to be thought of as a network; and as late as 1922, Paris was said to be spurning the telephone: 'Almost a half century after its invention the telephone remained a tool reserved essentially for professional men.' Retailers in France – and indeed in Britain – used it only to a limited extent in their buying and selling, and it was not until 1908 that Harrods, the great British retail store, installed pay phones for its customers. After 1918 the number of telephones per 1,000 persons continued to increase on both sides of the Atlantic, with an interruption during the Great Depression and the Second World War, and in the 1950s, long before the advent of the mobile phone, the rise began to be identified as a major social trend.

Radio

Selfridge's, a new London department store competing with Harrods, was more welcoming to communications after being opened by its American owner, Harry Gordon Selfridge (1858–1947) in 1909. With the support of the *Daily Mail*, it hosted radio broadcasts, as did the retail store in Pittsburgh where Frank Conrad's KDKA was supported by the Westinghouse Company. Different media interconnected. The store found that the gramophone records KDKA played for its listeners sold better in consequence.

A generation before radio broadcasting, however, there had been wireless with few intimations of broadcasting, pioneered in the 1890s by the Italian inventor Guglielmo Marconi (1871–1937). The 'improvements' in wireless which he brought with him to London in 1896 had a long history behind them, even predating the work of German scientist Heinrich Hertz (1857–94), who corroborated experimentally the brilliant theoretical work of the British scientist James Clerk Maxwell, who died young. Oliver Lodge, born in 1851, twenty years after Maxwell, was to die an old man in 1940, and it was he who demonstrated Hertzian waves at the Royal Institution in 1895, one year before Marconi arrived. Lodge also invented a 'coherer', as he called it, a sensitive detector of wireless signals, without ever quite realizing the potential, financial and otherwise, of his own work. For him, the coherer was a pedagogical device. In 1897 he first experimented with a 'tuned circuit', a means of selecting the wavelength of a station while keeping the other stations tuned out, an essential element in broadcasting.

There were wireless pioneers in other countries too, such as Aleksandr S. Popov (1859–1906) in Russia and Édouard Branly (1844–1940) in France, so that it could be claimed that Marconi, who acknowledged his debt to the Italian Augusto Righi (1850–1920), had only introduced another mode of doing what had been done before. Yet, as an anonymous writer in the *Quarterly Review* put it: 'It is well that the Press should occasionally wake to the rapid forward strides of practical science. Civilization has advanced more by the aid of the working engineer than of the talking politician.'

On coming to London, Marconi was talking directly to politicians, to civil servants, naval officers and soldiers as well as to scientists, including A. A. Campbell Swinton (1863–1930), a prophet of television (see p. 178), to whom he had an introduction and who extended him an invitation to meet Preece, who had informal talks with him at the Post Office. One of the naval officers, Captain Henry Jackson, had already begun experimenting with radio himself a year earlier, quite independently from anyone else, and he and Marconi now carried out field trials with the British fleet on similar lines to trials being carried out with the Russian fleet by Popov. Necessity, not the advancement of science, drove them. Iron-clad ships demanded new modes of signalling, just as the 'iron horses' of the railway had needed them two generations before.

Within this context, wireless, the culmination of nineteenth-century communications history, was thought of simply as a substitute for wired telegraphy, just as automobiles, the high point of nineteenth-century transportation history, were thought of as horseless carriages. It followed that radio would be of most practical use on the oceans or in large, sparsely populated continents. The fact that its signalled messages, all in Morse, could be picked up by people for whom they were not intended – its broadcasting dimension – was at first deemed to be not an asset but a disadvantage. Likewise, the automobile was a luxury product, and no one envisaged a car in a suburban house with a garage any more than a similar house would later be associated with a 'wireless set'.

In visiting England, Marconi wanted quick results, and, having taken out a patent for transmitting and receiving apparatus, when he founded his Wireless Telegraph and Signal Company in 1897 he concentrated on selling wireless apparatus to large-scale commercial and governmental customers. He had royalty in mind too: in 1897, more than one hundred messages passed between Queen Victoria at Osborne House on the Isle of Wight and the Prince of Wales's royal yacht outside Cowes, where the Prince lay ill in bed. Marconi had no vision then of wireless as a widespread medium. And in this he was not alone. In 1899, for example, *The Electrician* contended that 'messages scattered broadcast only waste energy by travelling with futile persistence toward celestial space'.

Preece, a founder member of the Society of Telegraph Engineers, which in 1889 changed its name to the Institution of Electrical Engineers, was cautious about the prospects of Marconi's patents within the context in which Marconi himself placed them; and even after Marconi had transmitted messages across the Channel to France in 1899, Preece warned that 'wireless telegraphy in its present form and limited speed' (a genuine limitation) could not be placed in the same category as 'the old system' of telegraphy. Bureaucratic rather than entrepreneurial in his approach to communications development, he believed as a fact that 'it is about the worst thing possible for an invention [like Marconi's] to get into the hands of a company. We have only to look at the telephone to be convinced of this.' There was, however, an immediate popular excitement about the medium used by Marconi to transmit his messages, 'the illimitable, incomprehensible, exquisite medium, the ether'. It seemed to the public as 'mysterious' as

Fig. 15 The young Guglielmo Marconi. He arrived in London from Italy in February 1896 with a bundle of wireless devices. He set up his Wireless Telegraph and Signal Company in 1897.

X-rays, newly discovered in 1895. It promised the nearest the world had got to telepathy. The potential of the medium only became apparent to most people, as it did to experts who claimed to speak with authority, when radio entered the home, first in the United States, and then in Britain and Holland.

Yet before new institutions had been created to offer 'programmes', an amateur network of radio enthusiasts, known as 'hams', had forged national and international links, most of them using Morse, others telephony. They were described with foresight in 1912 in an American book by F. A. Collins, *The Wireless Man*, as, potentially at least, 'the largest audience in the world'. There were then estimated to be 122 wireless clubs in existence in America. Young men – and boys – were prominent in founding and running them. Children had been exploited in the early years of industrialization. Now they were independent, active and vocal. They held the future not in their heads but in their ears. *The Wireless Man* was a book for children.

It became possible to think and write about size of audience only because of a series of inventions in the period between the 1890s and 1920s, some of them the product of careful scientific research, others encouraged by the special circumstances of the First World War when radio was employed for military purposes and governments took over the telephone and wireless business. Nonetheless, the future applications of radio technology might have been predicted if social factors had been taken into account, rather than underplayed when wireless was in the pipeline. For example, when the English scientist William Crookes (1832–1919), in a subsequently much-quoted article of 1892, offered 'the bewildering possibilities of telegraphy without wires, posts, cables or any of our present costly appliances granted a few reasonable postulates', he did not identify the postulates or suggest what would happen next. Meanwhile, Marconi followed his own line of development, stirring the American imagination when in 1899 he accepted a paid commission from James Gordon Bennett Jr., owner of the *New York Herald*, to cover the America's Cup yacht races, and capturing both American and European imaginations in 1901 when he transmitted the letter 's' 2,000 miles across the Atlantic from Poldhu in Cornwall to be received in Newfoundland, then independent of Canada. Sceptics shrugged their shoulders.

Subsequent publicity did not need to be contrived. In 1904, wireless hit the headlines when it was used to report the arrest of Dr Crippen, a murderer fleeing from England to Canada by sea with his mistress, and eight years later it was the Marconi station in Long Island which picked up the SOS messages from the sinking Titanic and sent the news on to the White House. In 1906, the second World Congress on Wireless Telegraphy, held in Berlin – the first had been held there in 1903 – had decided that SOS should be the standard distress call signal. Berlin was in fact outside the Marconi empire: the Germans had created their own Telefunken wireless system managed through a subsidiary of Siemens and Allgemeine Elektricitäts Gesellschaft, established in 1907, with indispensable government backing. It had a research and development budget and went on to establish radio stations in many parts of the world, challenging Marconi's existing patents and attempting to prevent him from acquiring new ones.

Before 1914 there were three outstanding inventors, one British, one American and one Canadian, who led the way towards sound broadcasting. In 1904, Ambrose Fleming (1849–1945), a professor who, as a student, had attended Maxwell's lectures, devised the thermionic valve which was described long before the microchip as 'the tiniest little giant in history'. A yet bigger step forward was taken two years later by Lee De Forest (1873–1961) in Palo Alto: he added a third electrode in the form of a grid between the cathode and anode of Fleming's diode valve, described in the United States as a vacuum tube. The latter was a British Marconi Company patent and there were patent conflicts which lasted even beyond the expiry of the Forest patent in 1922. Indeed, it was not until 1943 that the US Supreme Court decided that De Forest had sole claim for his 'audion' as he called it. This was more than an improvement: it enabled weak radio signals – not only in Morse but in words and music – to be amplified, and longer distances to be covered. It was with pride that De Forest called himself 'the father of radio'.

The third man in the trio, Reginald Fessenden (1866–1932), a Canadian who had worked with Edison in his Menlo Park laboratory, used a high-frequency alternator to put on the first broadcasting event in the pre-1914 decade, a wireless concert broadcast by him from Brant Rock, Massachusetts, on Christmas Eve 1906, and picked up in places as far away as the Caribbean. Fessenden himself played the fiddle, sang Christmas carols and presented Handel's Largo on his phonograph. 'If anybody hears me', he told his unknown audience, 'please write to Mr Fessenden at Brant Rock.' De Forest, who had broadcast from American naval vessels, reached a different and completely unknown audience of 'hams' when he sent out messages from the Eiffel Tower in Paris. De Forest, who is said to have lacked business sense but to have been 'a born ham', had seen the need for such a service before 1914. He had insisted, therefore, that he should go on presenting broadcast concerts after he had negotiated a deal with AT&T in 1914 whereby he sold the giant company his audion patents, while at the same time agreeing to stay out of point-to-point voice transmission by radio – that is, transmission from specific senders to specific receivers. De Forest wanted to concentrate on transmitting music – and opera, in particular – into people's homes, and in 1910 he broadcast direct from New York's Metropolitan Opera, with the Italian tenor Enrico Caruso (1873–1921) as one of the soloists. He already thought of broadcasting as a medium, and believed, before the technology was ready, that it could become big business.

In 1916, most British wireless experts, including leading figures in the Wireless Society of London, which had Crookes and Lodge as honorary members, were unconvinced that wireless telephony had a future of the kind that De Forest envisaged; it was not 'quite clear', one of them wrote in 1913, 'from what quarter the first definite demand' for wireless telephony would come. The President of the Society in 1914, Campbell Swinton, told its members that with a little imagination one could picture in the not too distant future wireless-receiving stations that would be specially set up in halls resembling picture palaces and that people would be able to go there and 'hear viva voce all the prominent speakers of the day, although they might be speaking hundreds of miles away'. Yet that was not to be the shape of the future. Wireless telephony, like telephony, was to invade the home.

This aspect of its future was realized after De Forest by Arthur Burrows (1882–1947), who worked for the Marconi Company during the war, collecting, editing and distributing intercepted wireless messages, and across the Atlantic by David Sarnoff, who was to become the first commercial manager of the Radio Corporation of America (RCA), a civilian version of the naval and military monopoly that had controlled American radio during the War. During the war Sarnoff had conceived of 'a simple Radio Music Box . . . arranged for several different wavelengths which should be changeable with the throwing of a single switch or pressing of a single button'. 'The problem of transmitting music had already been solved', he claimed, and no imagination was needed 'to forecast it'. And music could be supplemented by 'news items, lectures and scores'.

Sarnoff was thinking of broadcasting, although he did not then use the word, which was derived, like the words 'culture' and 'cultivation', not from technology or industry but from agriculture: broadcast seed was seed scattered freely, not in drills or in rows. The scattering, which had originally appeared to be a commercial disadvantage, was now being transformed into a rationale. Sarnoff wished to make 'radio a household utility in the same sense as the piano or phonograph'.

Ironically, it was the British forecaster, not the American, who incorporated advertising into his broadcasting vision. 'There would be no technical difficulty', Burrows explained, 'in the way of an enterprising advertisement agency arranging for intervals in the musical programme to be filled with audible advertisements, pathetic or forcible appeals – in appropriate tones – on behalf of somebody's soap or tomato ketchup.'

In the United States, there had been a completely new corporate turn after the formation of RCA, backed by President Wilson. The Corporation forcibly took over all Marconi's patents. If Marconi had been an American citizen, his highly successful American company might well have survived, for Americans put their trust in private enterprise. As it was, RCA was a government-sanctioned concern that used its exceptional power to establish close connections with AT&T, General Electric and Westinghouse. Faced with the surge of interest in broadcasting during the early 1920s, they had to concern themselves not only with patents and competitors but with competing claims for access to the radio spectrum. Two very different groups, Army and Navy officers on the one side and the amateurs ('hams') gathered in wireless clubs on the other, were among the claimants. By the terms of the Radio Act of 1912, the first such Act to be passed in the United States, 'ham' radio messages were restricted by law to wavelengths of 200 metres or less, a limit raised in certain states to 425 metres in 1915. Despite military and naval pressure, there had been resistance inside and outside Congress to any regulation. 'We have been brought up with the idea that the air was absolutely free to everyone.' Why should it not be? The same question was to be raised in Britain as well as in the United States after the First World War, when amateur broadcasting was not permitted for naval and military reasons. In 1921, for a spokesman of the Wireless Society of London, now largely committed to radio telephony, 'every Englishman is entitled to hear what is going on in his ether providing his listening apparatus does not annoy his neighbours'. In Britain it was by the terms of the Wireless Telegraphy Act of 1904 that all transmitters or receivers of wireless signals had to have a Post Office licence.

In all countries, whatever the system of control, most 'hams' used cheap crystal sets that they had made themselves. It was fortunate for them that in the late nineteenth century it had been discovered that several types of crystal would serve as detectors of wireless waves which could be listed and classified, as they were between 1908 and 1911. There was one well-known crystal rectifier on the market before 1914, the Perikon. It incorporated a piece of silicon, a substance with a more romantic future than the hams themselves had. After 1918, radio receiving sets began to be manufactured commercially, their styles reflecting changes in fashion as well as technology.

The big manufacturing companies had a direct interest in increasing the size of the audience for regular broadcasting which would incorporate not only 'hams' but also people who came to be called 'listeners', most of whom knew nothing at all about the underlying science. It seemed a landmark date in England when in 1920 the Marconi Company was allowed to broadcast concerts from M2X in Chelmsford. But, following protests from the Wireless Telegraphy Board, on which the Armed Services were strongly represented, permission for the Company to broadcast from Chelmsford was rescinded. The broadcasts, the Board argued, were not only interfering with defence messages, but were turning wireless, which was 'a servant of mankind', into 'a toy to amuse children'. The Board's protests led the 'hams' to protest in turn in March 1921, and after they had drafted a petition signed by 63 wireless societies, they forced the Postmaster-General, who himself had called the concerts 'frivolous', to think again. He yielded in December 1921, taking care to state that the resumption of the concerts would be 'for the benefit of the Wireless Societies'. He still had no sense of a 'great unseen audience'.

The first Marconi Company station to provide half-hour concerts after the resumption was Writtle, near Chelmsford, and its first concert, described modestly by its makers as 'an engineers' do', was broadcast on 14 February 1922. The nine engineers involved proved themselves to be bright and highly informal broadcasters: gramophone records were their staple, but the team also broadcast the first radio play, *Cyrano de Bergerac*. Peter Eckersley, natural leader of the team, was to become first Chief Engineer of the BBC, which was set up in the autumn of 1922 before Writtle closed.

The BBC, created as a monopoly after long discussions organized by the Post Office in 1922, derived its initial income not from advertising but from a government-imposed licence fee and royalties from the sale of wireless sets. It was made a monopoly because of the government's decision that, since there were competing claims for access to a limited spectrum, there should only be one broadcasting organization. In the United States, with no Post Office in the background – and with limited political will to regulate the spectrum – such a solution had not even been considered. The RCA could not act as a public monopoly. Nor did AT&T, as a 'common carrier', succeed in an effort in the early 1920s to promote programming by selling network time on a toll basis to would-be customers in the same way as it sold telephone time to subscribers. American broadcasting was to be developed quite differently from British. A remarkable radio boom in 1922, often described, as canal and railroad booms had been, as a 'mania', took the United States by surprise; and in response, a large number of stations of all kinds emerged, some associated with newspapers, others with retail organizations, some with cities, some with schools and universities. As one observer put it: 'Anything that could speak was called a broadcasting station.' As early as May 1922 the Department of Commerce had granted more than 300 licences for broadcasting.

Station turnover was high and, at first, all stations were required to use the same wavelength, 360 metres; by the end of 1922 there were 572 of them. The result was 'chaos in the ether', the 'ruin' which had been forecast before the war. Meanwhile, the demand for regular broadcasting increased. In 1922, no fewer than 100,000 receiving sets were sold. The figure for 1923 was more than half a million. By 1925 there were 5.5 million radio sets in use in the United States, nearly half the world's total. Powerful networks were soon to emerge, the first of them the National Broadcasting Company (NBC), launched in 1926 as a 'public service', the second the Columbia Broadcasting System (CBS), created in 1927 by the man who became Sarnoff's chief rival, William Paley (1901–90). He had started in radio by advertising his father's cigar business and had worked through the agency of United Independent Broadcasting.

The share of the networks increased from 6.4 per cent of broadcast stations in 1926 to 30 per cent in 1931. For the hams, now pushed into the
background, there might be continuing excitement in trying to pick up
messages from hundreds, even thousands of miles away, but for those
owners of local broadcasting stations who tried, as in Chicago, to concentrate on the near, not on the far, there was increased disappointment when
the networks developed broadcasting by formula. The hams treated the
reception of distant messages as a sport. For the radio networks, broadcasting was big business, with live sport as one of their attractions.

Advertising quickly became the financial dynamic. Criticized in many
sections of the press, it had been attacked, too, in 1922 and 1923 by Herbert
Hoover (1874–1966), future President of the United States, then an active
reforming Secretary for Commerce, the first to have to deal with broadcasting. In a memorable phrase, he declared it 'inconceivable that we should
allow so great a possibility for service and for news and for entertainment
and education to be drowned in advertising chatter'. It proved more than
conceivable, although in 1927, when government legislation setting up the
Federal Radio Commission was passed (a limited exercise in regulation), it
carried the language of 'public interest, convenience, necessity'.

Advertisers knew better. Edgar Felix, an early radio merchandizing consultant, looked back enthusiastically at the process of expansion before there
had been any regulation: 'What a glorious opportunity for the advertising
man to spread his sales propaganda. Here was a countless audience, sympathetic, pleasure seeking, enthusiastic, curious, interested, approachable in
the privacy of their own homes.' Westinghouse concurred. 'Broadcasting
advertising', the company asserted, was 'modernity's medium of business
expression. Operating through increasingly sophisticated campaigns, it
made industry articulate. American businessmen, because of radio, are
provided with a latch key to nearly every home in the United States.' Frank
Arnold, NBC's Director of Development, went so far as to call broadcasting
'the Fourth Dimension of Advertising'.

It was not seen as such either in Britain or in most European countries.
The Netherlands, having put out popular programmes as early as November
1919 from its one transmitter (until 1922), led the way in regular broadcasting, putting out programmes from The Hague in November 1919 by PCGE,
a station set up by Nederlandse Radio-Industrie. Until 1927 there was only
one Dutch transmitter, which was shared, unusually, although in line with
Dutch history, by five 'pillar' organizations, with their roots below, each
with a religious affiliation. British broadcasting took a different course.
Although the British Broadcasting Company did not receive its licence

from the Post Office until January 1923, it broadcast its first programmes on 14 November 1922. Burrows read a six o'clock news bulletin at two speeds (slow and fast) into an ordinary telephone receiver connected to the Marconi Company's 2LO transmitter. Far away in the Antipodes, New Zealand broadcast its first radio messages on the same day.

How to allocate scarce wavelengths was a matter of hard national bargaining, which became international in 1926. A Geneva Plan for European wavelengths, hammered out by engineers, was adopted in July of that year; and a year later a World Wireless Conference at Washington, the first such conference since 1912, examined what Hoover called 'the congestion of the lanes on which communications are conducted'. A further conference in Prague in 1929, one organized by governments and broadcasting authorities, left national administrations, including that of the Soviet Union, which had not been represented at Geneva or Washington, to make detailed allocations within a total of wavelengths allotted to them. Each year the Soviet Union celebrated 7 May, the anniversary of a Popov radio demonstration in 1895, and the first public broadcast was made in 1919, but there was little radio listening on a mass scale before the late 1930s.

In all countries concerned with the development of broadcasting, the activity was being left to newly organized public broadcasting institutions, local, regional and national, and these grew rapidly during the 1920s, employing the same radio technology within quite different structures. Some were commercial; some were government controlled; some, like the BBC, shaped by John Reith (1889–1971), were neither commercial nor governmental. Reith, who was the first general manager of the British Broadcasting Company and from 1927 the first director-general of the (renamed) British Broadcasting Corporation, a new form of corporate institution, gave his name to an adjective, 'Reithian': for him, 'public service' meant the power to operate broadcasting independently of government (see pp. 233). The new BBC operated under a Royal Charter and not under an Act of Parliament.

Whatever the structure of new broadcasting institutions inside and outside Britain, they had to share what has been called the 'role of cultural brokerage' with the gramophone record industry, the cinema, the performing arts, sporting bodies, periodicals and, indeed, newspapers. Each of these had its own history and its own organization. So too did what later came to be called telecommunications. There was convergence but there were also clashes. There were symbolic points in time too. On the day after Marconi died, 21 July 1937, almost all the wireless stations of the world were silent for one or two minutes. It was a unique moment in broadcasting history.

Sound Recordings

By that time, one of the common ingredients in broadcasting schedules was the gramophone record, but the pursuit of sound depended on others besides the broadcasters and those who controlled them. As early as 1894, two years before Marconi arrived in London, an American writer, Octave Ozanne, had noted what he thought of as the threat to printing, which had 'changed the destiny of Europe', by 'various devices for registering sound . . . which little by little will go on to perfection'. At the moment of silence in 1937, print had not died, but as another American woman writer, Hazel Kinsella, had put it three years earlier, there was what seemed to be unlimited 'music on the air'.

One of the first inventors to interest himself in the transmission of sound – words and music – was Edison, 'partially deaf', who was far more concerned with the words than with the music. He became involved in sound not through music but through work on the design of telephonic apparatus, and he was aware that a French inventor, Charles Gros (1842–88), had put in writing, in a sealed packet for the Académie des Sciences, plans for a paléophone based on the same concept as the one he himself had contemplated. Another Frenchman, the photographer Félix Nadar, a pseudonym (1820–1910), had conceived earlier in the century of an 'acoustic daguerreotype which faithfully and tirelessly reproduces all the sounds subjected to its objectivity'. Like Sarnoff long after him, Nadar suggested 'a box in which melodies could be caught and fixed, as the camera obscura captures and fixes images'. He called his machine a phonograph.

Edison, who, at the age of 30, was already being described frequently in American newspapers as Professor Edison, relied on an assistant, John Kreusi, to construct a recording machine, a cylinder covered with tinfoil and mounted on a screw so that, as it was rotated by a handle, it slowly moved along, allowing a needle to create a spiral groove which would make it possible to repeat sounds 'embossed' into it. At first Edison had thought of 'repeating' Morse dots and dashes, but when the new machine had been constructed he shouted into it instead the nursery rhyme 'Mary had a little lamb', astonishing the people who were with him by then replaying for them the words in his own voice. When Edison forecast ten uses for his phonograph, which characteristically he quickly publicized in the *Scientific American*, in first place was letter-writing and all kinds of dictation without the aid of a stenographer. The teaching of elocution, dear to Alexander Bell, who was following up the telephone with a graphophone, was placed higher on the list than music.

Music boxes and musical toys, to which Edison briefly referred, had a long history. There were, indeed, many ingenious examples of musical automata before the introduction of the piano. There were also cylindrical musical boxes, some of them playing a number of tunes, which in some boxes were indicated by a pointer. Making them did not stop in 1887. A Symphonium employing metal discs was introduced in Leipzig, a great musical centre, ten years after Edison's phonograph, and, after it had been improved, it sold in large quantities. The pianola, designed in the United States in 1897 and costing around £65 in Britain in 1900, advertised itself with the motto 'Anyone can play the piano'; and the question 'Why not convert your piano?' was posed explicitly in an advertisement for Kastner's Auropiano in 1910. An important Anglo-American musical business, the Aeolian Company, produced an aeolian which was to the organ what the pianola was to the piano. Later, the Company sold an Aeolian Vocalion Gramophone. In 1906, a massive 100-ton classical Telharmonium was demonstrated in New York.

There is no evidence that Edison had any knowledge of such musical devices. In contemplating the uses of his phonograph, one of the dearest to his own heart was the preservation of the language by reproduction of 'our Washingtons, our Lincolns, our Gladstones'. 'Fancy an interview with Gladstone or Bismarck reproduced not only in their words but with the very intonations of the great statesmen', the *Electric World* told its readers in 1890. Edison's talking machine actually recorded the politician Gladstone, the poet Robert Browning and the entertainer P. T. Barnum. In 1906, G. S. Lee, an American critic, in his *The Voice of the Machines*, took it for granted, as the novelist James Joyce was to do, that the phonograph enabled man to speak forwards to the unborn and listen backwards to the dead. By then there was a Musée Glossophonographique in Paris and the Vienna Academy of Science had created a phonographic archive.

From the very beginning, journalists were contemplating multiple uses for the phonograph. For *Leslie's Weekly* it would 'turn all the old grooves of the world topsy-turvy and establish an order of things never dreamed of even in the vivid imaginings of the Queen Scheherazade in the 1001 Nights Entertainments'. Yet it needed inventors with different cultural interests from those of Edison, notably Emile Berliner (1851–1921), an American of German origin, to identify the possibilities of recording classical music. Likewise, it needed jukebox proprietors with nickel-in-the-slot machines – the first of them was installed in 1889 – to discover the way ahead down Tin Pan Alley, an alley which actually existed, 28th Street off Broadway in New York. This was a two-way street for song-writers and performers that was to thrill future filmmakers. They were less interested in sheet music, which did not vanish into thin air with the coming of popular music records – what traditionalists dismissed as 'canned music'. Nor did concerts of classical music, the numbers of which increased on both sides of the Atlantic, as did the numbers of other 'musicals'. *Phonoscope*, a short-lived New York magazine, listed a chart of popular songs on record in its first issue of December 1896.

When Berliner, the son of a Talmudic scholar, who had entered the United States as a penniless immigrant, produced a recording machine, which he called a gramophone, with a disc in place of a cylinder, in 1887 – Edison allowed no one else to use the name phonograph – he opened up new possibilities. He was soon able to perfect master discs from which others could be pressed in quantity. The material he used in making them was harder and more durable than the waxes from which cylinder phonographs were made. Further developed technically by Eldridge Johnson, a 29-year-old proprietor of a small machine shop in Camden, New Jersey, who introduced clockwork drive and controlled speeds, the gramophone became the product name of all types of record-playing machines in Britain and was given wide currency in 1923 when Compton Mackenzie launched a monthly review, *The Gramophone*, at first a family affair run by himself, his wife and his brother-in-law. By then, although he did not know of their existence, there were gramophone societies or clubs on both sides of the Atlantic.

In both Europe and the USA, the underlying economics, including vulnerability to slumps – and to aggressive competition – was the same. The first person to appreciate this was not Berliner but Edison, who for financial reasons closed his Music Room as early as 1891 and discharged the staff he employed in it. He had continued after 1887 to manufacture record players and worked with Bell and two Bell associates to market them through a newly incorporated North American Phonograph Company. When, in 1901, Berliner joined with others in forming a new Victor Talking Machine Company, the company pattern was set which was to hold for decades.

The Victor Company, which under different names acquired a hold over the American gramophone industry for more than half a century, followed an approach that Michael Chanon has called 'a consumption model': the record was being dealt with like a book and not like a photograph. Successful performers were to make larger amounts of money out of their recordings, however, than most authors made out of their books. Thus, Caruso, who made his first quality recording in 1901 and his first million-selling record in 1904, went on to earn two million dollars from his records by the time of his death. Fred Gaisberg, who had joined the infant recording business as a teenager and went on to become a top international executive, was the person mainly responsible for Caruso's transformation from performer to recording artist: he had first listened to him at the opera in Milan in 1902.

The organization of music, classical and what came to be called simply 'pop', and the dependence of the fortunes of musicians, companies and performers on performing rights were not as well recognized in the consolidating American copyright statute of 1912. It needed pressure from the American Society of Composers, Authors and Publishers (ASCAP), founded five years later, to secure recognition. There was parallel pressure in Britain from the Performing Rights Society, founded in 1926. The parallels between American and British development were apparent in the world of sound, as they were in the world of pictures, with iconography as well as economics linking both. The black-and-white terrier listening with cocked ears to His Master's Voice became one of the best-known trademarks in a society where, during the first decades of the twentieth century, the numbers of people keen to buy records and to acquire home players was rapidly increasing. Their numbers depended on the range of prices and incomes. Edison's first model cost $40 in 1896: by 1899 you could buy his Gem Player for $7.50. Soon, models were being produced in all shapes, sizes and styles, some of them as cheap as they could be produced, some expensive, even ostentatious luxury products as the most lavish of the radiograms of the 1930s were to be.

A landmark was reached when the Odeon Company, formed in Berlin in 1903, introduced discs with recordings on both sides, an important development which was not followed up by Columbia until 1908, a year when the Pathé brothers, Charles (1863–1957) and Émile (1860–1937) in France did the same. In that decade, both Columbia and Victor launched 'celebrity discs'. (The Russians gave them red labels.) In 1913, Edison started making discs (along with cylinders until 1929), and in the same year HMV recorded the entire Fifth Symphony of Beethoven on eight single sides, played by the Berlin Philharmonic Orchestra. In 1917 Victor turned out its first jazz record. Six years later, in the space of eight months, King Oliver and his Creole Jazz Band, comfortably ensconced in Chicago, waxed no fewer than 37 titles for four different record labels, Paramount and Columbia being two of them. During the Second World War jazz was at a low ebb. This was the big band era in popular music. When jazz revived in post-war Britain, it owed much to Humphrey Lyttelton (1921–2008), who had gained his knowledge of the genre from gramophone records, and who went on to make a radio reputation through the BBC.

Electrical recording, a major breakthrough in recording quality, initiated by the Western Electric Company, was taken up by both Columbia and Victor in 1925, and in the same year General Electric introduced a greatly improved loudspeaker, marketed by RCA. Victor had marketed a machine with the horn built into the case as early as 1906. Gradually, the obstacles to easy listening to records in the home were being removed. A finer stylus tip greatly reduced distortion. After the Second World War – in 1948 – Columbia and RCA introduced fine-groove records made of a plastic: viny-lite. And there were major improvements to follow, particularly digital recording.

Quality mattered increasingly as purchasers compared one recording with another, but total numbers sold remained the main criterion of suc-cess. The statistics relating to record sales speak for themselves. Near the beginning, the number of records sold in the United States rose from around half a million in 1897 to 2.8 million two years later. A generation later, there was a slump in sales during the Great Depression, which followed the Wall Street Crash of 1929, only six million records were sold in 1932, 6 per cent of the total sales in 1927. In 1929 Victor joined forces with RCA, a merger facilitated by the development of the radio gramophone. In the same year, the Edison Company suspended the production of phonographs: Edison was then aged 82. Two years later, the Columbia Gramophone Company merged with the Gramophone Company to create Electric and Music Industries Ltd, EMI. The media as a whole were beginning to constitute a category: they were increasingly to be related to each other. EMI was the first company to manufacture cathode-ray tubes for television sets (see p. 204).

Photography

Television was to transform not only people's daily lives but also all dis-course concerning media, old and new. It will figure separately in the next chapter, which starts with the printed word. Here, in order to understand the new processes and patterns of visual communication in the century before television, it is necessary to go back to the instrument which made it possible: the camera. This itself had a long history behind it: the camera obscura (darkened room) had been an artist's tool for centuries. The new nineteenth-century camera was developed first in France and in Britain and then in revolutionary fashion in the United States. As early as 1802, a member of the Wedgwood family had written a 'Description of a Procedure for Copying Paintings onto Glass and for making Silhouettes by the Effect of Light on Silver Nitrate'; but it was a French experimenter, Joseph Nicéphore Niepce (1765–1833) who produced by what he called 'heliography' the first 'photograph from life' soon after the end of the Napoleonic Wars. (The word 'photograph' was coined by Wheatstone.)

Niepce informed the Royal Society in London of his success in 1827, but it was his younger partner, Louis Daguerre (1789–1851), whom he took on in 1829, who developed the first precise photographic images. Daguerre called these 'daguerreotypes' and, 'in the interests of the sciences and the arts', released details of his process for producing them in Paris at a joint meeting in 1839 of the Académie des Sciences and the Académie des Beaux-Arts. The state, whatever the regime, proud of French scientific prowess, as it always was to be, acquired monopoly rights in Daguerre's work, but immediately renounced them and declared photography 'open for the whole world'. The announcement was less dramatic than it seemed, for the invention had shrewdly been patented earlier in London, where it remained protected. Nevertheless, there was immediate competition. William Henry Fox Talbot (1800–77), who had worked in England independently but concurrently with Daguerre, employing a quite different process, using silver nitrate and producing 'negatives' on paper, demonstrated his 'calotypes' – what he called 'photogenic drawings' – to 'lovers of science and nature' at the Royal Society.

Calotype images were softer than daguerreotypes, although they took a long time to print. They were produced through what a distinguished British scientist, J. F. W. Herschel (1792–1891) called negatives, and as early as 1840 a Swiss, Johann Baptist Isenring (1796–1860), is said to have discussed a method for colouring them. A major breakthrough came in 1851, when Frederick Scott Archer, one of the first twelve members of Fox Talbot's Calotype Club, invented a wet collodion process which sharpened calotype images (collodion was guncotton dissolved in ether). This technique quickly made obsolete both the calotype and the daguerreotype, although there were no fewer than 10,000 daguerrotypists in the United States in 1853, among them Samuel Morse (see p. 158).

In the United States there was less emphasis on photographic art and more on pictorial photography, well represented in Matthew Brady's pictures of the Civil War, and on stereography which was dismissed by its critics as a passing 'fad'. Brady (1822–96), whose greatest project was to paint a succession of American presidents, has been described in the *Encyclopaedia Britannica* as 'probably the best-known photographer in US history'. Meanwhile, stereography was more than a fad. Stories could be told attractively by means of stereoscopes, and one double stereoscope was invented which enabled two people to view the same picture at the same time. A 'cosmorama stereoscope' was shown at the London Exhibition of 1862, a year when thousands of stereographs were produced.

Colour photography has its own history, as do photojournalism and medical photography. It was in 1861 that the first true three-colour photograph was taken by a great scientist famous in other fields, James Clerk Maxwell (see p. 158): it could be viewed only through a projector. The full development of colour photography was a twentieth-century venture, but throughout the nineteenth century there were many photographs taken, like those of Brady, that figure in what has come to be called photo history, the first of them, taken between 1843 and 1848 by David Octavius Hill and Rupert Adamson, photographs of all the ministers of the First General Assembly of the Free Church of Scotland. Between 1851 and 1854, P. H. Delamotte photographed week by week the erection of the Crystal Palace, after it had been transferred to Sydenham, providing a unique record. In 1868, Thomas Annan began to record the slums of Glasgow for the Glasgow City Improvement Trust, and in the same year the art photographer Julia Margaret Cameron (1815–73), who had photographed Herschel the previous year, photographed Charles Darwin. 'When I had them before my camera', Cameron wrote years later in the *Photographic Journal*, 'my whole soul endeavoured to do its duty toward them in recording faithfully the greatness of the inner man as well as the features of the outer man.' She attempted the same a year later with the poet Alfred, Lord Tennyson.

Two of the most famous photographs of the mid-nineteenth century were the Swede O. U. Rejlander's allegorical *The Two Ways of Life* and H. P. Robinson's *Fading Away*, while in France, Nadar, who photographed the French novelist Balzac without seeking to reveal the inner man, revealed much that had hitherto been hidden in his photograph of the city of Paris taken from an air balloon in 1862. Nadar also produced a magnificent photographic portrait (with a painted backcloth) of Count Savorgnan de Brazza, who gave his name to the capital of the French Congo. Brazza had with him two Congolese friends who, never having seen a painting, described every kind of picture that they saw as a photo.

Some Africans feared that when they were photographed they lost their identity; European children were taught the reverse. They figured prominently – and in different guises – in nineteenth-century photography. Lewis Carroll, a pseudonym used by the Oxford mathematician Charles Dodgson (1832–98), author of *The Adventures of Alice in Wonderland* (1865), was one of the best-known child photographers. Carroll's children, all girls, were very different from the carefully posed orphan children, boys and girls, whose photographs were collected in Dr Barnado's homes, or the child models who were used in photographer's advertisements. There was less diversity in the millions of *cartes de visite* that were first popularized in France by André Disdéri (1819–89). *Cartes* depicting celebrities were as collectable as autographs or postage stamps, and handsome albums were produced to contain them.

The biggest change in the social history of photography before the 'motion picture' was the arrival in the 1880s of the 'snapshot', a word – for some a term of abuse – coined in a different earlier context by Herschel. The size and price of cameras had already been falling when in 1884 an enterprising American, George Eastman (1854–1932), a bank clerk turned photographic manufacturer, ushered in popular photography with one of the most famous new cameras of the century, the Kodak, usable by everyone everywhere. Eastman thought correctly that Kodak was a name that would be memorable in every language. He had an advertising slogan for it too: 'You press the button, we do the rest.' A year later, he introduced the first commercial transparent celluloid film and proposed a list of the uses to which the Kodak could be put, a comparable list to that produced by Edison for his phonograph (see p. 184). Within the family, snapshots could be used as a record, recalling events that had happened over time; or by engineers and architects who could survey work in progress, and professionally by artists to save time in sketching before painting. Eastman's list ended triumphantly with the words: 'Anybody can use it. Everybody will use it.' When he founded the *Kodak News* in 1895, he doubled the daily output of cameras – to 600 – at his factory in Rochester, New York State. Two years later he organized in London what the *British Journal of Photography* called one of the most remarkable photographic exhibitions yet held.

Demonstrating operational business skills was Eastman's forte, as was his brilliance as an advertiser. His Brownie camera, which had no viewfinder, was designed in 1900 especially for children. His Kodak girl (1910), drawn by a cartoonist who regularly contributed to *Punch*, was well known and admired on both sides of the Atlantic. And the First World War increased rather than reduced his business. Five times as many Vest Pocket Kodaks were sold in the United Kingdom in 1915 as in 1914. By then, not only had the motion picture arrived, but films were being shown in places specially designed to present them.

Films

The origins of motion pictures were mechanical, not electrical, and belonged to the world of toys that had been given names that were far less memorable than Kodak, like Praxinoscope, Phenakistiscope and

Kaamatograph. The first man successfully to employ a camera sequence to convey the sense of movement – there had been many earlier unsuccessful attempts – was 'Eadweard Muybridge', whose chronophotographic series of horse movements, taken for the horse-loving Governor of California in 1872, proved that there were times when a horse was trotting when all its feet were off the ground. 'Muybridge', Edward Muggeridge (1830–1904), was an Englishman born at Kingston upon Thames, whose personal experiences included being charged with murder and acquitted. He publicized his photos in *Animal Locomotion* (1888) and *Animals in Motion* (1899) and opened a 'Zoopraxographical Hall' at the Chicago Columbian Exhibition of 1893, where a photographic display of leaping horses and gymnasts was a great popular attraction. In parallel, a French physiologist, Etienne Marey (1830–1904), publicized his own work in *Le Mouvement* (1894), and he recorded on a single film multiple images of birds in flight.

In 1894 Edison, who had set up his laboratory at Menlo Park in an earlier Exhibition year, 1876, put on sale his patented kinetoscope, a device that made it possible individually to watch, with an eye-piece, a moving film. Inspired by Muybridge and possibly by Marey, Edison set out to do for the eye what the phonograph could do for the ear. His practical ambition, however, was at first limited: he conceived of the kinetoscope in the context of a peepshow in a penny arcade, with one person at a time paying a coin and 'gluing' his eye to a small peephole through which he might see a girl dancing or two men boxing. Edison did not then believe that using his invention to project images onto a screen would be financially profitable, but between 1893 and 1895 he allowed two of his assistants, W. K. L. Dickson and William Heise, to shoot a number of interesting 20-second films in the world's first film studio, the Black Maria. Themes included 'Bar Room Brawl', 'Sioux Indians' and 'Edison in Laboratory'. Another assistant, Fred Ott, produced the first motion picture to be copyrighted in the United States in January 1894, 'Kinetoscopic Record of a Sneeze'.

In November 1895, Max and Emil Skladanowsky screened nine films in Berlin, using what they called a Bioskop system – they included gloved kangaroos engaged in a boxing match. A month later, Louis Lumière (1864–1948), seventeen years younger than Edison, introduced his 'cinematograph', hailed as a *nouveauté du jour*, to an audience of thirty-five at the Grand Café in Paris, going on in 1896 to present films to a bigger audience at the Empire Music Hall in London's Leicester Square. The London programme was very mixed, beginning with an overture and including a group of Russian dancers and juggling acrobatic acts. One of the films shown was *The Arrival of the Paris Express*, another *Boating in the Mediterranean*.

Lumière was one of two brothers who made films that would later be called documentaries. Maxim Gorki (1868–1936), the Russian writer, who saw and admired some of them, said that the film was 'born from life'.

There were other filmmakers, however, like Georges Méliès (1861–1938), who had a background in magic and who believed that illusion, the achievement of trick effects, was the strength of what came to be called 'the cinema'. By 1900, he was combining short lengths of film, often ostentatiously, to form episodes in a connected story. Other filmmakers looked to the circus, to the stage and, above all, to vaudeville. In fact, the film form was to prove as adaptable as the novel on which it also drew; and while for some filmmakers (to be treated by sophisticated critics as auteurs) their aim was avant-garde art, a new mass audience was being brought into existence through film, far bigger than that ever created by the theatre. Its creation took time, however, although Edison was a quick convert to supplying the developing new medium with ready-made films, as was G. W. Porter, working with him, from 1896 to 1909. Porter's *The Great Train Robbery*, combining the popular railway travel theme with the equally popular robbery theme, was an instant commercial success in 1903–4. It lasted for twelve minutes.

Film scholars, some of them highly erudite, argue about the making, interpretation and merits of particular early films, but they all acknowledge that the history of film, early and late, is more than the history of landmark films. There were active filmmakers before 1900 in many countries, including France and Britain, and although their films clustered, in retrospect, in genres, they were diverse in their backgrounds and intentions. In France, Léon Gaumont (1864–1946) produced before 1900 a series of short films featuring celebrities like Sarah Bernhardt. In England, G. A. Smith, who had been a portrait photographer and lantern-slide lecturer, produced two very different short films, Mary Jane's *Mishap* (1903) and *Grandma's Reading Glass* (1900). A nearby owner of a photographic business, James Williamson, produced, among other very short films, *The Big Swallow* (1901), which played around with his film apparatus itself. There were links too with the magic lantern in the Pathé Brothers' *Life of Christ*, the subject of a Méliès film in 1903. The magic lantern had often been used for religious purposes, and in Australia, *Soldiers of the Cross* (1900), once hailed wrongly as Australia's first feature film, was made by the Salvation Army Limelight Unit and incorporated lantern slides, film clips and a lecturer-narrator. The first decade of the twentieth century was particularly productive, although it was not until 1912 that the small Kalem Company's *From the Manger to the Cross* was hailed as America's first feature film.

As in the history of print publishing, religion was a main ingredient in early films, although entertainment had a still bigger place. The Pathé Brothers, who had produced *Magic Roses* in 1906, to be followed by *Magic Bricks* and *Magic Bottles* in 1908, made *Cache-toi dans la malle* (*Keep it Straight*, 1905), which presented a would-be lover wearing a smart white suit, locked in his lady's trunk to conceal him from her husband. Visual gags were a key element in the 'Cinema of Attractions', as the pre-Hollywood films have come to be called since Neal Burch and Tom Gunning reappraised them during the 1980s. They promoted a number of comic performers, one of whom, the French actor Max Linder (1883–1925), 'starred' (a term that has been applied to him) in more than 350 comedies in his role as 'Max'. He was acknowledged as a major inspiration by Charles Chaplin.

In France, where the 'Cinema of Attractions' reached its peak during the four years before the First World War, the Pathé brothers, who had originally dealt in phonographs (above), had by 1908 made their firm, called Pathé Frères, the largest producer of films in the world. Charles Pathé rented, rather than sold, his films to theatre operators, which was a successful shift in business operations, and the brothers, like another great French filmmaker, Léon Gaumont (1864–1946), manufactured studio cameras and equipment as well as made films. The Pathé logo, the silhouette of a rooster, was as familiar outside and inside France as was HMV's dog. With studios in New York and pre-revolutionary Russia, as well as in Paris, the Pathé Brothers, like Gaumont, were also active in Britain, among the first countries to generate filmmakers.

In southern England, where Brighton was an early filmmaking centre, R. W. Paul (1869–1943), a scientific instrument-maker by training, started his film life by duplicating Edison's kinetoscope, which was not then patented in England, and as early as 1896 produced a twenty-six-second film of Derby Day. He went on to produce many films, including one that ran for two-and-a-half minutes, *The Motorist* (1906). In northern England, a large number of lost films, including many dealing with industrial scenes, were found in Blackburn, Lancashire, in 2006; their makers had shot workers leaving their premises en masse after finishing work or at times of local festival. The workers had been prepared to pay for filmed collective pictures of themselves in their work clothes as well as in their holiday best.

Some of the English pioneers of film died young; but there were some who lived well into old age, among them the most celebrated of all film stars, Charlie Chaplin, born in London in 1889, who was to live until 1977. When he moved across the Atlantic, with an English background in vaudeville, Hollywood was still 'a pepper tree-lined village' with orange groves, only recently (1903) integrated into the growing metropolitan complex of Los Angeles. The first filmmakers had already moved there, such as the Selig Polyscope Company, founded in Chicago in 1896, which arrived in Los Angeles in 1907, but Chaplin started his long film career not in California, but in New York, where he worked in the Keystone Studios of Mack Sennett (1880–1960), starring in slapstick comedies. His first Hollywood film, *Making a Living*, did not come out until 1914. His reasons for moving there were bound up with his work, not with the desire to live in sunshine or to make still more money. Tiring of Sennett's 'custard pie wars', which followed a formula, Chaplin was to found his own studio and company, United Artists, in 1919, with Douglas Fairbanks Senior (1883–1939), Mary Pickford (1892–1979) – who had also acquired star status, the first woman to do so – and D. W. Griffith (1875–1949), fourteen years older than Chaplin, who had started his film career with Biograph with whom he made no fewer than forty films in 1909.

Griffith had moved to Los Angeles in 1910, where he made Hollywood's first film, *In Old California*. A year later, A. L. Christie of the Nestor Film Company turned a derelict Hollywood tavern into the first studio at the end of a dusty road called Sunset Boulevard. Other companies quickly followed: by the end of 1911 there were fifteen of them. In 1914 Cecil B. Demille produced *The Squaw Man*, running for seventy-four minutes, and a year later Griffith produced Hollywood's first classic (a term to become common in the future), *The Birth of a Nation* (1915). This was a long film, played entirely with white actors and with huge crowd effects, and it has been as frequently reinterpreted since 1915 as any Verdi opera. At the time, President Woodrow Wilson described watching it as being like reading history 'by flashes of lightning'. He did not comment on its length. The *New York Mail* called it 'the supreme picture of all time'.

From the start, the cinema business was strongly influenced by market considerations, although in Europe, where, until the outbreak of the First World War in 1914, Gaumont was producing more films than Hollywood, there was a bigger division between production and distribution than there was in the United States. Music-hall proprietors and showmen were the first people in Britain and France to put on films, and it was not until late in the first decade of the twentieth century that special halls for showing films were opened, the first of them in Britain at Colne in Lancashire. In the early twentieth century, films were first shown in the United States in fair-grounds and arcades, but Pittsburgh led the way in having a 'film theatre' in 1905. In France, Charles Pathé created his own projection halls. So too did Gaumont, who gave his name to a chain of them. Another word used in the naming of the theatres or halls was 'bioscope', of German origin. Slowly but inexorably the cinema business everywhere passed out of the hands of what Gilbert Seldes (1893–1970), American author of a pioneering analysis *The Great Audience* (1951), called 'aggressive and ignorant men without taste or tradition, but with a highly developed sense of business', into the hands of bigger corporations.

Edison, who played a major role in the process, lost control of his patents following Supreme Court decisions, and withdrew from producing and distributing films in 1916. In 1908 a Motion Picture Patents Company, MPPC, consisting of ten producing companies, had set out deliberately to establish and maintain a monopoly, in the interests, it claimed, of 'regularity and stability' in the infant film industry. The MPPC was strong enough to arrange a deal with Eastman that he would supply photographic materials only to its members. It also set up under its own auspices a voluntary Board of Censors, hoping to expand rather than reduce the market for its films by keeping control of what was on offer. The MPPC was not strong enough, however, to eliminate 'independents' from the film industry.

One of them, Adolph Zukor (1873–1976), who played a significant part in the breaking up of the MPPC, was to go on in his own good time to integrate production with distribution in the Paramount Company, which he founded. In 1919 he raised funds on Wall Street through an issue of ten million dollars of preferred stock, the first major attempt to finance cinema from the capital market, and two years later he controlled more than 300 cinemas. Complaints were now being made, as he had heard them made before, that it was too difficult for small and independent producers or distributors of films to enter into or remain in the moving picture industry or market, or to lease individual pictures of merit.

It was to remain too difficult, for, as in radio, corporate structures hardened. Another independent assisted in the hardening. William Fox (1879–1952) engineered the merger of his integrated Fox Film Corporation, incorporated in 1915, into Twentieth Century Fox. An earlier merger in 1924 had led to the creation of Metro-Goldwyn-Mayer (MGM), and two new moguls, Harry Warner (1881–1958) and his brother Jack (1892–1978), who founded Warner Brothers in 1923, made a breakthrough in 1927 when they released the first 'talkie', *The Jazz Singer*, starring the singer Al Jolson and ushering in the golden age of the movies. *The Jazz Singer* cost $500,000 to make and netted five times as much in box-office receipts, the ultimate test of any commercial film. In 1928, the capital assets of Warner Brothers were valued at $16 million; in 1930, with the financial crash of 1929 intervening, they stood at $230 million.

It became difficult for film interests in other countries to face up to Hollywood and to synchronized sound, although with the end of silent

Fig. 16 *The Jazz Singer*. Crowds gather to see Al Jolson in the world's first 'talkie', a Warner Brothers film, in 1927.

films the existence of the world's many languages, described in broadcasting circles as a Babel, gave non-American film producers an exceptional opportunity. Different national cultures were expressed in film, silent or talkies, often unconsciously, sometimes deliberately, with France throughout and Germany until the advent of Hitler in 1933 emphasizing the role of film as an art. In Soviet Russia, Lenin claimed that 'of all the arts for us the cinema is the most important'.

The sense of there being creative avant-gardes involved in film was strong everywhere. Indeed, there were some filmmakers who drew sharp distinctions between their products and the commercial films shown in cinemas. In the nineteenth century, novelist George Gissing (1857–1903) had anticipated what they would say in what he wrote about literature in his *New Grub Street* (1891). Yet terms derived from art and not from literature were applied to the avant-garde cinema. Thus, expressionism was associated with German film in the post-1918 Weimar Republic, when *The Cabinet of Dr Caligari* (1920) became a landmark film, as did Fritz Lang's *Metropolis* (1927), a haunting portrayal of city life.

Lang (1890–1976) was born a year after Chaplin; he moved to Hollywood before Hitler rose to power in 1933. Other film stars made their way there after 1933 when Hitler appointed Goebbels to take charge of entertainment, including film and propaganda. In the Soviet Union, the great film director Sergei Eisenstein (1898–1948) faced no difficulties when he made *Battleship Potemkin* in 1925, drawn from twentieth-century Russian history, but his *Alexander Nevski* (1938), with a musical score by Prokoviev, had a troubled history between 1938 and 1941. The Odessa Steps sequence in *Battleship Potemkin* is one of the most famous set pieces in the history of the cinema.

Like the novel, the film was an international force; among the films with a similar cultural impact were post-Second World War Italian films, such as Roberto Rossellini's *Open City* (1945) and Vittoria de Sica's *Bicycle Thieves* (1948), the Svenska Film Industry's films made by Ingmar Bergman (1918–2007), whose father was a Lutheran pastor and chaplain to the Swedish royal family, and the Japanese films of Akira Kurosawa (1910–98), particularly *Rashomon* (1951), which reintroduced Japanese film to a limited European and American audience. During the 1930s Japan had rivalled the United States in the numbers of films produced. They constituted three-quarters of the films shown in cinema screens in Japan.

In Britain, where culture was generally a suspect term in the 1920s and 1930s, a protectionist attitude towards the cinema was always evident in government circles from 1927 onwards. Hitherto, the government's only measure of control over the industry had been an Act of 1909 which gave local authorities the power to license buildings used as cinemas and to censor films. In 1927, the government, while refusing to offer financial assistance to the British film industry, acknowledged that there were grounds for intervening in its affairs because of the magnitude of what were described in Parliament as 'the industrial, commercial, education[al] and imperial interests involved'. In 1926, only 5 per cent of the films shown in Britain were actually made in the country. The British Cinematographic Films Act of 1927, described by the social historian Jeffrey Richards as 'a marked breach with the prevailing doctrine of free trade', controlled advance and block booking of films, introduced a quota system (maintained in a further Act of 1937) and created a Cinematographic Films Advisory Committee to advise the Board of Trade on the administration of the Act.

Nevertheless, Hollywood commercial films were the main staple of fare in Britain, as they were in South American countries like Brazil and Argentina; and it became clear to observers outside the film industry that it was via Hollywood that the cinema was influencing ways of thinking, feeling and, not least, dreaming in quite different social contexts. In the 1930s the largest British cinemas, provincial as well as metropolitan, were glamorous 'dream palaces', offering other entertainment besides films, including music played on mammoth Wurlitzer organs and popcorn to chew while the films were being shown. It is true that there were still cinemas that were flea-pits, 'cosy corners', with live pianists accompanying the film in silent days, but, as in Hollywood itself, the 'palaces' set the tone.

For example, at the Odeon in Bolton, Lancashire, opened in 1937 (one of twenty-seven cinemas in the town), there was room for 2,600 people; for Leslie Halliwell, the author of one of a cluster of *Film Guides*, its perfumed atmosphere was like that of a cathedral. In nearby Liverpool, traditional link between Britain and the United States, the number of cinemas had risen between 1913 and 1932 from thirty-two to sixty-nine (while the number of theatres fell from eleven to six). It was estimated that in 1932 no fewer than four out of ten people in Liverpool were going to the cinema once a week and one in four twice a week. In Hollywood itself, where the adjective 'atmosphere' was more appropriately attached to a major new cinema than in Bolton, Grauman's Chinese Theatre on Sunset Boulevard (1927) had a roof like a pagoda, and on the Boulevard itself stars left their hand and foot prints not just for their fans but for posterity.

When the dream palaces were going up, films were changing their character, among them Chaplin's films, which were to acquire a mythical character. Characterized as 'the Tramp' or as 'the Little Fellow', Chaplin was praised for his grace as well as for his humour, for his timing as well as for his pathos: Sennett considered him 'the greatest artist who ever lived'. His fame was to continue to grow, while a host of other stars – quite different from himself – had come and gone – for example, the matinee idol Rudolf Valentino (1895–1926), 'the great lover'. After America's unprecedented boom of the 1920s had been succeeded by the equally unprecedented depression, Chaplin's *Modern Times* (1936), presenting assembly lines in the kind of factory plant associated with automobile manufacturer Henry Ford, was to fascinate social historians as much as *The Birth of a Nation* had fascinated Wilson in 1915.

There was more than one turn in cinema history in the 1930s. A Production Code, drafted in 1930 by Will Hays (1879–1954), a former American Postmaster-General, was enforced through the Hays Office, which regulated what Americans could see on cinema screens. Foreigners had their own modes of censorship too; in Britain, a Board of Censors was set up as early as 1920. Technologically, the development of colour films, some of them glamorous and expensive, and incorporating dance, as in Fred Astaire's *Top Hat* (1935), as well as words and images, gave Hollywood a world lead. Animation was colourful in every sense: *Snow White and the Seven Dwarfs* (1940) by Walt Disney (1901–66) was a world success with adults as well as with children. Born in Chicago, Disney had moved to Hollywood in 1923, and with Mickey Mouse and Donald Duck had already given new life to the art of animation long before his *Wizard of Oz* (1939).

European cinema followed its own course during the 1930s after the Depression had stimulated the production of films that expressed the social conscience of their makers. Some of them were influenced by makers of documentaries, socially motivated and aiming at 'authenticity'. In Britain, John Grierson (1895–1972) was a pioneer of documentary filmmaking before being given charge of the National Film Board of Canada in 1939. In France, radio was influential too in shaping attitudes to film. Thus, for André Malraux (1901–76), who was to acquire political power after the war under de Gaulle, the talkies only became an art form when directors realized that their model should be the radio feature. Nevertheless, there was little in common between radio features and film documentaries. Newsreels were another category, and there were separate newsreel cinemas, some just outside railway stations. The earliest pioneering newsreel producers were French, with Pathé's *Animated Gazette* putting out a daily edition before 1914. Like its rival Gaumont, it presented a special women's edition during the 1920s. Fox-Movietone arrived from across the Atlantic in 1929 to produce a new British product, after Lord Rothermere, owner of the *Daily Mail*, had joined up with Fox to create British Movietone; the voice of its presenter Leslie Mitchell was one of the best known in the land.

Neither newsreel companies nor the film industry as a whole faced any serious challenge from television during the 1930s, although the word 'television' had been invented – in French – in 1900, and before that there had been a long prehistory of nineteenth-century experiment, going back, it has usually been claimed, to 1839 (see p. 189), the landmark year in the history of photography. Following Edouard Becquerel's experiments, Willoughby Smith, one of the telegraph engineers who supervised the laying of the transatlantic cable (above), noted in 1873 the correlation between the odd behaviour of selenium resistors and sunlight, and in the same decade a French lawyer suggested how selenium might be used in a scanning system. What he had in mind, however, was the transfer of single images, instantaneous but 'fugitive', rather than continuous images on a screen; and when, three years later, an Englishman, Shelford Bidwell (1913–96), demonstrated 'picture telegraphy' – necessarily of poor definition – to the Physical Society in London, it was the precursor of fax rather than of television.

Television

The technical basis of all television is different from that of the transmission of still pictures that Bidwell demonstrated. It involves the scanning of an image by a beam of light in a series of sequential lines moving from top to bottom and from left to right. Each section of the image, as the light passes over it, produces signals which are converted into electrical impulses, strong or weak. The impulses are then amplified and transmitted along wires or through the air by radio waves which are reconverted into light signals in the same order and the same strength as they were at their original source. Their capacity to appear to the human eye as a complete and moving picture on a screen depends on the retention of vision. No progress could be made until the valve amplifier, the key to radio telephony, had been invented.

There are two possible techniques of scanning – mechanical, by a disc, and electrical, by a beam – and before 1914 there had been experiments with both. Paul Nipkow, a Berlin science student, had conceived of the first mechanical scanner in Germany in 1884 – although he never made one. It was a mechanical instrument (Elektrisches Teleskop), a rotating disc, spirally perforated with small holes through which a strong light shone. Electrical scanning, which was to prove to be the key to mass television, was identified as such by Campbell Swinton in 1908. He suggested:

> the employment of two beams of kathode rays [note his use of the 'k', as in 'kinema'], one at the transmitting and one at the receiving station, synchronously deflected by the varying fields of two electromagnets ... So far as the receiving apparatus is concerned [and he did not call it a television set] the moving kathode beam has only to be arranged to impinge on a sufficiently sensitive fluorescent screen, and given suitable variations in intensity, to obtain the desired result.

When Swinton wrote those words, he did not know of experiments being carried out in St Petersburg by Boris Rosing (1869–1933), a professor at the Technical Institute, who applied for a patent in 1907 proposing a television system using a cathode tube as a receiver. The work on such tubes had started in Germany, but Rosing carried it much further, developing prototypes, only to see his work lapse in Russia during the First World War. After the Bolshevik Revolution one of his pupils, Vladimir Zworykin (1889–1982), who emigrated twice to the United States (on the first occasion he could not find work), successfully patented a complete electrical television system in 1923. Later he joined RCA, taken on by Sarnoff (in secret) to run a laboratory, and he developed a new camera tube, the 240-line iconoscope, which he described, without demonstrating it, to a conference in Chicago in 1933: it was, he said, 'a new Version of the Electric Eye'.

There is an immense difference between forecasting on the basis of scientific knowledge, as Zworykin did, and popular speculation concerning future pictures on a screen. Yet popular forecasting could be closer to reality in certain respects than 'expert' science, if wildly remote from it in others. A writer in *Lightning*, one of the many popular science magazines of the 1890s, was more right than wrong when he explained in 1893: 'Before the next century shall expire the grandsons of the present generation will see one another across the Atlantic, and the great ceremonial events of the world, as they pass before the camera, will be executed at the same instant before mankind.'

When, a generation later, the first publicity gathered around practical television, the situation had already changed. Television sets ('televisors') were being put on sale in the late 1920s: they had not been discussed much before. And the focus in Britain was now on a particular inventor, a Scot born in Helensburgh, John Logie Baird (1888–1946), a son of the Manse, like Reith in this but in nothing else. A lonely man, ingenious and diligent, if shabby – his first mechanical scanner was made out of a hat-box – Baird nonetheless appreciated the need for publicity, dependent as he was on raising funds from others, and consequently did more to publicize television on both sides of the Atlantic than any other single person. He liked anecdotes, telling, for example, of how he saw his fingers appear on the screen for the first time and, more dramatically, the head and shoulders of his office boy, who had been scared by the intense white light of Baird's arc lamp used in his studio. Baird was so pleased that he gave the boy half-a-crown.

It was even more of a landmark date in his life when, on 30 September 1929, after protracted negotiations with a reluctant BBC, Baird was given permission to launch an experimental television service. The President of the British Board of Trade, giving Baird his blessing, told viewers (still not described as such) that he looked forward 'to this new applied science to encourage and provide a new industry, not only for Britain and for the British Empire but for the whole world'. A year earlier, the eminent philosopher and mathematician Bertrand Russell (1872–1970) had warned his readers that while 'apparatus' had been constructed 'capable of transmitting more or less recognizable pictures of still life objects, such as a drawing, a page of writing or a stationary illuminated face', there 'did not exist nor, as far as one can see, is there likely to exist in the near future, any apparatus capable of transmitting a real life moving picture such as the Boat Race or the Derby'. Russell was as wrong as H. G. Wells had been at the beginning of the twentieth century when he discussed the future of aviation. Television became a reality when a Pirandello play was televised in July 1930.

Baird's relations with the BBC – and the Post Office, which had to approve of experimental television broadcasting as it had in the early days of wireless (above) – were complex not so much because the corporation was suspicious of television – some of the BBC's leading executives were – but because it was suspicious of Baird himself and, above all, of his business associates. One of them, Isidore Ostrer (for a time) ran the film company Gaumont-British and acquired a popular, soon unsuccessful, newspaper, the *Sunday Referee*.

Yet it was not only Britain that could upset Baird, who was interested in every aspect of television, including long-distance, colour and big-screen television. He found it just as difficult to work in the United States, where he was thwarted by entrenched American radio interests, as he had been in Britain. American inventors had their own differing experiences of what was happening in their own country. C. P. Jenkins, who had contributed earlier to the development of the cinema projector and who, like Baird, experimented with mechanical scanners, got nowhere, while Philo Farnsworth, born on an Idaho farm, who worked on developing an all-electric television system, using quite different apparatus from Zworykin, joined the Board of Philadelphia Battery Company, Philco, a rival of RCA, which produced radio sets, including sets for automobiles.

Farnsworth left Philco amicably and financially secure, and before doing so, he assigned his own patents to Baird, who had by then turned to electronic scanning. Meanwhile, EMI, with corporate wealth and access to RCA patents, built up a remarkable team, directed by another Rosing pupil, Isaac Shoenberg, who had worked earlier with the Marconi Company. It included Alan Blumlein, according to his colleagues 'a genius who showered idea upon idea'. Using an Emitron camera, the team set out to develop a 405-line system for Britain. At the same time, Telefunken in Germany, with gramophone as well as radio and television interests, was experimenting with a Zworykin design.

In Britain, the Baird and EMI systems were pitted against each other during the mid-1930s in a conflict that reached its climax in Britain when the two were brought head to head in trials – as locomotives had been in early railway history. There followed the publication in January 1935 of an official government inquiry which recommended the inauguration of a limited but ultimately 'general' service (without making clear-cut suggestions about how to finance it). The response of the BBC was to organize television transmissions from Radiolympia, the main radio trade fair, in August 1936. The first programme was called *Here's Looking at You*.

A bigger and longer trial started in earnest on 2 November, when, on the toss of a coin, the Baird system was given the first run: it described its installation as having been built 'with typical British thoroughness as solidly as that on a battleship'. The Marconi-EMI system, given the second run, confidently chose as its slogan 'The System of Today and Tomorrow'. The BBC studios to be used during the trial were at Alexandra Palace, a great North London centre of nineteenth-century entertainment, complete with organ and racecourse. Baird himself was working then in the nineteenth-century Crystal Palace building at Sydenham. The advanced new technology of television was thus developing in London within Victorian buildings.

The BBC producers staging the trial had few doubts that EMI would prove superior. One of them, Cecil Madden, said of working in the Baird studio that it was 'a bit like using Morse code when you knew that next door in the EMI studio you could telephone', while a knowledgeable BBC engineer, D. C. Birkinshaw, was sure that EMI would show the way things would go: 'No whizzing discs, no mirror drums, silence, lightness, portability.' Baird, who had done more than any other person in the world to publicize practical television, duly lost the contest – and with it far more. He went on working in television until his death, but his company was placed in the hands of the receiver in 1939. One of the engineers who had worked with Baird and who became a consultant on radar, part of a system that met war defence needs, put Baird's work into long-term perspective. Jim Percy wrote:

> He was right at the end of the mechanical age. He thought in terms of wheels and sprockets and devices that spun around. He really wasn't with the electronics age at all. He hardly knew how a cathode tube worked. But he created a demand . . . If it hadn't been for Baird shouting and yelling and putting his crude 30-line pictures over London, we wouldn't have had television in this country before the War. He demonstrated that television could be done if not the way it should be done.

In other European countries where there was no Baird, electrical television won more easily, and in Germany, where there was a less publicized contest, Fernseh, a subsidiary of the camera company Zeiss Ikon, like Baird, lost out to its rival.

Meanwhile, the production of cameras and television sets made progress both in the Netherlands and in Sweden, which were not at that stage anxious to carry out experiments with television systems. The Philips Company, with whom Karl Marx had family connections, built a Dutch iconoscope in 1935, and in the same year began 180-line experimental transmissions, later changing the definition to 450 lines, then 405, as in Britain. When war broke out in 1939, Philips television sets were on sale in both countries, capable of being used in either of them.

In Sweden, experimental broadcasts, licensed by the Swedish Board of Telegraphy and Radio AB, a subsidiary of the W. M. Ericsson Telephone Manufacturing Company, began in 1939. In France, there were experiments by Baird subsidiaries before an iconoscope was installed at the Paris Exhibition of 1937, and a new station was opened in the Eiffel Tower by the Administration des Postes, Télégraphes et Téléphones. Using 455 lines, the station was said in 1939 to have a peak capacity of 45,000 watts, making it the most powerful television station in the world. It continued experiments in television after the start of the war, as did German researchers.

In Britain, regular television, available only to London viewers, was halted for security reasons at the beginning of the Second World War in the middle of a *Mickey Mouse* cartoon, and not revived until 1946, still for a strictly limited audience. 'The Age of Television', described in the next chapter, was not to begin until the 1950s. The systems were different. In the United States and Japan, 525 lines were used; in Europe mainly 625. There were to be different concerns and different chronologies, but on both sides of the Atlantic the same problems of control were raised as had been raised in radio broadcasting.

Physical Communication

This chapter and the previous one have charted within a chronological frame the development of communications from the advent of steam power through to the early 1930s and sometimes beyond. There were, as we have seen, many different strands. The periodical *Scientific Siftings* chose to start, as this chapter did, with communications, when, as early as 1892, it observed how 'we are all learning to move together, act together, achieve in vast companies'; in the same year, *The Electrical Engineer*, charting what had already been done in relation to the spread of message services, could conclude that 'still the cry is for quicker communication'. There were more new forms of physical communication than there were of social communication, and a new sequence was beginning. There were also new places on the map. Detroit, car-making capital of the United States, was to vie for a time with Chicago, as Coventry, a very old city, did with Birmingham.

The advent of bicycles served as a prelude to the advent of the automobile, which at the end of the nineteenth century was still a luxury product. The making of bicycles offered an apprenticeship, too, to some of the inventors involved. Thus, in Britain, Edward Butler, who produced

Fig. 17 Alfred Harmsworth, first Viscount Northcliffe, greatest of British press tycoons, seen here in 1911 with members of the Astor family. His passion was automobiles.

the first petrol-driven engine capable of being attached to an automobile, had begun by designing a petrol-driven bicycle, and William Morris (1877–1963), later Lord Nuffield, before and after he repaired and sold motor cars, repaired bicycles in Oxford, where a new industrial suburb, Cowley, was to be brought into existence. Alfred Harmsworth, later Lord Northcliffe (1865–1922), founder of *Answers* and the *Daily Mail*, worked for the cycling magazines *Wheel Life* and *Bicycling Times* before he moved onwards into motoring, his greatest love, while at the same time becoming a 'media mogul'. In 1902, he published a still readable book, *Motors and Motor Driving*.

In the United States, Hiram Maxim (1869–1936), son of the inventor of the Maxim gun and himself the inventor of an automobile, wrote with hindsight in his autobiography that 'the bicycle could not satisfy the demand which it had created. A mechanically propelled vehicle was wanted instead of a foot-propelled one, and we now know the automobile was the answer.' Yet this was not to be the answer for those people who in the twentieth century could not afford to buy an automobile, even after it had ceased to be a luxury, for bicycles not only continued to coexist with automobiles (as old and new media coexisted), but were to remain for more than a quarter of a century the dominant form of transportation in Maoist China. Meanwhile, Japan became a major producer both of bicycles, some from the 1960s onwards luxury products in themselves, and of automobiles. By the 1980s, Japan was building 8 million cars a year, 2.5 million of them by Toyota.

There was a psychological angle, as well as an economic one, to the development of transportation as a medium, as there was to advertising and collecting. The bicycle could be considered, as Marshall McLuhan in the 1960s was to consider media like radio and television, as an 'extension' of man. The man on the bicycle was not just a man and a machine. He was a 'faster man'.

Technologically, the different parts of the bicycle, like the different parts of the railway (tracks, locomotive, stations, signals), had their own prehistory – steering (1817), pedals (1839), front-wheel cranks (1861), pneumatic tyres (1890) and geared front-drive (1889–96) – and there were many intermediate products, including French velocipedes (in English 'boneshakers') and tricycles. They were all associated not only with individuals (significantly 'new women' as well as men and boys) or with families, but collectively with cycling clubs, some of them socialist clubs, linked to Robert Blatchford's Clarion movement.

The word 'movement' retained its social and political force. Automobiles were never to acquire the same stamp even after Henry Ford, as influential a figure in his lifetime as Watt or Boulton (see p. 114), set the pace. His famous Model T, which took to the roads in 1908, was based on the principle, unattractive to fashion designers, that one automobile should be like another automobile, a standardized product sold at the lowest possible price. The conveyor belt made this possible. Non-standardized automobiles had been pioneered not in the United States but in France and Germany, with Gottfried Daimler and Karl Benz producing a four-stroke gasoline-burning engine in 1885. Rudolf Diesel used heavier liquid fuels.

Automobiles might have been electrical products, but for various reasons such an option was rejected. One of the three automobiles claiming to have been the first to be produced in Britain, that of Charles Santler, was initially, in 1889, fired by a steam engine and was only converted to petrol five years later. Santler had visited Benz. The first one that was said to have converted English people to the belief that automobiles – to be described in Britain but not in the United States as 'motorcars' – had a future was a French Panhard bought by Evelyn Ellis, an MP, which was shipped across the Channel in 1895. That was the year when Herbert Austin built his first Wolseley.

The social consequences of automobiles were a matter of argument from the start. What side you took depended on interest as much as reason. For owners, whose numbers multiplied, automobiles represented freedom, at least the freedom of the road: for their critics, they were symbols of privilege, intruders into the countryside, 'wandering machines racing with incredible velocity and no apparent aim' down country lanes. Their influential owners were well organized. Ellis, who exhibited his Panhard at the first British motor show at Tunbridge Wells, led the lobby which succeeded in 1896 in getting rid of an absurd Red Flag restriction limiting the speed of motor vehicles on the road to 4 miles per hour.

The first Motor Car Act was passed in 1904: it introduced driving licences, car number-plates and a twenty miles per hour speed limit. Most newspapers welcomed the legislation, as they did the introduction of the Highway Code in 1931, but what the leader pieces in the press said about traffic and taxation often contradicted what was said in automobile advertisements; and although the British almost always used the word 'motorcar', a Royal Automobile Club was founded in London in 1897 and quickly established close relations with the Automobile Club de France. Together they agreed that Nicholas Cugnot of Lorraine had been the first constructor of a 'true automobile', a huge, heavy steam-powered tricycle, in 1769.

Between 1904 and 1914, there were changes in style and tone both in leader articles and in advertisements, with even bigger changes in the 1920s and 1930s. The luxurious fast motorcar, the Rolls Royce, was still hailed as the classic car, production of which survived the Great Depression, but smaller and cheaper cars produced in the 1920s and 1930s by manufacturers such as Austin, Morris, Singer, Fiat, Citroen and, in the United States, Chrysler, introduced the automobile to a wider and wider range of customers, some of whom were also buying motorcycles and travelling on motorbuses and motorcoaches. By 1933 a famous British racing driver, Sir Malcolm Campbell, could write in a book, *The Roads and the Problem of Their Safety*, that the motor vehicle had become 'a vital link in the life of the nation'.

On the eve of the First World War, 25,000 automobiles were made in Britain, 45,000 in France and 485,000 in the United States, and between that time and the beginning of the Second World War, with the Great Depression dividing the period, there had been a sharp rise in the number of automobiles, in the miles of motorway – the Italians produced their first stretch of autostrada as early as 1934 – and in the scale and format of advertising.

The newest technology was symbolized in the aeroplane, which for the Italian Futurists represented 'The Future'. There was little in common, however between the aeroplanes of which they dreamed (or those on display in a great Fascist air exhibition held in Milan in 1934) and the wooden planes in which the Wright brothers, Orville (1871–1948) and Wilbur (1867–1912) had taken to the skies in 1903. There were nonetheless curious links between technologies. The Wright brothers worked from their bicycle shop. In England Sir George Cayley (1773–1857) had flown a glider successfully as early as 1853, while in Germany Graf Ferdinand von Zeppelin designed the airship named after him five years before the Wright brothers flew. It first went into the air in 1900.

During the First World War, 'air aces', relying on their prowess and daring, fought with each other above the earth as their ancestors, pre-Gutenberg, had fought land duels with swords. Future war would demonstrate the horrors of the aeroplane, and Guernica, the subject of a great painting by Pablo Picasso, expressed immemorially the devastation of a town and its civilian population. The unlikely final link was Le Corbusier, pioneer of modern architecture, who had once been an employee of a French aeroplane company: 'The aeroplane is certainly, in modern industry', he wrote, 'one of the most highly selective of products . . . [it] had stimulated invention, intelligence and boldness . . . imagination and pure reason. The same spirit built the Parthenon.'

It is not possible to tell the story of flight in purely linear terms, and it is taken up at various points in the next three chapters. The next chapter looks both backwards and forwards, concentrating on the three generally acknowledged functions of the various social media – information, education and entertainment. In the twentieth century they became an almost sacred trinity, three in one.

6

Information, Education, Entertainment

The constituent elements in the trinity that gives this chapter its title had not always been identified in the same language as that used in the late twentieth century. 'Information' had usually been described in the seventeenth and eighteenth centuries as 'intelligence', 'education' as 'instruction', and 'entertainment' as 'pastime', 'amusement' or 'recreation'. Similar terms existed in other European languages. In the nineteenth century the words 'elevation' and 'uplift' were two further key words in the vocabulary of communication, and 'trivial' information was separated from 'useful' information, not least in libraries. 'Entertainment' was deemed 'rational' or 'debased'.

Both education and entertainment had long histories stretching back to the ancient world, and they had institutions specifically devoted to them, some of them thought of in the nineteenth century as 'traditional', others as 'modern'. They included schools, universities, academies, halls, playing fields, arenas or stadiums, and concert halls and theatres. 'Information' had a long history too. The verb 'to inform', derived from Latin, originally meant, both in English and French, not only supplying verifiable facts, which might be incriminating, but 'forming the mind', one of the elements in education (in German, *Bildung*).

The practical importance of information was already clearly appreciated before the advent of industrialization, but the effects of the expansion of commerce and industry described in the previous chapter ultimately transformed notions of time and space. As Sydney Chapman put it in a book on the Lancashire cotton industry, published in 1904: '[D]uring the last century the amount and the accuracy of information at the disposal of dealers increased enormously; moreover, the time elapsing between an event and the general knowledge of an event has dwindled to a small fraction of what it used to be.'

This and the next chapter will be concerned both with continuities and with discontinuities. Computerization, with which this chapter ends, profoundly affected information, education and entertainment in that order, but there was little sense as late as 1972 just how profound its impact would be. It was associated at first with the automation of industrial processes, including the manufacture of armaments, and the writer of an excellent article on automation in the 1972 edition of the *Encyclopaedia Britannica* suggested that the difference between mechanization and automation was mainly one of degree. He drew particular attention to the development of instruments of control, looking back before Watt's centrifugal governor on his steam engine to Denis Papin's steam safety valve devised in the late seventeenth century, and of digital systems of control. He noted the land-mark study by Norbert Wiener (1894–1964), *Cybernetics*, which describes the science of automatic control and communications processes in animals and machinery. In *The Human Use of Human Beings* (1954) Wiener forecast that communications facilities would include not only messages between men and machines but also between machine and machine.

Long before automation became a subject of general discussion during the 1950s, work and leisure patterns, workplaces (not just factories, but offices and aeroplanes too) and leisure facilities (including specially designed lei-sure centres) had changed substantially. So too had research concerning them, often in academic institutions. During the 1960s and 1970s surveys of the use of leisure time in countries as different as Sweden and Japan as well as in the United States and Britain revealed that an increasing amount of time was being spent both on receiving information and on entertain-ment, which was increasingly viewed as a kind of industry.

Sport

Sport, in particular, illustrates the underlying trends. Locally organized and 'amateur' in the nineteenth century, it became largely professionalized in the twentieth. In the twenty-first century, professional managers, publi-cized as much as the talented and highly paid players they manage, hire or fire players on the basis not only of their talent, but of their 'work efforts'. Meanwhile, the managers themselves, some of them ex-players, are judged by other managers, and by players and their agents as well as by sport journalists in the same terms. Managers and players, though not agents, are treated as celebrities, and their private lives 'off the field' are spotlit in the media. They also earn money, as do the clubs for which they work, through advertisement of what they wear or eat. Television is the main medium, but musical recordings may also figure in the finance. A significant minority of players, not all of whom are team players, go on to become highly paid television or print journalists. Women have been increasingly drawn in as participants – tennis was the sport that led the way – as well as spectators. Some of them too end up as managers.

The twenty-ninth General Assembly of the European Broadcasting Union, held in Athens in 1978, was the first European occasion when all aspects of the organization of sport were covered, but by the end of the 1990s the organization had been completely transformed. The old term 'spectator sports', often used pejoratively in the nineteenth century, had passed out of use as the finance of many sports came to depend not on spectators but on corporate interests, the most important of which were the media themselves, particularly television. Sport, including the broadcasting and filming of it, became as commercialized as 'the food chain' had become under the influence of supermarket retailing.

Sponsors influenced the timing and scheduling of a sports calendar as well as the fortunes of sports finance. Small traditional sports, like darts and snooker in England, could acquire mass audiences. There was a technological dimension to the story. The 1912 Stockholm Olympics, for instance, saw the first use of electrical timing equipment for running events. New and smaller cameras, carefully grouped and placed, made it possible for viewers to see more of the action. This was merely a beginning. When slow motion replays of athletic events were introduced, they fascinated viewers and were studied by the athletes themselves. The camera itself became a referee.

This brief examination of the media and sport is part of a big picture. The dividing lines between information and entertainment became increasingly hazy during the 1950s and 1960s, both in newspapers and in the electronic media, and were later to become even more blurred. 'Infotainment' was the ugly hybrid word applied to the new product.

Newspapers

The visual element was dominant, but, as is revealed in the history of the press, infotainment was not an entirely new phenomenon. When Harmsworth launched his halfpenny *Daily Mail* in London in 1896, it was with the explicit object of entertaining as well as informing its readers. The *Mail* was the first daily newspaper to include a women's page, and 'stunts' were as much part of Harmsworth's strategy as features. The third element in the trinity, education, was incorporated into the strategy. One distinguished Liberal journalist, J. A. Spender, observed of Harmsworth and 'his imitators' that they 'influenced the common man more than all the education ministers put together'.

The press after Harmsworth remained a major influence in the twentieth century, although it was now contrasted with 'non-traditional' electronic media as well as incorporated in the general category 'the media'. It did more than reflect the concerns of society: it shaped them, probing as well as reporting. Indeed, investigating became 'the most highly praised and highly prized form of journalism, taking the place of opinion making, the most prized in the nineteenth century'. This was the verdict of Anthony Smith, then Director of the British Film Institute, in his book *Goodbye Gutenberg*, published in 1980.

In the history of the press, each country had its own landmark date. The position in the United States, however, was constitutionally different from that in Europe almost from the start. The First Amendment, incorporated in a Bill of Rights passed by Congress in 1791, stated: 'Congress shall make no law . . . abridging the freedom of speech or of the press.' The language seemed plain, and belief in the freedom of the press influenced all subsequent American history. Justice Oliver Wendell Holmes (1841–1935) introduced the metaphor 'free market place of ideas'.

In France, where Paris was the centre of the world of information, education and entertainment, the landmark date in press history was 1881, when, after protracted and comprehensive debates, a new Press Law began with the stirring words '*La presse est libre*'. Old restraints were removed, including the requirement for newspapers to deposit caution money against the possibility of fines for libel and other offences.

German experience was different. In 1848, all earlier German restraints on the press were removed in the year of revolutions, but they were back again within three years. In 1878, Bismarck, the Chancellor of the new German Empire, cracked down on the socialist press, and even after he lost power in 1890 the press was not totally free. Some countries, notably Tsarist Russia, had a clandestine press that was directly involved in politics. In Imperial India, new repressive laws were still being passed late in the century, and vernacular newspapers were controlled in 1878. Three years earlier, the Japanese Press Law of 1875 laid down that 'the Home Minister [might] prohibit the sale or distribution of newspapers or if necessary seize them when it is deemed that articles disturbing to the peace and order or injurious to morale' were contained in them.

In all countries, whatever the state of the law, it was difficult to control the press which, by 1900, was a force in society that would have to be reckoned with as much in a democratizing future as it had been in an authoritarian past. Print was to remain a basic medium long after electronic media had appeared, with journals, pamphlets, books and encyclopaedias flourishing alongside newspapers.

The Popular Press

As the cost of printing fell and mass readerships were built up, the content of those papers which did not claim to be 'quality newspapers' included more entertainment and less information. Their style, too, was less formal. Yet even so-called 'tabloids' were not a standard product, as some historians of newspapers have tended to suggest, and in important respects they followed older models.

G. W. M. Reynolds, the founder of the popular Sunday newspaper *Reynolds News*, which built up a large circulation by dealing in items other than political information, was no more the founder of the kind of journalism that was to be called 'new' than Harmsworth was twenty years later. It was the wrong adjective. Earlier in the nineteenth century, entertainment (or diversion) had figured as prominently as information in many newspapers, particularly those published on a Sunday: in 1812 there were eighteen, few of them designed for 'working-class' readers. *Bell's Life in London and Sporting Chronicle*, which appeared in 1822, advertised itself as 'combining with the news of the week a rich repository of fashion, wit and humour, and interesting incidents of high and low life'. In 1886, appropriately, it was to be incorporated into *Sporting Life*.

Another Bell production, *Bell's Weekly Messenger* (1796–1896), also focused on crime, scandal, sex, disasters, epidemics and the turf. So did the long-surviving *News of the World*, launched in 1843 (and closed in 2011 following revelations of phone hacking by its journalists) as well as Edward Lloyd's many publications. Lloyd (1815–90) had begun his working life, like a number of Chartists, as a newspaper vendor and bookseller in London's East End. His first venture into journalism was his *Penny Sunday Times and People's Police Gazette*, and two years later he launched his *Lloyd's Illustrated Sunday Newspaper*, the first newspaper to sell a million copies after it had changed its title to *Lloyd's Weekly News*. Lloyd raised his capital from the sale of Old Parr's Laxative Pills.

The role of journalists – the men who gathered news (there were few women before the 1890s) – was still controversial, like that of the editors who selected, arranged, presented and interpreted news, and they often moved from one newspaper to another. They were often copying each other too, sometimes deliberately. Controversy began long before sales rose. In New York, where the *Sun*, a successful penny paper, was launched in 1833 by a struggling job-printer, Benjamin Day, it reached a circulation of 34,000 copies five years later. Much of the information that it contained related to ordinary people – and the police. A totally fictional account of life on the moon, 'The Moon Hoax', was part of the entertainment that it provided. Day made no claims that he wanted the *Sun* to educate. James Gordon Bennett (1795–1872) wanted his *New York Herald* to be more ambitious. Born in Scotland, Bennett's own ambition was to make the press as a whole 'the great organ and pivot of government, society, commerce, finance, religion, and all human civilization'. Religion mattered seriously in this list: 'A newspaper can send more souls to heaven and save more from hell than all the clubs and chapels in New York.'

J. G. Bennett Jr (1841–1918) followed the same confident approach: H. M. Stanley's mission to Africa in 1869 to discover the missionary-explorer David Livingstone was financed by him. Technology was part of the Bennett vision also, as it was for many publishers. In 1854, Bennett Sr experimented with a method of printing using a metal plate impression of type rather than the type itself. This was genuine innovation, and by the 1870s printing by stereotypes had spread widely. In Paris, *La Presse* was using the stereotyping process as early as 1852.

From the start, newspapers in Paris and New York formed only one element in a national press which was never centralized and continued to rest on a local base. This, too, was the case in Italy and in England, where in 1864 there were ninety-six provincial dailies as compared with eighteen in London, and where Edward Baines, Nonconformist owner of the liberal *Leeds Mercury*, could proudly proclaim that out of a total annual newspaper circulation of 546 million copies, 340 million were provincial publications. Yet the English provincial press was to lose much of its influence in the late nineteenth and twentieth centuries, when, for a variety of reasons, the provision of information – and entertainment, too – came to centre on London.

Before the ending of what some observers considered a golden age of the press, one nineteenth-century newspaper, the *Manchester Guardian*, which had become a penny paper in 1855, acquired a national audience under the talented and highly responsible leadership of C. P. Scott (1846– 1932), but, before it had moved its printing office to London in 1960, it had already dropped 'Manchester' from its name.

In retrospect, what happened in the 1880s and 1890s provided a prelude to the twentieth-century history of the media. It was then that the ideal of an informed 'public' was giving way to the realities of 'the market' in the media, including books as well as periodicals. Publishing for some publishers was a business like any other: give (i.e., sell) to 'the public' what it wants. A common feature both of *Titbits*, the first snippets paper, published by George Newnes (1851–1910), and of Harmsworth's *Answers* was that they offered readers insurance as well as information, entertainment and education: anyone caught up in a railway accident who was carrying a copy of the journal would be offered financial compensation. Harmsworth, who underplayed the part of advertising in financing his business, saluted *Titbits* as 'the beginning of a development which is going to change the whole face of journalism'.

In the national interest, mass literacy was now deemed essential, just as continuing education and computer literacy came to be in the last decades of the twentieth century. In the long run, too, industrial advance called also for greater opportunities for relaxation, and only one year after England's 1870 National Education Act the first Bank Holiday Act was passed. Increasingly, through the media, leisure became linked in the twentieth century to new rhythms of work and play, and in the process it was commercialized.

Critics of the Press

The Swiss historian and sociologist Sismondi (1773–1842) observed bluntly in 1823 that, while 'the daily Press is a power' in Britain, its object was 'not public good, but to get the largest number of subscribers'. John Stuart Mill (1806–73) suggested equally bluntly that 'more affectation and hypocrisy are necessary for the trade of literature, and especially the newspapers, than for a brothel keeper', an image that was to recur. The *Times*, even as it was coming to be thought of as a fourth estate in itself, was never without a variety of critics, among the first of them the radical William Hazlitt (1778–1830), who wrote brilliant essays on 'The Spirit of the Age' in 1823. While admitting that *The Times* was entitled to the character it gave itself of being the 'leading journal of Europe', Hazlitt did not find it to his taste. 'It might be imagined to be composed as well as printed with a steam engine.'

Benjamin Disraeli (1804–81) put into the mouths of his characters in his novel *Coningsby* phrases like 'God made man in his own image, but the Public is made by Newspapers', 'Opinion is now supreme and opinion speaks in print', and the representation of the press 'is far more complete than the representation of Parliament'. As for Matthew Arnold (1822–88) quintessentially highbrow, he was unhappy, about the role of communications in general:

> Your middle-class man thinks it the highest pitch of development and civilization when his letters are carried twelve times a day from Islington to Camberwell ... and if railway trains run to and from them every quarter of an hour. He thinks it is nothing that the trains only carry him from an illiberal, dismal life at Islington to an illiberal, dismal life at Camberwell.

Such an attitude towards communications was accompanied in Arnold's case by a fear of the unenfranchised, and after some of them had been enfranchised in 1867 and 1884, he was equally uneasy about the first new voters – 'the democracy as people are fond of calling them'. 'They have many merits, but among them is not that of being, in general, reasonable persons who think fairly and seriously.' The 'new journalism' – and Arnold may have been the first person to use this term – was, he believed, 'feather brained' as it tried to attract the readership of the recently enfranchised.

In England, observers who thought or had thought of themselves as 'Christian Socialists' were more optimistic about the future than Arnold. Indeed, in 1867 J. M. Ludlow could claim that, while 'the cheap newspaper and periodical' could not perhaps be 'defined strictly as educators',

> for good or evil, and probably on the whole for good, they are very powerful ones. ... Notwithstanding the many sins and shortcomings of the newspaper press, the working man of today, with his broadsheet for a penny, is by its aid a man of fuller information, better judgement and wider sympathies than the workman of thirty years back who had to content himself with gossip and rumour.

With these great victories won, there was more than a touch of irony, even for optimists, in what was to follow. There was more gossip and rumour in 1900 than in 1800. Most of the newly enfranchised turned to the press for diversion – even escape – in larger doses than for information and knowledge. Thomas Wright, a 'workingman' friend of Arnold, who loved irony, put no trust even in the Education Act of 1870: 'The extension of elementary education ... if left to its simple self, will give us a large number of people able to read the police intelligence of the lower types of weekly newspapers, and willing to read little else.'

Journalists

Their ranks were to be augmented from the 1860s onwards by university-educated 'intellectuals'. They were not professionally trained, however, as they were beginning to be in the United States. A National Association of Journalists was created (in Birmingham) in 1886, later to be given a Charter and renamed the Institute of Journalists – it included editors as well as reporters – but a National Union of Journalists, a genuine trade union, was not founded until 1907. Even in the United States it was not until 1908 that the University of Missouri opened America's first school of journalism, headed by a dean. In the north, in New York, Columbia University was to become the main educational provider after 1912, although it was a graduate school. The man who conceived of a new role for Columbia,

Joseph Pulitzer (1847–1911), after whom coveted prizes were to be named (eight in specific fields of journalism, six in 'letters'), was born in Hungary and had taken over *New York World* in 1883. Pulitzer envisaged that the training of journalists would take for granted the contribution that the press had made to 'the idea of progress, especially the progress of justice, of civilization, of humanity, of public opinion, and of the democratic . . . ideal'.

One of the best-known names in the American pantheon of journalism was to be that of Walter Lippmann (1889–1974), the newspaper columnist who won two Pulitzer Prizes. His 'Today and Tomorrow' column, begun in 1931, was syndicated in 250 newspapers, one in ten of them outside the United States. 'Many people buy a paper', Lippmann recognized, 'because their own lives are so dull that they want the vicarious thrill of reading about a set of imaginary people with whose gorgeous vices they can, in their fancy, identify themselves.' Yet he probed more deeply than this, and his influential and often reissued book, *Public Opinion*, published in 1922, remains the best known of all books on the subject. Lippmann suggested that the power of the press was expressed less in the personality of the editor of a newspaper than in the flow of the news itself. In a complex modern world, news was inevitably selective, and readers, dependent on what was on offer – 'condensed stories' – found it increasingly difficult to make informed judgements of their own. They were offered 'stereotypes' – 'pseudo-reality' – on public issues when they needed to be wisely informed.

Lippmann's idea of the 'public sphere', like that of Habermas (see p. 80), was hard to sustain when it seemed that media distorted and advertisers manipulated. The idea remained an ideal, however, and most American schools of journalism – there were 84 of them by 1917 and 812 by 1987 – believed in maintaining ideals in a complex society and culture. An Association of Trades of Journalism was founded in 1912 and an Association for Education in Journalism in 1949, and in 1924 a *Journalism Bulletin* was produced, to be converted into a quarterly in 1930 and followed in 1974 by a periodical, *Journalism History*.

How to relate journalistic training to the changing world of communications remained – and remains – a matter of debate, not least in Britain, where media studies in universities were as slow to develop as courses in journalism. Between 1919 and 1939 the only university diploma for journalism in Britain was offered at London University. Had university studies been more readily available, there would have been much experience to draw upon, including the remarkable career of the pre-First World War journalist W. T. Stead (1849–1912).

W. T. Stead and Arthur Evans

Son of a Congregationalist minister, Stead began his career as a regular contributor to the provincial halfpenny Liberal morning paper in Darlington, the *Northern Echo*, becoming its highly successful editor in 1871. In that role he committed his paper to compulsory school education, collective bargaining in industrial relations, an eight-hour working day for coalminers and universal male and female suffrage. He left the *Northern Echo* in 1885 to become assistant editor of London's influential *Pall Mall Gazette*, a periodical widely read in the London clubs; the editor was the liberal politician John Morley (1838–1923), a very different kind of political journalist and a future biographer of Gladstone. When he was elected to Parliament, Stead took over the editorship. Morley himself had succeeded a very different kind of editor, Frederick Greenwood (1830–1909), known to his contemporaries as 'the Prince of Journalists'.

Remaining editor of the *Gazette* for only five years, Stead blended stirring leaders with muck-raking news items, many of them related to social and political campaigns, the most notorious being that against juvenile prostitution, which he labelled 'white slavery'. He was a pioneer of investigative journalism. Among those who wrote for him were Oscar Wilde, George Bernard Shaw and the novelist George Meredith. In an article in 1886, published in the *Contemporary Review*, entitled 'Government by Journalism', Stead argued that the press was far more than a check on Parliament. It was a 'Chamber of Initiative'. His *Gazette* was 'a Tribune of the people'. In 1890, with initial financial support from George Newnes and later from Cecil Rhodes, Stead founded the immediately profitable *Review of Reviews*, indispensable for historians of the world's press. He also wrote a sensational book, *If Christ Came to Chicago* (1898), but he failed in an attempt in 1904 to establish a newspaper of his own – what he called a 'paper of the home'. Having predicted that he would die by lynching or drowning, he was one of the passengers to go down in the *Titanic* in 1912.

In the twentieth century Harold Evans (1928–), who was dismissed from his post as editor of the *Sunday Times* in 1982 by his proprietor Rupert Murdoch, also began his journalistic career on the *Northern Echo*. There have been few more eloquent advocates of the public's 'right to know' than Evans, who in a 1974 address, published by Britain's Granada Television, wrote:

> Governments as well as citizens need a free and inquiring press. With a volatile, pluralistic electorate, and a complex bureaucracy, a free press provides an indispensable feedback system from governed to the governing, from consumers to producers,

from the regions to the centre, and not least from one section of the bureaucracy to another.

The political and social contexts of Evans's address were quite different from those in which Stead had moved. Contexts were always changing: political, economic and cultural. It had been even more different in 1860 when *The Times* was edited by John Thaddeus Delane (1817–79) and when *Punch*, an illustrated weekly founded in 1842, was describing itself variously as 'watcher', 'curator, 'protector', 'chastiser' and 'lancet'. Meanwhile, Delane maintained consistently: 'The first duty of the Press is to obtain the earliest and most correct intelligence of the events of the time, and instantly by disclosing them, to make them the common property of the nation.' He wrote these particular words in 1861 when, following the abolition of the paper duties, the *Daily Telegraph* welcomed the prospect of the production of paper being henceforth 'governed exclusively by commercial rules', and went on to argue that 'every class of literature would benefit too – Shakespeare, Milton and Shelley' as much as the 'railway literature available on W. H. Smith's bookstalls'.

Repeal, it went on, opened up for writers a 'proportionately extensive field for the activity of genius and of talent which they never before enjoyed'. Echoing Richard Cobden, who made moral claims for the freedom of the press as lofty as those for the penny post (see p. 153), and who believed that 'the influence of public opinion, as exercised through the Press', was the 'distinguishing feature in modern civilization', the *Daily Telegraph*, which went on to have the largest newspaper circulation in Britain, added that in future a newspaper would be considered as 'a far more formidable and trustworthy authority than any Attorney-General or official censor of the Press'.

It was looking back to the long struggle to abolish what radicals considered to be 'taxes on knowledge' when the most lively editors and distributors of a radical press, dealing in unstamped newspapers, then dismissed in Whig and Tory circles as a 'pauper press', had braved imprisonment. Their protest had been swallowed up in Chartism, an avowedly working-class movement, which fought for democratic freedoms. Most working-class leaders, pre- and post-Chartist, believed that 'knowledge is power', a motto emblazoned on every issue of the unstamped *Poor Man's Guardian*, first published in 1831. The most articulate working men, including ex-Chartists, hailed as a great victory the abolition of the stamp duty in 1855 on the anniversary day of Magna Carta, and they went on to hail the repeal of the paper duties in 1861.

The Twentieth Century

By the end of the nineteenth century, with the extension of the suffrage and voting by ballot, the political climate had changed again, and in the first decades of the twentieth century press headlines were more a feature of an extended press than long leaders or even longer reports of parliamentary proceedings. The emphasis now was on interviews with people 'in the news', while journalists told their stories in fewer words and in shorter paragraphs. Some stories were now making their way into advertising also. It is interesting that Harmsworth, who advertised the *Daily Mail* on poster hoardings and in the sky, did not like long and increasingly pictorial advertisements which directed attention to nationally 'branded products' in the press. He also played down the role of advertising in financing his newspaper. There were no such inhibitions in the United States, where the first advertising agencies were established between 1880 and 1914, and where advertising expenditure, on which the press had depended since the eighteenth century, broke all records. The total, which rose from $40 million in 1881 to over $140 million by 1904, reached the billion-dollar mark in 1916. Brightly lit Times Square, the centre of entertainment as well as of the offices of the *New York Times*, had no British counterpart. Nor did Madison Avenue.

It was an innovation in 1961 when the *Sunday Times* under Evans introduced a glossy colour magazine, packed with advertisements, an innovation soon copied by other British Sunday papers. Meanwhile, on both sides of the Atlantic, provincial newspapers, paid for largely through different versions of advertising, were distributed free, and periodicals took over some of the older functions of newspapers.

The United States led the way too with 'muck-raking' periodicals; and great muck-raking journalists, such as Lincoln Steffens (1866–1936), established their reputations through both newspapers and periodicals, notably a new magazine, *McClure's*, very different in content and style from old magazines like the *Atlantic, Harpers* and the *Century*. The muck-rakers were suspicious of tycoons of all kinds, including the press tycoons, whose British counterparts could generate extra suspicion when many of them had also received public honours. Harmsworth, who became a Viscount in 1917, was not the first of them. Algernon Borthwick, proprietor of the *Morning Post*, a confidant of Lord Palmerston, had been knighted in 1880 and made a baronet by Salisbury and a peer in 1898. The press tycoons were under attack in the early twentieth century not only from muck-rakers, but also from so-called 'new liberals' like L. T. Hobhouse (1864–1929). The press of 1909, Hobhouse claimed, was 'more and more the monopoly of a few rich men'. Far from being 'the organ of democracy', therefore – what radicals had hoped for – it had become 'rather the sounding board for whatever ideas commend themselves to the great material interests'.

This was, however, too simple a contrast to draw then and later. Some rich proprietors thought that they were representing the public more than Parliament did, while others, like the Quaker George Cadbury (1839–1922), who in 1899 acquired the *Daily News*, determined that it should propound his own principles. He immediately expelled betting information and tips from the newspaper, and Hobhouse was his first candidate for its editor. Cadbury went on to acquire provincial newspapers in the belief that it was better to spend money 'trying to arouse my fellow countrymen to take political action than it was to spend it on charities'. Another great Quaker family, the Rowntrees, believed in doing both. The *Northern Echo* was under Rowntree Trust control before 1914, as was the influential weekly *The Nation*, which in 1931 was to merge with the *New Statesman*, one of the most influential weeklies of the inter-war years, to be quoted as frequently in India as in England. Its editor Kingsley Martin (1897–1969), who wrote about the past (Palmerston and the Crimean War) as well as the present, was a sharp critic of English newspapers and their editors and proprietors.

Newspapers and periodicals founded before 1914 by C. A. Pearson (1866–1921), beginning with *Pearson's Weekly* in 1890, which had as its motto 'To interest, to elevate and to amuse', and going on in 1900 with the *Daily Express*, passed into other hands in the 1920s: those of the Canadian Max Aitken (1879–1964), who in 1917 became Lord Beaverbrook. Surviving Northcliffe, who was fourteen years older than himself, Beaverbrook was to serve during the Second World War in Winston Churchill's cabinet. He had already written a classic study of the role of politicians, including Northcliffe, during the political crisis of the First World War when Herbert Asquith was replaced as Prime Minister by David Lloyd George. 'Bravo, Lloyd George' had been the happy *Daily Mail* headline.

Northcliffe had been keenly interested in exploiting the power of the press not only in politics but in the advancement of new technology too. In aviation, he sponsored Louis Blériot's flight across the Channel in 1909, and the new medium of radio in 1920, when he arranged for the Australian singer Dame Nellie Melba, the 'Australian nightingale', to broadcast from Chelmsford. The headlines were worthy of the occasion, for in the *Daily Mail* there were not enough headphones in its office to go round on the great occasion. On the other side of the Channel, in Paris, a phonograph record of Melba's performance was made in a radio operations room below the Eiffel Tower.

If Northcliffe had not become mentally disturbed and died in 1922, the year of the foundation of the BBC (see p. 181), he might have played as important a part in the history of broadcasting as he had done in the history of the press. By contrast, Beaverbrook, who survived Northcliffe, had a more ambivalent attitude towards the new medium. He was opposed to 'radio manufacturers taking control of it', but he was totally distrusted by the BBC's first general manager, John Reith. After Reith stated in 1923 that 'freedom of the air would result in chaos', the *Daily Express* headline ran: 'Fighting Freedom'. A more open critic of Beaverbrook than Reith was the Conservative Party leader Stanley Baldwin (1867–1947), who made the headlines early in 1931, a year of financial crisis and political drama, when he accused Fleet Street newspapers of 'aiming at power without respon-sibility', adding that such power had been 'the prerogative of the harlot through the ages'. Supported by *The Times*, whose editor Geoffrey Dawson was close to official Conservative Party sources, Baldwin had himself been a target. Northcliffe's heir, Viscount Rothermere, along with Beaverbrook, threatened to oppose those Conservative candidates at the next general election who would not promise to campaign for 'Empire Free Trade'.

During the following decade, leading up to the Second World War, Rothermere was to support the English fascist leader Sir Oswald Mosley (1896–1980): 'Hurray for the Blackshirts', one *Daily Mail* headline ran. Meanwhile, Beaverbrook's *Daily Express*, very much the organ for his own opinions, was to promise its readers on the eve of Hitler's invasion of Poland that there would be no war. In Britain this was the age of the press barons, well described in the second volume of a magisterial study, *The Rise and Fall of the Political Press in Britain*, published in 1985 by an American histo-rian, Stephen Koss, who placed the adjective 'apparent' before the words 'baronial power'. The popular press in Koss's judgement could stimulate or provoke opinion, but it could not determine how its readers would react.

There was much else besides politics to appeal to them, including cross-words, a new popular pastime, and, above all, sport (football pools, a form of betting, and horse race odds were not broadcast by the BBC), and politics often came last when people chose to buy a particular newspaper. Although most of them were not knowledgeable enough to read between the lines, as the poet W. H. Auden suggested that they must, they did not necessarily share the politics of the newspaper proprietors or the editors. This was made plain in 1945 when, at the general election of that year, Winston Churchill, who had been praised to the skies by the *Daily Mail* and the *Daily Express*, was heavily defeated and the Labour Party won a record majority.

At that particular point in media history it is possible to compare press and radio as influences on the supply of information and the formation of public opinion. There were many reasons for the victory of the Labour Party in 1945, and Churchill, renowned for his wartime broadcasts to the nation, did not strike the right note in his partisan broadcasts before the general election, the first since 1935. Nor did it help him that he himself seemed to be getting advice on strategy from Beaverbrook. Clement Attlee (1883–1967), who had started his ministerial career as Postmaster-General, and his Labour Party colleagues, themselves surprised at the scale of their victory, enjoyed the powerful assistance of the *Daily Mirror* in 1945, a paper first issued in 1903, which had become a genuine tabloid in 1934. Its favourite strip character, 'Jane', was better known to the public in 1945 than Attlee himself.

Whatever the sources of press appeal in 1945 – and the limitations on its influence – the circulation of national newspapers had risen during the war, having climbed only slowly during the 1930s, when the circulation of provincial newspapers declined. Koss ended his book with the appointment of the first Royal Commission on the Press in 1947, which devoted 150 pages to the education and training of journalists.

He included a postscript, however, noting the later demise in the 1960s of two long-established newspapers. In 1960, the *News Chronicle*, heir to the nineteenth-century liberal *Daily News*, disappeared, and in 1964, the *Daily Herald*, founded as a Labour newspaper in 1912, with trade-union backing, was transformed into the *Sun*, when it was given a misleading new slogan, 'a newspaper born of the age we live in'. (Three years later, the funeral took place also of *Reynolds News*, a paper which had unequivocally belonged to an earlier age.) The *Daily Herald* had got into financial difficulties as early as 1930, during the Depression, when 51 per cent of its shares were acquired by Odhams Press, but the new *Sun* lost even more money, and after five years of uncertainty and strain it was sold in 1969 to Rupert Murdoch, still in the process of turning himself into a media tycoon.

In the same year Murdoch acquired the *News of the World*, with a far longer history than the *Daily Herald* (above), and in 1981, following in the wake of Northcliffe, he bought *The Times* from its Canadian owner Roy Thomson (1894–1976), who had himself bought the paper 10 years earlier. Having started his career in the Canadian newspaper and radio business, Thomson had secured a foothold in Britain through his acquisition of a major share in one of Britain's first independent television companies, Scottish Television, founded in 1956. It presented him, in his own unforgettable words, with 'a licence to print money'.

The twentieth-century concentration of media power became a matter of increasing public concern between 1961 and 1981. It blurred not only most of the possible lines between information and entertainment (with a little education thrown in), but most of all the political party dividing lines between left and right, and, not least, all the dividing lines between different media.

Murdoch's empire was to stretch into television and film. Thomson's had included the travel business too, the business on which he eventually concentrated. Cecil King (1901–87), Northcliffe's nephew, had acquired control of the large *Daily Mirror* Group in 1933, to be renamed the International Publishing Group (IPC) in 1963. The IPC had a stake also in Associated Television, and after taking over Odhams it was responsible for around 200 periodicals – weeklies, monthlies and quarterlies. This was such a formidable media array, therefore, that it persuaded King to involve himself in conspiratorial rather than party politics against Harold Wilson (1916–95), Labour Prime Minister in 1968. It was a foolish move on King's part, and he was forced out of the chairmanship of the Group. The best known of the IPC periodicals, *Woman*, had been launched by Odhams in 1937, price twopence; it had half a million readers by the end of the year. In 1945, it had three-quarters of a million readers, and at its peak in the late 1950s, three and a half million.

Completely outside the range of the IPC periodicals, the most distinctive weekly publication was the *Picture Post*, founded in 1938, with highly topical political articles and highly memorable photographs. During the Second World War it not only reflected wartime arguments and moods on the Left but had also had a strong influence on them. Through it, Stefan Lorant (1901–97), a refugee from Nazi Germany, using a small Leica camera, raised British pictorial journalism to a new height. The owner of the paper, Edward Hulton (1906–88), who had started his proprietorial career in 1937 with *Farmers' Weekly*, was knighted in 1957, the year that he closed *Picture Post*. Two years later the whole Hulton group of periodicals was taken over by Odhams before Odhams in turn was incorporated in IPC. The BBC acquired (briefly) the library of photographs.

The USA

It is interesting to compare *Picture Post* and *Life* magazine, founded in 1936 in the United States by Henry Luce (1898–1967), thirteen years after *Time*, and almost simultaneously with the monthly film newsreel, *March of Time*. Its prospectus was eloquent – 'to see life; to see the world; to eye witness great events; to watch the faces of the poor and gestures of the proud . . .

to see things thousands of miles away, things hidden behind walls and within rooms, things dangerous to come by . . . to see and be amazed; to see and be instructed.' With none of the campaigning drive of Lorant, Hulton or Tom Hopkinson (1905–90), the last editor of *Picture Post*, who was deeply interested in the education of journalists, *Life* lived up to the prospectus, which was distributed to advertisers before it reached the public. In a telegram sent early in 1936, Archibald MacLeish (1892–1982), poet and essayist, had told Luce that 'the great revolutions of journalism are not revolutions in public opinion but revolutions in the way in which public opinion is formed'.

Public opinion was to be formed in different ways, not one, just as entertainment and education were to be moulded in separate ways. *Life* itself, offering in colour a record for all time of history in the making, was to die in 1972 after seeking to compete frontally with television, most of which was then in black and white, not colour. Luce had to cope not only with television, but also with news magazines, including his own *Time*, and *Time*'s competitors, *Newsweek* and *US News and World Report*, the combined circulation of which rose between 1961 and 1970 from 5.38 million to 8.47 million. After Luce's own death in 1967, the first of these, *Time*, was at the centre of what became a huge economic conglomeration, consisting in the first instance of *Time* and Warner Brothers. Later, in 1996, it included Ted Turner, who, from an unlikely base in Atlanta, had created against the odds (and the old television networks) a global news network, CNN (Cable News Network), built from nothing.

In these changing circumstances the American newspapers had to adapt, as they had been forced to do when computerization arrived. The old newspaper office set-up, with its composing room, where reporters used typewriters and where copy was cut and edited, was to change as radically as the printing processes themselves. Yet before the first electronic editor's terminal was marketed in 1973, 'hot lead' had still not given way everywhere to 'offset' printing. There were still old smells and old noises in newspaper buildings, and these, later to seem quaint, provided the background to the brilliant political film *All the President's Men* (1976). As in the nineteenth century, copy was being laid out time and time again at different stages of the production process and sales were falling.

The Decline of Newspapers

The number of newspaper copies sold per household (smaller in size than in the nineteenth century) fell from 1.12 in 1960 to 0.88 in 1974. In social terms, the inner city on which the old local newspapers had focused had lost much of its grip on a wider urban area, which now included not only suburbs, but 'exurbia' – stretching out beyond them. This was the context within which Anthony Smith (see p. 213) studied the changes taking place in newspaper publishing both in the United States and in a number of other countries. As he showed, what was happening elsewhere was not dissimilar to what was happening in the United States and in Britain. Sweden lost fifty conservative, thirty liberal and several social democratic newspapers between the 1920s and the 1960s, and a loan fund and joint-distribution rebates were introduced by the state in 1970, to be followed by further state subsidies, particularly to low-circulation newspapers. There were also establishment grants for new papers. Norway pursued a parallel policy. Denmark did not. In Sweden and Norway, the extinction of party newspapers represented for many party members a total disaster.

International comparisons, increasingly drawn during the late 1970s, showed that after a decade of economic adversity the Swedes 'consumed' more newspapers per 1,000 of the population than any other people, except the Japanese; that they came next to the United States in the per capita number of telephones; and that 95 per cent of them had television sets. In such comparisons the media were now usually treated as one, with the United States as the main reference point. The rise of broadcasting – first radio and then television – had led to a decline in newspaper advertising from 45 per cent of all advertising in 1935 to 23 per cent in 1995, but the combined share of newspaper and television advertising in the total was more or less constant – 46 per cent as compared with 45 per cent.

Media in Competition

It was not only television which had posed a challenge to the press. Once the press had been forced to concern itself with other media, both in business and in cultural terms, it had to examine possible future changes in its own role. They were not new questions. In Britain, one of the first people to speculate on media relationships and their implications was Lord Riddell (1865–1934), then proprietor of the *News of the World*. Faced with sound radio, not with television, Riddell, unlike Beaverbrook, was friendly to the new medium, but he raised many interesting issues, some of which were being raised on the other side of the Atlantic:

> What effect is radio going to have on life? (By the way I do not like the description 'wireless': why describe a thing as a negation?) Are people likely to read less? Are they going to talk less? Are they going to be better or worse informed? Are they going to go

to the theatre and music less? Are those who reside in rural districts going to be more or less satisfied? Who can tell?

Wisely, Riddell went on to place his questions in an extended time frame:

> So far as the present generation is concerned, I believe that those accustomed to read and who like reading will continue to read whether they use the radio or not. But what about the next generation brought up on radio? Are they going to prefer information through the medium of the eye or that through the medium of the ear?

The next generation was to be able to acquire information (and, even more, entertainment) on the screen through the 'universal eye' of television, as well as through the ear. Indeed, already in the same issue of the *Radio Times* that Riddell posed his questions, a 'listener', then a new controversial word, suggested in a letter to the editor that it was 'not too much to prophesy that within ten years television will be as advanced as radio telephony is today'. The word 'viewer' was not yet thought of, but when the BBC started a second periodical in 1929, more highbrow than the *Radio Times*, the name given to it was the *Listener*.

When television did arrive, it raised more questions than those which Riddell had asked about radio. As Kenneth Baily, then television critic of the *Evening Standard* and associate editor of Television, put it in 1949:

> Thousands of people, and then people in millions, are going to become subject, to some degree, to their household screen. What will it mean to them? Good or ill? With this new power there are likely to be no half-measures; it will choose its way, and then do what it cannot stop itself from doing.

Technological determinism was not the answer, as the next section of this chapter will show, but more attempts were to be made to provide answers about the social consequences of television than had ever been asked about the social consequences of radio. The two media were different, but the story of broadcasting was one.

Radio

It is necessary to begin with what the BBC always called 'sound broadcasting' rather than with television, both because of its intrinsic interest and because the same institutions that had ushered in the age of radio broadcasting, each with its own history, were responsible also for ushering in the age of television. Some thought of themselves as institutions rather than organizations. In the United States, NBC and CBS thought of themselves in this way, and in Britain the BBC was universally thought of as such. As early as 1926, the then Archbishop of Canterbury, Randall Davidson, said so, and later the BBC was to be compared with the Church of England over which the archbishop presided. In 1940, R. S. Lambert, a former editor of the *Listener*, turned to a different institution for historical comparisons, claiming in his book, *Ariel and All His Quality*, that 'in the field of art, intellect and politics' the BBC exercised through patronage 'all the power once exercised by the Court'.

One of the great radio reporters of the Second World War, equally well known on both sides of the Atlantic, the American Ed Murrow (1908–65) was almost an institution in himself, recognized as such for his broadcasts from London during the Battle of Britain. For MacLeish, by then Librarian of Congress, it was Murrow's broadcasts that 'destroyed the superstition of distance'. Now invaluable as historical records, at the time they made everything alive. MacLeish himself had opened a new chapter in American radio with a verse play, *The Fall of the City*, broadcast in 1937, with Orson Welles cast as a radio announcer. Another CBS broadcast in 1938, in which Welles again figured as an announcer, was a much-transformed version of H. G. Wells's *The War of the Worlds*. His announcement of Martian landings on earth generated listener panic. In retrospect, the Welles broadcast was said to have made 'a greater contribution to an understanding of Hitlerism, Mussolinism, Stalinism and all the other terrorisms of our time than all the words about them that have been written by reasonable men'.

Within two years, most European broadcasting stations were in the hands of the Nazis, and the demand for 'real' news was greater than ever. In providing it, radio for the first time had a marked advantage over newspapers, an advantage that was somewhat resented in the United States but was greatly appreciated in Britain. Before the Second World War, the BBC had been restricted in its news operations, particularly their timing and content, by the press and by news agencies. Now, with the support of the Ministry of Information, it was liberated, although as a liberator the ministry was new and unpopular, and it was not through it but through a newly founded Political Warfare Executive (PWE) that the BBC became host to many European broadcasting organizations and broadcasters, themselves seeking political liberation. It stood out now as the 'Voice of Freedom', going on to broadcast at its wartime peak in as many as forty-five languages, including, for audiences outside Europe, Tamil, Thai and Japanese. At home, it had the responsibility for maintaining morale; among the wide range of entertainment programmes that it broadcast, comedian Tommy Handley's *ITMA* (*It's That Man Again*) was one that passed into legend. How the BBC interpreted 'views' in wartime through a range of speakers, most of them not professionals, was a matter of public importance. American radio, too, turned increasingly to broadcasters from outside the pre-war profession. The propaganda of democracy was a propaganda in which Hollywood excelled.

War provides a necessary but unusual vantage point from which to survey these aspects of broadcasting, just as it does for a survey of technological change – for example, radar, air power and rocketry. A war of words was being fought between 1939 and 1945, and in democratic as much as in totalitarian countries the microphone became a potent weapon. It had already been so employed during the 1930s by Hitler and Goebbels, as it had been before them in the Soviet Union. At the very first Nazi radio exhibition in 1933, Goebbels, who was then engaged in destroying the independence of the press, had stated forcefully that radio would be to the twentieth century what the press had been to the nineteenth. At the huge, cleverly staged Nuremberg party rallies, the microphone was handled like a megaphone – just as it was in the Soviet Union.

Wired radio, to which the BBC was almost obsessively opposed, was favoured in totalitarian countries because it could be controlled, and the people's radio sets, which were being produced during the late 1930s, kept other countries' radio out. Neither Lenin nor Josef Stalin (1879–1953), both of them associated with pamphlets on propaganda published under their names, set out to be active broadcasters, however, and Soviet programmes were dull, replete with dubious statistics and appealing only to party activists. The press was rigorously controlled. In the United States, where newspapers were largely hostile to Franklin D. Roosevelt (1882–1945), who came to power in the same year as Hitler (1933), the president used the microphone in his 'fireside chats' quite differently from the way Hitler (or Stalin) did, seeking to make his listeners feel that he was present with them in their own homes. This was not the only way he used radio. The eight 'chats' he gave between 1933 and 1936 represented only 8 per cent of his radio addresses in that period: one of them, on a public holiday, was heard on 64 per cent of American radios.

None of these uses of the radio had been part of the pre-war British experience, however, so that in dealing with the move from peace to war, the BBC, which during the first years of its history had been required by government to keep out of all controversial broadcasting, had to increase its size and adapt its structures and its policies more than any other great broadcasting organization. It had begun its overseas broadcasting with a shortwave Empire service in 1932 – Reith's idea, not that of the government – and six years later it began foreign-language broadcasting with an Arabic service, pledged to broadcast 'the truth'. In wartime, it had to expand its overseas broadcasts in

Fig. 18 In the stadium. Adolf Hitler, assisted by his Minister of Propaganda, Josef Goebbels, used the microphone as a megaphone. Here, alone, separated from his huge audience, he addresses a rally.

unexpected ways, and in its domestic programming it found it necessary to abandon much that had been considered fundamental in its Reithian years – a special pattern of broadcasting on Sundays, for example, and unwilling- ness to broadcast too much (self-censured) 'pop music'. At the start of the war, obeying government defence instructions, the BBC had broadcast only a single programme, but as early as January 1940 it launched a new Forces Programme as an alternative to the Home Service. Broadcast throughout the world, this completely changed the BBC's pre-war programme balance.

Fig. 19 At the fireside. Franklin D. Roosevelt uses radio to chat to his fellow citizens. He put his trust in what he considered democratic communication.

After the Second World War was over, the Forces Programme became the so-called 'Light Programme', one of three programmes for the home audience, of which the Third was a minority cultural programme, more prestigious abroad, perhaps, than it was in Britain. Through these moves, the 'great audience', the praises of which had been sung by Reith as much as by the American critic Gilbert Seldes, was now being split up, although Sir William Haley (1901–87), then director-general, would never have used the word 'fragmentation': it was his hope that listeners would graduate from one programme to another, Light to Home, Home to Third. Thorough 'fragmentation' was to become possible only after further technological change. Meanwhile, in the post-war United States the large radio networks remained firmly in control, although during the war the US War Department had its own servicemen's network with 1,800 outlets in 1944, and foreigners could thereby listen to American programmes throughout large parts of the world.

In the war-time USSR, despite overseas propaganda broadcasting, no efforts were made to introduce relaxing programmes for Soviet citizens. The maintenance of morale never rested on the provision of entertainment. Soviet printing presses were 'vying with machine guns and artillery as weapons of war', and poets, novelists and composers were mobilized in the cause. Overseas programmes carried the same message. Nevertheless, it was significant when Stalin used the words 'brothers and sisters' and not 'comrades' in his first radio address on 3 July 1941, and a few weeks later a main radio feature was the reading of letters from men and women at the front. After the war, there was to be a greater emphasis on Russian 'culture', defined and monitored from above by Andrei Zhdanov (1896–1948) and his associates.

The Role of Reith

In examining British, American and Russian expansion in broadcasting, it is necessary to go back to the beginnings. In Britain, there was one outstanding personality, John Reith, briefly the wartime Minister of Information from 1940 to 1941, who could relate personal history to institutional history as he looked back. He was only 33 years old in 1922 when he was appointed general manager of the British Broadcasting Company, five years before he became director-general of the new British Broadcasting Corporation, required by Royal Charter to provide information, entertainment and education. He stayed in the post until 1938, when he moved to Imperial Airways.

He had set out his views about broadcasting, which he never changed, in his *Broadcast Over Britain* (1924), written at great speed while he was under the kind of great pressure that suited him so well. When he entered broadcasting, Reith wrote, there had been no 'sealed orders to open': 'very few knew what [it] meant: none knew what it might become'. Even by 1924, however, he anticipated its challenges in long-term historical perspective:

> Till the advent of this universal and extraordinary cheap medium of communication a very large proportion of the people were shut off from first-hand knowledge of the events which make history. They did not share in the interests and diversions of those with fortune's twin gifts – leisure and money. They could not gain access to the great men of the day, and these men could deliver their messages to a limited number only. Today all this has changed.

Reith had a strong sense of mission. He believed that to have used broadcasting simply as a medium of entertainment would have been to 'prostitute' it. He did not wish to offer people merely 'what they wanted'. In short, the BBC had to set standards. 'It should bring into the greatest possible number of homes . . . all that is best in every department of human knowledge, endeavour and achievement.' There was more than a touch of Arnold in this, although Reith probably did not realize it. For him, in his own words, 'the preservation of a high moral tone' was 'obviously [note the adverb] of paramount importance'. He attached great importance to religion. He never ever used the words 'mass media' or 'mass communications'.

A monopoly was the natural instrument to achieve Reith's mission, even a 'brute' monopoly – he chose the adjective himself years later – for only a monopoly could defy a cultural Gresham's law laying down that the bad drives out the good. What were the bad and the good was, of course, a matter of argument. Even at the time, Reith's stand, refusing to seek 'the lowest common denominator', seemed authoritarian to his critics, and with the passage of time it appeared rigid and ultimately obsolete. Yet it won unofficial and official qualified support, as Vail's defence of the AT&T's position had usually done in the United States. In August 1922, a *Manchester Guardian* leader affirmed confidently, before Reith had been appointed, that 'broadcasting is of all industries the one most clearly marked out for monopoly', and twelve years later, in the light of experience, *The Times* observed that it had been wisely decided 'to entrust broadcasting in this country to a single organization with an independent monopoly and with public service as its primary motive'.

Perhaps more to the point, the official Crawford Committee, appointed in 1926 to inquire into the future of British broadcasting, agreed with Reith's line of thinking that monopoly was a matter of mission more than of technology. It was not the response to spectrum scarcity. While conceding that 'special wavelengths or alternative services' might provide an escape from what it called 'the programme dilemma', the committee trusted that they would 'never be used to cater for groups of listeners, however large, who press for trite and commonplace performances'. In 1927, when the recommendation of the committee to set up a public corporation by Royal Charter was implemented, the new corporation was hailed by the Fabian socialist W. A. Robson (1895–1980) as 'an invention in the sphere of social science no less remarkable than the invention of radio transmission in the sphere of natural science'.

Radio in the USA

In the United States, broadcasting had developed on different lines, but there too 1927 was a landmark year. A Federal Radio Commission was set up, designed to be temporary, but which was renewed annually with

Fig. 20 John Reith, architect of British broadcasting, appeared in many cartoons, including *Punch*, where he could figure as Prospero. (The BBC's house magazine is called *Ariel*). 'The isle is full of music, sounds and sweet airs that give delight.' This cartoon shows him outside the new Broadcasting House.

changes until 1934 when, following a new Federal Communications Act, the Federal Communications Commission, the FCC, took its place.

Already by 1927 American radio had diverged quite significantly from that in Britain. It was providing mainly entertainment, although the word 'service' was widely used in what the Federal Radio Commission said about its own role. Like the national network companies that shaped the pattern of programming, it rejected all systems of financing that depended on licence fees. The finance of broadcasting through advertising involved rating the appeal of every sponsored programme and taking those programmes off the air that did not attract sufficient listeners to satisfy the advertisers. A number of specifically educational stations continued to operate, but advertising set the tone as well as the terms of US broadcasting which was thus incorporated within the US business system.

There was one other difference between the United States and Britain. American radio had a very different attitude to political (including election) broadcasting, for which, it believed, politicians should pay. To try to maintain a balance, the FCC developed a 'fairness doctrine', imposing a two-part duty on broadcasters – to devote a reasonable time to controversial issues of public importance and to provide reasonable opportunities for contrasting viewpoints on such issues to be heard.

Other Systems

A business model was followed by most broadcasting organizations in Latin America, although political broadcasting was treated differently from such broadcasting in the United States. Two models, the American and the British, were followed in the Caribbean.

The British and American systems were only two of many broadcasting systems which evolved during the 1920s and 1930s. There were many hybrids, as there always were in telecommunications. Canada is particularly interesting since, given its powerful neighbour, it was never likely to follow the United States as a model. It used broadcasting quite deliberately, like transportation earlier, to reinforce national identity. Spill-over broadcasting from the United States greatly disturbed the Canadian Radio League and influenced directly the Canadian Radio Broadcasting Act of 1932, the setting up of the Canadian Broadcasting Commission (CBC), and the subsequent creation of the Canadian Broadcasting Corporation in 1936. This was in large part modelled on the BBC, but from the start it incorporated a commercial element: a segment of specifically Canadian advertising was introduced.

Before 1945, the Soviet system, built on Marxist–Leninist foundations, did not serve as a model, as it was to do (enforcedly) in Central and Eastern Europe after 1945. Nor did Nazi radio. Italian radio, propagandist though it was, offered no model either, although, because Mussolini broadcast propaganda in Arabic, it drew the BBC into broadcasting in Arabic also. French radio, never a model, had been run since 1928 by a public broadcast service organized by the Post Office in competition with thirteen private commercial stations. The audience was relatively small, and in 1939 the public service was placed under the control of a newly established Office for Public Information. Following the German invasion of France in 1940, which was backed by clever German radio propaganda, the service lost all credibility.

Each radio system, even the French, had its advocates. It was NHK (Nippon Hoso Kyokai) in Japan, before and after the Second World War, with its board of governors, that seemed the closest to the BBC. NHK was founded in 1926, dependent on licence fees, but, unlike the BBC, it was subject to government control, and this was tightened even before the Japanese invasion of Manchuria in 1931 when the number of licence-holders had reached a million. There was pressure before and after Japan's war with China in 1937 to concentrate on broadcasts that would extol 'the national spirit', including 'theme of the day' broadcasts which incorporated the national anthem, patriotic songs and calls on the Emperor's subjects to bow in the direction of his palace. Ironically, the Second World War was to end with an unprecedented broadcast by Emperor Hirohito (1901–89), which few listeners understood because of the highly formal court language that he spoke.

After post-war Japan had been occupied by American troops, the status of NHK as a 'juridical person' was confirmed in the Radio and Broadcasting Law of 1950, which was designed to guarantee freedom of expression in broadcasting; and only after that date did NHK face competition from commercial broadcasters, most of them associated with newspapers. Likewise, it was while Germany was occupied – and in its case divided – that the framework of its post-war broadcasting system was set for it by two very different occupying powers. In East Germany, the main function of radio (and later of television) was defined as 'the formation of socialist state consciousness'. In federal West Germany, a highly decentralized radio system was devised after 1945, largely under British influence, with nine regional public law broadcasting stations, each offering two of the three very different programmes.

There could be no 'great audience' in such circumstances, but there were other distinctive elements from the start in the media set-up in West Germany. Broadcasting was suspect to the press, which was dominated by powerful financial interests, represented in particular by the Springer group, based in Hamburg and Berlin. The fifth article in the Basic Law of the new federal German state in 1949 specifically made a free press an integral element in the constitution, but it had not foreseen the triumphs of the Springer group: Springer's *Bild-Zeitung* (a German *Picture Post*) was to sell as many as four million copies a day. There was another apparently distinctive element in Germany which was reproduced in other areas in

Eastern and Central Europe – the presence of spill-over listeners and, later, viewers. There were observers, official and unofficial, who were particularly interested in their presence. The case of Canada could be used for reference.

Post-war Italy had a completely different media set-up from its wartime German ally. Fewer newspapers were sold there to a smaller proportion of the population than in any other European country – in 1975, just 99 per 1,000 compared to 441 in Britain – but some of them were important institutions, recognized as such, and Mussolini's Ordine dei Giornalisti, in which all Italian journalists were compulsorily enrolled, survived. There was also a mass weekly, *Oggi*, to be set along *Paris Match*. The Italian broadcasting agency, Radiotelevisione Italiano (RAI), promoted the policy of targeting a unified Italian public, but it was often compromised by overt political interference.

The Division of Labour in Broadcasting

Whatever the country, whatever the regime, whatever the period under review, the *raison d'être* of all broadcasting was the offer of programmes to a large unseen audience, and in all countries there was an operational division of labour behind the scenes, as there was in the film industry. There was a division between producers, however they were described, usually working behind glass screens; presenters, working in front of them; and performers, not all of them necessarily full-time professionals. Engineers were always behind the scenes too. There might also be scriptwriters, although over time scripts as such were largely abolished. Electronic recording was largely responsible for a cultural change that affected more than style of presentation.

In the United States, where, from the start, broadcasting was integrated into the business system, there was a different division, that between performers and presenters, the latter often the highest paid of broadcasting 'celebrities', and salesmen, given various titles, who collected advertising revenues. It seemed inevitable, therefore, that a programme ratings system would be developed in the United States which could become more sophisticated than the programming itself. Sponsors of programmes would seek to measure statistically the impact of radio programme scheduling as they would later measure the audiences for television programmes (peak and non-peak), and this would largely determine the bill of fare that they would offer. The A. C. Nielsen Company, founded in 1923, devised the first direct audience measurement machine, the Audimeter, in 1941, and by the time it turned to television in 1950, it had become as established an institution as the advertising agencies which preceded the rise of broadcasting and which organized often highly expensive radio and later television campaigns. The agencies which brought forth a distinctive marketing language were subject to the same process of concentration as operational radio (and later television) companies.

The Reithian BBC avoided ratings as guides to policy, and carried out no listener research of its own until 1937, but the post-Reithian BBC developed a sophisticated internal grading system which considered the quality of particular programmes as well as the numbers listening to them. Its beginnings can be traced back to the year before Reith left. Under him, as later, there was nothing monolithic about the broadcasting process in Britain. The structural distinction was not between performers and presenters on the one hand and salesmen on the other, but between those people, 'creative' or not, who were directly involved in programme-making and those who 'administered' programmes and sorted out their finance. Some individuals straddled or, more frequently, crossed the divides. One of the most eloquent among creative administrators of the post-war BBC, Huw Wheldon (1916–86), who joined the Corporation in 1952, insisted that the BBC was 'the sum of its programmes, no more no less'. The patterning of programmes, which for him necessarily incorporated arts programmes, was never fixed, although there were particular programmes scheduled at the same times each week, some with a very long life, some brought back to life in the twenty-first century. Many listeners did not want to see them die, and when they were dropped it was often amidst controversy.

Programmes

The word 'programme' thus had two usages in Britain, first, with a capital P, as in the Light or the Third Programme, a day-by-day and week-by-week planned and scheduled entity which, in the days of television, would be described as a 'channel'; and second, for the individual constituents in what was planned and scheduled. Many individual British programmes have had their histories written, but there have been few comparative studies across national frontiers of the balance of constituents in the planned and scheduled Programmes, the balance of which has changed for complex reasons over the years; those broadcasters planning and scheduling them have had to take account of the loyalty of listeners to particular programmes, and of their timing. They also have to recognize the use of radio as background noise: it is switched on but not listened to.

Throughout the history of broadcasting, some individual programmes (with a small 'p') have found a place in all countries. Weather forecasts are one example. Indeed, they precede broadcasting. For farmers in mountainous Switzerland and rural America, they were a major selling ploy for radio sets before broadcasting established itself. So, too, were sporting events, despite the frequent lack of cooperation on the part of sporting vested interests. From the start, religious programmes were broadcast in many countries. In Britain, the BBC's week ended during the 1920s and 1930s with a religious Epilogue and a long Amen. In Roman Catholic countries, there were differences of opinion about whether or not the Mass should be broadcast. Meanwhile, Radio Vatican, following in the wake of the Vatican newspaper *Osservatore Romano*, developed its own restrained style of general broadcasting.

The main form of pre-war broadcast entertainment in Britain was 'Variety', an odd name, which, like vaudeville, had its origins in the theatre, and the first BBC programme broadcast (30 January 1923) was appositely called Veterans of Variety. It was described by *The Times* in 1934 as 'the bread and butter of broadcasting'. In the United States, it was the name of a professional periodical. Cabaret had a different class appeal, while in the United States, the *Amos 'n' Andy Show*, with its origins in nineteenth-century black-and-white stage minstrel shows, survived depression and war, heading pre-war ratings; after twenty-one years, it remained in Nielsen's top ten in 1950 before transferring to television. Its programme form was open-ended, leading the way to the serial.

One of the reasons for changes in the balance of radio programming was television, although long before television audiences came to exceed radio audiences, portable transistor radios had changed the pattern of radio usage not only in the United States and Britain, but in the Arab world too, where, as Daniel Lerner pointed out in his then influential book *The Passing of Traditional Society* (1958), they became symbols of modernization. The desert as well as the beach was the place to observe how they were used.

Later in the 1940s, one of the drives to make established broadcasting institutions change their programming was finding a way to deal with 'pirate' radio stations. Radio Caroline (1964), broadcasting from the North Sea, was the first of a cluster of such stations to defy authority and broadcast mainly pop music to Britain and other European countries. After attempts to handle the situation by law – and such attempts were rarer in Britain than in the United States – the BBC itself created a new Radio 1 in 1967, which provided much the same fare as the pirates had done (largely pop music) and even employed some of the pirates themselves. By then, there were four radio channels (1, 2, 3 and 4) instead of three (Home, Light, Third).

Radio 4 was allotted the mainstream element in the Home Service, the programme to which listeners turned for 'comprehensive coverage of news and comment on the news', and Radio 3 took over what remained of the old Third Programme, which had itself become a generic music programme in 1964 and 1965. Local radio was introduced also, for the first time since the earliest days of the old British Broadcasting Company.

The changes made during the 1960s, a shake-up, were highly controversial inside and outside the BBC, but the new pattern quickly established itself. For Frank Gillard, who had made his name as a wartime broadcaster, reporting from the Front in the brilliantly organized programme, War Report, British radio had the great advantage of being 'relatively cheap and simple', an advantage which was of special importance in education, while television was 'costly and cumbrous'. Gillard believed that in providing information it could be more detailed and delve into greater depth, regional and international, than television, and that it would never be superseded by it.

There was just as big a shake-up in the Netherlands, where there had been a unique broadcasting structure before 1939, largely shaped by religious bodies. With the experience of the pirates in mind, a new Broadcasting Act of 1967 introduced two new stations, TROS and VOD, designated to entertain. One of the most powerful drives in radio in the Netherlands, as in Britain, came from radio journalists anxious to launch a continuous news programme, but it was not until 1974 that the Minister of Culture insisted that TROS should include any news bulletins at all. 'Trossification' left its impact on traditional broadcasters, although the Act defined the purpose of broadcasting as that of offering a 'comprehensive programme' in 'reasonable proportions' of 'different programme categories'. They were 'to satisfy the population's cultural, religious or spiritual needs'. That was a different trinity from that in the title of this chapter, as was 'entertainment, information, discussion'.

In the United States, the purposes of radio broadcasting could never have been so defined. Nor did American radio, by the 1990s largely local, live up to the challenges of the time as the much-criticized BBC and Dutch radio did. Before the war American 'soap opera' had received its name from fifteen-minute daytime dramas sponsored by Colgate-Palmolive and Procter and Gamble. There was a Palmolive Hour, too, and a Maxwell-House (coffee) Hour. News was slow to enter the charts after Lowell Thomas, despite press complaints, began reading news regularly on NBC in 1930, and it was not until 1934 that it took its place in radio schedules, often in headlines and snippets. Some celebrities figuring in radio programmes were to pass directly from radio into television. For example, The Fleischmann Hour introduced Milton Berle, who began as a nightclub and theatre comic, and ended as an NBC star.

After the post-1945 advent of coast-to-coast television, a new stimulus was given to local radio, but as the prime night-time listening audience for radio fell from seventeen million homes to three million, little was done to improve the range of programming until the number of available channels increased. The coming of the transistor radio, first offered as a de luxe item in the United States in the early 1950s, and the rapid development of automobile radio guaranteed that pop music, including 'country and western', punctuated by brief news bulletins, would remain staple fare. Only over time – and with the sense that the narrow scope of the radio spectrum no longer mattered – did generic classical music provide an alternative, as later still did 'community radio'.

The subtitle of a 1964 article by Desmond Smith on 'American Radio Today' in *Harper's* magazine was 'The Listener be Damned'. His was a very different message from that of the editor of London's *Daily Mirror*, Hugh Cudlipp, author of *Publish and be Damned*. Smith argued that:

> The aims of radio are identical in kind, but different in magnitude from television's. American radio, as any listener can tell, is an even more docile slave of the commercial dollar. Radio's standards are worse than television's, if that is possible, because radio can only survive, in an atmosphere of shrill salesmanship, as a bargain advertising medium for the local merchant, department store [back to the beginnings of radio] or used car lot.

In 1946, the share of local advertising in radio revenue had been 34 per cent: in 1963 it was 70 per cent. Nevertheless, profits from local station operations were high, and it was ironic that, with radio in the doldrums as a creative medium, the FCC had partially to freeze the granting of new licences in 1962.

The Rise of FM

Perspectives were to change somewhat in the 1970s, a decade that began with the creation of a National Public Radio and ended with the number of FM listeners exceeding the number of AM (amplitude modulation) listeners for the first time. Frequency modulation was less vulnerable to interference in their reception.

The long story of FM involved business more than technology. An engineer, Major Edwin H. Armstrong (1890–1954), originally a friend of David Sarnoff, became an enemy as Sarnoff came to see FM, which was demonstrated to him in 1933, as a danger to the network system; and although Armstrong was allowed to build an experimental station in New Jersey in 1939 and FM became popular, war held back progress. Thereafter, it stagnated until 1957. Appalled by the attitudes of the FCC and driven relentlessly into the law courts, Armstrong committed suicide by jumping off a skyscraper. In the history of FM there were parallels with the slow development of UHF in television, although FM made listening, particularly to classical music, far more satisfying, while UHF in many places made viewing less so.

The Influence of Radio

It is now possible to make a number of generalizations about the age of radio broadcasting before television became the dominant medium. Nonetheless, it is almost impossible, as it is in the case of television, a medium far more frequently studied, or, indeed, in the case of the automobile, also far more frequently studied, to separate out its influence on attitudes and habits from other influences on culture and society. Perhaps the word 'age' itself gets in the way. No age is of one piece. Like the postal system – and there was no postal age – radio broadcasting set out to reach the whole population even in the most remote places in a quite different way from the press and the cinema. Everywhere it might seem like 'a good companion', consoling as well as entertaining, informing and educating, and everywhere it carried with it unique blessings for the blind, the sick, the lonely and the house-bound. In retrospect, at least, the pictures of people listening to the radio linger as much as the words offered on it.

The extent to which radio broadcasting established a common culture in countries where this was held up as an ideal is debatable. In Europe, Asia, Africa, Australia and Latin America the range of programming was limited, largely by class, however defined, yet jokes were shared, as were stories, before the process of fragmentation set in. Quite apart from the creation of huge new industries, its economic consequences were substantial. Even where, as in Britain, there was little or no integration with the business system, through newspapers and periodicals – and, not least, through exhibitions – broadcasting opened up consumer markets, including the market for radio and radiograms. There was also a special appeal to women. As early as 1928, the *BBC Handbook* included an advertisement 'to the women of Britain', who, having installed 'wireless' and thereby 'kept your husband away from the club', were urged to go one step further and 'make your home comfy and cheerful by having Hailgloss Shades and globes in your lights'. The advertisement bore the caption 'The Pleasures of the Hearth'.

For its fiftieth anniversary in 1972, the BBC invited Alasdair Clayre, writer, singer and broadcaster, to produce a number of radio programmes examining the impact of broadcasting on people who had grown up with it. He began with *Children's Hour* (1922), presented by 'uncles' and 'aunts' – would-be family figures, reinforcements for parents, not substitutes for them. Politics came next in Clayre's survey, with Marshall McLuhan, one of the people being interviewed, arguing unconvincingly that radio broadcasting had pushed into the forefront 'tribal chiefs', but drawing no distinctions between broadcasting policies in Britain and the United States or, indeed, between those in Britain and Canada. Music came third in Clayre's reckoning. There had been an unprecedented access to classical music, and the audience for it had greatly increased: gramophone and radio had been interdependent. A commercial British radio station, Classic FM (1992), was to prove how interdependent they remained after the BBC lost its sound monopoly. Meanwhile, background music, including 'Muzak' – 'wallpaper for the ears' – was a largely new phenomenon in all countries and in aircraft travelling between them. Aircraft had their own scheduled programmes, including music programmes and radio 'repeats'. The traveller could choose between them.

Looking back more closely not at Clayre's book, but at the trinity of entertainment, education and information, which provides this chapter with its title, entertainment certainly changed in character after the arrival of sound broadcasting in the home, although not as dramatically as it was to do during the 1980s and 1990s. In the 1920s and 1930s the cinema was usually an alternative popular attraction, with the 'Big Five' (Metro-Goldwyn Mayer, Paramount, Warner Brothers, RKO and Twentieth Century Fox) dominating production in Hollywood and distribution around different markets, and with syndicated newspaper columnists publicizing (and sometimes damning) the stars of the screen. The announcement of the Oscars, first awarded in 1927 by the American Academy of Motion Picture, Arts and Sciences, was always an occasion not only for a lavish display, but as a media event, replete with media gossip. Radio publicity never had the same popular appeal.

As for education, despite much rhetoric about the uses of radio in education, the educative role of radio broadcasting, like television broadcasting, was always greater than its formal educational role. Even in Britain, where the BBC concerned itself both with school and adult education almost from the start, the conception of the 'Talk' as an art form, limited in length and carefully scripted, combining information, education and entertainment, was more significant than classroom instruction: it was as strange to

French listeners as it was to Americans. A later American innovation, 'the talk show', shared few of its features, but it made its way across the Atlantic.

The first national broadcast to schools in Britain was in April 1924, and by 1939 there was an elaborate apparatus of schools broadcasting, organized by a largely independent Central Council for Schools Broadcasting. It did much to keep schools alive and alert during the Second World War. Towards the end of the war there was also a system of Forces Educational Broadcasting, keenly supported by the Adjutant General of the Army, a scheme that was not phased out until 1952 when a new 'Further Education Experiment' was begun. Both the Forces scheme and the Experiment focused research not only on educational needs but also on the intelligibility of broadcasts. How many could people actually understand? The answer was fewer than the people producing them realized themselves. Broadcasting, researchers well knew, was never simply a mode of transmission. As its historians have pointed out, it served at least some of the functions set out by Habermas when he wrote of a 'public sphere' (see p. 80). While most of the broadcasters were middle class, accents had to be 'standard' and there was no talk of interactivity; nevertheless it 'widened horizons' (this became a cliché) and stimulated not only hobbies but reading. Librarians usually deemed it to be an ally, not a foe. A radio programme could lead to a run on bookshops as well as on libraries.

In the United States, early radio had been developed enthusiastically by many educational institutions; but, as we have seen, by the late 1920s they were losing in influence as well as in numbers; and the new FCC of 1934 (see p. 235), concerned with telecommunications as well as radio, favoured stations catering for 'the entire listening public within the listening area of the station' and showed no interest in supporting educational stations. Nor did Congress show much interest either. Despite philanthropic as well as academic support, by 1935, in the words of the American professor of communication Robert W. McChesney, they had 'washed their hands of broadcast policy'.

The Rise of Television

Sound broadcasting on both sides of the Atlantic and in many other parts of the world, whatever its pattern, was so well established by the mid-1930s that it was never easy for those engaged in it – whether as proprietors, managers, presenters or performers – to decide how television would or could fit in. Moreover, although there was a minority of dedicated enthusiasts for television, they were not able to apply the pressure that the far larger number of 'hams' had applied in the early days of radio. They had applied it in boom years. Now in years of depression even the growth in sales of automobiles was under threat.

Despite Sarnoff's employment of Vladimir Zworykin (see p. 201), it was always the off-putting word 'experiment' that stood out when television was mentioned in the 1930s, on both sides of the Atlantic. It was only when the decade that ended in war was almost over that television was on public display at the New York World Fair in 1939. There was even a 'Television Hall of Fame', and Roosevelt spoke. Yet it was not until 1941, the year in which the United States entered the war, that NBC and CBS, keen rivals, began limited but scheduled television broadcasting in New York. It was not one of the networks, but an ambitious newcomer without a radio base, DuMont Laboratories, in which Paramount Pictures was an investor, that continued regular television programmes throughout the war. Sarnoff and William S. Paley (1901–90), founder of CBS, were away on noncombatant media-related war service, and the third network, ABC, turning to television in 1943, had too many financial problems to be an effective initiator.

When the Second World War ended, there was still little sense of excitement about television in radio and film circles, and below the surface, indeed, there may have been apprehension. Decisions had to be taken from above, and, given strong radio interests, the FCC did not help either. It was involved in protracted arguments about technology, including colour television and the choice of VHF rather than of UHF, and when it froze the setting up of all new stations between 1945 and 1949 this did particular harm to DuMont. The problems went deeper. In so-called informed circles there was a misconception about the prospects for television. Only the higher income groups would be attracted to it, it was believed. This was shown to be a serious misconception even before the freeze ended. With few programmes on offer, the production of television sets rose remarkably from 178,000 to around fifteen million between 1947 and 1952, and in the latter year there were more than twenty million sets in use. More than a third of the population now possessed one: the figure for 1948 had been 0.4 per cent, with a significant proportion of the sets not in homes but in bars. Expectations were changing. In 1948 *Business Week*, enraptured by a post-war boom, could call television 'the poor man's latest and most prized luxury' and proclaim the year 'Television Year'. RCA fell into step: the price of its stock in that year rose 134 per cent on the basis of sales of sets.

A real mass audience was beginning to grow dramatically each week, while cinema attendances were going down. Hollywood might claim that 'Movies are Better than Ever', but in 1953 President Eisenhower, in no sense a populist, wrote in his diary: 'If a citizen has to be bored to death, it is cheaper and more comfortable to sit at home and look at television than it is to go outside and pay a dollar for a ticket.' Average weekly cinema attendance fell from ninety million in 1948 to forty-seven million in 1956. The number of cinemas had peaked to 20,000 in 1945, then fallen to 17,575 in 1948, and had slumped to 14,509 in 1956. From within Hollywood, attempts to push for pay television failed in face of radio network power, although that took time to assert itself. And some film companies set out to secure television licences. Thus in 1948, Twentieth Century Fox tried to buy ABC. One way out, that of selling films to television companies, was not taken until the mid-1950s. By then, no one was talking of 'The Age of the Cinema', and Hollywood, far from being a 'Dream Factory', had been torn apart by Senator Joseph McCarthy, who had drawn up a 'black list' of so-called pro-Communist performers. McCarthy himself used television, but his appearances eventually proved counter-productive, and he was subsequently destroyed in part by the journalists Ed Murrow and Fred Friendly, who used the medium (without the backing of their company, CBS) to expose him. Some companies had not shown the hearings, and Murrow's own role in McCarthy's fall, through his programme *See It Now*, has been exaggerated.

There were many kinds of television programme, among which the McCarthy hearings were unique, although not as many kinds as there were in radio, and there were different line systems in different countries. The United States used 525 lines – as did Japan – and many European countries used 625. By the 1960s programme traffic across frontiers increased, but there was no television equivalent to turning the knob, a distinctively radio experience. For home viewers drama was popular at first, provided not from Hollywood, but from Broadway, and if the *New York Times* could complain that watching stage scenes being enacted there was not unlike looking at a series of picture postcards, there were optimists who thought of the new medium as 'cultural theatre'. There was room also in that earliest stage in American television history for local differences in the content and style of programming, differences quickly lost as the networks took over, helped in this by a technological advance, the development of magnetic videotape. Television programmes could now be broadcast at any time and in any place.

Already before then, however, staple American television programmes were stereotyped. They included game shows, like *Beat the Clock*, quizzes, which were soon to raise ethical issues, and soap operas. One of the best-known programmes, not only in the United States, was *I Love Lucy* (1957). The long-running *Ed Sullivan Show* on CBS was 'rushed on to the air' in 1948 in an attempt to counter NBC's Milton Berle. 'Television is going the same way as radio as fast as it can: that is towards entertainment', the editor of the *Louisville Courier-Journal* remarked in February 1956.

This was a complaint in 1950 of Gilbert Seldes, who had served as a CBS director during the war, and who observed with interest, later in the 1950s, how Hollywood, returning to the scene, was dominating the new medium on its own terms. By then, the United States was televising far more film material (including old movies) than live features, including Westerns like *Gunsmoke*, which ran for twenty years. Warner Brothers was the main provider; ABC, with a new president, who had Hollywood connections, was the main purchaser. And a new generation of 'independents' was producing low-cost films, which, if successful, earned substantial profits when shown in the cinemas. *On the Waterfront* (1948), with Marlon Brando, from the start a celebrity, was one.

The British Model

Not all non-American broadcasting companies wanted to move in the same direction as the United States, certainly not 'as fast' as they could. Nor did Italian filmmakers, who were at the height of their creativity in difficult post-war years (see p. 198). In Britain, the BBC, operating in a land not of boom but of austerity, followed a completely different strategy from the United States when it put its trust in George Barnes (1904–60), a cultivated broadcaster, who was more at home directing its radio Third Programme than he was inside a television studio, and who moved on from being head of television to become head of a new university, Keele.

Haley, the BBC's post-war director-general, was uneasy about the medium itself, even though it was the BBC that had pioneered the pre-war regular but small-scale television service in 1936 (see pp. 203–4). When, after a seven-year wartime break, 405-line television – Britain used its own lines, giving a clearer picture than in the United States – was restored in June 1946, the first item to be shown was the interrupted Disney cartoon of 1939. It was called a 'resurrection'. The number of television licences in Britain had reached only 14,560 at the end of March 1947, but the million mark was attained at the end of 1951, with a preponderance of low-income-group viewers: a BBC survey showed that 70 per cent of them had not been educated beyond the age of 15. It was claimed at first that television aerials were status symbols put up for show, but there was very soon no doubt about the extent of genuine viewing. This became possible in large parts of Scotland, Wales and the north of England in 1952. There was now the potential for a mass audience.

A unique impetus to viewing was Queen Elizabeth's coronation, literally 'in sight of the people', in 1953. Around twenty million people were said to have watched it. (There was a large American audience, too, supplied with film transported by air.) Given that only just over two million British television licences had been issued at this time, large numbers of people must have been watching outside their own homes, some of them in cinemas, public halls and public houses. The commentator Richard Dimbleby (1913–65) had become well known to radio audiences during the war and had moved naturally into television, becoming even better known as a presenter of Panorama, one of the BBC's leading information programmes, first broadcast in the same year as the coronation. His two sons, David and Jonathan, were to become equally well known as broadcasters. The number of radio-only licences reached its peak in 1950 (11,819,190) and fell to fewer than 9.5 million in 1955 when the number of combined radio and television licences was more than 4.5 million. That was the year when Parliament, after protracted and often bitter debates, took away the BBC's monopoly.

In a Conservative White Paper of 1952, one of a whole series of White Papers on broadcasting, what was later to be described as a 'Trojan Horse' clause had pointed to the 1955 outcome: 'In the expanding field of television, provision should be made to permit some element of competition when the calls on capital resources at present needed for purposes of greater national importance make this possible', and it was from inside the BBC that the man emerged who was to play a major part in breaking its monopoly. Norman Collins (1907–82), for a time Head of the Light Programme and of BBC Television, created a Popular Television Association in July 1953, which won the support of *The Economist*, the editor of which asked the deceptively simple question, often asked in the United States and in continental Europe, 'Why should broadcasting be treated in a different way from other media, including the Press?'

The Association operated in a different way from a pressure group, fighting its campaign against the BBC's monopoly in populist terms. One member of it attacked the BBC because 'it set out unashamedly to make people think, and from that it was only a short step to telling them what to think'. The Americans, the campaigner failed to add, would never have permitted that, but the new competitive British television channel was not to be devised on American lines. Indeed, to many people – including French observers, hostile to all Anglo-Saxon pressures both on language and on culture – America served as a warning to Europe rather than an example, as it had done in the early years of radio (see p. 174). During the early 1950s, there were many British critics of commercial television who felt a sense of threat, and they were influential enough to ensure that when regionally based commercial companies, described as 'independent' companies (some with press interests), were enfranchised, they were placed within the orbit of an Independent Television Authority (ITA), set up by Act of Parliament in 1954.

The word 'Authority' stands out in its name. It was the ITA that would control advertising on which the revenue of the companies would depend, limiting it to short advertisements placed between programmes. These would not be sponsored by business firms. 'Commercial breaks', however, now became a feature of the British viewing experience. Their length and character were regulated, but by the 1990s the process of regulation had been softened – with exceptions, like the end of tobacco advertising in stages, the first of them in 1965. Children's advertising was subject to far more critical scrutiny than it was in the United States. Meanwhile, the BBC was never reluctant to advertise itself – and its programmes – in what became increasingly lavish 'trailers' that intervened between the scheduled programmes of the day.

Whatever its impact on viewers, competition in British television worked to the financial advantage of television producers and performers and a range of outside organizations, particularly in sport, while sharpening competition inside the BBC itself between professionals employed in television, many of them young, and those working in radio. For Antony Jay (1930–2016), a member of the pioneering BBC television team that produced the unscripted, popular programme *Tonight*, introduced in 1957, 'the BBC had been improved more by competition from within itself . . . than by competition directly with ITA'. Yet it was through the competition of ITN, the competitive news organization, that a new vitality was given to British news broadcasting, radio as well as television. Hitherto, news presentation had been superior in the United States, where Walter Cronkite (1916–2009), a genuine professional, had long ago embarked on a successful career of influence and, indeed, authority.

In Britain, as in the United States, a sense of professionalism in both branches of broadcasting was becoming increasingly strong during the 1960s and 1970s. It was possible, therefore, through professional skill more than through institutional policy, for the BBC to retain after 1955 a competitive advantage in sport (*Grandstand*, 1958) and in comedy. British 'sitcoms' were more popular than drama series, and some of the latter gripped viewers abroad as well as at home: John Galsworthy's *Forsyte Saga*, seen in New York and Washington, was also watched in Moscow. *Hancock's*

Half Hour, which moved from radio to live television in July 1956 and ran until 1961, focused on a comedian of genius, Tony Hancock (1924–68), one of whose most memorable programmes was about 'ham radio'. Another successful BBC television series, *Z Cars* (1962), focused on new-style mobile police, offering a contrast to Ted Willis's *Dixon of Dock Green*, which dealt with old-style policemen on the beat.

In programmes like these – 'mirroring change' – the BBC, with an alert, if controversial, new director-general, Sir Hugh Greene (1910–87), who took over in 1960, was responding to the social circumstances and institutional changes of the 1960s more imaginatively than the commercial companies. Nevertheless, not everything that succeeded was planned to achieve this result. The programme *Dr Who* (1963), which went through as many changes as the 'time lords' who featured in it, started as a children's programme, but eventually became a cult, as did *Star Trek* in the United States. This successfully passed from television to the cinema and survived the disappearance of its original cast.

The BBC went further than the United States when, freed of restraints, it introduced satire. *That Was The Week That Was* (*TW3*, 1962), was a programme that treated all institutions and all people in authority irreverently, including the then prime minister Harold Macmillan (1894–1986). Like the new weekly *Private Eye* (1961), it caught the mood of the time. In drama, where there was more of a sociological than a satirical emphasis, Independent Television (ITV) had secured the services of a creative Canadian producer, Sydney Newman (1917–97), to run its highly successful Armchair Theatre, but he was 'poached' by the BBC in 1961 and went on to broadcast a similar, and equally contentious, series, *The Wednesday Play*. Drama flourished, but there were persistent critics of television programming on moral grounds, the most pertinacious of whom, Mary Whitehouse (1910–2001), founded a National Viewers' and Listeners' Association. She mobilized what became vigilantes of the homescreen.

Despite ample evidence of the power of creativity coupled with controversy, the Pilkington Committee, skilfully lobbied by Greene, expressed concern in its report, published in 1962, that a decline in the BBC's ratings share would lead inexorably to a continuing lowering of standards. Also, turning back to an old argument, familiar during the parliamentary debates on the end of monopoly, it claimed that the companies were making excessive profits from 'the use of a facility which is part of the public and not the private domain'. It was clear in the early 1960s that the BBC itself had not yet accepted the verdict of Parliament in 1954; and in its voluminous evidence to the Pilkington Committee, seven times the length of Tolstoy's *War and Peace*, and including a film, *This Is the BBC*, it stuck to what Greene considered to be the high moral ground, quite different from the moral ground which Mrs Whitehouse, 'defender of the decent', chose to tread.

Independence for Greene was all. He knew, of course, that whatever the Pilkington Committee might say, the BBC itself would have to develop an adaptable strategy to defend public service broadcasting and the licence system on which its life depended, whatever government was in power. Harold Wilson (1916–95), Macmillan's Labour successor, accepted ITV enthusiastically, while Tony Benn (1925–2014), to the left of his party but an enthusiast for new technology, did not believe – in a memorable phrase – that broadcasting could be left to the broadcasters. By the early 1970s, when local BBC radio, part of the structural reorganization introduced during the 1960s, was being opened up to competition, as it was in other European countries, it was the unified nature of the British broadcasting system, including television and radio, rather than the differences between the BBC and the ITA (now renamed, after the development of local commercial radio, the IBA) that began to stand out – at least for some knowledgeable commentators and for IBA's second director-general, Sir Brian Young (1922–2016), a former headmaster of a public school, appointed in 1973. Governors, even chairmen of governors, were now being switched from one institution to the other. Programmes, too, could start on one channel and move to another. The only difference between the IBA and the BBC now seemed to be the continuing difference in its mode of finance. The BBC did not take advertising: the companies did. The BBC depended on a licence fee: the companies were driven by profit.

Both 'sides' adapted themselves to changing circumstances, including the arrival of regular colour television in 1967, far later than in the United States, and the introduction of a separate and more expensive colour licence in 1968. For some time, income from this new source sustained the BBC's finances, while other public broadcasting systems in other countries as different as Canada and Portugal were facing serious cuts. There were several attempts in the United States to rewrite the 1934 Federal Communications Act, all of which failed.

The Explosion

The differences between Britain and the United States, where the networks remained immensely strong, was as enormous as ever, although joint enterprises were just around the corner. First, however, came what was called at the time an 'explosion'. After the US domestic television market seemed to have reached saturation point in the mid-1950s, powerful American television interests looked abroad, including Europe, where in February 1955 there were 36 million sets in use in the United States as against only 4.8 million television sets in use in the whole of Europe, with 4.5 million of these in Britain.

By the mid-1960s the explosion had happened: there were television stations in more than ninety countries, and the great global audience now consisted of more than 750 million people. Outside the United States CBS already had affiliates in Havana, Mexico City, Puerto Rico and twenty Canadian cities. It was outside Europe that the American style of commercial television, intent on offering the entertainment it believed viewers wanted and on avoiding all causes of political offence, spread most easily. In 1966, the well-informed Wilson P. Dizard, in a jargon- and hype-free book, *Television, a World View*, dedicated to Murrow and written after the first phase of the 'television explosion' was over, estimated that by the early 1970s the 'great audience' would have doubled and that 'TV's influence would stretch from Minsk to Manila, from London to Lima, and on to the Nigerian up-country city of Kaduna where even now bearded camel drivers and local tribesmen sit in fascinated harmony before a teahouse television set watching Bonanza'.

Dizard noted that there were differences in programme styles as well as institutional structures in a world industry dominated by the United States. In Latin America, for example, the *telenovela*, an indigenous form of domestic drama and cheap to make, became immediately popular. Individual episodes, lasting between half-an-hour and an hour, were shown each day except Sundays and public holidays: they were made only the day before. They sometimes offered alternative endings, requesting viewers to express their opinions on which ones they liked best.

In Japan, samurai made their way across the centuries on to the 'small screen', as they did in the cinema, and to other countries too. So did 'monsters from the deep'. In Japan, NHK had introduced television in 1953, to be followed later in the same year by the first commercial station, and there had been excitement on the Tokyo streets when thousands of people gathered to watch a live television broadcast of a wrestling match. Five years later, a Japanese royal wedding gave as great an impetus to viewing as the British royal wedding had done earlier: a million TV sets were sold. In that year, 1958, it was reported that Japan was becoming 'as TV obsessed as the US'. NHK, which spent more money on research than any other broadcasting organization, showed that in 1960 a Japanese adult spent three hours and eleven minutes a day on average watching television, and children even more.

In France and Germany television development followed lines that might have been anticipated given the post-war history of radio broadcasting in both countries, and in France, in particular, a far longer period stretching back at least to the revolutionary and Napoleonic Wars, and even before that to Colbert. In 1946, all French political parties had supported legislation that nationalized French radio and television, but seven years later, with television policy following radio policy, there were only 60,000 television sets in French homes. It required a five-year national television plan in 1954 to project forty-five transmitters, but it was not until it was abundantly plain that audiences were being lost to neighbouring broadcasting organizations, like Luxembourg and Monaco, that the tide began to turn.

After de Gaulle, who appreciated the political potential of television, had become head of state in 1958, the first efforts were made to modify the system, and in 1964 a so-called autonomous new organization, L'Office de radiodiffusion télévision française (ORTF), was set up. By then, there were five million French viewers as compared with nearly ten million in West Germany and nearly six million in Italy. In West Germany, on Allied orders, television, like radio, had been left to the governments of the Länder, with the first television station, Nordwest Deutscher Rundfunk, beginning its operations in December 1952.

There could be no further change in France until after the resignation of de Gaulle in 1969, following the disturbances (*les événements*) in Paris in 1968, which recalled the revolutionary years of the nineteenth century. The big change still did not come, however, until after the death of de Gaulle's successor, Georges Pompidou. President Giscard d'Estaing then abolished ORTF in 1974, and in a far-reaching 'new deal' set up seven autonomous organizations, one to run radio, two to run television channels, one to run regional television, one to work an independent production company, supplying the rest, one to deal with the technological side of the operation, and one to handle research and archives. To preside over the whole elaborate, but still monopolistic, structure, a High Audiovisual Council was created.

This was only one of a number of reorganizations in television structures. The most dramatic was in Italy. In 1974, decisions of Italy's Constitutional Court, which confirmed the need for public service broadcasting based on objectivity and impartiality, nonetheless opened the way for private broadcasting and, following a 1975 Broadcasting Act, for an extraordinary eruption of private companies. Most of them did not survive, but in 1978 there were no fewer than 506 local television stations and 2,275 radio stations. There were now more stations per person than in the United States. Ten years later, the Spanish counterpart of the Italian Court made a similar decision, noting that since the constitution was silent on the question of broadcasting, no structure was explicitly forbidden. The constitutional principle of free speech might be deemed, it stated, to include the principle of the freedom to broadcast, a judgement unrecognized in the United States, where telegraphy, telephony, radio and television operated under different legal principles from publishing.

The Italian scenario, which continued to evolve, was not copied in Spain; and in Italy itself, Silvio Berlusconi, future Prime Minister, started a quasi-national channel, Canale 5, in 1980, going on to buy other Italian channels in 1983 and 1984. His business concern, Fininvest, then controlled three channels to RAI's three, a duopoly situation, which was sanctioned in law in 1990. RAI survived, however, as it survived the downfall of the two main Italian political parties, the Christian Democrats and the Socialists, and a long spell in office of Berlusconi from 2001.

In Britain a Labour government had commissioned in 1974 a *Report on the Future of Broadcasting* by a committee headed by Noel Annan (1916–2000). Reporting in 1977, it rejected schemes put forward within the Labour Party, including the formation of a National Broadcasting Council and Commission and the splitting up of the BBC; and in 1980 the new Conservative government, headed by Margaret Thatcher (1925–2013), former Secretary of State for Education, taking account of its recommendations but modifying them, decided to introduce a new Channel 4, outside the control of the IBA, but dependent for part of its revenue on advertisement. It would commission programmes from independent producers, growing in numbers and soon to grow still more, rather than make them itself.

Channel 4 soon proved itself a highly innovative institution, drawing on programmes commissioned from abroad as well as from Britain, and some of the new British independents, with diverse areas of speciality, among them 'wild life' and 'social documentary', were highly creative, in time constituting a new sector with overseas as well as with British interests. They were more genuinely independent than the early so-called Independents had been in the American film industry (see p. 196).

Annan made much of the diversity of voices and the lack of moral consensus in the Britain of the early 1970s. In France, however, where there was a strong distinction between the left and the right, President Georges Pompidou claimed in 1970 that being a journalist in ORTF was 'not like being a journalist anywhere else': ORTF was the 'voice of France'. Giscard d'Estaing's new ORTF did not live up to the hopes placed in it. Broadcasting remained firmly in the hands of government, so that after the election of a socialist president, François Mitterrand, in 1981, all the senior directors in French television were dismissed and replaced by socialists. A new study commission, appointed to set out a reform programme in France, recommended a High Authority for the Audiovisual Media, old and new, and changes in the disposition of funds between the various programme sectors. In the subsequent legislation based upon it, the language of monopoly was abandoned, but there was an increased stress on public service. Only a public authority had the right, it was reiterated, to take decisions about radio and television programmes 'for the French people'. Such sentences stand out, as they did in broadcasting reform legislation in other countries. There were no clauses dealing with finance, however, and many ambiguities in the sections on structures.

As television spread, leaving only a few countries like Tanzania and Guyana beyond its reach – both of them by governmental choice – there were some countries where only one voice was allowed to be heard and only a few privileged faces to be seen on the screen. Thus, in Thailand official regulations stated in 1965 that the first objectives of broadcasting were: (a) to promote national policy and common interests in the area of politics, military affairs, economics and social welfare; (b) to promote the loyalty of the citizens to the country, the religion and the king; (c) to promote the unity and mutual co-operation of the army and its citizens; and (d) to invite citizens to retort to and oppose the enemy, including those doctrines which are dangerous to the security of the nation.

Debates

Contemporary comment on television, in countries where its pattern depended on debate, was now stressing its global rather than its national implications, as Marshall McLuhan (see p. 2) did when he popularized (not his word) the concept of 'global' in his 'global village' in 1960. (He had published *The Mechanical Bride: The Future of Industrial Man* in 1951.) His most-publicized books, which followed in sequence, beginning with *The Gutenberg Galaxy* (1962), directed attention to the intrinsic characteristics of particular media, including print, radio and television, dwelling on their range ('hot' and 'cool', a distinction of his own) rather than on their content. Nevertheless, when he generalized about village or globe or railways, he was influenced by the unique experiences of Canada.

Railways, McLuhan stressed, fostered the development of new kinds of cities and new kinds of work and leisure quite independently of the freight that they carried. He did not idealize the global village as a place of harmony. It was a place filled with new and intense tensions and with new forms of violence. McLuhan, whose words and images linger, was one of the first writers to draw attention to 'the media', a term which, he was told by a friendly critic of the first draft (1954) of *Understanding Media*, required careful explanation as it was not in the average teacher's vocabulary. It was not so much what he said about television as television itself that provoked viewers. McLuhan himself looked beyond the television offered in his own time to computers and to satellites.

Television has provoked more comment and stimulated more argument (and more cartoons) than any other medium in history, beginning perhaps in Britain with the comment of the *Daily Mirror* in 1950: 'If you let a television set through your door, life can never be the same again.' The judgement made by American actor and comedian Ernie Kovacs (1919–62) that television is a medium 'because it is neither rare nor well done' is memorable. So, too, is the description of it given by architect Frank Lloyd 'Wright (1867–1959) as 'chewing gum' for both eyes. The cartoons in the *New Yorker*, like older cartoons in *Punch*, began with the medium as gadget rather than as message and ended with the experience of viewers.

Criticism was strongest in the United States, where the emphasis in network television, as in network radio, was on stereotyped entertainment, leading Newton Minow, chairman of the FCC in 1961 – a quite exceptional chairman – to speak of network television as a 'vast wasteland'. In London, Milton Shulman, a lively newspaper critic of particular programmes, called British television 'the least worst television in the world', but he noted also, as did Lloyd Wright, how 'for most people the act of watching the box' had become 'a habit rather than a conscious discriminatory act'. For Shulman, television was 'the ravenous eye'. For others, it was 'the evil eye', *mal occhio*, destructive not only of the individuals who gazed into it but of the whole social fabric.

Much of this criticism is now dated. Some of it, however, sounds curiously topical. For many critics, television was a reductive agency, trivializing the news as well as the other constituents of programming; for other critics, however, it was a negative force, distorting not only the news but also the issues that lay behind it. At the same time, it spawned a superabundance of entertainment. For the American media theorist Neil Postman (1931–2003), writing in 1986, we were now 'amusing ourselves to death'.

If that had been all that there was to television, there would never have been as many debates as there were in most countries about decency, language, taste, sex and violence, or the standards or codes dealing with them.

Nor would the law have been so prominently evoked, in particular in the United States. There, as we have seen, broadcasting was from the start treated quite differently from print; and cable television, when it arrived (see p. 302), was treated differently from network television, not only in the courts but by the FCC too. Most legal action originated there. Both inside and outside the courts much of the debate centred on the role of the family, an institution in flux, about which it was even more difficult to reach consensus or even to generalize than it was about television itself.

It was easy to say that children needed to be protected when television intruded into the home, but ideas on how to protect them might divide families. The legal issues were complex, and the complexity increased with the advent of cable and, ultimately, the Internet. The debate on the influence of television on children, who as we have seen, figured prominently throughout the history of the media, was opened by the London-based social psychologist Hilde Himmelweit in her *Television and the Child*, published with Nuffield Foundation support in 1958. She also considered the influence of television on adolescent and adult social and on political behaviour, including violent protest.

The United States contributed much to both debates, but no agreement was reached in either of them, there or elsewhere, despite public demand to 'do something' and a vast amount of empirical research. In general, protecting children was given more attention than educating them: content labelling and rating systems were proposed and implemented; time zones were introduced, within which certain types of programme could not be broadcast; and, most recently, technical filtering devices were devised. The last of the devices was technological, the invention of the Violence-Chip (V-Chip), an electronic device designed in Canada, which could be installed in television sets to identify television programmes which parents deemed objectionable. Politicians seized upon this device for their own purposes, and in 1996, in a Communications Decency Act, Congress mandated that such a chip should be installed in every new television set sold in the United States. In 1997, the Supreme Court ruled the Act to be unconstitutional on the grounds that its provisions would abridge freedom of speech.

There were many moves and countermoves. As early as 1956, British television abandoned a so-called 'Toddlers' Truce', an hour of television silence between six and seven o'clock in the evening. There were complaints, as there were when BBC Radio dropped *Children's Hour*. Similar issues have arisen in film and there have been similar complaints about the effects of particular films on children. As early as 1919, a now defunct periodical – called, significantly, *Education* – complained of 'the tendency of children to imitate the daring deeds seen upon the screen', with the imitation 'not confined to young boys and girls, but [extending] even through adolescents and to adults'. Different categories of films were subsequently classified, including those X films not to be seen by children.

The best-known example of American action to use television positively in the interests of children leads back a generation before the Children's Television Act of 1990 to the Children's Television Workshop that devised the series *Sesame Street*, starting in 1969. A commercial product, deliberately designed to be entertaining as well as educational, the programme, teaching pre-school children how to read, depended on team cooperation and collaboration similar to that of academics in the British Open University (see p. 318). In the course of its long life, it has been shown in 140 countries and it became a model for programmes like the Mexican *Plaza Sesamo*, the Brazilian *Vila Sesamo*, *Sesamstraat* in the Netherlands and *Iftah Ya Simsin* in Kuwait.

Nevertheless, it inspired almost as much controversy as enthusiasm, particularly in countries which had different attitudes towards children from those in the United States and did not wish to treat them as young consumers. It is refreshing to turn to the simplicities of Dr Maire Messenger Davies's British paperback of 1989, *Television is Good for Your Kids*, which itself used evidence derived from research like that carried out in Australia by Bob Hodge and David Tripp. Their in-depth study of 600 5–12-year-olds concluded that 'the bête noire of lobby groups, the cartoon, turns out . . . to be a healthy form, ideally adapted to children's growing powers'.

Media Research

Empirical research on radio and television use or on the appeal of particular programmes has sometimes, but not always, avoided theory, but, with the expansion of twentieth-century universities and other institutions of higher education, many of them developing departments of media studies, it is not surprising that theory, including Marxist theory, was given a prominent place and that the wide range of theories on offer frequently did not seem to relate pertinently to the experience of people working in the media. The earliest American research was carried out at the University of Columbia in New York, where the sociologists Robert K. Merton (1910–2003) and Paul Lazarsfeld (1901–76) met in 1941. In 1948, they coauthored a remarkably wide-ranging article, 'Mass Communications, Popular Taste and Organized Social Action'. In Britain, where early sociological research was largely empirical, a Glasgow University Media Studies Group opened up in 1976 a sometimes bitter debate about 'news bias' in a book called *Bad News*, which was followed up by several sequels.

Exploration of cultures and subcultures was the intention of Richard Hoggart (1918–2014), the founder in 1964 of the Birmingham Centre for Cultural Studies, the first academic institution in Britain to deal explicitly with the task. Hoggart started his career in adult education, as had several other writers on the media, particularly Raymond Williams (see p. 29), and from 1960 to 1962 he served as a member of the Pilkington Committee on Broadcasting, the conclusions of which he largely shaped. Before that he had published *The Uses of Literacy* (1957), which drew on women's magazines for much of the material that it put under review. Universal literacy had come to be taken for granted in England (prematurely); Hoggart showed its current limitations years before the BBC introduced its first literacy initiative, the kind of campaign which was still regarded as necessary, perhaps more necessary, in 2001.

Daniel Boorstin's book on the media, *The Image* (see p. 76), was often quoted alongside Williams, although it was written within a very different American frame. It directed attention not only to 'pseudo events' manufactured by the media, but to 'celebrities', known, unlike 'heroes', by their images rather than by their achievements. 'Formerly a public man needed a private secretary for a barrier between himself and the public. Nowadays he has a press secretary to keep him properly in the public eye.' Techniques of communication, including 'spin', have become far more sophisticated, if not always more effective, since then. As for the 'events', they were to be described by the Israeli scholars Elihu Katz and Daniel Dayan as 'media events' and treated as reinforcements of 'social integration'.

Neither Katz nor Boorstin drew on statistics. Others did, often heavily, including UNESCO, which produced a series of reports on mass communication, the first of them in 1954, *Newspaper Trends 1928–1951*. These reports demonstrated that Canada was by far the main supplier of newsprint both before and after the war and that, among the 120 countries that were consuming more than fifty tons of newsprint in 1951, the United Kingdom was consuming less in 1951 (599,000 tons) than in 1938 (1,250,000 tons). In the same year, 1938, Political and Economic Planning, a non-partisan organization, produced the first empirical report on the British press. Three post-war British Royal Commissions, reporting in 1949, 1962 and 1977, drew useful comparisons of readership across the century. In 1920, one in two adults read a daily newspaper of any kind – it could still be considered a luxury; in 1947, twelve daily newspapers and twenty-three Sunday newspapers were being read by every ten adults.

The main intellectual shaper of the Birmingham Centre was Stuart Hall, who was to move to a professorship at the Open University. In 1971, he published a fascinating article in the second issue of *Cultural Studies* entitled 'The Social Eye of Picture Post', and in the third issue another long article called 'The Determinations of News Photographs'. Both articles threw light on the evolution of newspapers and of 'photojournalism', more highly developed in Germany before the Nazis took power than in any other country. Meanwhile, the Centre subjected entertainment to closer analysis than at any earlier time in Britain. It also traced British strains in media studies and the German origins of media research back to Max Weber (see p. 41).

In Germany, the twentieth-century Frankfurt School, Marxist in its origins and orientation, was once described by the sociologist Ralf Dahrendorf (1929–2009) as 'the unholy family of critical theory'. Yet when Theodor Adorno and Max Horkheimer, who were driven across the Atlantic in 1934, returned from the United States to Frankfurt after the Second World War, they stored their old papers in the basement and invited the young Jürgen Habermas (see p. 80) to join them. Ill at ease, Habermas moved on to Marburg and Hamburg. His first major work, *The Structural Transformation of the Public Sphere* (1962), set out his ideal of a rational informed discussion of public policy.

This was the moment when cultural studies were emerging in European universities, Italian and Dutch as well as British and German, and interest in the image (through the newspaper, television and film) and in 'history from below' was generating new approaches in scholarship. University teachers and, above all, students were being recruited in increasing numbers from hitherto socially underprivileged sections of society. There was a social convergence, therefore, that preceded the technological convergence examined in the next chapter. Nevertheless, in the United States one of the best-known and most influential pre-war researchers, Bernard Berelson (1912–79), who had made his reputation with his studies of media content, announced in the *Public Opinion Quarterly* in 1959 that communications research was 'withering away'. It was not. Years later, in the summer of 1983 one of the contributors to a special number of the *Journal of Communication* entitled 'Ferment in the Field', James W. Carey (see p. 17), asked whether the spokesmen of cultural studies would be able 'to think through a theory or a vocabulary of communications that is simultaneously a theory or vocabulary of culture'. Would they cover all the relevant questions?

French scholars had long engaged in theory by different routes, and three of them, conscious that they were writing from within an electronic society, stand out, largely because of the influence they exerted on others. They were Guy Debord (1931–94, above), Jean Baudrillard (1929–2007) and

Pierre Bourdieu (1930–2002). Debord's *Society of the Spectacle* (1967) argued, with little empirical evidence to back it, that in societies where 'modern conditions of production prevail, all life presents itself as an immense accumulation of spectacles. Everything that was directly lived has moved away into a representation.' Thus, the spectacle became the world. The observation should be contrasted with the modest remark by an American writer on television, Richard Adler, that 'the small screen severely limits the effectiveness of spectacle'.

Baudrillard, who judged McLuhan's 'the medium is the message' to be 'the key formula of the age of simulation', turned to television as the medium of 'electronic simulation', pointing to 'the dissolution of television into life [and] the dissolution of life into television'. From a different intellectual tradition, Bourdieu, in a short, highly compressed, bestselling book, *On Television* (1996), mentioned Debord only once and Baudrillard not at all. This was and is not unusual among theorists of the media, who prefer parallel play to engagement with each other. Yet the editors of the British journal *Media, Culture and Society*, launched in 1977, made a valiant effort across the years to keep British media scholarship in contact with continental theory and to find a place for young scholars.

While French university professors were beginning to discuss the media during the late 1960s with sharp differences of outlook, university students who were involved in *les événements* of 1968 in Paris were learning – like civil rights marchers in America – through experience, not research, how to use television to ensure that they were seen and heard. Inevitably, they were attacked, mainly in newspaper correspondence columns. Was it television, their critics asked, that was stirring them up and making them behave in a way that they would not have done had there been no 'Small Screen, Big World'? Protesters against the Vietnam War were soon to appear frequently on the American screen. Who were they stirring up?

There was ample debate on this question on the screen and more than ample blaming of television and, indeed, of all the media, which reached a climax when President Nixon's first vice-president, Spiro Agnew, launched a premeditated but not unpopular attack on them in 1969. Richard Nixon (1913–94) himself often used the phrase 'the press is the enemy'. Why, he asked, should the press and television set the agenda? Why should they determine the tone of argument? Politicians were elected, citizens paid taxes. What was the claim of journalists to exert power? These were questions that persisted long after 'revolting students' had passed from the centre of the stage. Indeed, they were topical at the end of the century and the beginning of the next.

How religion was affected by television had provoked a more uneasy long-term debate in America than the effects of television on politics, particularly Republican politics. Jerry Falwell, star of *The Oldtime Gospel Hour*, which claimed fifty million viewers, had for a time mobilized 'moral majority' power. And in the 1990s, televised religion, 'the electronic church', became visible in Garden Grove, California, where the Revd Robert Schuller built a huge cathedral with 10,000 windows. By then, praised by Murdoch, he was giving weekly broadcasts to an audience of millions, which stretched far beyond the United States. Religious television continued to change. No cathedral could contain it. Schuller was a less stirring and less provocative gowned figure on the screen than the eloquent but personally vulnerable Jimmy Swaggart, or the presidential hopeful Pat Robertson. The most global of televangelists, the American Billy Graham, never needed a cathedral. A football stadium would do just as well, and a raincoat just as well as an academic gown.

Debate Renewed

Whatever the style, there were persisting questions about journalists, whatever their medium, and their relationships with government and religious groups. In particular, the Vietnam War, a long war which went through different phases, was the first war to be seen, if in selective form, on home screens. Followed as it was by the domestic scandal of Watergate, it raised basic questions about the dependence of the media on official sources and the extent of press and television influence on American politics. So, too, did the later reporting of President Clinton's personal life.

Robert Manoff and Michael Schudson began the book that they edited, *Reading the News* (1986), with a discussion in different form of the three old questions raised by Harold Lasswell (see p. 6): 'Every newspaper reporter should answer the questions, What? Who? Where? When? and Why?, adding How?, and should do it in the first paragraph as early as possible.' Manoff and Schudson noted that the questions, all of which might figure in the catechism of schools of journalism, hid 'within their simplicity and their apparent commonsense a whole framework of interpretation'. The wide range of interpretation, which had little to do with technology, was explicable only in terms of values, their glossing over as well as their expression. News values remained more or less the same, but the lapse between an event and its reporting shrank.

The range of questions relating to television, some of them the same as the issues raised in relation to the press, often had little to do with technology. It is interesting to compare the structure and dynamics of television as described in 1966 in Dizard's *Television, a World View* (see p. 253) with Francis Wheen's *Television: A History*, which appeared in 1985 in conjunction with an ambitious fourteen-hour British Granada television series that broke a taboo that television should never investigate itself. The series was three years in the making and involved hundreds of interviews in Europe, America, Asia and Africa. It demonstrated that, as television had made its way around the world both to democratic and authoritarian countries, leaving only a few countries untouched, it had won new friends and made new enemies. The comment was now multicultural. Thus, the magazine *India Today* described the Indian television service in 1982 as being like 'a slack, inexorably slow and malfunctioning government department, no different from the local passport office': 'the tedium is the message'. And in the Philippines, a Jesuit priest claimed that President Ferdinand Marcos worshipped the media 'idolatrously', 'the way other people believe in God'.

A Japanese who was quoted as saying that television addiction had turned millions of his fellow countrymen into imbeciles might have taken as part of his evidence an opinion poll of 1982. When Americans and Japanese were asked what single item they would take to a desert island (of the kind mapped by Sue Lawley in Britain's radio programme *Desert Island Discs*), over 36 per cent of the Japanese chose television, while only 4 per cent of the Americans did so. At that time, 2-year-old children in Japan were, on average, watching three hours, thirty-one minutes of television a day, either alone or with their mothers.

Much of Wheen's book was devoted to particular programmes, like the long-running *Coronation Street* (1960), and to the handling of particular events by television in fact, fiction or what was called 'faction', a combination of both. Prominent among the programmes were documentaries on the events of war. From the early years of post-war television, the Cold War was always in the background, and its influence could inspire propaganda and generate entertainment.

So could the Second World War. In Britain, *Dad's Army* (1968) returned to it, as did many British programmes, a preoccupation that was disturbing to German critics. Thames Television's *World at War* (1982) was produced by Jeremy Isaacs, who was first Director of Channel 4 and a strong critic of the Glasgow Media Group's *Bad News*. The First World War had been the subject of a twenty-six-part series, organized jointly by the BBC, the Canadian Broadcasting Corporation and the Australian Broadcasting Commission. It drew on the reminiscences of more than 50,000 survivors, in a way impossible in previous centuries. A very different war, the Korean War, was the setting of a highly successful and often repeated American sitcom, *M*A*S*H* (1972), which ran to 251 episodes and did not close until 1983.

During the troubled 1960s, civil rights battles in the United States was transformed through television exposure. The assassination of Martin Luther King in 1968 was caught on the screen, but Kennedy's assassination had first to be announced in sound only – by Cronkite – before endless television pictures were released. Terrorism provided a major theme on many occasions, long before 11 September 2001, for the cinema as well as for television. So too did space. NASA's officials were uneasy at first about using television, but for political as well as televisual reasons they soon changed their mind. When John Glenn went into orbit in 1962, the world as well as the United States saw his blast-off; and seven years later the first pictures from the moon provided a prelude for what was hailed as 'the greatest show in the history of television': the Apollo XI landing. It was seen by 125 million Americans and 723 million other people around the world. This was a scientific and technological as well as a media event of the kind described by Elihu Katz and Daniel Dayan.

Fig. 21 The moon landing, 1969. The Americans tell the world they are in space. The successful Apollo project enabled Neil Armstrong to be the first human to walk on the surface of the moon. The Russian Yuri Gagarin had been the first human to orbit the earth.

Landmarks in Entertainment

Entertainment, eventually bound up inextricably with news and sport, has its own landmark events, frequently recalled on television and on film. One American programme in particular, *Dallas* (1979), 'the ultimate soap opera', has also been a subject of sociological research in many universities. Dealing dramatically with sex, wealth, power and family, irresistible in combination, it was shown, often in dubbed form, in more than ninety countries ruled by governments of all political persuasions. Meanwhile, a very different kind of British comedy programme, *Monty Python's Flying Circus* (1969), with an appeal greater even than that of the equally innovatory Goon Show on radio, also captured an international audience. It used linking animation and revelled in absurdity, just as apparent when the television series was extended into film. *Till Death Us Do Part* (1966), yet a third kind of comedy programme, British as it was in essence, inspired American and German programmes: *All in the Family* and *One Heart and One Soul*.

Entertaining was a task that crossed frontiers. In Britain the BBC did not hesitate to import entertainment programmes from the United States. And under a communist regime, Serbs, Croats, Bosnians and Slovenes watched *The Forsyte Saga*.

Education

Educating, not entertaining, remained the priority for some of the first defenders of television against charges made against it that it had an inevitable corrupting influence on society and culture and took up far more of viewers' time than they spent on any other activity. Yet there were different answers to the question. Should educating be treated as a separate task, segregated in separate channels or in separate broadcasting organizations? Japan introduced an entire NHK channel devoted to educational television in 1957. Britain took a different route and incorporated education into general programming. The idea of launching a separate educational channel had been supported by independent television companies, but had been opposed by the Pilkington Committee, and it was 'independent television', not the BBC, which initiated a television service for schools in its regular programming.

In 1964 the new Chairman of the Schools Broadcasting Council, Charles Carter, the Vice-Chancellor of Lancaster, a new university, urged, in face of much schoolteachers' opinion to the contrary, that television 'opened up opportunities' that were 'as exciting as anything since the arrival of the cheap printed book'. In the United States, the FCC reserved more than 200 television stations for educational broadcasting in 1952, but most of them lacked adequate finance and would not have been able to operate without help received from the Ford Foundation, which supported a National Education Television (NET) to produce programmes and initiated pioneering formal and informal educational schemes in Latin America, India and Africa. So, too, did the Council for Educational Television (CETO), a British organization, financed by the Nuffield Foundation.

The American situation changed when a commission set up in 1967 by the Carnegie Corporation proposed the creation of a Corporation for Public Broadcasting, and the Ford Foundation earmarked funds for a Public Broadcast Laboratory. The public broadcasting system (PBS) that resulted, with strictly limited funds, concerned itself as much with informing as with educating. It did not entirely leave out entertainment either, some of the entertainment consisting of drama imports from Britain.

Information

It was not events in the United States or in Britain, but Third World reactions to American dominance ('hegemony') in the generation and distribution of information that pushed information into the centre of international debate from the mid-1970s onwards. UNESCO, where much of the debate was concentrated, now became the forum for a North–South dialogue (a new term) in which the developed countries had the power and the developing countries a majority. This was the beginning of UNESCO's 'Second Development Decade', covered, chronologically and analytically, in Thomas McPhail's *Electronic Colonialism* (1987).

Even as early as 1959, before the beginning of the first Development Decade, UNESCO had been asked by the Economic and Social Council of the United Nations to prepare for the UN's General Assembly 'a concrete programme of action' to promote 'the development of mass media of information all over the world', but little was done until, in the changed economic circumstances of the 1970s, most of the countries which had long described themselves as 'nonaligned' placed on a broad international agenda disparities not only of wealth and of income but also of information, pre-electronic as well as electronic. This was at a time when new attitudes towards the development process were taking shape in the United States and in Britain. The word 'modernization' had fallen out of favour, particularly in the sense given to it by Daniel Lerner (see p. 5), and the word 'underdeveloped' had given way to the word 'developing'. These were the countries where radio seemed a superior medium to television.

The need for new approaches to communications issues and policies was emphasized in pioneering fashion in *Intermedia*, the journal of the International Broadcast Institute, which, significantly, changed its name to the International Institute of Communications in 1978. It explained in its leaders, with evidence culled not from the United States but from the Third World, that 'without information – without the opportunity to select, distribute and discuss information – one has no power. Those who lack information are often the most conscious of this relationship.' Most of the leaders were written by its committed Swedish director Edi Ploman, who had previously worked in Swedish radio and television, and who subsequently moved on to become a vice-rector of the United Nations University, with its headquarters in Tokyo. In the words of one of his leaders:

> [It had long] been a frustration of the developing countries that their 'window on the world' is filtered through lenses chosen and fitted by the developed, industrial countries. Their own information infrastructure – their newspapers, television and radio stations; national and international microwave links and satellites; news agencies; training institutes; film production units – are few and scattered. Few countries have UNESCO's minimum requirements of ten copies of daily newspapers, five radio sets, two television sets and two cinema seats per thousand people. A journalist in Bombay can telephone London or New York more quickly and more easily than Kabul or Dar es Salaam.

In this statement, which did not yet include the phrase 'media environment', all the media were related to each other, and UNESCO was given a special role – that of setting standards. Ironically, one country, Iran, which after the fall of the Shah in 1979 was to proclaim Islamic values in face of modernization, was for a time the main focus of studies of development and the role that the media might play in the development process. The first editorial in the journal *Communications and Development Review*, which appeared in 1977 under the editorship of Majid Tehranian, was entitled 'Communications and Development: The Changing Paradigms', and this was followed by the report of a probing interview with Daniel Lerner. A later article was headed 'Modernity and Modernization as Analytical Concepts: An Obituary'.

Turning from Tehran to Paris, where, also ironically, the man who took over after the overthrow of the Shah, the Ayatollah Khomeini, was living in exile, the 17th General Session of UNESCO in 1972, one year before the international oil crisis effectively brought the 1960s to a close, had passed a 'Declaration of Guiding Principles on the Use of Space Broadcasting for the Free Flow of Information, the Spread of Education and Greater Cultural Exchange'. The declaration asserted that cultural sovereignty and international control of the accuracy of news broadcasts were necessary. No fewer than fifty-five states accepted the declaration, and only seven, with the United States most prominent among them, were opposed. There were twenty-two abstentions, among them the Soviet Union.

The demand for 'cultural sovereignty' was a protest against 'cultural imperialism', a concept developed in the United States by academics such as the American sociologist Herbert Schiller (1919–2000), who also (in 1976) used the phrase 'cultural domination'. In Latin America, where cultural imperialism was at the centre of media and communications studies, commercial television was the most prominent target of attack. In the strong words of the Chilean delegate to a United Nations Working Group, competitive, commercial television, 'dragging down standards and offering the dregs of mass culture', constituted a 'source of concern for our educators, sociologists and statisticians and for all of us who participate in a cultural policy that seeks to ennoble rather than to degrade our people'.

Imbalanced information was a parallel complaint, gaining in weight as statisticians, among them Scandinavian communications scholars like Kaarle Nordenstreng, collected details of information 'flows'. Geographers were to play an increasing part in communications research, not only studying flow routes and comparing them with the trade routes of the past, but also exploring through what came to be called 'phenomenological' geography – the relationship between people and the world they lived in.

A landmark work was Joshua Meyrowitz's *No Sense of Place* (1985), which argued in the wake of McLuhan that electronic media affected people not primarily through their content, but by dissociating physical place and social place. 'When we communicate through telephone, radio, television, or computer, what we are physically no longer determines where and who we are socially.' Critics of 'imbalance' continued to point out, along the lines of *Bad News*, that most of the news relating to the Third World was negative. It dealt only with such subjects as disasters, political and military intrigues, scandals, shortages and famines. Complaint shifted later to an attack on direct broadcast satellites, seen as a threat to national cultural identity, and to the distribution of frequencies on the radio spectrum, still conceived of as a scarce communications resource.

The spectrum was a matter not for UNESCO but for the World Administrative Radio Conference (WARC), organized by the International Telecommunications Union (ITU), which had previously been concerned largely with technical questions. Now, communications policies came to dominate its conference agenda. This was a shift of importance in the history of the ITU, which, at a plenipotentiary meeting in Nairobi in 1982, set up an Independent Commission for Worldwide Telecommunications Development under the chairmanship of a British former diplomat, Donald Maitland. Its sixteen members included his vice-chairman, the Costa Rican Minister of Information and Telecommunications, the chairman of the Advisory Council to the Indian Prime Minister for the Planning Commission, and, from the USA, a former chairman of AT&T. The commission's report, *The Missing Link*, which appeared in 1984, showed that while there were six hundred million telephones in the world in 1982, half the world's population lived in countries that between them had fewer than ten million telephones. It went on to say that, given what it called the 'dramatic advances in the technology of telecommunications [which were then] taking place', the appropriate technology for a Third World country might enable it to 'leap frog' more developed countries in its economic development.

Telecommunications had been brought to the forefront of the argument in *The Missing Link*, which appeared eight years after UNESCO, also in Nairobi, had carried a highly contentious resolution that included what to many 'developed' countries was a notorious Article XII, which laid down that 'states are responsible for the activities in the international sphere of all mass media under their jurisdiction'. It set up a commission, headed by an Irish politician Sean McBride, who was given what he rightly described as 'the formidable task' of examining 'the totality of communications problems in modern society'. Among its members were McLuhan, the Colombian novelist Gabriel García Márquez, a well-known Japanese journalist, Michio Nagai, and the director-general of the Soviet news agency TASS.

They were agreed on the need 'to approach communications globally', but, even before they were appointed, it was clear that in Cold War conditions they had no hope of winning universal support for any recommendations that they might make. When their report, *Many Voices, One World*, appeared in 1980, their recommendations quickly passed into history. Indeed, the nonaligned countries were themselves divided after Indira Gandhi's repression of press freedom in the last phase of her long prime ministership of India between 1966 and 1977.

When UNESCO, attempting to square the circle, passed a fuller resolution in 1978 leaving out Article XII, the United States, followed by Britain, left the international organization, which never again set out to deal with the 'totality of communications problems in modern society'. The initiative in international intellectual debate now passed to academic spokesmen of 'free trade in ideas' – what the most able of them, Ithiel de Sola Pool (1917–84), a professor at the Massachusetts Institute of Technology, who favoured deregulation of all media, called in 1983 'technologies of freedom'. For Pool, who mentioned UNESCO only once en passant in his book with that title, published in that year, what the news media did, whoever owned them, was to create counterweights to established authorities. It was authoritarian governments, not traditional cultures, which were in danger. The cultures would flourish not on protection, but on a fostering of their production capabilities and on reciprocal exchange. No culture could remain isolated. This continued to be the line taken by the United States in the late 1990s in a periodical *Correspondence*, edited by the American sociologist Daniel Bell (1919–2011). In the spring of 2000 it drew on survey evidence to claim that, of 186 countries in the world, only 69 had a 'free press'.

Pool did not consider it necessary to scrutinize systematically media operations in democratic countries, nor did he dwell on global issues. He placed stress on 'electronic media as they are coming to be . . . dispersed in use and abundant in supply', allowing for 'more knowledge, easier access and freer speech than were ever enjoyed before'. Although he was in no sense a technological determinist, he hailed the demise of the typewriter and the prospect that 'not too far in the future nothing will be published in print that is not typed on a word processor or typed by a computer'. Looking ahead towards a new millennium, as futurologists had been doing since the 1960s, he estimated that by the early 1990s there would be more than 600 million telephones in the world and 680 million television sets, along with millions of computer work-stations. Pool had little to say about entertainment or the threat to local cultures from homogenized culture, although he welcomed the 'end of spectrum scarcity' and the advent of 'electronic abundance'.

The Information Society

When Pool looked forward to an age of greater media choice, with information, not entertainment or education, at the core of his thinking, the term 'information society' was in the air, as it had been in 1977 when a young American, Marc Porat, commissioned by the United States Information Agency, published a paper called 'Global Implications of the Information Society', in its first form. By then, the word 'information' had also been incorporated into the terms 'information technology' (IT), first used in management circles, and 'information theory', mathematical in content.

The new term 'information society' had a more general application. It gave form or shape to a cluster of hitherto more loosely related aspects of communication – knowledge, news, literature, entertainment – all exchanged through different media and through different media materials – paper, ink, canvas, paint, celluloid, cinema, radio, television and computers. From the 1960s onwards, all messages, public and private, verbal and visual, began to be considered as 'data', information that could be transmitted, collected and recorded, whatever their point of origin. Control of information, it was claimed, would be the essence of wealth and power in the future.

Once again, in the late twentieth century as in the sixteenth, it was the French language that became a carrier of extended and changing concepts through the words '*informatique*' and '*informatisation*', which influenced not only ways of thinking and feeling about communication, but the procedures and decisions of businessmen and the policies of governments. There was a clear link in French between these terms and computerization. Indeed, an essential French text by Simon Nora (1921–2006), Inspector-General of Finance, and Alain Minc, extolling an information society as the ultimate civilization, had immediate policy implications for the French government, and was called in English translation (1980) *The Computerization of Society*. Nora had written it as a report for the then President of France, Giscard d'Estaing, with the title *L'Informatisation de la société*.

There were other forces, however, behind such changes in language. In the biological sciences, the discovery of DNA as the carrier of genetic information gave a new impulse to what was called an 'information paradigm'. Information was considered the organizing principle of life itself. The word 'paradigm' itself was an unfamiliar word that had rapidly passed into general language. This followed the immense success of *The Structure of Scientific Revolutions* by the American philosopher of science Thomas S. Kuhn (1922– 96), which sold nearly 600,000 copies between its first publication in 1962 and 1984, the English novelist George Orwell's year of communications doom. In fact, 1984 was a formative year, when the communications pattern, responding in particular to new technology, proved to be very different from that which Orwell had sketched fifty years earlier.

A different strand, more central to the emergence of the concept of an information society, was bound up with the development not of biology or of information technology, but of economics and sociology (with politics seldom absent). Daniel Bell was aware of the work of the Austrian-American economist Fritz Machlup (1902–83) when he published *The Coming of Post-Industrial Society: A Venture in Social Forecasting* (1974), in which he examined the way in which the services sector of the economy was becoming more important than the manufacturing sector. He employed the prefix 'post', which was to become increasingly fashionable, in his title.

Bell's analysis of the social implications of structural change, which paid little attention to the continuities within corporative capitalism, whatever the dominant technology might be, were challenging, as was his account of the social framework of what he too called the 'information society'. Not surprisingly, his analysis led to criticism from Marxists like Herbert Schiller, who published in 1981 *Who Knows: Information in the Age of the Fortune 500*, focusing on the financial pillars of the new society. Meanwhile, Machlup, who had first introduced the theory of a 'knowledge economy' in his book *The Production and Distribution of Knowledge* (1962) demonstrated that in the course of a century the number of workers engaged in agriculture in the United States had fallen from 40 per cent to about 4 per cent, and that the proportion of information workers was rising, as it was in Britain.

The description 'information workers', the broadest of categories, far too loosely defined and analysed, sounded far more appealing than 'service workers'. The Austrian-American Peter Drucker (1909–2005), the most successful and prolific of all the analysts of change, had drawn attention to their presence in 1969 in his book *The Age of Discontinuity*, the first part of which was devoted to 'the knowledge technology'. 'Learning and teaching were going to be more deeply affected by the new availability of information than other areas of human life.'

Yet for Drucker there was a considerable way to go. One large international company was already shipping computers at the rate of 1,000 a month, but there was still no equivalent in the computer field of Edison's light bulb. Such an equivalent would be an 'electronic appliance' selling for less than a television set, 'capable of being plugged in wherever there is electricity and giving immediate access to all the information needed for school work from first grade through college'. Drucker clearly saw, too, that it would give access to much else in society besides information for school use, but he had no sense of what such an 'electronic appliance' might be able to do.

The unfinished story of the development and impact of computers is told in the next chapter, which deals also with the conception of a 'digital age'. One of the most interesting of pointers to the future (in retrospect) was a small, schematic and highly motivated book, *The Information Society as Post-Industrial Society* (1980) by Yoneji Masuda (1905–95), a Japanese sociologist, working in a country which already by then was producing millions of computer microchips. It was published by the Tokyo Institute for the Information Society, which forecast that in the not-too-distant future work would be dispersed in 'electronic cottages', that the media would be 'demassified', and that human awareness would be heightened as a global flow of messages accelerated.

It is not surprising, given this vision, that another new label – 'post-industrial society' – would take over and would stick until new metaphors were coined. Masuda himself pointed to the one already mentioned when, in a brief section called 'Globalisation: The Spirit of a New Renaissance', he put the spotlight on globalism: 'Information has no natural boundaries. When global information space is formed, world-wide communications activities among citizens will cross all national boundaries.' 'As distinct from conventional geographical space, "global information space" would be space connected by information networks.'

Coexistence and Convergence

Following on chronologically after Chapter 5 – and in places overlapping with it – this chapter has shown that while technical innovation comes in 'waves' ('clusters') associated with economic trends, historical labels tend to be attached to societies according to what seems, for a variety of reasons, to be their dominant communications technology. The 'age of railways', described in Chapter 4, was one. The 'age of radio' and 'the age of television', as it has usually been called, have overlapped. The 'space age' was ushered in, as we have seen, by television. In none of the ages, some of which were thought of – at least in retrospect – as golden, has one medium eliminated another. Old and new have coexisted. The press remained a powerful force during the 1960s, and in some ways increased in importance after that date. Television, sometimes called 'the fifth estate', did not supplant radio, often dismissed when television was young as 'steam radio'. Cheaper to operate than television, it remained the dominant medium in Third World countries. The railway continued to be an important means of transportation in 'First World' countries even while – or even because – the number of automobiles increased more rapidly than ever before. Letters still went by post everywhere, although post offices in small and capital letters faced increasing financial problems. Yet, as technological advance speeded up (with occasional lags), old technologies were being challenged and, above all, their institutional framework was having to be thought out afresh.

There was a backward-looking as well as a forward-looking aspect to the historical process. Interest began to grow during the 1960s and 1970s not only in steam locomotives, refurbished trams and vintage cars, but also in the range of fears and expectations of earlier generations when what had become old technologies were new. 'Retro' was to become a favourite prefix a decade later in the United States. From the start, the word 'generation' was applied to computers as well as to people. Meanwhile, it was seldom appreciated that whatever the 'age', similar issues were raised concerning the relationship of 'ownership' of the media to 'content', of 'content' to 'structure', and of 'structure' to technology. All were bound up with 'control'. The need for information in every age has been associated with the effort to control the present and future for personal, political and economic reasons.

The next chapter in this book brings in what even at the time was thought of, and has been thought of since, as a major breakthrough in human history, the advance of digitalization. Yet its title, 'Media Convergences', at the simplest level concerns the coming together of technologies and of their capabilities during the 1960s, 1970s and 1980s. The word 'technologies' must be in the plural because there was a wide range of them and it was not clear which one would win. Convergence involves far more, however, than technology, dazzling – or intimidating – although some of the technologies were both. Inventing the future seemed to be the challenge, as it had been when Erasmus Darwin (see p. 117) wrote his verses before the end of the eighteenth century.

The two words 'information' and 'convergence', which had already been brought together in the 1960s, were to be linked increasingly often during the 1970s and 1980s. Meanwhile, just as the advent of television had stimulated historians of the media to re-examine the implications of the invention of printing, so the development of new electronic technologies, culminating in the Internet and the World Wide Web, stimulated their successors to re-examine the implications of the sequence of nineteenth-century inventions covered in previous chapters. Thus, in 1986, an American professor, James Beninger, traced back meticulously to the nineteenth century and earlier the origins of both technical and social control, some of it built-in, with feedback through new mechanical and electronic devices.

The 'governor', a pioneering mechanical device in Watt's steam engine (see p. 114), was an example of control before the advent of electricity multiplied both the number of devices and the opportunities they offered. With the Internet then at the centre of the picture, in 1998 Tom Standage wrote a book on the telegraph and its 'online pioneers' with the title *The Victorian Internet*: 'Modern Internet users', he maintained, 'are in many ways the heirs of the telegraphic tradition, which means that today we are in a unique position to understand the telegraph. And the telegraph in turn can give us a fascinating perspective on the challenges, opportunities and perils of the Internet.'

7

Media Convergences

Convergence is a useful, if overworked, word which has been used in com-munication circles for many years. It was freely employed by Ithiel de Sola Pool (see p. 270) before it became fashionable, and in 2008 it was employed by the British government in the naming of a new Convergence Think-Tank, set up to examine the implications of technological development for the media and communications industries.

From the 1980s onwards, it had been applied most commonly to the development of digital technology, the integration of text, numbers, images and sound, different elements in the media which had largely been considered separately in the previous periods of history covered in this book. Digitalization, or digitization, with its origins in nineteenth-century mathematics, has been a continuing and unfinished process which started with computers and what was described during the 1970s as 'a marriage made in heaven' between computers, partners in other marriages also, and telecommunications.

Dictionary definitions of 'communication' itself, in the singular and without the prefix 'tele', had changed substantially during the previous twenty-five years. In 1955, the *Oxford English Dictionary* defined it generally as (1) 'the action of communicating, now rarely of material things' and (2) 'the imparting, conveying or exchange of ideas, knowledge etc. whether by speech or writing or signs'. By the time a supplement to the *Dictionary* appeared in 1972, however, communication was described specifically as 'the science or process of conveying information, especially by means of electronic or mechanical techniques'. The difference was enormous.

The word 'convergence', which was not given a separate entry in the 1972 supplement, was subsequently applied to organizations as well as to processes, particularly the coming together of the media industries and the telecommunications industries, and it also had broader uses in relation to whole societies and cultures, including British society and culture. D. L. LeMahieu, examining the concept of a common culture in Britain and the limits to it in an illuminating book *A Culture for Democracy* (1988), included a chapter called 'Sight and Sound: Studies in Convergence', while Daniel Boorstin, in his fascinating but now dated book *The Republic of Technology* (1978), used it in the most general sense possible – 'the tendency for everything to become more like everything else'.

As multiple media were being brought together and society became more 'mobile' through travel and migration, the favourite term that was to make its way into the convergence rhetoric of the 1990s was 'highway'. Different societies and cultures which started their historical journeys separately were now said to be travelling together on the same 'information superhighway'. As early as 1972, an American freelance journalist, Ralph Lee Smith, saw innovations such as cable television (above) as a way of providing an 'electronic communications highway' for 'a wired nation' along which all kinds of services could be provided for home, office and factory.

During the 1960s the development of technologies to provide many such services was still at an experimental stage, although theory was well advanced. Even during the 1980s there was still no certainty as to which technologies would be successful. It was only after 1993 that the term 'super-highway' really took off, after a new American president and vice-president, Bill Clinton and Al Gore, had introduced it into politics, within the context of the Internet.

Computers

Computers must come first in any historical survey of converging media, for once they had ceased to be thought of merely as calculating machines or as useful office adjuncts – and that was not until the early 1970s – they enabled all kinds of services, not only communications services, to take on new shapes. In order to do so, however, computers had to become smaller and cheaper. And in the achievement of that task, the United States, not Britain – or Europe – dominated the course of events.

On both sides of the Atlantic, the first computers had been huge, and were designed for military purposes. As in earlier history, the stimulus was war, not profit, although profits could be made by ingenious entrepreneurs. Academics were in the forefront of their development. Colossus, ENIAC and, after the Second World War, Manchester University's one-tonne 'Small Scale Experimental Machine', nicknamed 'the Baby' (1948), MANIAC (1952) and UNIVAC (1953), were giant, some said monster, machines, dependent on thousands of not always reliable valves, still called in America vacuum tubes (see p. 177). In 1950 they were correctly described by the brilliant British computer pioneer Alan Turing (1912–54) as 'universal machines'

Fig. 22 The Colossus electronic code-breaker was used at Bletchley Park, Buckinghamshire, to help Britain and its allies win the Second World War. It used 1,500 valves. Meanwhile, the University of Pennsylvania developed ENIAC (Electronic Numerator Integrator and Computer) between 1942 and 1946. The Soviet Union developed MLSM.

which rendered it 'unnecessary to design various new machines to do various computing processes'.

Transistors

The word 'computer' first meant not a machine but the person who computed: the word typewriter had a similar history. The design of what we would now call computers changed radically, however, after the replacement of valves by transistors. In the first phase of their development, transistors were even less reliable than valves, but in the long run they made possible a necessary revolution in scale. Computers could become 'lap tops' and they could become light enough to be carried around by their users.

The making of the first transistors depended on advances in semiconductor physics following team experiments in the Bell Laboratories and elsewhere. John Bardeen and Walter Brattain, who became Nobel prize-winners in 1950, had devised solid state amplifying devices two years earlier, made out of germanium and looking like two cat's whisker detectors. The commercial demand for them was small at first, and it was not until 1959 that sales of transistors (the first customers for them were makers of hearing aids) exceeded those of valves. The unfamiliar name 'transistor', which their devisers gave to them, was initially adopted by the public to refer not to the devices themselves, but to the small battery-driven portable radios incorporating them. These were first marketed seven years later. Bardeen was appalled that the users' main fare was rock music. Like Edison before him, he was uninterested in the 'trivial'.

Miniaturization

Confidence in the new technology did not grow at once even after it became known that an engineer working for Texas Instruments, Jack Kilby, had applied for a patent in 1959 for the integrated circuit, 'a body of semi-conductor material . . . wherein all the components of the electronic circuit are completely integrated': Kilby had written in his log book in July 1958 that 'extreme miniaturization of many electrical circuits could be achieved by making resistors, capacitors and transistors and diodes on a single slice of silicon'. A patent for miniaturization had already been granted to Robert Noyce (1927–90), one of the founders of Fairchild and later (1968) of Intel, who wrote perhaps the best known of early articles about the significance of microelectronics, using the word 'revolution' to describe it, in a special issue of *Scientific American* in 1977. The first full-length feature on the subject had appeared in *Fortune* magazine two years earlier. This and other business magazines are good sources for the historian, although their predictions have to be read critically.

David Nye, author of *Electrifying America* (1990), has rightly described technological prediction as a 'Promethean problem'. With the advent of the integrated circuit, a complete circuit that is manufactured in a single package, a silicon chip, one-sixth by one-eighth of an inch, containing 2,250 miniaturized transistors, now had the same power as ENIAC, which had taken up an entire room. With in-built logic circuits, the new chip made possible the development of computers for all kinds of purpose. Their minuscule central processing units took instructions from specially written ROMS (read-only memories). Nonetheless, their first uses proved strictly limited. In 1963, only 10 per cent of circuits on sale were integrated circuits. When thousands of circuit elements were integrated on one tiny chip, the integration was said to be large scale. The logic system employed rested on algebra set out by the British mathematician George Boole almost a century before the first digital electronic computer was built.

The microprocessor, which was subsequently to be described as the heart of the computer, was eventually devised by Marcian (Ted) Hoff in 1971. It was first applied, as an eighteenth-century French mechanical invention might have been, in a clock that could sound like a piano. Nevertheless, manufactured and marketed by Intel, it made possible not only an enormous increase in computer power but also a decentralization in its use. Intel's RAM (random-access memory) chip, introduced in 1970, substantially reduced the cost of the memory component, and from now on there were to be computers of all sizes and 'generations': the Japanese, in particular, warmed to the concept of generations of things.

Noyce, who had a way with words as well as the ability to invent things, compared the purpose of the minuscule microprocessor with that of the automobile: it was 'the simplest way to get from here to there'. Hundreds of thousands of components could be carried on a microprocessor, and as their versatility became recognized, a stimulus was given to digital over analogue technology in all the media which were soon to become their main users. Print, film, recording, radio and television and all forms of telecommunications were now being thought of increasingly as part of one complex. Yet different media benefited in different ways. What was called 'digital compression' – elimination of data, including the audio-data, from a file in order to save space – was of particular value in relation to radio and television.

In 1964 Gordon Moore, a chemist who was another co-founder of Intel and its first president, had formulated what came to be called Moore's Law, which was to hold true during the 1960s and 1970s, that the number of transistors that could be placed on a single chip would double every eighteen months. Moore, like Teal, Kilby, Hoff and bevies of other semi-conductor physicists, was working in what had recently been fruit groves in Silicon Valley, California, an area that was now beginning to stand out on a new global communications map as prominently as the Eiffel Tower, London's Broadcasting House, the Bell Laboratories or – closer to home – Hollywood, which had itself been built on orange groves.

It was of major significance in the history of communications that it was new businesses – less hierarchical, more innovative, more informally structured and more 'bottom-up' than established businesses – that pointed the way forward in computer development, a development that, as we have seen, was always slower on the demand than on the supply side. During the first phase of computer history, IBM, the International Business Machines

Company, had a huge business advantage. The product of a 1924 merger, which included the successor to the digital punched-card Tabulating Machine Company, founded by Herman Hollerith in 1896, it had a distinctive corporate culture which served it well in dealing both with governments and with big companies. Nonetheless, its products belonged to what one historian of the media, Brian Winston, looking back for comparison to the early years of printing, called 'the incunabula period' in the history of the computer. When this ended, IBM was marketing no fewer than seven separate lines of computers, but none of them pointed forward to what the microprocessor made possible – the personal computer.

Japan

There was from the start a marked divergence between American and British computer history, with Japan playing an increasing part in the international scenario. The first computers in the world to be built and marketed commercially, the Manchester Mark Is in 1950, were British, but although their manufacturers, the Ferranti Electronics Company, went on to build a large Atlas computer which everywhere attracted great interest, the company did not have access to the massive American military, naval and space establishment identified by President Eisenhower as 'a military-industrial complex'. Meanwhile, Japan, unburdened by the costs of such an expensive complex, became not only a producer of microchips but a major player in the whole communications game, acquiring virtual monopoly rights in the production of consumer, not military, products, including tape recorders and VCRs.

An interesting survey of Japanese involvement in microelectronics, published in 1985, identified six periods in Japanese technology after the imperial restoration of 1868. The fourth of them, from 1955 to 1964, was that of the post-Korean War economic boom: near its beginning, a governmental Science and Technology Agency was set up in 1956. The sixth period, from 1975 to 1985, saw a further advance, with the country now ready 'to counter US initiatives'. There was more than a touch of pride in the comparative chronology. 'The Japanese entry into the field of computer research was not late by world standards', the survey stated, 'and much [had] depended on the cooperation of American computer manufacturers, notably IBM.'

The advent of transistors had led to the production in 1964 of a transistorized television set by Sony, a new company. It was Sony that introduced the Walkman, a personal, portable stereo, which transformed the way of listening to recorded music. Personal mobility, walking on the street as well as riding in an automobile, was to influence the direction of much future technological development, notably the mobile phone. There was easy personal access to 'pop music' wherever you went. The fact that most of the pop music was American was an example of unplanned international collaboration. Its celebrity providers appeared in person in concerts planned in several continents.

An American paper of 1977 entitled 'Communications for a Mobile Society' referred to 'long commutations between residence and work place within expanding metropolitan areas' inside the United States, 'a large amount of intercity travel using an advanced highway system' and 'a high degree of dependence on trucks to transport goods'. There were approximately 105 million automobiles and 25 million trucks and buses, most of them equipped with 'standard radio receiving units for entertainment services'. The paper referred to the 'cellular system', which increased mobile communication capacity, to FM cellular technology and to the use of 'narrow band digitized voice systems'. 'Mobile phones' had not then begun to be promoted vigorously – although there were 100,000 of them in use – but Citizens' Band radio had proved so popular that nearly a million people had applied to the FCC for CB licences in January 1977. For the author of the paper, Raymond Bowers, 'the growing use of CB had implications that extended beyond the domain of the service itself'.

Among the 'social and cultural factors supporting technological development' in Japan, the Japanese survey concluded, were 'a society based on equality', 'specialized technology in small and medium-sized companies', 'a tradition of respect for human relations' and, not least, 'cultural respect for technology', evident in the late nineteenth century in the early introduction of the telephone (1890) and the telegraph (1893) (note the order). 'Skill at miniaturization' came last in the list drawn up by the Japanese National Institute for Research Advancement (NIRA). The factors identified by NIRA operated within a Pacific context which was then being favourably compared with that of Europe. NIRA added to its list the development between 1965 and 1973 of a substantial Japanese automobile industry, rapidly global in scale, which was to prove highly competitive with the American and European automobile industries. What has happened in Japan since the beginning of the twenty-first century makes this analysis look incomplete and dated.

Even on the supply side the history of the evolution of the computer cannot be told simply chapter by chapter, step by step, or even 'page' by 'page', without gross oversimplification. Like the early history of the evolution of the railway, the history of computerization encompassed different features – design, memory, language, logic circuitry, software – and different new devices, like the modem (modulator/demodulator), necessary for transmitting computer data over telephone lines, and the mouse, an input device to control a pointer on a computer screen. Different people and places played their part in the story over different periods of time. It was a story of evolution, not of revolution, the word used by Noyce, but Noyce himself was right to insist that the history was not 'linear'. Design was always crucial, as everyone involved in any computing business, old or new, recognized.

The beginnings of 'memory' went back to the 1940s, even before MIT's Jay Forrester started working on project 'Whirlwind', concerned with the stability of aircraft. It was Forrester who secured the incorporation in computers of magnetic core memory in 1953. Programme languages had a shorter and more complex history; it was John Backus, working in IBM, who developed in 1957 a new 'internal program' computer language, FORTRAN (formula translating system). The first of many such languages, PLANKALKU had been devised by a German engineer, Konrad Zuse, who has largely been forgotten. Joseph Licklider, a psychologist at MIT, author of a seminal article of 1960 on 'ManComputer Symbiosis', has not. He became head of the Information Processing Technology Office (IPTO) at the Department of Defense's Advanced Research Projects Administration, ARPANET (see p. 310).

Licklider's vision of 'human brains and computer machines . . . coupled . . . tightly' was shared by a group of computer pioneers employed at the Xerox Palo Alto Laboratory, founded in 1970 by another psychologist, Bob Taylor, and led by Alan Kay. It was they who developed the mouse, originally called 'an X–Y position indicator for a display system'. Xerox, concerned exclusively in its daily operations with copying, did not choose to exploit these pioneering efforts commercially: its ideas were taken up by other companies, including Apple and Microsoft. Meanwhile, Douglas Engelbart, a wartime radar specialist, had invented the phrase 'intelligence amplification', and in 1962 he set out a 'conceptual framework' for networked computing. He used a 'tool kit', as he called it, to demonstrate his oNLine System (NLS) in San Francisco in 1968.

It is difficult to do justice to the many software providers whose numbers multiplied after the invention of the microprocessor, keenly aware that they represented the 'creative side' of the new technology. They gave a new meaning to the word 'software' itself, a word already in use – the opposite of hardware. No computer could function without some kind of programming software. As Reed Hundt, President Clinton's first Chairman of the

FCC, was to put it, without software programmers, computers would sit, 'like inert creatures, awaiting the Creator's life'. A quick way of catching the excitement of creation is to turn to some of the advertisements in the special number of the *Scientific American* on microelectronics in which Noyes wrote his pioneering article. Texas Instruments advertised 'the new generation of programmable calculators with revolutionary solid state software in a plug-in master library'; Apple Computer Inc showed pictures of a 'home computer that's ready to work, play and grow with you'.

To think in terms of precise chronological landmarks in the history of computing may be misleading. Whereas in Cold War conditions, military, naval and space orders responded to public events, market processes, continually changing, cannot be explained in the same way.

Even before the great increases in sales of personal and business computers, it was already beginning to be recognized before the end of the 1970s that communications history, into which media history was now being slotted, had entered a new age. Computers were now serving not only as business instruments, but as 'the mainspring of a whole range of media activities', stimulating or shocking the imagination, particularly in the United States, as locomotives had done in nineteenth-century Britain. Sometimes computerization was affecting traditional media, not least print. The term 'electronic book' was coined by Andy Van Dam, who had founded a company in Rhode Island called Electronic Book Technology. Meanwhile, traditional books, magazines and newspapers were increasingly being edited, designed, printed and distributed according to computer routines.

The PC

The pace of development depended not only on advances in technological knowledge, but on entrepreneurial drive within an always changing economic climate. The greatest technological advance was the introduction of the personal computer. Yet in a collection of essays published in Britain in 1979 called *From Television to Home Computer*, this was picked out as only one in a range of gadgets in consumer electronics, with video-cassette recorders (VCRs) being dealt with before PCs. Many of the gadgets were being dismissed as 'vanilla paraphernalia'. Yet 'smart', a very different adjective from 'vanilla', was soon to be applied to things more than to people, to everything from cards to houses. The author of the essay on the personal computer in the 1979 collection found it necessary to strike a reassuring rather than an excited note: owning a personal computer, which could cost as little as a cheap colour TV, did not mean that you had to know all about them to benefit from it. A personal computer – and one of the first was called 'The Pet' – was as 'simple to set up as a hi-fi system, if not simpler'. 'Just as when you buy a hi-fi system it is worth looking for reputable manufacturers and dealers.' The industry was growing fast, and 'your knowledge as a user' would grow too.

It is instructive to compare this view from the home with views from the laboratory or from the library, or, above all, from the office workplace, where 'word processing' became a major computerized activity, quickly making the typewriter, by that time a highly sophisticated object, obsolete. Yet word processing, with debatable effects on the content and style of writing, was often conceived of as part of the same complex as fax, originally a spin-off from telegraphy, not as part of a computerized technological complex. William Olsen, one of the first businessmen to put a mini-computer, the PDP8, on the market (in 1963) looked to educational users as the most promising clients at the time. Still newer companies had groups of computer enthusiasts in mind. An Amstrad range was launched in 1984.

The first computer shop was opened in Los Angeles in July 1975, and the first home computing magazine, *Byte*, appeared a month later. 'Byte' and 'bits' went together, and in 1973 Anthony Smith was to publish a book of essays called *From Books to Bytes*. The word 'bit', which was first 'concatenated' in 1946 by John Stukey, a Princeton statistician, had no literary connotations. It was an abbreviation of 'binary digit', the smallest unit of digitalized information. Nevertheless, from the start, one of the successes of the Internet was to be the selling by Amazon of millions of books, new and old. For several years, its founder, Jeff Bezos, could do no wrong. His senior editor, James Marcus, moved from New York to Seattle to join him and described his experiences in *Amazonia: Five Years at the Epicentre of the Dot.Com Juggernaut* (2004).

Cornucopia

Cornucopia – abundance – a word traditionally applied to products and to resources, was quickly applied to the electronic media which had been restrained in their early history by a scarcity of wavelengths. What Anthony Smith called 'the comfortable logic of scarcity', going back to the beginnings of broadcasting, was abandoned. As new communications technologies multiplied, they made possible greater individual choice of what to see and hear – and of when to see and hear it. Whether that choice would either be 'genuine' or 'beneficial' was a matter for argument as listeners and viewers alike came to be thought of as 'customers'. Would not more media 'channels' provide more and more of 'the same'? For Smith, choice was the 'chimera of the age'. New 'devices', some extensions of old ones, were repudiating the notions both of a great audience and a of common culture.

With cornucopia some established media institutions had to confront difficult circumstances which were sometimes called crises. The press itself was often deemed to be in 'crisis' – on both sides of the Atlantic – and in the United States it was feared that the press might go 'the same way as the rail-road'. Yet it was no more on its way out there than it was in Britain, where there was fierce trade union resistance to technological change affecting both printers and journalists. Another even older institution committed to universal service, the Post Office, faced more difficult technical and financial problems. As early as 1970 a presidential commission reported that 'the United States Post Office faces a crisis. Each year it slips behind the rest of the economy in service, in efficiency and in meeting its responsibilities as an employer. Each year it operates at a huge financial loss.'

Broadcasting

The institutional framework within which broadcast programmes were produced and distributed, whether by public broadcasting agencies, which had to face up to new forms of competition, or in the United States by the big television networks, was not in crisis but was under constant scrutiny. Cable, treated by the networks as a competitor, held out the 'promise of convenience, entertainment in abundance and many other remarkable uses of the cathode ray tube'; but, like satellites, it raised fundamental questions of 'public interest'. Should it be treated differently from radio and television? The Supreme Court was never sure, although some Supreme Court judges were. Examining options, another favourite word in any scrutiny, many Americans believed that the prospect of further abundance, even superabundance, was an incentive to deregulation, another of the key words of the period. Competition, even if Darwinian, would usher in a new age of communications. This scenario seemed promising to most commentators in the United States, including Neil Hickey, a frequent contributor to *TV Guide*, an invaluable source for historians.

The thought of a *Götterdämmerung* for the networks appealed to Hickey: 'It is certain that today's 20-year-olds will enjoy a far saner, more multifarious communications environment than anything we know today. . . . The public will be addressed, at last, in all its variety, potentiality and dignity rather than as an immense herd of dim-witted sheep to be delivered to the highest bidder.' Although this hope was misplaced, optimism was not confined to the United States. In London, *The Economist* could describe in 1982 a Cabinet decision to wire Britain with fibre optics as offering 'as much potential for Britain as it moves into the next century as laying the railway network did in the last'.

The first Thatcher government was then in power and as much committed to competition as Reagan's United States. Its thinking was strongly influenced by the report of an Information Technology Advisory Panel (none of its members had broadcasting experience) on 'Cable Systems' handed to it late in 1981. The panel, of course, saw no need for public funding of cable enterprise. Nor did the government of the United States. Nevertheless, governments, however much they might be committed to deregulation, found it difficult to stay out of the scenario. In Britain, where transportation was becoming a topical issue in Parliament, much of the domestic infrastructure supporting the media system was and remained Victorian, as the press was always quick to point out. There was scope for immediate disaster as well as for long-term crisis.

Debating Change

The technological and cultural context continued to change and was the subject of many press articles, political pamphlets and books (with the book trade itself often being described as 'in crisis'). In 1983, when a new gallery of communications was opened in London's Science Museum, Eryl Davies wrote an informative brochure, *Telecommunications: A Technology for Change*, which began with telephones and ended with radio towers and television dish aerials. He included sections on laser links as well as satellites, stressing the possibilities of 'far more capacity' or 'bandwidth'. 'When every source of information is reduced before transmission to a stream of digital information just like computer data,' he concluded, 'there is no reason why all information should not share the same highways and exchanges.'

Similar points had been made in two revealing collections of papers, published in 1976 and 1979. The first of them was *New Perspectives in International Communications*, published by the East–West Communication Institute in Honolulu. The second collection was *Communications for Tomorrow*, edited by Glen Robinson and published under Aspen auspices.

These were only two collections out of an unprecedentedly huge assembly of writings on media themes, many of the best of which are to be found in topical pieces in the magazine *Intermedia*, which ran a series of special surveys, covering a very wide range of countries, on subjects like

high-definition television, the frequency spectrum and teletext. It was particularly informative on the 'Arab world' and on Japan.

Global Communications

By the end of the twentieth century, China was moving actively into a controlled world of communications, not only as a customer in the market, but
as a player. In 1976, television, which had previously been largely an urban
medium, had been converted into a national network linking a central
product unit in Beijing with 20 provinces or municipalities throughout
China, which were capable of relaying signals to local stations. India too
was an active player. In 1976, All India Radio (AIR) lost its monopoly over
radio and television and a new broadcasting organization, Door Dashan,
was set up to manage television separately. At that time, there were only
57,000 television licences. The two bodies were to have equal status and
both were to report to the Minister of Information and Broadcasting. The
new director-general of Door Dashan had previously been deputy director-
general of AIR and had been involved in the preparations and management
of SITE (the Satellite Instructional Television Experiment).

The Robinson volume, *Communications for Tomorrow*, emphasized the plurality of different technologies rather than their convergence. As Robinson
himself put it:

> The heart of communications policy issues is a scheme of social control of the struc-
> ture and performance of communication industries: common carriers, specialized
> common carriers, value-added networks, satellite facilities and services, telecommuni-
> cations equipment, television and radio broadcasting, cable TV, pay TV, citizens band
> mobile radio etc.

The 'etc.' was significant.

Institutions

So too were the institutional implications, not only for those concerned
with broadcasting. The biggest of them was AT&T, the gross revenues of
which in 1977 surpassed the gross national product of 118 of the 145-
member nation-states of the United Nations; and its break-up, on 1 January
1984, in the middle of a decade of continuous change, followed the biggest
anti-Trust case in American history. As early as November 1974 *Businessweek*
had complained that the regulating process was no longer able to contain
AT&T's power. That was the month when the law case *United States v. AT&T*
(with AT&T, Western Electric and Bell Labs as defendants), which was to

drag on for a decade, was filed in the District of Columbia federal district court. In 1985, the 'Bell system', which under different names had evolved over more than a century, came to an abrupt end. The AT&T chairman described the reorganization of 1984 as 'the most complex restructuring job in any business anywhere'.

A detailed study of the case and its outcome suggests that few people before the late 1970s saw 'the extraordinary ways in which the technologies would soon converge'. It was their plurality that stood out then, as it did for Robinson, and because of the plurality a sense that a host of separate options would have to be considered and decided upon not only by the various players in the communications game, as it was often thought of, but by thousands of users who would often find bewildering the choices (this time in the plural) that they could now make.

Communications about Communications

Users now had available to them a greatly extended range of sometimes highly specialized periodicals that offered them advice and some users became players themselves. As John Howkins, then editor of *Intermedia*, put it in 1979: 'Every few days a new publication appears, or an old one is relaunched, to report on the ever growing business of communications.' Meanwhile, the business pages of newspapers were increasingly devoted to commenting on communications technologies, and with them came communications supplements. Like sports supplements, they employed a common language of discourse whatever the language of the news pages, which itself were changing.

There were some people who, for occupational reasons, felt it necessary to follow events carefully at a less media-dominated level. Thus, in Canada in 1985, John Black was examining what was happening to communications neither from a law court, a laboratory, nor a newspaper office, but from one of the oldest of communications centres, a library, that of the University of Guelph in Canada. Black clumped existing new technologies under nine headings: satellites, laser-based transmission, fibre optics, microwave digital terminal systems, local area networks, other broadband links (CATV, community antenna television, for example), extended uses of existing telephone networks, cellular radio (initially for voice; in the future for data and much else as well) and new 'off-line' distribution devices. Black was among the best informed of those librarians who, like the most forward-looking of museum directors, were confronting the new technologies in a pioneering, if controversial, way. Like all other commentators, he recognized that it was developments in microelectronics and, as a result, 'vastly increased computer power' that had made possible most of the changes realized by that date.

For many computer users – and not all of them turned expectantly to the business pages of the press – it was video games that turned them towards the computer. There was no reference to games, however, in *Daedalus*, the journal of the American Academy of Arts and Sciences, in a number published in winter 1992, which had the title 'A New Era in Computation'.

Games

None of the writers of the learned articles in *Daedalus*, noted that, as in the case of the telephone, there was a play element in the early development of inventions. More important than books – or education – in the early history of personal computers was entertainment, directly in the line of vision of entrepreneurs such as Nicholas Bushnell, one of the developers of the video game, who in 1974 began selling a microprocessor-driven toy called Pong: this could be attached to a television set. By 1980, his company, Atari, was retailing $100 million of video games and simple home computers.

Adults as well as children were to become keen players of computer games, such as Space War, said to have been created by an MIT student of the 1960s; and Doom, in the early 1990s one of the first games to use 3-D. There were marketing reasons for concentrating on children and young adults, as there had been in the film industry. It had been said a generation earlier that 'the child born at the same time as broadcasting takes it so much for granted that he cannot think of a previous age. He is apt to think of it as our days.' And the same was true of children born at the same time as the first computer game. Nevertheless, not all children were actively responsive to new technologies, and geniuses – such as a Dutch boy, Wouter Couzijn, reported in *The Times* in 1996 – were exceptional. Couzijn constructed a walking, talking, self-locating robot, built from yellow Lego pieces but with a microcomputer system installed. At the age of 13 he had built his own laptop computer with twelve parallel processors that could run simultaneously or share one task between them. The press and television like to publicize prodigies, including young computer hackers; they also came to devote critical attention to video games. The relative 'prioritizing' (a new word) within the household between television sets and personal computers took time to work itself out and economics (pricing) was as important as technology.

Games, however technically sophisticated – and by the 1990s they were only one item in computer advance – had been described in a BBC publication, *Television in the Eighties: The Total Equation* (1982), as 'the natural descendants of the electronic machines in the amusement arcades', which themselves had a long pedigree. But it was their role in the home, where they supplanted other games, that was to prove different. By 1983, video games were being played on the television screen in fifteen million American homes, only one in fifteen of which possessed a personal computer. Ball games with sound effects and onscreen scoring become immediately popular, and the microprocessor, making them cheaper and changeable, extended the genre. Violence was always as familiar an ingredient as sport. Given the increasingly highly organized 'leisure market', in which the media were involved either directly or through mergers, it was inevitable that business should seek new opportunities. Bushnell sold his Atari company to Warner Communications.

There was a characteristically bewildered argument, however, particularly in Britain, about the likely effects of video game-playing, particularly on children. 'Violent' was not the strongest adjective to be applied to many of them: 'vile' was common. *Video Fever* was the title of a paperback by C. Beamer, published in 1982, which had as its subtitle *Entertainment, Education, Addiction*. The book, both practical and speculative, is particularly interesting historically because of the contrast between its two brief appendices. The first, 'A Brief History of Video Games', was too brief to be of much value. The second, 'How the Games Work', which dealt with the underlying technology, was written clearly and concisely, far more so than most early personal computer manuals, which were considered 'consumer unfriendly'. The chapter in the main text which summed up value questions was called 'Family Activities: A Fresh Look'.

The PC Explosion

Radio Electronics in July 1974 introduced a computer along with a manual under the heading 'Your Personal Minicomputer', while *Popular Electronics* in January 1975 advertised a new product of its own as 'The World's First Minicomputer Kit to Rival Commercial Models'. The first commercial model to succeed became available in July 1976 when Steve Wozniak, who had worked for Bushnell, and Steve Jobs, both natives of Silicon Valley, launched the factory-assembled Apple I, which sold initially to computer enthusiasts in local clubs. In the same year Apple II was launched with the capability to carry out a variety of tasks. One of its backers was Mike Markutta, formerly Intel's marketing manager, who had left Intel a millionaire at the age of 32. Jobs was 22.

Apple Macintosh, showing an apple in its advertisements, became a public company, maverick by instinct, valued in 1980 at $1.2 billion. In 1984 it launched one of the most remarkable advertisements of all time – a television commercial, '1984', which was, in fact, broadcast only once during the Superbowl game. Apple was reluctant to use it, but it had cost $500,000 to make, and it cost $600,000 to put on the screen. The viewer saw first a tubular tunnel in which minute human figures were marching. They were prisoners, wearing heavy, thick-soled boots. They had been 'mind-washed' by an Orwellian Big Brother. The viewer saw the process and, as part of it, a beautiful blonde girl who represented resistance.

There were many layers of meaning in this ad (which can still be seen on YouTube) which placed it in the middle of a cultural context brilliantly examined by Asa Berger in *Manufacturing Desire* (1996). In commercial terms, Big Brother was IBM, and the prisoners were either IBM employees or the American public. The blonde image was that of Apple. The contrast was binary, and the presentation, directed by Ridley Scott, suggested an art form rather than a commercial. There was one brief verbal 'announcement' to make: 'On January 24th, Apple Computers will introduce Macintosh and you will see why 1984 won't be like 1984.'

Virtual Reality

Apple was to retain its mystique as it grew, but, ironically, it was the established firm, IBM, slow to develop personal computers, which had applied the adjective 'virtual' to 'reality' during the late 1960s, when it began to refer to nonphysical links between processes and machines, and which in 1983 had announced a Virtual Universe Operation System, OS/VU, incorporating in its announcement the words 'planetary system' and 'galaxies'. Also in 1983, 31-year-old Jaron Lanier had talked of virtual reality when working on new approaches to computer use; and in 1983 his company (VPL Research) produced a range of virtual reality product accessories or 'tools', far removed from the range of IBM. Lanier had been in the video games business. One of his colleagues came from NASA. There was a close association, therefore, between the exploration of outer space and what came to be called inner space.

Microsoft

It was left to a small firm, Microsoft, to which IBM had turned in 1980, to provide an operating system. Within three years – back to the fateful

1984 – 40 per cent of all personal computers were running Microsoft programmes. When, two years later, Microsoft became a public company, Bill Gates, 19 years old when he founded it, became an instant millionaire. It was obvious by then, when there were fewer than a million computers in use worldwide, many of them incompatible, all of them quickly becoming obsolete, that software was the key to increased use of all computers, small and big, and Microsoft quickly became the biggest supplier. Its Windows operation was by then on sale around the world. While Microsoft dominated the market, there were early competitors, notably Netscape, whose initiator Marc Andreessen had developed 'Mosaic' browsing software while he was an undergraduate. When Gates announced in 1995 that Microsoft was 'hard core about the Internet' and that it was introducing an Internet Information Server, Internet Explorer, Netscape's Navigator was already in production.

Convergence

Three years before this announcement was made, in October 1992, after huge political and social changes had taken place in the world – and there had been many legal wrangles in the computer market – London's *Financial Times* produced a survey of 'Computers and Communications', which began by acclaiming 'the slow but inevitable convergence of computing and telecommunications' (note the adjectives used as well as the nouns), adding that the convergence would provide the 'motive force' for 'an implosion of new information processing practices and technologies'.

Five Japanese businesses were then in the world's top ten producers of microchips, with Toshiba and Hitachi second and third. The established European multiproduct firm Philips, with its headquarters in the Netherlands, came tenth, and South Korea had already entered the picture. Japan had become a leader too in the video games industry. 'Nintendo successes pile up' was one American headline in 2001.

An earlier development was compact discs with memory, which were capable of storing for home replay the content not only of newspaper files, but of whole encyclopaedias. Games could be played on them too. At first, they had limited capacity for showing film, but they revolutionized the transmission and distribution of music, classical and pop. DVDs (digital video versatile discs) were soon to be marketed with six times the amount of storage of a CD-Rom. Price, as always, was a key factor in marketing. So, too, as always, was advertising. In 1992, however, there was less optimism about the saleability of the whole range of computerized products than there had been two years before and there was to be later. The computer industry was in flux, like many other industries, in a brief period of economic depression following a dramatic Wall Street crash in 1987. New technologies were cutting profit margins as well as costs, and while prices plummeted, structural unemployment reached peak figures. Nonetheless, optimism about the long term seemed justified as talk moved to 'interactivity' and 'networking'.

The change in mood was obvious ten years later when Peter Schwartz and Peter Leyden, in a brief 'History of the Future, 1980–2020', published in *Wired* in 1997, could write breathlessly of a new 'long wave', 'the biggest boom in the world's history'. New 'titans of industry', many of them young, were eager and determined to push the new wave forward with government backing. Inflation was now being kept in check, and all the time globalization was being forced forward. In the new century, it was predicted, there would be further innovative breakthroughs, including alternative energy and a landing on Mars.

Exploring Space

The ability to get to Mars would depend on advances in space communications, and these already had their own history, as, indeed, did fiction relating to Mars before there was any talk of convergence. It changed significantly when Kim Stanley Robinson wrote his novella *Green Mars*, a prelude to his trilogy of 1990s novels: *Red Mars, Green Mars* and *Blue Mars*. For a brief spell in world history from the 1950s to the 1980s, communications satellites, 'comsats', impossible to launch without computers, were attracting more attention than the computers themselves.

Satellites were the most glamorous (some said 'sexy') expressions of technology after the launching of Sputnik by the Soviet Union in October 1957, the surprise 'happening' which led the American government to respond as quickly as possible. NASA, the new American National Aeronautics and Space Agency was set up within a year. The launching also led to a burst of popular American interest in space which television drew upon and magnified. In what had already become a famous prediction made and published in 1945, Arthur C. Clarke, then treasurer of the British Interplanetary Society and a future writer of science fiction, had foreseen a chain of three manned geo-stationary radio satellites; in 1968, his science fiction novel *2001, A Space Odyssey* was turned into a Stanley Kubrick film. In 1961, NASA had planned Telstar, a satellite, costly to build, which could circle the globe in less than 2.75 hours. It contained more than 2,500 transistors, but no integrated circuits. The British and French Post Offices, still secure in the prospects for their own future, agreed to build related ground stations, one not far from the place where Marconi had sent out his transatlantic messages decades before.

Cables and Satellites

A later ground station in Bahrain, to be built by the Marconi Company, was owned not by the government of Bahrain but by British-based Cable and Wireless, which gained in business strength when it became clear that satellites, for all their glamour – and a fall in cost as new systems were introduced – would not supplant cable in which Britain had had a long-term interest. Fibre optics guaranteed the continuation of cable, and the first optical cable link to carry commercial traffic, two colour-television channels, was installed in Sussex, England, in 1976. The first fibre-optic cable television system in the United States was operating in Birmingham, Alabama, in 1984. Four years later, a fibre-optic cable was laid across the Atlantic by AT&T and its partners, and thirty companies inaugurated a cable across the Pacific a year after that. The oceans still mattered as well as the skies. There was to be a tenfold increase in transatlantic cable capacity between 1996 and 1999.

The first experimental telecasts using Telstar were exchanged on 11 July 1962, when there was a familiar initiating dialogue, this time overheard by millions and recorded. An American television announcer broke into the televising of a 'drama' to declare that the British were 'ready to bounce a program off Telstar'. The viewers went on to see as well as to hear characters sitting around a table across the Atlantic. 'On my right is that dour Scot, Robert White. On my left John Bray, who is in charge of our planning in the space field. It is half-past three in the morning. Good luck.'

The satellite was managed by a new company, the Communications Satellite Corporation (CSC). Half its stock was owned by AT&T and other communications carriers; the other half was open to public purchase. The Kennedy administration, committed to a 'man-in-the-moon' programme, was not anxious to depend entirely on AT&T; and while the Soviet Union was creating a planned twelve-hour orbit system (Orbita), other options were being explored in Washington. A control framework was set out in the first Communications Satellite Act of 1962. CSC was neither a private monopoly nor a public agency, but there was a market for its stock which quickly rose in value. Syncoms I and II were launched in 1963, as was Telstar II, and in the following year Syncom III transmitted the popular Tokyo Olympics. The World Cup soccer matches in 1966 drew on six transatlantic television satellites for reporting the games.

Television, however, was an intermittent, not a continuous, client: the 'instantaneous pictures' which viewers saw depended on journalistic – and financial – priorities. With the coming of satellites, the press, too, had its own unprecedented opportunities, and it was possible for a new American daily newspaper, *USA Today*, to be launched in 1982, printed simultaneously via low-powered domestic satellites, in seventeen cities: it came to be divided into separately folded sections with media being dealt with in 'life', in 'business', in 'sports', or intermittently in the 'news' section. In every country the press was turning 'the media' into a staple news item, with information about regular programmes being accompanied by gossip, increasingly revolving around 'celebrities', and sometimes, more rarely in the United States than in Europe, by serious criticism, comparable to literary criticism. Particularly in the case of film criticism, much of it relied heavily on theory. The new media world was a new world of media studies.

It was never possible in the history of satellites to ignore international issues, including the obstacles to development, and in August 1964, five years before the FCC announced a domestic 'open skies' policy, an International Telecommunications Satellite Organization (Intelsat) was established under intergovernmental agreements that became definitive in 1973. Ownership was initially determined by telephone usage: in 1964, the United States through Comsat held 61 per cent and Britain held 8.4 per cent. The Soviet Union did not participate – this was the height of the Cold War – and in 1968 it created an alternative international body, Intersputnik, which was joined, however, by only seven countries. Intelsat continued to attract a large number of countries, many nonaligned, and by 1975 no fewer than eighty-nine countries, large and small, with varying telecommunications needs, were members. The first of its geo-stationary satellites, Intelsat I (1965), weighing only about ninety pounds, commissioned by NASA and made by the Hughes Corporation, was named Early Bird. It was successful enough to ensure further Hughes contracts for the next generation of Intelsat satellites launched in 1967.

The geo-stationary satellites were located in a precise and limited orbit above the equator, the only orbit that allowed a continuous contact between a satellite and a single ground station. The number of slots on the orbit were finite and were consequently bargained about behind the scenes and at World Administrative Radio Conferences (WARCs). Each slot had what were called a terrestrial 'footprint', and this largely determined the price that it fetched. Another factor was the content that it might offer. There were sometimes surprises in the allocation of slots. Thus, in 1985 WARC allotted seven orbital slots to the island of Tonga, a 'port of call' in the Pacific, which Tonga then leased to profit-seeking corporate interests.

In his *Media and Sovereignty* (2002), Monroe Price looked far back in time and compared satellite routes through the air to the trade routes of the seventeenth and eighteenth centuries. International satellite organizations were all required by contract to provide 'equitable access' to users, but there were few limitations on domestic satellites, and when the first low-powered US domestic satellite was launched in 1974, it was owned not by Comsat but by Western Union. A year earlier, Canada had launched the world's first domestic satellite, Anik (Brother), an Inuit name, but it was built in the United States and was used there by RCA before the Western Union satellite was put into orbit. In 2000, Intelsat, based in Washington, became a private satellite communications company after almost forty years of existence as an intergovernmental organization. It was then operating seventeen existing satellites and planned to build ten more.

This was a time of reassessment as well as of planning for the future. Almost a generation before – and the term 'generations' was applied to satellites themselves as well as to computers – *Intermedia*, in a special number of August 1975, reported problems of an international kind – it did not use the word 'global' – similar to those of 'environment, energy, disarmament and seabeds and oceans'. For its editor, 'analyses of the significance of satellite communications' provided 'as many interpretations ... as there are theories about the role, function and effect of communications upon society and individuals'. He noted that Algeria was the first African country to use a satellite system for national purposes and that in Asia, SITE proposals for educational broadcasting to six different regions in four languages were well advanced. Broadcasting, using a NASA satellite, was to start in 1975 and would cover health, hygiene and agriculture. SITE had a real but limited success, and subsequently figured prominently in all accounts of recent educational history.

In the United States, it was only after a convergence of satellite and cable interests, the latter completely deregulated under the Reagan administration, that effective use of a satellite system began. Meanwhile, satellite television development in Europe, despite high costs, moved ahead independently, making it impossible for an American-backed organization to launch a communications satellite and operate from a Luxembourg base. Instead, a Franco-German agreement was reached in 1974 to construct a multi-purpose cooperative satellite system, Symphonie, which would provide sound broadcasting and telephone circuits between Europe and regions of Africa and later of Latin America. The project failed. Ten years earlier, a European Space Agency had been set up 'to probe space and to launch and operate satellites', and it launched its first rocket, Ariane, in 1979 and its first satellite in 1983.

In 1980, the European Community had issued a statement on Europe and the new information technology – 'telematics' – in which it stated not only that the information technology revolution was under way, but that it could not be stopped; and in 1982 it declared that the projection of European culture through a European television policy offered the key to European integration: 'The sharing of pictures and information will be the most effective means of increasing mutual understanding among the peoples of Europe and will give them a greater sense of belonging to a common social and cultural unity.' It was in the light of this declaration that the first operational European satellite cable television delivery system, SATV, was set up, and the European Broadcasting Union started ambitiously an experimental European Service, Eurikon, later called Europa, employing the European Space Agency's orbital test satellite, OTS-2.

The first evening's programmes included speeches, an hour and a half of 'high culture' (mainly Haydn), an episode from Coronation Street, a World in Action programme and fifty minutes of pop music. For once, content was deemed as worthy of acclamation as technology.

Despite, or perhaps because of the emphasis on quality it was unlikely that all the countries in an expanded European Community would fully accept the principle of integration through European television, which was restated in a landmark directive, Television Without Frontiers, adopted in 1989, the dramatic year when the wall dividing the two Germanys was breached and communism collapsed. The principle seemed fundamental to pan-Europeans, but it was commercial companies not governments that set the pace in what was happening in radio and television and what was happening in telecommunications. The commercial market appeared to have triumphed. Research by Pan European Television Audience Research (PETAR) between 1987 and 1995 revealed poor viewing figures and cultural differences between different member states of the Community. As far as telecommunications were concerned, the British government, which had appointed its first Minister for Information Technology in 1980, led the way, putting its trust in the business sector; and in 1984, having already sold its shares in Cable and Wireless, it privatized British Telecom.

Related plans to develop direct satellite broadcasting through a risk-sharing consortium failed in 1988, however, even though the consortium included powerful players like British Telecom, British Aerospace, GEC/Marconi and the Rothschild Bank. A new consortium, British Satellite Broadcasting (BSB), which included several television companies and Pearson, a conglomerate which included a newspaper business, the Westminster Press, the *Financial Times* and *The Economist*, as well as an established book business, Longman (which went back to 1724), succeeded in 1990 in launching a satellite, also built by Hughes Communications. Yet, it found the costs of operating it and supplying programmes so high that later in the year it was forced into a merger, BSkyB, with its commercial competitor Sky Television, owned by Murdoch, who was by then as powerful a figure in television as he was in the press.

Murdoch's media interests were multiple, including film (Fox) and the News Corporation, then based in Australia, and before the new merger he had already demonstrated that commercial satellite broadcasting could be a profitable enterprise, able over time to outbid the BBC, particularly in contracts with sporting organizations, and to challenge it in the presentation of news. By 1993/4, three million British households, one in seven, were subscribing to BSkyB, and more than 30 per cent of television households in sixteen European countries were viewing Murdoch programmes, the highest proportion of them (92 per cent) in the Netherlands, which, like Belgium, Denmark, Sweden and Switzerland, already had high cable penetration. (Half of Dutch homes had been wired for radio in 1939.)

The relationship between satellite use and cable numbers requires analysis as well as survey. In the United States, where, as has been noted (see p. 297), the fortunes of satellite and cable were intricately interconnected, it was not until 1976, when Home Box Office, linked with Time Inc., decided to hitch its future to RCA's Satcom I, that a large cable concern acquired national distribution capabilities comparable with those of the three big television networks at a fraction of the cost. Other companies quickly followed HBO's lead, some companies becoming multi-service operators specializing in 'movies' and sport. A familiar process of business concentration ensued, and some stations became cable 'super stations', among them WOR-TV (New York) and WTBS (Atlanta). Crossmedia ownership was common. So were deals with Hollywood. In the most active city areas, cable subscribers were able to have access to a wide range of programme channels, whatever their content, and, in consequence, the National Citizens' Committee for Broadcasting, an organization blessed by consumer guru Ralph Nader, suggested that citizens should ask for twice as many local channels as prospective cable companies were offering their community, and exact from the winner a higher franchise fee than the highest fees paid elsewhere.

Charges for customers varied from city to city, and in some cities new cable systems were often expensive to construct. That was part of the economics. It was estimated in the city of Dallas, for example, with 400,000 homes, that a take-off would cost $100 million. The financial prospects were attractive enough, however, for no fewer than six groups to bid for the franchise, and when the City Council granted it to Warner Amex, a local company asked for a referendum. Already Dallas, known in many countries through the soap opera with that name, had twice as many pay television companies as any city in the United States. It led the way, so that by the mid-1980s, nearly half of American homes had cable television, and the top ten multiple-system operators served nearly half the cable subscribers. The comparative Canadian figure was 60 per cent. Not all such channels were to prove successful or profitable. Nor did greater choice provide the variety that it might have done. For Brian Winston, writing in 1998, American cable channels had 'almost totally failed to alter the established genres and forms of television broadcasting in any significant way'.

The distribution of cable outside the United States in the mid-1980s was uneven. In Italy, where cable was thought of simply as a version of broadcasting, there had been one company, Tele Biella, as early as 1971. In the Netherlands, municipalities owned more than half the cable systems. In Finland, which was taking pride in its wholehearted adoption of new technologies, the satellite audience was as low as 1 per cent, but the cable audience was 40 per cent. France did not adopt a comprehensive law relating to cable until 1982. Progress was slow in Germany and in Sweden. In Britain also, cable was slow to develop even after the government, in the name of competition and choice, granted eleven pay cable franchises in 1983. Two years later, seven were operational, and ten years later there were thirteen in operation, some part time. Some of them formed transatlantic consortia with major American companies.

Both for programming and for business reasons, there was often an international – as well as a local – dimension to cable development. Ted Turner's Cable News Network (CNN), based in Atlanta, was deliberately global in scope, and made its reputation in Baghdad during the first Gulf War. Following its merger in 1995 with Time/Warner, itself international in outlook, the new conglomerate was capitalized at $36 billion. Time/Warner was itself the product of a merger in 1990. The unexpected new merger with CNN would guarantee a bigger annual turnover than the Walt Disney Company, known throughout the world, which had recently bought Capital Cities/ABC, owner of what was then the largest American network. Time/Warner already held 18 per cent of CNN, and Turner is said to have made bids on more than one occasion to acquire CBS. Under the CNN banner in

1995, he was running two news channels and two movie channels, one of them the Cartoon Network. He also owned the film archive of Hollywood's MGM, which could now be placed alongside the Warner archive.

Murdoch, who by then had become a US citizen, had been mentioned in the press as one of Turner's suitors: in 1995 he had joined in an American 'gang of four' alliance with Brazil's Globo, Mexico's Televisa and the United States Telecommunications Inc. All this represented a business, not a technological, convergence. Globo and Televisa were huge Latin American concerns with tentacles everywhere. In 1997 Murdoch sold out his American satellite business, ASkyB, which he had set up in January 1996 when he promised Americans 200 channels. He had envisaged it as a major element in a global communications strategy which was as ambitious as that of any government, or, indeed, group of governments. He had secured control of Star TV in Hong Kong in 1993 and he had launched JSkyB in Japan in December 1996 as a joint venture with the Japanese company Soft Bank. Sony came in soon afterwards. When Murdoch abandoned ASkyB in 1997, therefore, one television executive concluded that the satellite business was 'a theoretician's delight and a practitioner's nightmare'. But this was only partially true, even after Murdoch sold out his controlling interest in Star IV. By the mid-1990s, there were eleven million Asian viewers linked together through Asia Sat-2, and in 1991 the BBC launched World Service Television, which quickly claimed to have millions of viewers in Asia, Australasia, America and Africa. Significantly, China preferred Murdoch television to that offered by the BBC.

The United Kingdom, where cable had been slow to develop, had a far smaller satellite audience in the early 1990s than the Netherlands, probably because the BBC and ITV were offering free a more generally acceptable service without payment of a subscription. The BBC had opposed wired radio before 1939 on the grounds that, if uncontrolled, 'it might be disruptive of the spirit and intentions of the BBC's Charter'. Now it objected strongly, but in vain, to cable television, whether terrestrial or based on satellites. It was finding it increasingly difficult, however, to maintain its traditional stance as a guardian of the public interest, and by the end of the century it had been embroiled in more than one political controversy. Worse was still to come.

Differences in the national approaches to satellite and cable were as significant as earlier variations in broadcasting systems. In consequence, the overall trends in each country were as interesting to watch as the interplay of personalities. The proportion of British households subscribing to satellite services accounted for nearly 6 per cent of viewers in 1993: three years later, it accounted for over 11 per cent. In Japan, where an experimental satellite, Yuri, launched in 1978, was said to be the first to be 'dedicated' to communications, NHK had taken the lead in new development in scheduling cable and direct-to-home broadcasts in 1991. This was followed later in the year by Japanese Satellite Broadcasting, which began operating a twenty-four-hour channel. In 1996 it had more than two million subscribers.

In lists of new technologies drawn up during the 1960s, 'other broadband links', CATV (Cable Television) had figured well below satellites. At first, cable television stations, wherever they operated, were local and one-way and offered viewers an initial selection of up to twelve programmes, eventually to rise, it was suggested, to one hundred. The promise of better reception mattered then at least as much as greater choices. As cable developed during the 1970s, however, there were enthusiasts who believed that it was the core of a revolution both in telecommunications and in broadcasting. One of the enthusiasts, already mentioned, the American Ralph Lee Smith, coined the slogan 'Wired Nation', which he used in a widely read article in *The Nation* in May 1970, which had an appeal outside the United States. Nevertheless, as we have seen, the first steps had been faltering, and Smith's prediction was dismissed in some circles as 'Cable Fable'. In 1970 itself, there were 2,639 cable systems in the United States, with 5.3 million subscribers, only 8.7 per cent of American television households; in 1975 there were 3,506 systems, with 9.8 million subscribers. The comparable figures ten years later were 4,300, 17.2 million and 23 per cent, and there was now a place, as in periodical and book publishing, for niche content channels, like the History or Discovery Channels, since limited local audiences could now be aggregated. The concept of a virtual community crossing national frontiers preceded the Internet.

The development of cable raised major policy issues for the FCC, which, without any guidance from Congress, did not care directly to confront cable interests. In 1959, the FCC had ruled that since cable was neither broadcasting nor common-carrier communication, the FCC had no jurisdiction over it. In 1968, after fears were expressed in network circles that cable growth could put 'free' network television out of business or siphon off from it popular outside events, particularly sporting events, it intervened directly in the cable business, going so far as to restrict cable stations from importing 'distant signals' – that is, all signals outside their own designated service areas. Such 'freezing' proved unpopular in a variety of circles, and in 1972, as an uneasy compromise, following discussions between different interests, the FCC decided that cable systems could import at least two distant signals. They were still to be subject to regulation, however, including the requirement to set aside some channels for education, local government and 'the general public'.

After another four years – and a number of law suits – many, but not all, of these restraints on cable were removed, but even this was not enough for the increasing number of believers in deregulation, beginning to be a buzz-word. In 1977, a three-judge panel of the Court of Appeals in the District of Columbia declared that all the protective restraints on cable were invalid, that there was no 'constitutional distinction between cable and newspapers', and that in First Amendment terms cable television was not broadcasting. Fears of a different kind were being expressed by then, in particular that, with the increasing convergence of electronic and print media, print would become entangled in regulations similar to those applied by the FCC to broadcasting.

In these circumstances, with Congress still unwilling or unable to intervene, there were constitutional lawyers who urged that spectrum scarcity should no longer be treated as a rationale for regulating broadcasting. In city areas, they might be able to watch up to fifty channels. Genuine choice seemed to be opening up locally, as cable, while fragmenting the mass audience, permitted some channels to be used for more than entertainment.

Satellite and cable were obviously big business. Yet, as Timothy Hollins wrote in a well-informed study, *Beyond Broadcasting: Into the Cable Age* (1984), no more people in Britain than in Italy 'had any inkling' before 1982 'that cable was more than just another name for a telegram or a piece of wire'. By 1984, however, a year when everything seemed to be converging, significant numbers of observers on both sides of the Atlantic were beginning to argue that it would be the 'vanguard of a new technological revolution'. Many of the people who were enthusiastic about new technologies argued that the revolution would start with what was usually described as 'viewdata' – with 'teletext' being part of 'new developments associated with the television receiver'. Teletext was a system for broadcasting pages of information (words and graphics) on a television screen, making use of spare lines not previously employed in regular broadcasting. Videotex, a more comprehensive term, was the delivery via telephone line or cable of computer-stored information to be displayed on a television screen or specialized videotex terminal.

Because of the access to computerized data that videotex made possible, and the way that it was provided by information service agencies, much that was said about its advantages – and problems – anticipated what was to be said later about the Internet and the World Wide Web. So, too, did the questions it raised. Would viewdata become 'a mass medium or an individual medium or, as the Japanese say, a mass individual medium?' a writer in Intermedia asked in 1979. One of its slogans was 'the world of information is now at your fingertips', but the technology on which it rested at first was analogue, not digital. Interest in videotex centred, in the writer's view, largely on its likely 'evolution of identity'. As different electronic services grew, he and some other observers hoped that they would 'edge towards equilibrium'.

There was in fact no equilibrium. Instead, there was a further rush of new technologies, not all of which were to take off in what had been called as early as 1970 'a data-based society'. Some stayed at uncompleted points of development, even at the prototype stage. One, in particular, high-definition television (HDTV), which offered better colour and clarity of picture through 1,125 lines (instead of 525 and 625) and a wider screen, more like a cinema screen, was successfully demonstrated in the United States and elsewhere, but to the chagrin of the Japanese, who worked hard and long to develop it, for a variety of reasons there was no breakthrough. Nor had there been in 'cinorama', 'sensorama' or 'holography', although Denis Gabor, using lasers, had produced a forty-seven-second hologram movie in Moscow in 1976, showing a woman carrying flowers.

The fact that HDTV was capable of delivering video images carrying five times as much information as conventional images could do did not count. There were more compelling facts. A shift of system would have involved not only heavy investment but a new spectrum allocation. Technical standards in different countries were different; and, most important of all, as has been noted, the technology then proposed was analogue, not digital. Digitalization, or digitization, as some people continued to describe it, was already considered to be the likely basis of much new technology during the 1980s, but the process of switching to it was slow. A turning point came in 1997 when the British government, in its plans for digital broadcasting, chose to go ahead with the provision of more channels rather than with the introduction of high-definition television.

Viewdata

Before that turning point, it was a fragmented telecommunications system, with telecommunications and broadcasting having radically different cultures, that reared the Viewdata family. And in Europe, in particular, Post Offices, sometimes in cooperation with private business, were the ambitious parents. In the words of the British Post Office, the family they were rearing was sprawling and under constant scrutiny in the press. It was the

British Post Office, soon to lose the telephone side of its business, which placed on offer in 1979 the world's first operational Viewdata system, Prestel, following an experimental period, common to older technological developments and parallel to new ones. This was 'the year of Videotex', when the much-heralded convergence of computer and communications technologies was discussed at what was described as 'the first ever international forum on video data'.

Prestel would have been called 'Viewdata' had the Post Office been able to copyright the name, but it was not the only Viewdata system then being developed. The IBA in Britain had Oracle, the French Teletel, Finland Telset, CBS in America had Teletext, and Canada Telidon. In all these cases, the hallmark of the systems was 'not technological wizardry but social utility'; and Prestel, 'the pioneer', which did not incorporate microprocessors in its terminals, was never alone in refusing to incorporate new technology. The subsequent chronology of viewdata development is not easy to sort out, for there were delays between demonstrations and installations, and gaps between rhetoric and performance. Ambitious announcements were often made and reported while planning was at an early stage. Sets were expensive, and modes of charging were complicated and controversial to calculate and implement. In France, there was to be cross-subsidization, but in Britain there was none. In the United States, popular interest was difficult to arouse. A local experiment, like that of the Los Angeles Mirror, which started in California in 1984, was halted after several years of loss-making.

There were two types of viewdata systems; those that were telephone-based, like Prestel and Telidon, and those that were broadcast-based, like the BBC's Ceefax and IBA's Oracle; and it was ITU's consultative committees that chose videotex as the generic name for them all. The former type of system, claiming greater simplicity, relied for the data which it offered on information providers, who acquired 'pages', for the data which it offered: there was no central editor or coordinator of content. The Post Office's role was similar to that of a common carrier, therefore, and in this and other respects there were anticipations of the Internet both in the language used and in the procedures. The first problem that the Prestel method posed for an information provider, one of its managers noted, was how to direct the user to the information as quickly as possible. In the days of the Internet, the manager of a software system might have said the same. Prestel, potentially 'a mass medium', was much closer to printing and publishing, the Post Office then argued, than it was to radio and television. This was given as one of the reasons why some newspaper interests, among them the *Financial Times* and *The Economist*, decided, sometimes defensively, to become information providers, while others were opposed. In particular, the German press was bitterly hostile to the viewdata system introduced by the German Post Office in 1984.

Two points were emphasized by an early British information provider who was not on the defensive and who saw new business opportunities in the venture. First, there was no 'tyranny of peak hour transmission time', 'prime time', either for an information provider or for a user. Second, the user had to be active. Unless he made decisions and pressed buttons on a control page, the same page would sit on the screen for ever. The number of data pages was strictly limited, however, and it required enterprise on the part of the information provider to introduce 'simple graphics' as well as text. In Canada, Telidon, developed by specialists attached to the Research Centre of the Canadian Department of Communications, was alone in offering visual as well as verbal information.

VCRs

A very different range of video-communications devices, owing nothing to Post Offices or governments, were video-cassette recorders (VCRs) and video discs, to be followed by CD-Roms. The first of them were put on sale in 1972 after years of experiment both with cassettes and discs, as American, Dutch, Swedish and Japanese companies engaged in a race to capture a new consumer market. Sony introduced a magnetic tape into its cassettes in 1969, while RCA, fully familiar with the use of tape, persisted with discs until 1984. Philips in the Netherlands demonstrated laser videodisc technology in 1978. In America, the first laser disc was on sale in time for Christmas 1980. Their use raised issues of copyright and of piracy, particularly in relation to music, which had been aired in a very different social and economic context in the eighteenth and nineteenth centuries. There was no problem in individuals 'time shifting' – that is, recording television programmes that they could see on the home screen later than they had been broadcast. In practice, however, the main use of VCRs was to be the playing of pre-recorded commercial films, bought or hired, a source of profit for cinema interests, particularly Hollywood. Home-produced video developed later, and eventually made its way as a form of public entertainment onto network and cable channels. The growth statistics were striking. By 1985 there were more video-cassette stores in the United States than there were cinemas.

Between 1980 and 1995, the number of VCRs in the United States increased from 1.8 million to 86 million, the most impressive of all the media statistics of those years. By 1990, 70 per cent of American homes possessed a VCR. Outside the United States, British demand had risen even faster than in the United States, and outside Europe, 85 per cent of all homes in Saudi Arabia had a VCR by 1985. In the same year Nigeria sold 1.5 million VCRs. The head of Germany's overseas broadcasts (Deutsche Welle) wrote of a 'video invasion of Africa'. There were videoteques selling or making VCRs in most of Africa's capital cities: more than two hundred in Ghana's Accra, seventy in Abidjan, capital of the Ivory Coast, and more than fifty in the capital of Mali, Bamako. Ethnic groups, some of them far away from their place of birth, now had separate access to video in their own language.

The social effects of the diffusion of VCRs have received less attention than the technology – there was a battle of standards – and the economics, which involved heavy investment in research. Because in many countries tapes could be hired as well as bought, video shops became a more prominent and ubiquitous feature in townscapes than bookshops. Many shops sold both. Newsagents were in the hiring business, too. Hollywood, initially resistant to video-recording as it had been to television, boomed through video sales. So, too, did the musical industries in audio as well as in video when music could be heard and recorded. The long-playing record, itself hailed as a major invention when it superseded '78s', soon became as obsolete as the typewriter. Video cameras became part of the family kit also. The most successful of what have been called 'the spin-offs of the video cassette' was Sony's video camera of 1984, the small camcorder, 'the TV version of the Polaroid'. And the day of the digital camera was still to come. There was one feasible invention which did not take off – the videophone – much 'flashier' than a voice-alone phone, although AT&T had begun to market an analogue-based Picturephone in the 1960s, projecting a market of up to 1 per cent of all domestic phones by the 1980s. Failing to secure customers, it decided to drop manufacture of the phone in 1973, but the idea never lost its appeal and was taken up again in the 1990s, when, according to an 18-month European survey of 1992/3 covering Britain, France, Germany, the Netherlands and Norway, videophone calls, lavishly advertised, would last longer than telephone calls and would require 10 times as much bandwidth. Yet videophones were far more expensive than cellular mobile phones and their quality was unreliable. There was clearly a limited market for them, as there was for video-conferencing. Further developments were forecast, like 'telephonoscopique kiosks', although they would clearly need a different name if they were to make their way onto the streets, as Internet bars and cafés were about to do.

Mobile Phones

Given the great future for mobile phones, which were to acquire uses not at first anticipated, including digital cameras as part of their repertoire, in retrospect it was those communications experts who focused on mobility who were the most prescient. Citizens' Band radio had led the way in the United States, with yachtsmen and hunters following in the wake of truck drivers; and in the wake of the international oil crisis and a consequent reduction of the speed limit on American roads, the first mobile telephone system was licensed in 1983, just ten years after the installation of Citizens' Band. By 1989 there were a million American cellular phone users, but the great mobile telephone boom came later, by 1996 there were nearly six million mobile phone users in Britain and, five years later more than forty million. One phone every two seconds was sold between April and June 2000. This was a distribution-led phenomenon that inspired a frontpage heading in *The Times*: 'Half the country is mobile mad.'

A different *Times* commentator preferred to describe what was happening as a 'mobile love affair'. Britain was by now ahead of the United States in the proportion of mobile phones per one hundred people, and in mainland Europe both Finland and Italy were ahead of Britain. In Japan, where there was a huge increase in the diffusion of cellular phones after 1996, the main group of purchasers were between 20 and 24 years old, and it was observed that they used their phones mainly to keep in touch with a small group of friends, described in Japanese as 'cellular mates'. The market, expanded with the aid of massive advertising, was built up on the basis of a single service – voice communication – but there was an implicit promise that this would soon change. Wireless applications protocol (WAP) would turn mobile data and multimedia into major revenue providers for the companies. Music would figure prominently too. Its economics would change even more than the technology transforming music distribution.

Young people were affected most by the introduction of new services, particularly the provision of short text messages (SMSs), the first of them sent from a personal computer to a mobile phone on the Vodaphone Network in 1992. In what was treated by observers as a 'fad', an old word in the history of technology, teenagers became 'hooked' on them. Around 400 messages were transmitted in Britain alone by March 2000. In March 2001, the *Sunday Times* described (with photographs) a teenage girl who was sending more than one thousand short text messages each month. Such messages, which could not be more than 160 characters long, included a variety of symbols, and grammar and spelling were totally irrelevant. There were critics who warned about the possible side effects of the new technology, and many questions were asked, such as: Is there a health risk in radio waves near the ear? Should children use mobile phones? Should mobile phone companies be able to erect transmitter masts without planning permission? Should mobile phone users be controlled in railway carriages? In aeroplanes, they were forbidden to use them.

In every country non-users complained. The correspondence columns of newspapers provided a regular location for the complaints. So, too, did phone-in radio programmes, now a major constituent in the programming of the media. The fact that 'experts' differed gave zest to the question-ers and, perhaps less often, to some of the people being questioned. The shrewdest observers wondered whether most of the experts deserved to be described as such. Suspicion of experts, who aired their views regularly on BBC programmes such as *Today*, might well have been stronger.

The Internet

The presence in the background of the Internet influenced all media dis-course. Yet, as late as 1991, a book written by leading figures in computing, *Technology 2001: The Future of Computing and Communications*, published by MIT, made no references to the Internet. Nor did the words 'World Wide Web' or 'cyberspace' figure in the index. Interactive television seemed the ultimate convergence ploy. Nevertheless, in the same year David Gelernter published a book for technologists, *Mirror Worlds*, a fascinating extended research paper in which, without using the word, he forecast the rise of the Web; and by the end of the 1990s Eli Noam, then Director of Columbia University's Institute for Tele-Information, could make the judgement that 'when the media history of the 20th century will be written, the Internet will be seen as its major contribution': it was loose and under no single own-ership, and it seemed to be a communications complex which grew from below not from above. Netsurfing was one of its main attractions. Public access to browsing software (Mosaic), described in the business sections of the *New York Times* in December 1993 as 'the first window into cyberspace', made it possible to attract users and providers, software pioneers whose origins have already been described. The Netscape Navigator, relaunched in 1994, became the browser for nine out of ten browsers.

Quickly leaving physics behind, the Internet, 'more phenomenon than fact', developed its distinctive psychology, as 'the wild west frontier' had done in the nineteenth century, and along with the psychology what came to be called its 'ecology'. More portentously, by 1997 it began to be treated as a paradigm (see p. 272). In its origins, however, it was set up initially in 1968/9, with indispensable financial support from government, as a limited network (ARPANET), sharing information between 'hi-tech' (another new word) universities and other research institutions. By 1975 there were two thousand users, many of them physicists and engineers, and because of the nature of the information which they were sharing, it was an essential element in its rationale that it could survive the removal or destruction of any computer within the system and, indeed, the nuclear destruction of all communications 'infrastructures'. That was the view from the Pentagon. The view from the universities was that the Net offered 'free access' to academic and research users. It was they who were the communicators.

Whatever the vantage point, from above or from below, it was of crucial importance both immediately and in the long run that the 'architecture of the system' (the term often employed) differed from that of the telephone network. Any computer could tap into the Net anywhere, with the information being exchanged 'sliced' at once into 'packets'. The sending system broke information into encoded pieces: the receiving system put them together again after they had travelled to their destination by the quickest route via a series of computer 'nodes'. This was the first packet data system in history, although the idea of breaking up messages into 'packets of information', 'message blocks', had been in the mind of computer researchers since the mid-1960s, among them Donald Watt Davies of Britain's National Physical Laboratory, who used the term 'packet switching'.

The first interface message processors (IMPs) arrived at the Los Angeles campus of the University of California in January 1969, the year of the first moon landing, when Professor Leonard Kleinrock installed and used them in his laboratory. Within two years, ARPANET was fully operational. Electronic mail (email) was its staple mode of communication. Not all email messages dealt with defence matters. They lent themselves to personal communication after 1973 when Vint Cerf, a computer scientist at Stanford University, then 30 years old, devised a radically new way of reconstructing the protocols, as they were called, that linked computer networks. In cooperation with Robert Kahn of ARPANET, five years older than he was, he devised the Transmission Control Protocol and the Internet Protocol which ARPANET adapted in 1983. Many of them were to stay. Thus the @ in the address for transmission became routine. Three years later the further abbreviations 'com' for commercial, 'mil' for military and 'e' for educational were introduced.

The value of the Net outside military units and universities depended on a broader awareness of its commercial possibilities, and the first online commercial service provider, CompuServe, at first catering for what has been called 'a private club', partly owned by Time/Warner (see p. 300), started operating in 1979. A formidable rival, American Online, linked to German and French groups, followed. There was also a third, 'Prodigy'. The three of them, keen rivals, had a combined subscriber base in 1993 that doubled in two years to 3.5 million. Given their strength, it is possible, at least in retrospect, to trace what looks like a logical phasing in the complex history of the Internet, as there was in most branches of communications history, with a new phase opening when the Net attracted business interests and its uses were extended.

The ecology was transformed not from a United States base, but from CERN, a European particle physics research institute, nestling under mountains in Switzerland, where an English engineer, Tim Berners-Lee, born in 1955, devised what he called the 'World Wide Web' (www) in 1989. 'Suppose I could programme my computer to create a space in which anything could be linked to anything', he speculated. 'Suppose all the information stored on computers everywhere were linked.' Berners-Lee did not then know that Vannevar Bush of MIT, who had been intimately involved in the early history of the computer and who had headed the US Office of Scientific Research Development during the Second World War, had pondered on similar lines in an article in the *Atlantic Monthly* in 1945. Contemplating the way in which wartime technologies could be used in a world of peace, Bush had projected a photo-mechanical machine called 'the Memex', memory extender, a vast encyclopaedia of text, images and sounds.

For Berners-Lee, 'weaving' the Web was primarily neither a high-security nor a profit-making task, but a means of widening user opportunity. He sought to keep the Web non-proprietary, open and free. Yet, like those American entrepreneurs who developed the Internet for profit – and in his autobiography he referred briefly to Cerf and Kahn – he was driven by a fervent belief in its potential: it could and should be 'worldwide'. His development of hyperlinks, highlighting words or symbols within documents by 'clicking in', was the key to all future progress, although he noted that the Web would deal not only in texts but also in sound and in images. In 1993, *Time* magazine, which hailed him as the Web's sole parent, paid him the highest tribute that it could in calling his achievement 'almost Gutenbergian'. Berners-Lee had taken a 'powerful communications system that only the elite could use and turned it into a mass medium'.

Not everyone wanted it to be converted in the way to which *Time* was pointing. To some of the pioneer users of ARPANET, the adjective 'mass' carried with it the same connotations as it did when attached to broadcasting.

The more Internet users there were, the more of a wasteland would lie ahead. Some claimed that the Internet would 'pollute the human spirit', while Neil Postman coined the word 'technopoly' in 1993 to cover what he called 'the surrender of culture to technology'. Such critics were in the minority, however, and there was more euphoria than alarm in most critical comment. Most of the pioneer software providers considered that the Internet liberated and empowered individuals and offered unprecedented benefits to society. So, too, did enthusiasts for an uncontrolled Internet. In his *Twilight of Sovereignty* (1995) William Winston argued confidently that through technological convergence we would journey towards 'more human freedom', 'more power to the people'.

There were sharply contrasting approaches, therefore, to the future of the Internet. Like the railroad, it would bring strangers together: you never knew whom you would meet on it. Like the media – and through the media – it would carry information, entertainment and education. It would be undirected by any government. This was an attraction even for some of its critics. Yet could it remain undirected by government or by 'big business'? For Benjamin Parker, an American writer with a self-declared 'passion for democracy', new titans of telecommunication were emerging, eager to exercise 'monopoly control not just over material goods like coal, oil, steel and the railroads, but over the essential instruments of power in an information-based civilization'. Would the fact that it was interactive save it? The question was asked at the end of the twentieth century within the context of a 'digital era', a new label to attach to society and culture. Another label was 'global society'. Yet some observers looked backwards as well as forwards.

In an issue of the *New Yorker*, 'The Digital Age', in December 1999, one of the writers described how email, 'the return of the word' after a long visual age, looked 'way back' to Swift and Pope and Lord Chesterfield, each of whom it endowed with a Web page which helped to bring together families scattered throughout the world far more than letters sent through post boxes. It seemed important during the late 1990s to ensure that children should become 'media literate' at school and should learn there how to use the World Wide Web; there was a great symbolic event in March 1996 when President Clinton and Vice-President Gore joined others in installing telephone wires linking California's schoolrooms with the Internet. The President promised that all American classrooms would be so connected by the next century through the National Information Infrastructure (NII). This was at a time when Clinton's Secretary of Education could describe the Internet as 'the blackboard of the future'. Entertainment was not mentioned on this occasion.

It was a coincidence that in 1996 the New York Public Library, one of the world's largest libraries, celebrated its centennial, and *Daedalus* joined in the celebrations with a special number called Books, Bricks and Bytes. Its first article, by Peter Lyman, University Librarian at Berkeley, California, raised the question 'What is a Digital Library?' In attaching the adjective 'digital' to the noun 'library', he suggested, the future seemed to be reconciled with the past. In the previous century, the United States had created a marketplace of ideas upon three institutions – libraries, publishing and copyright law. Would digital libraries, electronic publishing and information highways – he put quotation marks round each of these terms – constitute the marketplace of ideas for an information society? A later article on the story of libraries in South Africa by Peter Johan Lor, Director of the State Library in Pretoria, did not employ these terms. Instead, Lor reproduced Maslow's diagram of a Hierarchy of Needs which had at its base 'physiological needs: hunger, thirst and so forth'. It was difficult to use a library analogy in countries where such needs were paramount and where there was large-scale illiteracy.

There was certainly a contrast here with the United States, which in its cities at least, was more concerned with wants than with needs. In the US more than in any other country, e-commerce was often seen as the culmination of the consumer revolution, a shoppers' heaven which, in the words of Bill Gates in *The Way Ahead* (1995), would enable 'all the goods in the world [to be] available for you to examine, compare, and often customize'. Nevertheless, Gates, self-taught, who regarded computers as liberators, used a substantial part of the huge personal fortune that he acquired to endow educational projects. In 2006, eleven years after publication of *The Way Ahead*, he announced plans to step down two years later from Microsoft, the great concern he had launched in 1975, to concentrate on a new career as a philanthropist.

The 'meteoric' growth of the Web overshadows most other aspects of recent media history. Ten years after Clinton and Gore's symbolic gesture, *Fortune* could describe the Internet as 'old news': its 700 million users were changing business and society so fast that it was sometimes hard to keep up. By then, the real world was celebrating the arrival of a new millennium and the United States had suffered a devastating terrorist attack ('9/11') on New York and Washington.

A New Age?

It was in New York that a 'Millennium Summit' was held at the United Nations headquarters in September 2000, attended by 150 heads of state. There had been much written about the end of an old millennium and the beginning of a new since the 1960s, when a number of commentators, including self-styled 'futurologists', looked forward in their analyses and predictions to the year 2000. Yet ironically, perhaps, when it came – amid celebrations – there was less talk about the future than there had been in the 1960s and 1970s. It was the immediate present that loomed largest, and 1999 ended with fireworks and lavish displays of entertainment in the world's capital cities, the scale and impact of which claimed clamorous headlines. Fewer balance sheets of technological, economic and social gains and losses were drawn up than at the end of the previous century. At the summit in New York, where a number of millennial goals were set, the first of which was the eradication of extreme poverty and hunger, the goal to which Lor had pointed in 1996 (none dealt with the media), Britain's Chief Rabbi, Jonathan Sacks, who was present, noted that the large crowds he saw in downtown Manhattan had gathered not to watch political or religious leaders on their way to the United Nations building, but to catch sight of celebrities gathered for the MTV Video Awards. The television corporation MTV (Music Television) dealt mainly in entertainment.

There could be controversy even about whether entertainment had become mixed up with politics. At the beginning of the year, the Millennial Dome erected in London's East End was a matter of continuing media controversy, although the project had been backed by Conservative and Labour governments in turn. The Dome attracted fewer visitors than had been anticipated; those who did buy tickets were impressed not only by the sophisticated acrobatic entertainment, but also by those sections of the Dome which were devoted to education and transportation. The most lasting of a wide range of millennial projects, a large number of them local, was concerned with transportation: a chain of new underground stations was opened between Westminster and Greenwich. The BBC had attempted to broaden the millennial agenda. It opened a BBC History 2000 website, an ambitious oral history, 'The Century Speaks', recording twentieth-century lives and voices. This was the first century in history when such a venture had been possible. The technology had not been available before.

Whatever was said or not said about the new millennium, or of the role of the media in interpreting it, there was a general recognition that the planet was not the same after 11 September 2001, when suicide bombers, in a terrifying attack, destroyed the great towers of the World Trade Center in New York and part of the Pentagon buildings in Washington. 'Tragedy is history's pivot', wrote Michael Wines, Moscow correspondent for the *New York Times*. For other journalists – and historians – this was the 'real' beginning of the new millennium, a chronological time span that the Islamic calendar did not recognize.

Globalization

The world had to recognize the presence within it of Islam. Culturally, it was not one world. Different countries stressed their own uniqueness. The globe, rather than the world, inspired one of the buzz words of the 1990s, 'globalization'. Theories about its role abounded, including the alleged emergence through it of a new 'global public sphere'. In 1999, Anthony Giddens, then Director of the London School of Economics, devoted his prestigious BBC Reith Lectures, somewhat misleadingly entitled 'Runaway World', to the initiation of 'an electronic global conversation' about it. Ignoring the long history of globalization which had preceded industrialization and which had fascinated Marx, Giddens, who believed that globalization was explicable less in terms of economics – he had recent economic integration in mind – clearly appreciated that globalization was a subject not only for conversation, but also for debate. He delivered some of his lectures not in London but in other cities of the world – the first time this had happened – and in some parts of the world they provoked not only a fundamentalist recoil, a religious response with political ramifications, but a wave of more general criticism. Globalization was often identified with Americanization, and the responses focused on economic and political issues, with cultural ramifications.

Responses varied, indeed, from 'globalization might be inevitable but we don't have to like it' to claims that all 'the success stories' in the recent history of economic development were countries that had 'got into the world economy'. The need to take global action to cope with melting of polar ice and greenhouse gases, a difficult subject for international communication, was not then at the top of the agenda. By 2009 India and China figured increasingly in international debate along with the United States with the debate being as much concerned with the social costs of globalization as with the advantages it offered. It was an American newspaper headline that put it most succinctly: 'Globalization Just Is: Is It Just?'

There were critics of approaches to globalization who denied that it 'Just Is'. Regular viewing of European and American satellite television, they noted, was for the most part limited to small elites. Regionalization was more significant than globalization. The influence of the nation-state had not diminished. Language was still a barrier to communication. The hybrid word 'glocalization', coined by sociologist Roland Robertson in 1994, needed, therefore, to be closely analysed. Critics' approaches to what was always a contentious concept were well summarized in Kai Hafez's *The Myth of Media Globalization* (2013), which included an excellent bibliography, including important works in German and articles in Arabic. His own conclusion is plain: so far, no global public sphere has been established. In reaching this conclusion, he relied not on theories but on empirical data about globalization, sadly limited though they were both in quantity and quality. For him, what some scholars had come to think of as a new paradigm might come to be seen as a myth. Among the subjects Hafez discussed, with strictly relevant footnotes, were foreign reporting, foreign broadcasting and satellite television. At the end, he returned to economics and to an article by two English economists, Paul Hirst and Grahame Thompson, 'Globalization – A Necessary Myth', published in 2000 in one of the first Globalization Readers. Despite Hafez's concerns, he agreed with them that the answer is: 'Yes: it is.'

The story of global economics necessarily accompanies the story of global communications, and in the summer of 2000 global economies suffered a shock. The Swedish Internet concern Boo.com collapsed, followed by a remarkable fall in the value of shares in Amazon, one of the best-known Internet companies, which dealt in books (see p. 285): they lost a fifth of their value on Wall Street in one day. 'Dealers await Amazon waves', was one newspaper headline. Yet a headline of July 2001 could read: 'Amazon beats expectations, closing in on profitability.' The business had just worked out a deal with AOL, Time/Warner. In a 'thinkers' guide to the e-conomy', *The Economist* in April 2000 had referred not to its fluctuations, a recurring word in the history of capitalism, but to its 'gyrations'. Such nuanced language did not help when, in 2001 (and later, in 2008), the fates of cyber-millionaires, 'a dot.com plutocracy', some of them incredibly young, were daily in view during the sharp swings in share prices on Wall Street and the stock exchanges of the world. 'High-tech' NASDAQ shares had begun to be listed as a distinct group in the United States in 1993. (The National Association of Securities Dealers Automated Quotations is an American online stock exchange.) Main Street was less involved then, or, indeed, in 2001, than Wall Street was. This was not to be the case in 2008.

The economics behind the technology of the Internet was only one dimension of debate about the Internet taking place around the turn of the century. The politics of spin or of sleaze captured attention, as did the manoeuvres and scandals of politicians. In his book *Communication and Control* (1991), Geoffrey Mulgan, having examined what he called 'a lattice of world networks', went on to consider techniques like offering unattributable leaks and even unanswerable lies. For him, these were all part of the 'mediating process', all developing 'in tandem with the technologies which carry them'. Significantly, the role of the press in that mediating process received more critical attention during the 1990s on both sides of the Atlantic than the role of other media and the new technologies on which they rested. For this reason alone, leaving out all questions of 'hype', the most recent period in the social history of the media cannot treat the Internet as the climax. It was a period when, as always, there were diverse strands and multiple options.

In what was thought of as a multimedia society and then as a digital society, a main cause of alarm for many disinterested observers was neither the gyrations of the media market nor the dangers of 'technopoly', but the rise of what the American critic David Halberstam called 'a culture of allegation and assertion at the expense of an older culture of verification'. Halberstam was writing in his introduction to a study, *Warp Speed* (1999), which included among its chapter headings 'The Rise of Anonymous Sourcing', 'There Are No Gatekeepers Here' and 'The Argument Culture'. The authors of the book, Bill Kovach and Tom Rosenstiel, quoted a Lippmann comment of 1920 that 'public as well as private reason depends on the importance of having an accurate, reliable account of "events". Not what somebody says, not what somebody wishes were true, but what is so, constitutes the touchstone of sanity.' Habermas would concur. Any such judgements, like condemning journalists for relying on anonymous political sources, television producers for failing to present 'hard news' during presidential elections, and Internet providers for dealing not in information and ideas but in 'garbage', including pornography, require to be placed in a broad historical context and seen, as far as possible, in perspective.

It is valuable, therefore, to return in conclusion to the fate in the last years of the twentieth century of the familiar trinity of information, education and entertainment. Information raised the same issues as before, with continuing argument about the interpretation of particular events as well as about the 'information economy' and 'information society', the latter term being described by a South African professor of journalism and media studies, Guy Gough Berger, as one of the most 'slippery phrases yet to grace contemporary discourse'.

One new book of 2000, *The Social Life of Information*, gained in interest since one of its two authors, John Seely Brown, had been Chief Scientist at the Xerox Corporation. His argument was that the gap between 'hype' about communications technology and 'end-user gloom' was largely due to the 'tunnel vision' that 'information-driven technologies' breed: news stories compete and conflict. There is no single agreed narrative. Both 'events' – like the tearing down of 'the Wall' in Germany in 1989 and the subsequent collapse of the Soviet Union, or the Tiananmen Square protests in Beijing, also in 1989 – and 'issues' – such as the spread of Aids – were sometimes turned confidently into drama also, with fictional elements being introduced but not always identified. The record of the information that was presented, sometimes misrepresented, sometimes bypassed during the last decade of the twentieth century, shows how easy it was to turn information into entertainment, the staple of the visual media.

Education was usually under scrutiny in radio, television and the press. There always seemed to be unique educational opportunities in digital convergence, despite fears in all societies and cultures of 'digital gaps', domestic and international – gaps between those who were literate in the new technology and those who were not and, probably, never would be. Yet there were complaints that computer literacy was becoming a substitute for, not a complement to, verbal and visual literacy. There was a contrast between the 1960s and the 1990s. When the state had intervened directly during the 1950s and 1960s to widen access to higher education in the interest, as its leaders saw it, not only of individuals but of societies, its intervention had coincided with the emergence of television, and the word 'convergence' had been used then in a spirit of hope, the same kind of hope that had been evident in the early years of radio. There had also been a related and encouraging shift in language at the same time, as the word 'learning' began to be more generally used, sometimes, but never universally, in place of the word 'teaching' (or, indeed, the word 'knowledge'). The new language was developed further and as part of the shift phrases like 'learning how to learn' and, with it, 'lifelong learning' began to be taken seriously. There was even talk of a 'learning society', a phrase used by the second Rector of the new United Nations University, the Indonesian Soedjatmoko (1922–89), who invited the Swede Edi Ploman (see p. 268) to Tokyo to join his staff as a Vice-Rector to head a new 'knowledge division'. The words 'learning society' were subsequently to be used in the title of an official paper produced by the European Community in 1995.

Learning at a Distance

The British Open University, planned meticulously but imaginatively during the 1960s, led the way in recruiting distance-learning students, in the first instance on the political initiative of Britain's Prime Minister Harold Wilson, who was determined both to widen access to higher education and to employ new technologies: he talked, the first British politician to do so, of a white-hot technological revolution, fully aware that it was largely taking place outside Britain. No formal entry qualifications were demanded by the new Open University. In the words of its first Chancellor, Geoffrey Crowther, a former editor of *The Economist*, who welcomed Wilson's initiative, it was open to students, open to ideas and open to methods. The University enrolled its first degree students in 1971, and its hundred-thousandth student graduated in 1989. Capable of adaptation, the Open University had greatly extended its non-degree work during the 1980s to include professional education. It went on to extend its area of operations during the 1990s, setting up a United States branch in 1999 and providing courses in business management in Russia.

Distance learning had been launched earlier than 1971 in Canada, Australia and New Zealand, and in 1989 a 'Commonwealth of Learning' was created, with its head office in Vancouver, to foster 'the channelling of resources to projects and programmes in distance education in Commonwealth countries'. The report leading to its establishment was called for by a Caribbean Secretary-General of the Commonwealth, 'Sonny' Ramphal, and its first executive head, James Maraj, was a Caribbean also. Financial resources were restricted, but the enterprise was genuinely global in scale. Brunei was an early contributor. By 1991, other national open universities had come into existence, among them the Indira Gandhi National Open University, established in India in 1985, and the Israeli Open University, along with so-called 'mega' open universities in Thailand and China, with huge numbers of students enrolled. In Japan, a University of the Air, founded in 1984 and modelled on the Open University, used NHK's second educational channel. More than institutionalization had been involved: there were significant changes in perception. 'Traditional' universities themselves came to take up distance learning in the name of 'outreach': the word 'traditional' applied to them as well as to what were beginning to be called traditional media. Some of the universities also changed their ways of teaching within their own campuses in response to an increased number of students, a general phenomenon. Seminars, traditional in Germany, became as common as lectures.

With the arrival of the Internet, there were extended possibilities of lifelong learning, formal and informal, whenever experience or expectation called for it, and there were claims that the World Wide Web, with access open to it, would serve for many as a 'university without walls'. Yet during the European Community's European 'Year of Lifelong Learning', member governments of the European Community, particularly Britain, were more interested in schools than in universities and in skills than in degrees. Meanwhile, Cisco Systems, one of the most effective of the American Internet companies, founded in 1984 by a group of computer scientists from Stanford University, was deeply involved in education in all the countries where it operated, seeking, it said, to help change 'the way we work, live, play, and learn'. Cisco also appreciated the necessity of working through and not against other educational institutions. The languages of advertising and of education might converge – the last version of 'convergence' – as they did not only in Cisco advertisement, but in a press release announcing the publication by Eurydice, the European Commission's 'information network on education', of *Two Decades of Reform in Higher Education in Europe* (2000). The publication drew in statistics too, and the press release was entitled: 'Convergence across European Higher Education Systems viewed in the Light of the Facts.'

8

The Return of the Social

If one phenomenon stands out from the throng of events and happenings in the media history of the early twenty-first century, it is 'social media'. In the 2000s and 2010s, many of the most famous and recognizable brands in media, and in the world, were social media – among them Facebook, Twitter and YouTube. These were not world-leading corporations in terms of their revenues, and the number of people they employed was modest, not going above a few thousand worldwide. Still, arguably, they were among the most influential in shaping publics and daily lives on a global scale. Some of the basic and everyday ways that people connected with others and with the world became named after digital and social media brands: 'tweeting', 'skyping', 'googling'. A certain return of the social to the centre stage of mediated communication took place, then, in the 2000s and 2010s. This final chapter charts a course through those two decades, using the concept and the realities of the mediated social as a main point of orientation.

In the period of convergence before the start of the new century, covered by Chapter 7, media industries were actively promoting the notion of media use as something that should be tailored to the individual. The technologies of the Internet were seen ideally as a means of enabling individuals to seek out and receive the content to suit their tastes, when and where they preferred. Personal choice was often linked to overarching notions of freedom and liberty, in discourses on the Internet as well as in the incumbent mass media, as deregulation and increased competition took hold there from the 1980s. The notion of this autonomous individual, unmoored both from the bonds of media producers and from other members of the media audience, was supplemented in the early 2000s by an ideal conception of the media user as sociable, sharing and communicative. In more historical terms, it should be noted that this amounted to a reframing in more positive terms of media users who had been grouped together in negatively inflected ways. Whereas the social instincts of media-consuming crowds were associated with unruliness and manipulability in the eighteenth and nineteenth centuries, in the early twenty-first they could be seen as active and constructive.

A case in point was the title of a 2006 bestselling book by the journalist James Surowiecki, *The Wisdom of Crowds*. Various forms of tailoring of media to individual use would continue to be central, even extended in some important respects that will be explained in this chapter. But the new emphasis on the social was not merely a media-industrial discourse; it also captured a broader imagination, one that opposed traditional power holders and hierarchies. Among the more thoughtful of those who believed in that empowerment was the Harvard law professor Yochai Benkler. He linked networked social collaboration online to a promise of greater freedom and democratization, but also emphasized that the promise came with no guarantee of being fulfilled. Among the obstacles, Benkler counted not only the incumbent media industries, who would try and hold on to their market positions, but also the commercial logic that was spreading online.

His solution was collaboration that built on ideal or at least non-commercial motives, as in the unpaid entry contributions that comprised the online encyclopaedia Wikipedia. Following its launch in 2001, Wikipedia became the largest reference site on the Web. Run by a nonprofit foundation and enabling in principle all Web users to contribute, Wikipedia drew on the encyclopaedia genre's rich traditions for collaborative production going back to the Enlightenment. The site expanded the encyclopaedia tradition by using Wiki software to build an impressively extensive site with a high degree of inclusiveness. This type of online collaboration was not always satisfactory for highly controversial topics and when professional standards were needed – factual errors were a recurring problem. Another problem (not exclusive to Wikipedia) was the manipulation of search engines by commercial interests. Still, Wikipedia remained a prime example showing that serious contributions to public discourse could be made by so-called 'crowdsourcing' and 'peer-to-peer production'.

The term 'social media' is in itself something of a misnomer. All media are social in the sense that their production and reception have a social dimension. They are routinely made in collaboration, received and made sense of in social settings. Also, many media are social in that they represent people being together, in film dialogues, broadcasting studios or massively multiplayer online games. Even a child gaming offline in the bedroom or a solitary parent watching a television game show on the floor below are not exempt from the social, since the concept of competition has to be realized on their respective screens in ways that are collectively recognizable.

At the same time, different media technologies do make a difference to how the social is articulated, and a longstanding discussion exists in media theory as to what that difference is. In a famous article from 1956, sociologists Donald Horton and Robert Wohl spoke of the relationship between the senders and audiences of broadcasting and film as a 'para-social interaction', a form of communication that bore some of the traits of informal social interaction, even though broadcasting technology worked on a principle of separating broadcasters from their audiences. The media performer onscreen might act in an accessible, informal, friendly manner, and the audience would regularly respond to the onscreen famous people as if they were friends, according to Horton and Wohl.

With the so-called 'interactivity' of digital media, which allowed audiences to become active users who engaged with digital technologies and with each other, a main limit of broadcasting had been overcome. The transition from so-called 'Web 1.0' to '2.0' at the turn of the century increased the emphasis by the ever more entangled media and tech industries on user-generated content that was shared in a mediated social setting. In her valuable history of social media, *The Culture of Connectivity*, José van Dijck pointed out that since social media connect people on the basis of automated systems, 'the meaning of "social" thus seems to encompass both (human) connectedness and (automated) connectivity'. She also made the point that such automated connectivity could run counter to the logic of interpersonal social relations. On Facebook, a 'friend' could be a family member, a person one knew intimately or a person one had never met.

The Web-based services of the 1990s had enabled the user to connect with others via, for instance, email or list-server groups, but did not actively push such connections as social media would later, and did not generate significant revenue from users connecting and sharing. From the early 2000s came service providers whose business idea was precisely to connect people, to put interactivity in the service of social connectivity and provide platforms for doing so to as many people as possible. These social media start-ups – which would evolve into major corporations – relied on new technologies that had the power to transform the ways that social interaction was harnessed, particularly via technologies of automation. The result was features like the personalized news streams on Facebook and Twitter. The rapid spread of smartphones with apps in the early twenty-first century enabled also those who were on the move, and those not owning a personal computer, to be connected via social media platforms.

An emphasis on the social aspects of media output was evident also in a number of other arenas. Again, it would be too simple to speak of this as new, since there had been, for instance, an emphasis in the gaming industry of the 1990s on developing games with multiple players connected via the Internet. Still, 'Web 2.0' media would provide an arena for more and more everyday social occasions to be conducted online – among them teamwork using collaborative software, management of the family's appointments via messaging services and organization of one's financial affairs by chatting online with a bank employee. Hobbies and leisure interests were increasingly activities that included the uploading and sharing of audio, still and moving image files. Apps were developed for dating, while romance and forms of sex were taking place in private chats. With the introduction of smartphones in the 2000s, their mobile and locative (e.g., their geographic location) functions connected people on the move in places and situations where before they could not be reached.

The result of these media technologies becoming commonly available in Western societies was a higher degree of media saturation. The owner of a smartphone could be excused for having a hard time remembering which application to open in order to retrieve the latest message: it could be a text message, an email, one of the dedicated message apps or a direct message option offered as part of some social media app. In the twenty-first century, the mediated social would penetrate deep into the micro-level of individual, mobile, everyday and intimate lives via digital technologies, as well as into the macro-level of politics and public life.

Everyday Mobility and Gaming

Mobility was in the minds of media industry decision-makers at the turn of the century. In 1998, at the Consumer Electronics Show in Las Vegas, Microsoft's CEO Bill Gates proclaimed: 'People want information everywhere they go. They want it on a small device. They want it in their car. They want it combined with their wireless telephone.'

As was described in Chapter 7, mobile phones had been spreading throughout the 1980s and 1990s to become a major means of telephony in the West and in East Asia. A significant part of everyday mediated communication had become wireless and portable, that is, continually available in pockets or handbags, strapped to the arm or carried in the hand. These media were close to the body in a new way. Marshall McLuhan described media as an 'extension' of man' (see p. 207) – and mobile phones turned out to be a prime example of this. So-called 3G or third-generation technology for distributing mobile phone signals was implemented from 2001, and made it possible to stream content to mobile units from the Web. A number of new services were built on this technological foundation, among them the podcast, digital audio files downloadable to mobile media. A decisive shift towards a popular use of phones to access, stream, upload to and download from the Web came with the introduction of the iPhone in 2007. It also offered what personal stereos like the Walkman and the iPod had already been providing for some years: the possibility of accessing a personally tailored music archive, mainly of music files using the audio coding format MP3.

Thus the iPhone and its later mobile competitors like Huawei and Samsung became powerful ensembles not only for downloading, storing and sharing music, but also for photographic images and other personalized data. The use of mobile media that were linked to the Web and to locative information became a commonplace: according to the telecommunications industry analyst Canalys, 2011 was the year when global sales of mobile phones outnumbered sales of personal computers. In itself, the smartphone is a device of unprecedented complexity, with telephony merely one of its many functions. Losing one's iPhone not only means being unable to call, surf or listen to music; it might well also mean not finding one's way around town, having no calculator or address book, no access to the ticket for an imminent plane trip, etc. Smartphones introduced not only extended forms of individual tailoring and facilitation, but also new technological dependencies and vulnerabilities.

Many of those vulnerabilities are social ones. Mobile media became surrounded by discussions about breaches of civility, the perceived impoliteness of, for instance, breaking off a conversation to read a text message, or shutting out other people by listening to music in headphones. These social tensions are real enough, and testament to the changes mobile technology caused to the order of social interaction. At the same time, behind such matters of politeness came other basic shifts in the configurations of the individual and the social. In a study of personal stereos with headphones or earplugs – such as the Walkman, a precursor to smartphone music listening – Michael Bull, a professor of sound studies, characterized the experience of moving around as an 'accompanied solitude'. This was a medially assisted way of being alone in that it tended to shut out other people, a way of replacing everyday experience with one's own choice of music. That meant taking a kind of control over the everyday by using otherwise boring or frustrating stretches of time for pleasurable aesthetic experience. At the same time, playlists of music built up by the user allowed for layering a kind of personal, musical narrative onto experience. That narrative may have social dimensions, despite the solitude involved in listening to it. Someone listening to a party playlist would, in a sense, be accompanied by that party setting even while being alone.

Other features of the smartphone directly invited new forms of social engagement. Text messages and the messaging functions of numerous apps connected mobile users on the go with others. Given a working wireless connection, it became possible at any time to communicate with others, either as individuals or in groups, and even with larger audiences, for instance via the message sections of blogs and digital newspapers. The technology also made it possible, as long as if someone was present at the other end, to communicate in 'real time', so that mobile users could keep in constant touch with one or several others while moving from A to B. This extended availability created some genuinely new kinds of social situation, and presents challenges that go hand in hand with the benefits of being able to connect across time and space. The flip side of being able to contact others at any time, even when on the move, is that others can always get in touch with you – or, at any rate, can always try to do so. The result is a certain form of extended social surveillance, where intimacy with friends and loved ones has been converted into the default expectation of always being available, always making oneself open to communication. This 'perpetual contact' – the title of a research anthology on mobile media – made possible what was termed 'micro-coordination' in mobile media researchers Richard Ling and Birgitte Yttri's contribution to that anthology.

The ease and expectation of mobile contact has made it possible for families and circles of friends to make appointments and sort out their logistics in new ways. Relations became more flexible and negotiable, but, by the same token, they also often demand more work. Instead of a definite, advance arrangement to meet at a certain time and place, the appointment could be negotiated in rounds of messaging back and forth, up to the last minute. These mechanisms were first observed for text messaging in the 1990s, but later social media took over with their larger circles of 'friends' and facilities for creating groups of different sizes and compositions. The micro-coordination of such mediated social circles became highly complex. Users now simultaneously manage groups for siblings, various circles of friends, colleagues and acquaintances, while gauging in this relatively unsettled social terrain how much to get involved or withdraw, whether to respond to the latest message or not.

The advent of digital image technologies led to discussions concerned with their relationship to what they represent, with more intensity the more closely the representation seems to correspond with real life. Digitalization brought a fresh urgency to this question, since it enabled representations that were life-like in more immersive and interactive ways. The 1980s saw the first 'virtual reality' technologies, in the form of headsets used for projecting simulations of a computer-generated environment, sometimes in combination with gloves or suits to provide a more tactile and whole-body experience. The figure of the 'cybernaut' putting on a headset and disappearing into virtual reality became a cultural preoccupation in the 1990s. This was propelled not only by the technology itself, but also by creative representations of its possibilities – for instance, in the novels of William Gibson (who coined the phrase 'cyberspace') and in films like *The Matrix*. Their common theme was the computer-generated world that had become so realistic and immersive that humans could not distinguish it from the 'real world', which consequently threatened to fade from sight.

This is not quite how media developments panned out in the 2000s and 2010s, however. The most immersive virtual reality (VR) technologies largely stayed with the specialized uses they had long been put to – for example, in aviation and robot navigation. They did not make the move into large-scale media consumption, although media industry development continued; Facebook, for example, bought the VR headset manufacturer Oculus Rift in 2014. Computer-generated simulations did turn out to be important and widely influential across media, but in less dramatic and controversial ways. One example was locative media, which spread with the adoption of smartphones and used inbuilt geolocation technologies like GPS. The American transportation network company Uber, for instance, and Google Maps enable users to be visually indicated on virtual maps that also provide suggestions for how to get from point A to point B. The film medium is another prime example: three-dimensional (3D) animation was key to the development of animated film, with leading companies like Pixar and Dreamworks basing their film production lines on this technology. Computer-generated imagery (CGI) made it possible to generate virtual environments for real film actors, and also to transform their physical appearance, as in the famous case of the character Gollum in *The Lord of the Rings*.

Another medium impacted by VR technologies was video games. As described in Chapter 7, video games became established in the 1970s as a media industry and a media technology in the home, particularly in youths' basements and kids' bedrooms. Generically speaking, developments were led by complex fight and quest games for consoles, like *Tomb Raider* and *Myst*, which demanded considerable time and effort to master. At the same time, gaming had become dominated by young males, both as producers and users. Towards the end of the twentieth century, games had also become more immersive in sensory terms, with 3D graphics and, later, high-definition imaging.

A change came when the industry turned its attention to so-called casual gamers in the 2000s. This was done in order to expand markets beyond the relatively limited group of hardcore gamers. Games designed for this group was often dominated by stagings of conflict and violence that tended to be divisive – a minority of users were turned on, but more were turned off by them. In his book *The Casual Revolution*, Danish game researcher Jesper Juul described this as a moment where the simpler and less dark early video games were rediscovered, and combined with online and mobile distribution. This was the case for the highly successful casual games *Angry Birds* and *Candy Crush Saga*, the latter accessed via Facebook. Also, console games were now designed more consciously with a view to the kinds of social interaction they generated in a group of gamers, as evidenced in *Singstar* and *Dance Dance Revolution*, which require gamers respectively to sing and dance.

This cultivation of casual players helped spread video games further throughout households and everyday life, including mobile life. When his book was published in 2010, Juul felt justified in concluding: 'To play video games has become the norm; to not play video games has become the exception.' In industrial terms, the video game industry by and large presented a story of growth in decades where other media industries experienced major setbacks. By 2019, video games, by most accounts, were a larger enterprise than either the music or the film industry. It is also worth noting for an activity with a male reputation that females had always been gamers. The globally top-selling game for many years in the 2000s was *The Sims*, the majority of whose users were female.

The broader integration of video games into everyday life changed their social significance. While controversies over problematic use and addiction persisted, there was more of the kind of everyday gaming few would see as deeply worrying. Casual gaming and the family-friendly activizing strategies promoted via, for instance, the Nintendo Wii console made the everyday presence and status of video games more like that of traditional board and card games. With this kind of prominence came a cultural impact that went beyond the revenues of their industries and the time spent gaming by individual users. Video games became a cultural point of reference and a source of aesthetic inspiration throughout the culture and media landscape. The sonic synthesizer world of early games was incorporated into the soundscape of mainstream pop music, and game-aesthetic features were used in popular film and television.

In addition, the logics and attractions of games found their way into work and business life as tools for selling products, for helping with motivation and promoting learning in organizations. For instance, ad campaigns for products were fashioned as games in which consumers were encouraged to play some product-related game and earn points that could be turned into discounts. This development, which has been termed 'gamification', had much of the transient business trend about it. It was an instance of how games, once considered to be a somewhat subcultural interest and a genuinely creative one to its defenders, could become a mainstream tool for businesses that were more interested in monetization via points and scoreboards, and less in the imaginative and aesthetic dimensions of games.

Mediated Selves and Intimate Lives

In simple terms, the environments offered by digital and social media can be seen either as worlds of their own, or as parts of our own world. For many of those experiencing media developments around the turn of the century, several of those taking place in digital media seemed to point towards the former possibility. In sensory terms, both immersive computer games and simulated environments like the Internet-based 3D *Second Life* appeared to be such worlds of their own. Then there were media of social interaction that were available in the 1990s in the form of chat rooms, bulletin boards and so-called multi-user dungeons (MUDs). These enabled some much-discussed forms of role play and experimentation with anonymity that seemed for a time to constitute a separate realm of human experience. Users could be represented in these worlds by so-called 'avatars' that were named and kitted out for virtual life by their users. 'Cyberspace' was a popular buzzword in the early 2000s, used to describe these digital worlds. In the parlance of the day, they were inhabited by 'cybernauts', who travelled from our realms into digital ones, like astronauts leaving this planet to discover others, where different existences were possible.

Virtuality was in itself a very real and important part of media-technological developments, and the history of, for instance, computer games can hardly be understood without it. As a means of leaving one's own social and physical world behind, however, at the time of writing this fourth edition it remains more an eventuality than a reality. The rise of social media has turned out to be a case of mediated sociality being closely interlinked with interpersonal social life, rather than separate from it. On the major social media sites, users more often than not use their real names, message with actual friends and post about their real jobs and holidays. Meanwhile, the concerns of virtuality – particularly a loss of the sense of reality – receded somewhat in public consciousness. In their place came other concerns, and in many ways the downsides of social media dominated debates over media development in the first decades of this century.

As a professor of social studies at the Massachusetts Institute of Technology, Sherry Turkle has been an influential and in many ways symptomatic thinker, whose work has made a turn away from an initial embrace of digital media as worlds of their own. Like many intellectuals writing influentially about current media development since Marshall McLuhan in the 1960s and Neil Postman in the 1980s (see pp. 13, 17, 257), Turkle's writings are positioned somewhere between academic contribution, cultural-social diagnosis and civilizational critique. In 1995, she published *Life on the Screen*, which suggested that a life led in engagement with digital media was profoundly different from a nondigital one. Although far from uncritical, it argued that being anonymous in this digital life could in certain circumstances be freeing and empowering, for instance in the forms of gender play it made possible.

By the time she published *Alone Together* in 2011, Turkle's views of social life had darkened significantly, as she herself made clear in the book. She had developed a bad feeling about the kind of loneliness she now saw among young digital and social media users. It seemed to her the result of choosing comforts promised by technology over the uncertainties of intimacy with actual others – seeking comfort in robotic pets like the Tamagotchi, or texting instead of actually talking with others. Turkle's concerns reflected a wider anxiety in the early 2000s over whether core values of subjecthood and social life were being eroded by media-technological developments, values such as authenticity, intimacy, trust and privacy.

Turkle's account, although successful in capturing a moment when the popular imaginary shifted, was also partial. It did not leave much room for considering digital technologies as tools for a self-expression that was meaningful to users. Yet clearly, many users were engaging with them for that reason. A key dimension in the development of digital technologies on both sides of the millennial shift was that of enabling non-professional users to articulate their sense of self and identity. Along with the 1990s phenomenon of reality television, the interactive affordances of digital media gave so-called 'ordinary people' an increased visibility in the media and, to varying degrees, also an increased control over the conditions of representation.

Two main genres of such digitally mediated participation were blogs (short for 'weblogs') and digitally made non-professional self-portraits, called 'selfies'. They became expressions of popular creativity on a grand scale. Blogs had no upper word limits and mobile phones allowed for extensive image capture and storage. The most striking feature of these digital means of expression, therefore, was the enormous quantity of texts and images they allowed non-professionals to produce and publish on the Web. Also, both blogs and selfie-publishing apps like Instagram involved regular publishing and archives that accumulated. Hence, over time they produced a comprehensive mediated image of the person in question, and of his or her everyday life.

This combined quantity and everydayness in some senses allowed users a greater degree of control over how their lives and selves appeared to others. At the same time, they became vulnerable to accusations that this intensified self-representation was a sign of vanity and self-centeredness. It is probably not a coincidence that the sociologist Erving Goffman's 1956 book *The Presentation of Self in Everyday Life* had a new lease on life fifty years later in intellectual and scholarly commentary on these 'personal media', as they have been called. Goffman's book was about the ways social life is a kind of performance that involves all of us adapting to the social situations at hand. The 'presentation of self in digital life' seemed to be a version of interpersonal social life where performers faced a more uncertain kind of situation on social media, potentially facing both friends and strangers, 'lurkers' and 'trolls' – but where they also had more extensive control over how they came across.

From the late 1990s, new Web publishing tools such as WordPress had made it possible for owners of a computer to publish online without needing programming or HTML skills. From that point, the blog – simply defined, a website updated with posts regularly displayed in reverse chronological order – rapidly developed and had a particular prominence in the early years of the century. Some of the self-communicating functions of blogs were taken over by social media accounts and profiles, but blogs remained a significant digital genre: in February 2019, the blog search engine Technorati reported tracking twenty-two million English-language sites and more than a billion links. Some blogs were celebrity-authored and theme-driven (focused around tech, fashion, crafts or politics, for example), but from the start a main subgenre was produced by 'ordinary' people who related their personal life experiences – mainly in their own periodic blog posts, but also by engaging with others in blog comments sections. The personal blog became a main means of self-expression and connection with others. Its distinct appeal came from being updated continuously, so that readers and commenters could access a life as it was being lived, in sync with their own.

While the blog had its media-historical predecessors in the journal and the autobiography, selfies could be seen as the latest instantiation of a long tradition of self-portraits in art and visual media. From the standpoint of an interest in visual media history, a major shift took place as portable and affordable cameras were marketed to popular audiences from the early twentieth century onwards. This democratization of photography inserted the medium into the self-imaging process of ordinary people, and into the everyday life of families, as the emergence of family photo albums attested.

When digital and then mobile phone cameras came on the market, the number of images that could be easily captured and stored rose drastically. Most adults in Western countries now had the ability to generate large image archives documenting their lives, and to digitally exchange images with others. On the one hand, this allowed for an intensified communication of everyday and intimate lives. At the same time, editing and filtering tools became available, both integrated with the cameras themselves and in dedicated apps. The selfies sent to others and displayed via social media platforms are thus often noticeably crafted. They are the result of a process under which subjects have worked on images of themselves to make them look more pleasing, striking or entertaining. As the digital media researcher Jill Walker Rettberg has pointed out, these images present viewers with a filtered reality in both the image-technological and the cultural sense of the word.

Both blogs and selfies are surrounded by suspicions of self-absorption and superficiality. In some of these reactions, gender dimensions are apparent. Here, as in many other circumstances, it is easier to denigrate the self-expressions of young women. In a number of cases of self-representation, a circling around the self can be hard to disentangle from its broader societal conditions. A case in point is the way in which these genres are used by individuals with a disease who want to communicate with others in the same situation and, in doing so, cope with their own illness. Since the late 1990s, the availability of personal media has made it possible for patients to chronicle their life with illness through a combination of periodical posts on blogs or social media with photos of themselves and their life in and out of treatment. Typically, these are very personal and intimate accounts, sometimes harrowing ones. At the same time, these autobiographies are often motivated by a wish to communicate with others in a similar situation, to offer companionship and support. They represent portraits of everyday lives that are dependent on hospitals and the medical professions, of people who might struggle to deal with these circumstances, or with other societal systems like the welfare bureaucracy. These personal media uses are, at the same time, both political and deeply personal.

Personal media expressions connect at numerous points not only to society and to politics, but also to the worlds of businesses and organizations. From the early times of the Internet, everyday human interaction captured by personal media has been seen by some entrepreneurs and Web enthusiasts as harbouring a great economic potential. Symptomatic of this line of thought was the online *Cluetrain Manifesto* of 1999, which used the heated rhetoric of the Internet as a revolutionary force by couching its arguments in the form of ninety-five theses, borrowing from no less a historical figure than Martin Luther. 'Markets are conversations' was the manifesto's number one thesis. The idea was that traditional businesses were not able to speak in human voices and interact, but that the Internet enabled just these types of communication, and was therefore the future of business.

The manifesto's thinking about digital media and media history was simplistic, but its claim that the subjective voice of the digital participant could be used for business turned out to have merit. Organizations and businesses established blogs and social media accounts, attempting precisely to commercialize conversations in personal and social media. In the first decades of the twenty-first century, there were also numerous examples of ordinary people using digital technologies in an attempt to become extraordinary, non-professionals aiming for careers. They would often harness an ensemble of social media, updating frequently, keeping track of the user statistics that social media networks make available, trying to establishing a distinct mediated persona and building what became to be known as a 'personal brand'.

In doing so, some bloggers, social media 'influencers' and 'youtubers' would be able to generate revenue through advertising, sponsoring or product placement, in addition to the excitement and fun of media visibility. A few were also able to approach the kind of fame that the established celebrities of mass media enjoyed, such as the Kardashian family. More often, this was a kind of second-tier fame, as illustrated by the blogger Perez Hilton, whose assumed name was a reference to the TV personality Paris Hilton. The term 'microcelebrity' has been used to characterize the more transient and seemingly less legitimate kind of fame that personal and social media afforded.

At the same time, the terrain inhabited by these career media participants, as one might call them, was highly precarious. Their sources of income tended to be unsteady, their economic activity often took place in legal grey areas, and their social status was uncertain. On the one hand, many achieved the media visibility they had been actively and eagerly seeking. At the same time, the negative social sanctioning from others via social media could be harsh. In her 2017 book *(Not) Getting Paid to Do What You Love*, the digital communication researcher Brooke Erin Duffy interviewed female social media entrepreneurs and found them suspended 'between amateurism and expertise, between authenticity and strategic self-branding, and between internal drivers and external demands'.

Within families, the adoption of social media and mobile technologies has created new patterns of media use. They have moved the family further away from media consumption as an occasion for physical gathering, prototypically around the TV in the living room. Video games and Internet connections on desktop computers contributed to this splitting-up in the 1990s. Social and mobile media further accelerated the process whereby media interfaces became available not only in more and more rooms of the house but also outside it, via smartphones. A comprehensive survey made public by the EU Kids Online network in 2011 found that the average European 9–16-year-old at that time spent eighty-eight minutes online per day, that 49 per cent of these went online via computers in their bedroom and 33 per cent via a mobile or handheld device.

Thus there has been a process of individualization, whereby TV content could now be accessed separately by each family member in different locations. Young family members might be streaming from personal laptop computers or via the YouTube app on their smartphones, while older ones would more often continue using conventional broadcast television. In terms of the ways media consumption has happened within the family, this is a progress partly of social fragmentation, partly of new social configurations. The children's rooms, for instance, became media-saturated in themselves. The Internet and mobile media consumption happening in this 'bedroom culture', often together with peers, is often unavailable to parents.

In some measure, the physical splitting up of the family's media consumption was counteracted by social media, which has made it possible for family members to stay in touch outside the home, and enables an extended surveillance of children by adults. Long-standing apprehensions among parents and in public debates over children's exposure to pornography continued into the 2000s, as did concerns over excessive time spent with media, particularly in terms of teenage boys gaming. Some scares intensified, such as those over bullying having moved to the Internet and children making contact via the Internet with adults who were scheming to abuse them – so-called 'grooming'.

Sometimes, the real worries were more unexpected. Breaking with the stereotype of children as innocents, the EU Kids Online network found a significant number of cases where bullying was done by children to their peers – and by children who had, in a majority of cases, been bullied themselves. Limits on screen time and installing browser filters became means of control for parents looking for something tangible that could protect their children. Such measures were limited, however, since much of children's use still took place away from the control of parents. For instance, pornographic content had reached a level of online availability that was very hard to counteract. Also, these new forms of surveillance and censorship provoked questions of whether or not children have privacy rights and are entitled to a measure of personal dignity.

At the same time, the Internet was becoming more and more important as a source of information and socializing. This means that depriving children of access has major disadvantages for their learning and literacy. Not only would they be deprived of information needed to develop key literacies and engagement in society; everyday social activities that sustain them would also be undermined – such as making appointments, keeping in touch with friends and loved ones. As with adults, children depend on digital media to be part of social life. As the EU Kids Online II final report concluded, 'opportunities and risks online go hand in hand'.

Algorithms

An increasing concern with media corporations' surveillance of users would mark the first decades of the new century. It had historical roots in the rise of large-scale media industries of the twentieth century. Since they were capital-intensive efforts to reach large-scale audiences, these industries needed to gather systematic information about audiences' tastes and behaviours. In the mass media, some information could be obtained one-off when starting a newspaper subscription, or when viewers paid a licence fee to a public service broadcaster. The second main means of information was data gathered by the industry about the media use itself. With newspapers, this was traditionally limited to the occasional survey, while broadcasters monitored viewing patterns in more detail, for instance by connecting mechanical 'people meters' to television sets in selected households. While this amounted to a fairly extensive surveillance of who watched what programme and channel at any given time, digital technology would provide significantly more extensive means of registering information about user behaviour. And crucially, it helped facilitate a sharing of this information to an extent that was unprecedented in the media industries.

The key element of this digitalized process of garnering audience information was automation, particularly via the use of algorithms. In simple terms, an algorithm is a series of formal steps – in a digital media context, of computations – taken to solve a task or problem. By the turn of the century, the dramatically increasing computational power of micro-processors enabled an extremely fast and automatic processing by means of algorithms that, for instance, helped Google scan vast swathes of the Web for replies to each query. Those replies could then be accompanied by advertising that was targeted with the help of the user information that the algorithm had provided. Algorithms came to play a crucial role both for search engines like Google, in the workings of social media networks and for so-called content aggregators like Amazon, Netflix, iTunes and Spotify. Their users' histories of searches, postings, likes, retweets and other activities left a wealth of digital traces that were available for potential use. This was the promise of so-called 'big data' that could be 'mined' through the use of algorithms. Data mining by means of algorithms proved to be a powerful booster for media start-ups. Founded in 1998 in California by Larry Page and Sergey Brin, Google LLC rapidly went from a small start-up to a major search engine that first rivalled competitors like Yahoo and Alta Vista and then overtook them. Google became the dominant global actor in Western markets, with google.com the most visited website in the world by 2016, according to the Web traffic analysis company Alexa Internet. As it expanded, the Google corporation branched out into products like digital maps, translators, books and the mobile operating system Android.

Algorithmic sifting through enormous amounts of digital information had become possible because of long-term and concerted efforts to increase signal capacity. The major telecommunications companies penetrated markets with broadband cables that could handle not only the mostly text-based Web of the 1990s, but also, increasingly, images, video and audio. These efforts were often supported by Western governments eager to digitalize their nations. Around the turn of the century, Web access and speed were treated as key measures of societal progress. Indeed, connective speed for a while was exalted much as it had been when the railways had been built, or when Italian futurists in the early twentieth century dreamed of greater and greater speeds of flight. By 2015 there would be 3.2 billion users of the Internet globally, as estimated by the International Telecommunication Union, with broadband connection having become the norm for a large majority living in the West. In parts of the world that lacked this infrastructure, such as sub-Saharan Africa and rural Latin America, developments would be slower and largely concentrated around access to the Internet via smartphones. And it should not be forgotten that the poorest in the Third World continued to live worlds apart from Western media saturation.

Although algorithmic processing was available around the turn of the century, the strategic use of it to boost revenue streams and user numbers significantly increased from around 2005. 'Boom and bust' cycles shaped the development of digital media, and the 1990s had been dominated by website providers who faced a major downturn with the bursting of the so-called 'dot-com bubble' in 2000. Social media start-ups then provided the next surge, transforming from small-scale operations to world-spanning corporations. Much of this staggering success was attributable to the scale at which algorithms could be used for surveillance-based recommendations that were personalized yet could reach unprecedented numbers of users. Twitter built a significant part of its appeal by providing rankings of trending topics that were based on algorithmic searches of hundreds of millions of tweets. The information paths enabled by these automation tools significantly changed the structures and professions of the media industries. As they became progressively integrated with the computer and telecommunications industries, computer engineers became central figures. Their competencies in coding and programming were highlighted and sometimes idealized as the key media skills of the future. Other new professions received more limited attention and were carried out on much less favourable work terms, such as frontline call-centre work and the moderating and censoring of undesirable digital content.

Following the mining and processing of user data was a process of tailoring and providing recommendations to the user. By the 2010s, users became familiar with a wide range of such recommendations, designed to boost and steer media use. Examples included Twitter's 'trending tweets', Spotify's 'recommended songs' and Amazon's 'customers who viewed this item also viewed . . .'. The more users generated by these kinds of tactic, the more user data could be mined that were of interest not only to the corporations themselves, but also to a host of third party companies willing to pay for such data. The ecosystem of social media developed as an intricate set of connected businesses. Social media network providers collaborated with data analysis companies, and also interconnected with each other, as when Google merged with YouTube in 2006.

The automated ways of connecting people afforded by algorithms was very hard to understand for those doing the socializing – in some cases near impossible. This opacity to users was to become highly controversial. Again, secrecy was not something entirely new to the media industries, which had always been protective of information that could affect their competitive

standing. In some significant ways, the workings of the social media industries exacerbated opacity, however. Their surveillance was so extensive that
it became very hard for outsiders to trace, or even to realize that it was
happening. In her 2017 book *Technically Wrong*, digital media designer Sara
Wachter-Boettcher catalogued a range of opaque ways that algorithm-based
services ran counter to users' interests and even to their basic dignity. Her
examples ranged from happy-style invitations by Facebook to celebrate a
user's year marked by grief, to transgender persons being forced to tick off
conventional gender boxes in order to access services. Particularly offensive
were the instances in 2015 when images of Afro-Americans were automati-
cally tagged as 'gorillas' by Google Photos. The tag had been applied by
an image-learning algorithm (an example of 'artificial intelligence') whose
automatized choice-making went badly wrong, so that Google had to make
a public apology.

Beyond such anecdotal instances of how automation and algorithms
could cause scandal lay other opacities. As the services offered by the social
media industries expanded, they tended to install themselves as de facto
infrastructures, as several researchers have pointed out. This means they
went from being one of several providers to being the de facto environment
that housed the service. The Chinese application WeChat, a mobile platform
that reached one billion active users in 2018, is perhaps the most striking
example of a social media platform that was able to install itself as an all-
purpose infrastructure of communication. It offers not only social media
connection and group and private messaging, but also video games, video
calls and conferencing, e-commerce payment, video and photo sharing.

Another example is Google Maps, which has come a long way towards
becoming the cartographic default standard for the 'geospatial Web' since
its introduction in 2005. That development was made possible by a combination of geolocation technologies and user-generated input that have
provided not only traditional map functions but also starred rankings for
restaurants, museums and other facilities in the vicinity of the user. These
added features increased the market standing and revenue of Google while,
at the same time, naturalizing it, making it something to navigate without
really considering whose perspectives and interests it served. In roughly
the same period, Uber succeeded in becoming a transport infrastructure
in important Western urban areas. Industry actors termed this a 'platform
revolution', and there is no doubt that digital applications have grown in
prominence significantly in recent decades, driven particularly by the adoption of smartphones and tablets. Still, it may make more sense in the long
run to speak of platforms working to achieve the status of infrastructures,

in a process driven by motives of market dominance and revenue. In such cases, the maintenance and repair of services that were default options to its users, in much the same way as roads and waterworks were, would also be dependent on commercial considerations.

The powers of algorithms extended from the microsocial relations of staying in touch and moving around to the ways in which algorithmic media tied in with larger societal forces. Indeed, several media researchers were willing to argue that the mining and selling of user data from social media had become so important as to signal that a new economic logic had taken hold in Western societies. Harvard Business School professor Shoshana Zuboff raised the stakes in her 2019 book with the programmatic title *The Age of Surveillance Capitalism.* To Zuboff, capitalism now crucially depended for its working on the capture and processing of information in ways that were far more extensive than in earlier epochs. According to her, they also had to be opaque, so that the extent of repression could not be apparent to those who were paying for the generating of profit with their privacy, while believing life was merely being made more convenient for them.

The social media networks that have become dominant, and the algorithmic technologies underpinning them, operated for the most part outside regulatory regimes. For a long time, there were few or no demands for editorial or content management. In addition, tax rates for these media corporations were very low in the various countries into which they expanded from their starting point in the United States. The reasons for this relative lack of regulation were many. First, although many European states had a strong tradition throughout the twentieth century of regulating the media via monopolies and then licences, by the time the social media corporations had become established this tradition had been largely displaced by an ethos of deregulation and free market competition. Second, the globalized activities of major media corporations largely escaped the reach of regulators and politicians bound by national borders. Also, international policy bodies such as WTO and the EU put more emphasis on promoting free trade than on regulating it. In so far as policy was impacting social media, their spread was instead encouraged by the free trade ideology underlying international trade agreements like NAFTA and GATT.

For a long time, regulators of digitalization mostly focused their attention on copyright infringement in connection with the copying and downloading of 'pirated' data files. In addition, the activity of social media corporations seemed for many years not necessarily to be concerned with public interest. Their basis was as much in the computer and telecommunications industries as it was in the media industries, where the need to regulate content was more established. As will be discussed later in this chapter, a series of political scandals and controversies throughout the 2010s would change this relationship between social media corporations, regulators and politicians.

Facebook

The first major example of a media corporation that originated in the IT sector and used it as a springboard for moves into different digital media and services on a global scale was Google, launched in 1998. The years 2004–6 saw in short order the launch of both Facebook and YouTube, which in January 2019 had, respectively, 2.2 billion and 1.9 billion users, according to Statista. In their early years, they both became globally dominant in the area of social media networking, although there were some notable exceptions to this Western dominance. Chinese social media sites like WeChat and QQ reached comparable levels of use, mainly thanks to their command of the world's largest domestic market.

By virtue of its sheer audience size, its influence in the media sector and the political controversies surrounding it, Facebook was arguably the most important social media network site of them all. Many of the sites that later gained a mass following had started out as small-scale operations for networks of friends and acquaintances. This was the case with the service originally called Facemash, launched in 2003 by a student at Harvard University, Mark Zuckerberg, and initially available for that university's students only. Zuckerberg wrote the software for Facemash, a site that compared and ranked female students, using, for instance, student photos obtained by breaking into the university server. In an instance of absorbing but rather selective history writing, the film *The Social Network* explained much of Facebook's early development as a result of Zuckerberg's duplicitous and asocial manoeuvring, some of which was alleged and some of which (like the stealing and illicit use of Harvard student photos) undeniable.

A less individualistic explanation would be to say that the early history of Facebook was shaped by the founder's background in a certain type of male hacker culture, and by the algorithmically based gathering and use of personal data as a foundation for business start-ups. The ideology of Facebook and Zuckerberg has been characterized by José van Dijck as a 'liaison between geek culture and counterculture'. Zuckerberg articulated a rationale for Facebook that borrowed from ideals of the early Internet as non-hierarchical and participative in an empowering sense. These were reformulated as relatively abstract ideals of sharing and connecting. Sharing

Fig. 23 Mark Zuckerberg.

was good because it brought people together and fostered mutual under-standing, argued Zuckerberg, so the bigger Facebook became, the better it was for the world. In a 'Letter to investors' written in 2012, Zuckerberg claimed that 'Facebook was not originally created to be a company. It was built to accomplish a social mission – to make the world more open and connected.' This self-understanding of Facebook as basically an idealistic enterprise could be found also in other major corporations emerging around the millennium, as evidenced in Google's slogan until 2018: 'Don't be evil.' Whether or not the intention was genuine, the self-legitimating rhetoric set these corporations up for accusations of hypocrisy when their practices came under greater public scrutiny.

The first years of Facebook were marked by rapid expansion, as the site went from an exclusive platform for Harvard University students to being universally accessible for everyone aged 13 or above with a valid email account. In 2008, international headquarters were established in Ireland, and Zuckerberg announced on the company blog that Facebook had reached its 100 millionth active user. Investments from venture capital-ists like Peter Thiel made the expansion possible, but as for Internet-based companies more generally, it was not clear in this period where the profits would come from.

A major change in corporate strategy seems to have come around 2008–10, coinciding with the hiring of Sheryl Sandberg as Facebook's Chief Operating Officer. From her former position with Google as vice-president of online sales and operations, Sandberg brought a keener sense of what it would take to monetize a corporation at the scale Facebook was heading towards. This meant developing algorithms for several key purposes. One was in tracking users more comprehensively in order to generate data that were more commercially attractive. Another was applying algorithmic selectiveness to the Facebook site itself, so that the content of each user's news feed depended on which Facebook content that user had previously liked or commented on, as well as on the user's other activities on the site.

Crucially for Facebook's reformed business model, algorithmically generated user data were the basis of targeted adverts, so that, for instance, some hobby listed by a user in the profile might lead to ads for matching products in that user's news feed. The eerie feeling of being spied on that could sometimes result was testament to the extensiveness of the tracking that lay in the background, and how opaque that process mostly was to the user. In his 2018 highly critical account of Facebook's history, *Anti-Social Media*, Siva Vaidhyanatham has pointed out that this form of advertising logic was different from the one dominating most of the media industries in the twentieth century. The old model was based on 'methods of persuasion', on appealing to consumers without knowing with any precision whether they were interested. With automated surveillance and data mining, 'advertising became much more about aligning interest with offers', writes Vaidhyanatham. It was now possible to target consumers whose user data had already revealed them to be interested.

This was undeniably a way of making advertising more relevant for those it targeted. At the same time, critics of twentieth-century advertising had pointed out that the logic of giving the customer what the customer wanted hid a different kind of operation. Media companies were effectively turning its audiences into commodities, selling their media attention to advertisers, as the political communications researcher Dallas Smythe pointed out in the context of the mass media of the twentieth century. The question for the twenty-first century, then, was how, and with what consequences, social media corporations were using digital technologies to commoditize the user.

One main answer to that question lay in the ways data were sold by Facebook to third parties. In technical terms, this involved making Facebook's application programming interface (API) available to them, together with other digital tools that made it easy for these partners to mine

Facebook for user data. Through a service called Open Graph, Facebook partnered with a number of such partners to integrate services, so that, for instance, Facebook login could be used to access Spotify. At the same time, this enabled the corporations to share information, so that user activity on Spotify could be accessed by Facebook and vice versa – all without the users' knowledge. Keeping close track of Facebook's licence agreements and terms of service only yielded a very limited knowledge of how data were used, and in reality few users had the time, motivation or technological insight to pursue the issue.

The years after 2010 saw a spate of more or less scandalous incidents where Facebook was publicly exposed for having allowed third parties access to user data without users' knowledge. Until 2014, for instance, Facebook had collaborated with game developers not only by featuring them on their site, but also allowing them to data-mine the friends lists of those who played the games via Facebook. Covert use by Facebook of user data was even harder to spot in cases where the corporation accessed data outside the site itself. In 2018 came the most infamous of the user data scandals, when the *Guardian* first reported that the firm Cambridge Analytica had accessed data from more than eighty-seven million users, including data about their Facebook friends, ostensibly for use in research. Cambridge Analytica used the information to create detailed user profiles, which were sold to political actors for targeting. One such actor was the campaign organization behind Donald Trump's successful presidential bid in 2016; another was a group of Russian operators who used Cambridge Analytica's data to try and undermine Hillary Clinton's bid for the presidency. On top of this came several instances of people using the Facebook Live streaming service to attract attention to their suicides and murders, some for political reasons.

The weight of political controversy gradually registered. In a statement on his own Facebook page in 2017, Zuckerberg wrote: 'For the past decade, Facebook has focused on connecting friends and families. With that foundation, our next focus will be developing the social infrastructure for community – for supporting us, for keeping us safe, for informing us, for civic engagement, and for inclusion of all.' Here, the language of connectivity was being supplemented by formulations about safety, in an appeal to those who felt their rights were being threatened by Facebook's exploitation of their user data. As for 'civic engagement', it remained controversial as to whether the corporation was willing and able to engage effectively with its role as a political and democratic actor.

At the time of writing in 2019, there are signs, although uncertain ones, that Facebook's dominant market position is threatened. The media industries have long been supply-driven, with audience demand difficult to foresee. Major cyberspace experiments like Second Life, social media sites such as MySpace and search engines like Alta Vista have risen fast, then faded into insignificance or shut down. The enduring interest in Facebook lies in the fact that this corporation led in promoting a combination of automated algorithm processes, media-industrial strategies and social uses that are likely to be of more general and enduring importance.

Transformations of Digital Publics

The Internet has been acknowledged as a political force ever since its advent and early spread. From its early days, those who commanded the technology and had strong political opinions were quick to use it for airing their views. The early Internet was surrounded by expectations that it would in time lower the threshold for access so that everyone could voice their opinions publicly. To use the vocabulary of public sphere theory, the Internet was discussed as an embryonic public sphere, by virtue of its potentials for deliberation and democratic participation. Here, an old discussion was being revived by new media. As was discussed in Chapters 2 and 3, the print and visual media of early modern Europe were key to the workings of the time's public spheres. That was a time of controversy and unsettledness over the terms of public discourse and access to participation – not unlike the last decades of digital and social media.

Roughly speaking, the possible upsides of the Internet for the public sphere dominated public discussions in the first decade of the twentieth century, while its downsides became a focus of attention in the second. A series of scandals and controversies caused this shift in expectations. Together, they produced a marked sense of disillusionment with the Internet as a democratic tool.

A major, early blow came with the protests after the Iranian election in 2009 – the so-called 'green movement' or 'Iranian spring' – and then from 2011 a string of demonstrations and uprisings throughout the Middle East that became known as the 'Arab spring'. Much attention and hope centred around the ways in which social media, particularly Twitter, were used by activists to spread a message of reform and democratization in the face of authoritarian regimes. Actual democratization did not, however, come to pass in Iran or most of the Middle East following these events, so that the optimism about the Internet's powers proved to be largely unfounded in this case. In 2014, the idea that the Internet was a place for extended and progressive participation took a different kind of hit with the controversy called 'Gamergate'. Threats against an American female game developer expanded to an extended series of online abuses from right-wing factions of the gamer community against feminists and other political progressives, highlighting problems of online harassment and misogyny.

Simultaneously with these events, concerns were mounting over the surveillance tactics and privacy invasions of major corporations like Google and Facebook. Along with Twitter, Facebook was also repeatedly criticized for failing to prevent harassment. A series of revelations, mostly by newspaper journalists following leaks, led to a combination of defusing attempts and public apologies, but not to major changes in corporate tactics. From 2016, the stakes were raised when exposés revealed that the leading social media platforms had been used for political manipulation by actors who created false accounts and hashtags, planted fictitious news stories and used 'bots' (software robot devices posing as people). The US presidential election of that year was followed by the Cambridge Analytica scandal mentioned above, and Russia was found to have been using social media actively in campaigns designed to influence the outcome of the American election. Similar scandals over manipulation of the news stream also appeared in connection with the 2016 Brexit vote in the UK.

At the time of writing the fourth edition of this book, President Donald Trump has been using Twitter as a main platform for promoting a brand of public speech, sometimes called a 'Twitter presidency', that had been demonstrated to involve routine lying. The same president has also tweeted accusations at the news media for producing 'fake news' and for being 'the enemy of the people', illustrating how a type of discourse had risen to the highest prominence that was very hard to square with ideals of how deliberation should work in a mediated public sphere. Parallels were drawn with the rise of propaganda in the inter-war period, drawing on that concept's negative connotations of manipulating public opinion. Theorists of propaganda at that time had not necessarily used the term negatively: for Edward Bernays, systematic and professional influence on the mass public was inevitable in a modern society (see p. 2). The authoritarian encroachments of twenty-first-century digital surveillance makes it hard to place that kind of trust in society's political and media elites.

The discourse of the inter-war period did not forefront a notion of the public as rational and deliberative. That was provided for the post-war period by Jürgen Habermas, who argued that a public sphere was capable of such rationality, if granted a measure of autonomy from the state, the market and the sphere of private life (see pp. 2, 80–1). The more optimistic intellectuals of the Internet around the turn of the century were often critical of markets, but tended to see the Internet as inherently impossible for states to control. Many of the scandals and controversies of the 2010s turned out to involve state manipulation of digital media, however, particularly by authoritarian regimes. As it turned out, the Internet was amenable to a series of machinations by states that had a tradition of surveillance and coercion. This was pointed out early by Evgeny Morozov in his 2012 book *The Net Delusion*, which was part polemic against those he termed 'cyber-utopians', part review of authoritarian state uses of the Internet throughout the world. Morozov himself is a native of Belarus and developed from being an early believer in the democratic Internet to realizing just how pervasive state infiltration of digital media was becoming in his home country and its dominant neighbour Russia.

Morozov described the Belarus KGB carrying out surveillance of the social media pages of students from the political opposition. He pointed out that, in the past, information about friends and contacts had to be coerced out of citizens, whereas now they are listed on social media and readily available. Morozov commented that this really ought to have been no surprise for those interested in the political context of media – and, one could have added, the historical dimension also. Both the tsarist and the Soviet political tradition featured a wide range of state surveillance and repression tactics for the mass and print media. The age of the Internet has turned out to be not so very different.

Morozov's examples of countries with an authoritarian Internet include Russia, Belarus, Venezuela, Iran, Burma, Saudi Arabia – and China, which is of particular importance because it has both a sophisticated media and informatics sector, as well as the world's largest national pool of media users. Post-Mao China saw a large-scale movement towards Western-style markets, but without an attendant development towards democracy. Instead, the Communist party and state apparatus together sought to preserve authoritarian rule, and to extend its control from mass to digital media. In the early 2000s, China led the world in jailing Internet activists, and became infamous for applying authoritarian measures of surveillance and manipulation of the Internet on a huge scale. A survey of the Chinese Internet published in 2017 by Gary King, Jennifer Pan and Margaret E. Roberts estimated that the Chinese government had fabricated and posted online approximately 448 million social media comments in support of the regime per year in 2013–14. Crucially also, China pursued a policy of keeping major international media actors like Google and Facebook out, allowing instead for national social media like Sina Weibo and WeChat, and the search engine provider Baidu, all of which could be more easily monitored and coerced. This set of digital censoring and blocking technologies combined with restrictive policies became known as the 'great firewall of China'.

The Chinese case demonstrates that authoritarian control over digital media is not only based on overtly repressive measures like wholesale censorship and state violence against dissidents. In an account of contemporary Chinese media history, Yuezhi Zhao makes the important point that much of this control is decentralized and often informal, depending in part on active participation from Internet users surveilling and reporting on others. She argues that the Chinese authorities' answer to the decentralizing tendencies of the Internet has been the decentralization of control itself. It was a sobering lesson from the authoritarian Internet of the 2000s and 2010s that its users often turn out to be willing and active accomplices of the state. And with signs of authoritarianism on the rise also in both the European and the American contexts, it is becoming harder to see the West as exempt from these darker sides of digital media.

Concurrently with these developments, academic work on social media interactions has been honing in on the properties of social media that underlie the various cases where they have proved to be dysfunctional. In addition to describing the processes of algorithmic automation already discussed, they zone in on tendencies towards fragmentation, and on the opaque relationship between public and private in interactions online. This research is responding to current notions of the digital public sphere as having become infected with 'echo chambers' and 'filter bubbles', as social media and search engines feed users information tailored to what the algorithms say are their individual needs. In principle, each person online would, over time, encounter fewer and fewer experiences and opinions that are different from their own. Thus, the Internet is liable to fragment its users, encourage hyper-partisanship and prevent a real deliberation over common and public concerns – so went the argument. Although such strong and general arguments are not confirmed by academic research, they continue to be a part of debates on the media, at a time of growing concerns over polarization and the perceived loss of a common ground in Western political life.

As for the issue of how digital media disrupts the relationship between public and private spheres, a concern with the difficulties of separating the two has been discussed also for the case of television. In digital and social media, other kinds of tension between public and private were in evidence, however. For instance, on large, multi-purpose social media sites, users would find themselves sharing information in their role of employee, citizen, friend and partner. Since in interpersonal social life these roles tend to be played out in more separate contexts, the result was what digital media researchers danah boyd and Alice Marwick termed 'context collapse'.

One could say the opposite development might also be true – that with the fragmentation of media, distinctions between private and public became drawn with more and more variation, in different local contexts. And again, it is arguable both how much was actually going on in terms of a collapse, and indeed how much of a problem such a collapse would be. For instance, the decades after the 1960s had been marked by the feminist insight that the private was public, that something like domestic violence and sexual abuse were public concerns, and not just private matters. But much like the eighteenth century, the early twenty-first was a time of widespread anxiety that destructive social behaviours associated with the private sphere – fervent emotions, aggression, invasive intimacies – were undermining public discourse.

Gradually during the 2010s, these concerns translated into a greater pressure for regulation. As has been mentioned, digital media developed largely outside the reach of Western national regulators. Generally, the corporations themselves tended to present their services as purely infrastructural. Although they might argue for the social and human benefits of connecting people digitally, at the same time they want to avoid taking the same sorts of responsibility for the content they carry that journalists and editors are committed to. For a long time, the pushback against such a strategy came mainly in the extreme circumstances of child pornography and 'grooming', and messages in support of terror. Also, there have been intermittent calls for stricter taxation, since these corporations as a rule pay very limited taxes, which, as some politicians argued, are disproportionate to their power over more and more national media markets.

An important step first came in the realm of privacy, when the EU introduced its General Data Protection Regulation (GDPR) in 2018. It required that concrete steps be taken by the corporations to secure informed consent about the use of personal data. Following the scandals and exposés of the Brexit referendum and the Trump election, pressure on the corporations escalated in an attempt to make them take more active and practical responsibility for the content they provided. They responded in part by allocating more resources to monitoring and surveillance, in part by making some concessions regarding their public role. In a statement on his Facebook page at the end of 2018, Mark Zuckerberg referred to having more then 30,000 employees working on 'preventing harm'. He professed his engagement on behalf of 'preventing election interference, stopping the spread of hate speech and disinformation'. Zuckerberg did not address taxation, however, nor the sale of data to third parties, and he did not actively acknowledge editorial responsibility. It remained uncertain how even a large staff of moderators would be able to effectively patrol something as vast as Facebook's social arenas. At the tail end of the 2010s, it remained unclear how and to what extent the social media corporations would embrace their responsibilities vis-à-vis the public sphere, particularly if that meant jeopardizing their strategies for expansion and sources of income.

The development of digital public spheres, then, depended partly on technology, but also on institutional and regulatory frameworks, on societal and historical conditions. Illustration of this is provided in the development of journalism, which is of course key to the mediated public sphere, in the digital era as it had been since the eighteenth century. Digital technologies present a set of pressing risks and opportunities to which journalists and editors must adapt. News consumption shifted from television as the main source to social media and the Internet, which has become increasingly central as distributors of news. In 2017, the Pew Research Center reported that 43 per cent of Americans were using online news reports as a news source, particularly from social media. This meant narrowing to 7 per cent the gap up to television as the previously dominant source. Radio and newspapers were, respectively, at 25 per cent and 18 per cent, and declining.

Journalists and outlets with a starting-point in newspapers or broadcasting, and with a basis in the professional culture of journalism, thus faced a dilemma: letting social media platforms share their news stories, or be marginalized for lack of an up-to-date means of distribution. The journalism researcher Axel Bruns argued that one significant development in journalism since the late 1990s was the shift from traditional 'gatekeeping' to 'gatewatching' and then to 'news curation'. In their production for the mass media, journalists working in an editorial setting would, so to speak, guard the gates of information, select a few from a great number of possible stories, process them according to professional norms and then present them to audiences. According to Bruns, digital tools that became available from the 1990s produced a number of experiments in news blogging and idealistically based 'citizen journalism' that were based on continuously compiling and drawing attention to stories that were generated by non-professionals. This gatewatching principle, very different from the more closed-off and one-way traditions of mass media journalism, guided web initiatives like Indymedia and Buzzfeed. These largely constituted a separate, Web-based ecology, an alternative that mainstream journalism was often reluctant to acknowledge.

A major change then came with the rise of social media, which forced the two into closer contact. Journalists were now compelled to let their news stories be distributed on networks like Twitter and Facebook, which meant being shared or ignored by users who were now 'curating' their news diet via their news feeds. It also meant being promoted or marginalized by whatever algorithms the social media corporations were using. This change in technologies presented journalism with a new arena and means of distribution. The increased accessibility of technologies for monitoring and tracking the Web by means of algorithms also placed a new set of possible tools in the hands of investigative journalists. Furthermore, one could argue that the move to social media contributed to the shaking loose of journalists from conventional ideas of print media and its relation to new generations.

Journalists also faced a number of dilemmas as they entered the world of social media, however. One was that the fast-moving and often emotionally charged choices that characterize social media use often fit awkwardly with an established journalistic ethos. Another area for difficult balancing acts came when the hosting social media accounts made journalists responsible for user comments that include hate speech, 'trolling' and breaches of law. Pre- or post-moderation would then have to be considered, which could be both expensive and difficult to enforce if traffic on the page was extensive. Yet another key dilemma lay in the fact that by ceding control over news distribution to a third party, journalists not only saw major shares of advertisement revenue leaking to those third parties, but had to face the fact that they were actively aiding in their own demise.

Finally, digitalization coincided with a time when the resources available for journalistic production were becoming scarcer, just as they were having to be stretched over more and more platforms and media. Major Western newspapers, such as the *New York Times*, the *Guardian*, *Le Monde* and *Die Welt*, not only had to move from print to the Web in order to survive; increasingly, they also had to become media houses offering video, live streaming and podcasting. In the early stages, this was largely an uphill struggle. As a result, even though social media presented significant possibilities for journalism, actual developments may have been more shaped by the need to save money and adapt to short-term competitive challenges.

Coda: Fragmentations and Collectives

In many ways, as we approach the 2020s, and produce this fourth edition, we find ourselves in a time marked by disillusion with the Internet and with the promises of personal and political empowerment. For a while, the Internet was believed to be a unifier in the sense that it was technologically able to incorporate all earlier media by turning their outputs into bits and bytes. Writing in the typical visionary register from the last years of the twentieth century, the Web designer and self-styled 'Web guru for hire' Jakob Nielsen claimed that 'most current Web formats will die and be replaced with an integrated Web medium in five to ten years'. At that time, both commentators and industry decision-makers were smitten with the idea of an 'über-box' from which all the Internet would be accessed, and therefore all information, once it had been digitally converted.

As the digital media researcher Anders Fagerjord has pointed out in a critical discussion of Nielsen and the 'über-box', this kind of argument was an instance of not very sophisticated technological determinism. Actual developments in the early years of this century went largely in the opposite direction. Digital devices in households proliferated instead of converging. Television and radio sets did not disappear, but had to fight for space with computers, set-top boxes and game consoles. Access points to digital technology also proliferated, so that, for example, Messenger texts could be read via both the mobile and personal computer, via both the Messenger app and Facebook. And then there was the much-discussed tendency of algorithms to present different kinds of information to different people. It all added up more to divergence than to convergence, more to fragmentation than to unity. The social media networks may have advertised themselves as providing a new kind of common ground, but given the way international public debates about these actors have gone in the first two decades of the twenty-first century, fewer and fewer people are convinced.

Discussions paid less attention to the kinds of historically deep-rooted collectives that had long been formed around major events with the help of media, and continued to do so in the new century. In the broadcast-dominated twentieth century, radio and television audiences became so large, and live broadcasting brought them so vividly in touch with the event, that it was possible to speak of TV audiences watching elections, coronations and natural disasters as constituting a national 'imagined community', to use the historian Benedict Anderson's phrase. It should be said that not everyone watched, and the premises offered to those who did could be questioned, but clearly a certain experience of national collectivity via the media was made available.

The splitting up of this national audience, like its establishment, was a long time coming. Its heyday had been in the decades after the Second World War, which also in many ways marked the apex of European public service broadcasting. From the 1980s on, the process of splitting up audiences began with the introduction of commercial television channels distributed by cable and satellite. In the 1990s, a proliferation of digital platforms was added to the proliferation of channels. In this process, the whole concept of 'television' became blurred, as it was now possible to do one's viewing on terrestrial TV, via satellite, digital TV, or, in the twenty-first century, through a smart-TV app. By virtue of this historical development, national audiences scattered across both channels and media.

There were counter-strategies, however. Broadcasters and newspapers sought to redefine themselves as 'media houses', branching out into Web-based activities, among other things using them to make available their large archives. They also adopted several of their commercial competitors' strategies, developing an overall brand and scheduling for audience movements between their various channels, platforms and sites. The public service institutions' degree of success varied, and not only depending on their abilities to compete. Generally, public service institutions did better in countries where their remit was less controversial and their standing with political authorities was stronger.

Throughout this time of change and threat to public service institutions, discussions over their legitimacy would revolve around their ability to serve as a common forum in society. When the independent report *The Future of Television* was put together by academics in consultation with British public institutions and the TV industry ahead of the BBC's charter renewal in 2017, this was their summary statement of television's continued relevance: 'Television remains at the heart of British life, serving a democratic purpose, stimulating local and national conversations, and providing collective experience.' To a large extent, though, this would have to happen in different ways than by gathering one national audience around one live broadcast. Public service broadcasters had started to think in more flexible terms, conceiving of the whole of their output across channels and platforms as constituting a kind of collectively available arena, one that could cater to a diversity of experiences and viewpoints.

Building collectives across media is by no means a strategy only for public service institutions. A main means of large-scale revenue in commercial markets is the blockbuster film, whose content and brand are internationally attractive and indeed regularly made with international audiences in mind. These films/multimedia products have attracted large fan audiences that can be effectively monetized by other means than mining user data. *Avatar*, *Harry Potter*, *The Hobbit* and *The Lord of the Rings* and *The Pirates of the Caribbean* are among the internationally highest-grossing films/series of this century so far, in part because they are multi-platform enterprises that have generated sales not only from movie attendance but also from downloads, book sales, video game sales, and merchandise. At the same time, their popular narratives are in many ways quite traditional: they reach into myth, fable and folk story for their collective appeal. There could be no *Pirates of the Caribbean* series without the centuries-old folklore surrounding pirates on the high seas, or that tradition being summed up in the 1883 book *Treasure Island* by Robert Louis Stevenson.

A key means of gathering large audiences around collective experiences across media is sport. In a time of specialized programming and increased competition on TV, sport has in many ways been a winner, since it has both broad appeal and fans who were willing to pay in order to see their favourite teams and athletes. Sport appeals to basic collective experiences with deep historical roots, experiences of competition and teamsmanship. Sport also presents perhaps the most successful attempts to create collective experiences via media on a global scale. Events like the Olympic Games and football world championships continue to be strong draws. Even if they hardly represent an equal playing field in terms of audiences' physical and mediated access to these events, they are nevertheless phenomena of a genuinely global reach. At the same time, they tend be surrounded by controversies concerning the conditions under which athletes and audiences are gathered. The democratic deficiencies and business practices of the International Olympic Committees, for instance, has come under intense debate. So too did the choice of authoritarian national organizers, as with China and the Beijing Olympics in 2008, and Russia with Sochi in 2014.

Even when considering the significant collective thrust of major sport and entertainment, it is the great political and natural upheavals that still stand out as collective mediated events of the first importance. The turn of the millennium was framed by the 9/11 terror attacks in 2001 against New York and Washington, DC, which ushered in a period of greater volatility in international relations, and brought intensified tensions between religion and politics. Since the advent of modern news distribution, media had functioned as a key facilitator of the particular kind of event that seemed to threaten the basic security and well-being of the people.

Media coverage of such events would still carry a unique force. On the one hand, they relay messages to their audiences of threats against life, health and safety, and they also provide the same people with a main source of information about those threats. Early twenty-first-century events such as 9/11, the war in Syria and the Asian tsunamis were uniquely powerful in giving the media a main role in appealing to and mobilizing collectives.

In the special circumstances of such events, an individualized media diet becomes a hindrance, and fragmentation of the media environment can produce a sense of frustrating disconnection. In such a situation, the media coverage of an unfolding dramatic event functions as a means of being in touch with the moment and the possible transformations it may bring. At the same time, these are often moments of intense conflict in and around the media, over their powers and responsibilities, their influence and sometimes also their failure to influence.

The kinds of collectives and senses of unity provided by the media should not be idealized. An absolute unification of media's outputs and their reception is the dream of dictators, not democrats. It is an important measure of plurality that a divergence of opinions and viewpoints is expressed in the media. Also, even in a media-saturated society, the centrality of media should not be overstated. Power can still reside elsewhere and benefit from avoiding the media rather than seeking them out. Nevertheless, there are limits to how fragmented communication can be if collective identities and actions are to be possible. In this sense, a key question is – and will still be – that of the social, and its medial underpinnings.

Chronology

c. 5000 BCE	Invention of writing
c. 2000 BCE	Invention of the alphabet
c. 764	Earliest known example of woodblock printing (Japan)
868	First known printed book (China)
c. 1040	Invention of movable type (China)
c. 1390	First pictorial woodcuts
1390	First Renaissance medal
1403	Movable type cast in bronze in Korea
c. 1456	Gutenberg prints Bible
1460	Antwerp Bourse founded
1467	First press established in Rome
1468	First press established in Paris
1476	First press established at Westminster
1492	Columbus lands in America
1492	Oldest surviving globe (Behaim)
c. 1500	First etchings
1506	First printed map to include information about America
1517	Luther's ninety-five theses printed
1522	Luther, New Testament in German
1525	Twelve Articles of German peasants printed
1526	Tyndale, New Testament in English, published (in Worms)
1534	'Affair of the Placards' in France
1544	First *Index of Prohibited Books* published in Paris
1554	London Exchange founded
1557	Charter granted to Stationers' Company of London
1562–94	Religious wars in France
1563	First printed timetable of postal service in the Habsburg Empire
1564	First general *Index of Prohibited Books*
1564	First press established in Moscow
1566	Iconoclasm in France and the Netherlands

1568–1648	Eighty Years War between Spain and the Netherlands
1570	Ortelius, *Theatrum Orbis Terrarum*
1576	First London theatre
1579–94	'Kralice Bible' published in Bohemia
1585	Teatro Olimpico opened at Vicenza
1594	First opera performed in Florence
1598	Globe Theatre, London
1605	Cervantes, Don Quixote
1609	First newssheets (in Germany)
1611	Authorized Version of the Bible published
1617	First logarithmic tables
1618–48	Thirty Years War
1620	*The Corrant out of Italy* published
1626	Ben Jonson, *The Staple of News*
1631	*Gazette* begins publication in Paris
1637	First public theatre opened in Venice
1638	First theatre opened in Amsterdam
1640	Bicentenary of printing celebrated
1640	Root and Branch Petition, London
1641	Grand Remonstrance, London
1642–60	English Civil War
1642	First mezzotint
1644	Milton, *Areopagitica*
1648–52	Fronde in France
1662	Gazette d'Amsterdam
1663	First Turnpike Act
1668	*Giornale de' letterati* in Rome
1665	*Philosophical Transactions of the Royal Society of London* began
1672	*Mercure Galant*
1672	Louis XIV attacks the Dutch Republic
1679–81	'Exclusion crisis' in England
1683	Louis XIV moves into Versailles
1684	*Nouvelles de la République des Lettres* began
1688	'Glorious Revolution' in England
1688–97	War of the League of Augsburg
1689	Procope's Café founded, Paris
1695	English Licensing Act lapses
1695	*Flying Post, Post Boy*, founded in London
1701–14	War of the Spanish Succession
1704	Boston Newsletter founded

1709	British 'Copyright Act'
1710	Sacheverell's sermon
1711–12, 1714	*The Spectator*
1711	First press established in St Petersburg
1712	Stamp duty imposed
1719	Defoe, *Robinson Crusoe*
1726	First press established in Istanbul
1731	*Gentleman's Magazine*
1740	Tercentenary of printing celebrated
1740	Richardson, *Pamela*
1749	Fielding, *Tom Jones*
1751–65	*Encyclopédie*
1755	Johnson's *Dictionary*
1761	First aquatints
1764	*Il Caffè* published in Milan
1765	Repeal of the Stamp Act
1766	Lunar Society of Birmingham founded
1768	Royal Academy founded
1771	First edition of *Encyclopaedia Britannica*
1775	Steam engine completed by Watt and Boulton
1776	American Declaration of Independence
1779	First Derby Day horse race
1780	First British Sunday newspaper
1787	Constitution of the USA
1788	First Amendment to the US Constitution
1788	John Walter founds *The Times*
1789	French Revolution
1790	First steam rolling mill in Britain
1790	First patent law in the USA
1792	Cable-making machine invented
1794	Revision of the calendar in France: Year One
1794	Chappe's long-distance signalling system in France
1796	Senefelder invents lithography
1798	Paper-making machine
1798	Stamp tax on newspapers raised in Britain; imports of foreign newspapers prohibited
1800	Stanhope's iron press
1802	Cobbett's *Weekly Political Register*
1802	*Edinburgh Review*
1803	Fulton propels a boat by steam power

1804	Trevithick's steam engine runs on rails
1805	Completion of Britain's Grand Union Canal
1807	'Clermont' plies on the River Hudson
1809	*Quarterly Review*
1811	Koenig's steam press
1812	Luddite riots
1814	*The Times* printed by steam
1815	Increase in stamp duty
1816	Isolation of selenium, the moon element
1816	Cobbett's cheap (twopenny) *Political Register*
1819	Carlsbad decrees abolish freedom of the press
1819	Six Acts: new stamp duties
1820	Ampère's laws of electrodynamics
1820	First iron steamship
1821	Saint-Simon, *Système Industriel*
1821	*Manchester Guardian*
1823	Babbage begins building his mechanical computer
1827	Chromolithography: Niepce produces permanent photographic image on a pewter plate
1829	First typewriter
1830	Liverpool and Manchester Railway
1831	*Ottoman Gazette*
1832	British Reform Act
1834	Hansom cabs introduced in London
1834	Lloyd's *Register of Shipping*
1835	*New York Herald*
1836	First railroad in Canada
1837	First French passenger railway
1837	Electric telegraph
1837	Pitman's shorthand
1838	Brunel's 'Great Western'; crossing of the Atlantic
1839	Daguerreotypes and collotypes demonstrated
1839	Opening of telegraph line between Paddington and West Drayton (thirteen miles)
1840	Britain introduces penny post
1840	Wood pulp used in Germany to make paper
1840	First unofficial newspaper in Turkish
1841	*Punch*
1841	*New York Tribune*
1841	Bradshaw's first Railway Guide

1842	British Copyright Act
1842	Mudie's circulating library opened
1842	*Illustrated London News*
1843	Morse's first telegraph message transmitted, using Morse code
1844	Britain's first Railway Act
1844	Cooke and Wheatstone formed Electric Telegraph Company
1846	Rotating cylinder press
1846	Siemens insulated electric wiring
1846	Smithsonian Institute, Washington
1846	*The Economist*
1846	*News of the World*
1848	Year of revolutions
1849	Berlin and Frankfurt linked by telegraph
1850	*Harper's New Monthly*
1850	First British Public Libraries Act
1850	Patent for first typewriter with continuous paper feed
1850	First submarine cable between Britain and France
1851	Great Exhibition in London's Crystal Palace
1851	Wet plate photography
1854	Boole's *Laws of Thought*
1854–6	Crimean War
1857	First transatlantic cable (failed)
1858	Phonautograph
1861–5	American Civil War
1861	*Harper's Weekly*
1864	Maxwell expounds electromagnetic wave theory
1864	London's Metropolitan Railway
1865	British Red Flag Act limiting speed of vehicles on roads
1865	First successful transatlantic cable
1865	International Telegraphic Convention
1867	Marx's *Das Kapital*, vol. I (in German)
1868	N. W. Ayer and Son, first multi-service advertising agency, founded in Philadelphia
1868	First American newspaper to use woodpulp paper
1868	First British Telegraph Act
1869	First postcards
1869	Transcontinental meeting of railroad lines in USA; Golden Spike celebration

1869	Opening of Suez Canal
1870	Velocipede
1870	Britain's first national Education Act
1870	Fall of Napoleon III: Paris Commune
1872	Muybridge demonstrates moving pictures of animals
1873	Recognition of the photo-sensitive properties of selenium
1873	Globe Telegraph and Trust Company
1874	Universal Postal Union founded
1876	US Centennial Exhibition
1876	Bell's telephone: first transmission from Boston to Cambridge (two miles)
1877	Prototype of Remington typewriter
1877	Dry plate photography
1877	Edison's phonograph
1878	First American telephone exchange in New Haven
1878	Hughes's microphone
1879	Siemens's electric tram in Berlin
1880	Hertz describes radio waves
1880	Half-tone black used in *New York Daily Graphic*
1883	Sydney–Melbourne railway opened
1883	Hoe's newspaper folding machine
1884	Nipkow's rotating disc
1885	Gottlieb Daimler develops lightweight petrol engine in Germany
1886	Bern Convention on Copyright
1886	Eastman's hand camera (Kodak)
1886	Canadian Pacific Railway opened
1886	Daimler's four-wheeled automobile
1888	Use of celluloid in photography
1888	*Financial Times*
1889	American Copyright Act
1889	Edison's motion picture camera
1890	First electric underground trains in London
1892	First automatic telephone switchboard
1892	Pulitzer buys the *New York World*
1892	British Post Office acquires control of all telephone trunk lines
1893	Telefon Hirmondó, Budapest
1893	*McClure's Magazine*: 'muckraking'
1893	Spanish–American War (the 'correspondents' war')

1893	Kinetoscope
1894	Expiry of Bell's patents
1894	First railway over the Andes
1895	Discovery of X-rays
1895	Skladanowsky brothers exhibit films in Berlin
1896	Athens Olympic Games
1896	Marconi arrives in London with wireless devices
1896	Harmsworth's *Daily Mail*
1896	Lumière's cinema show in London
1896	Hollerith forms Tabulating Machine Company to make punch cards
1896	London–Brighton automobile rally
1896	Langley's flying machine
1897	Marconi founds Wireless Telegraph and Signal Company
1897	Type-setting machine (Monotype)
1898	Airship (Zeppelin)
1899	British Telegraph Act
1899	Magnetic recording of sound
1899–1902	Anglo-Boer War
1900	Paris Exhibition
1900	Fessenden broadcasts voice messages
1901	Marconi transmits messages from Cornwall to Newfoundland
1901	Mercedes-Simplex automobile
1901	First motor bicycle
1901	Trans-Siberian railway reaches Port Arthur
1903	First world congress on wireless telegraphy
1903	Wright brothers' petrol-driven aeroplane
1903	Detroit called the automobile capital of the world
1903	First motor taxis in London
1904	First work on Panama Canal
1904	Harmsworth's *Daily Mirror*
1904	Fleming's thermionic diode valve (vacuum tube)
1904	First New York subway
1904	British Wireless Telegraphy Act
1905	First motorbuses in London
1905	Neon signs
1906	British Patents Act
1906	Fessenden broadcasts words and music
1907	De Forest patents triode valve

1908	Harmsworth acquires *The Times*
1909	Ford's 'Model T'
1909	Blériot crosses the Channel by aeroplane
1909	Cinematograph Licensing Act in Britain
1909	Imperial Press Conference in London
1911	British Copyright Act
1911	First Hollywood studio
1912	Post Office takes over British telephone companies
1912	First American Radio Act
1912	Loss of *Titanic*
1912	*Daily Herald*
1912	First diesel locomotive in Germany
1913	Ford introduces moving conveyor belt
1913	London Wireless Club
1913	First Eiffel Tower wireless signals
1914–18	First World War
1915	D. W. Griffiths, *Birth of a Nation*
1917	UFA company formed In Berlin
1919	Alcock and Brown fly across Atlantic
1919	Ross Smith flies from Britain to Australia
1919	First successful helicopter flight
1919	First motor scooter
1919	Radio Corporation of America founded
1920	Dame Nellie Melba broadcast in Britain
1920	KDKA, Pittsburgh
1920	Writtle broadcasting station
1920	British Board of Film Censors
1922	British Broadcasting Company founded
1923	*Radio Times*
1923	*Time* magazine
1923	First transatlantic radio conversation
1924	First stretch of Italian motorway completed
1925	*New Yorker*
1925	Greenwich time signal
1925	BBC's long-wave transmitter opened at Daventry
1925	First general assembly of International Broadcasting Union
1926	Geneva plan for international distribution of wavelengths
1926	First broadcast on NBC Red Network (formerly WEAF/ AT&T)

1926	Hugo Gernsback's *Amazing Stories*
1927	British Broadcasting Corporation
1927	CBS (Columbia Broadcasting System) purchased by William Paley
1927	Federal Radio Commission
1927	First transatlantic wire and wireless telephone service
1927	Al Jolson in the first talkie
1927	Cable and Wireless merger
1927	London acquires automatic telephone system
1927	First Oscars awarded
1928	Baird demonstrates television
1928	Mickey Mouse created
1929	Wall Street Crash
1929	Kodak 17 mm colour film
1929	Warner Brothers announces end of black and white films
1929	*Graf Zeppelin* flight around the world
1929	*The Listener*
1930	Picture telegraph service between Britain and Germany
1930	Photo-flash bulb
1930	First television play (Baird system)
1930	Hays cinema code in Hollywood
1932	F. D. Roosevelt's presidential election victory
1932	Opening of Broadcasting House, London
1932	BBC short-wave Empire Service inaugurated
1932	International Telecommunications Union
1933	Hitler appointed German Chancellor
1933	London Passenger Transport Board
1933	British Film Institute founded
1934	Mutual Broadcasting System
1934	International wavelengths agreement signed
1934	Nuremberg Rally
1934	Regular airmail from Britain to Australia
1934	Federal Communications Commission
1935	Radar
1935	35 mm Kodachrome film
1936	Ford Foundation founded
1936	*Life* magazine
1936	BBC television inaugurated
1936	Berlin Olympic Games
1936	Chaplin, *Modern Times*

1938	First BBC broadcasts in a foreign language (Arabic)
1938	First Volkswagen Beetle
1938	PEP report on the British press
1938	Orson Welles's Martian invasion broadcast
1939	Frequency Modulation (Armstrong)
1939–45	Second World War
1941	Welles's *Citizen Kane*
1943	Contract signed for ENIAC (Electronic Numerical Integrator and Computer)
1943	Colossus put into action at Bletchley
1945	Vannevar Bush, 'As We May Think'
1945	Arthur C. Clarke forecasts satellites
1946	Television service restarts in London
1947	Royal Commission on the Press in Britain (reported 1949)
1947	Transistor devised by Bardeen and Brattain
1948	First long-playing record
1948	Norbert Wiener's *Cybernetics*
1948	Claude Shannon pioneers information theory
1948	Universal Declaration of Human Rights
1950–3	Korean War
1950	European Broadcasting Union formed
1950	Copenhagen plan for frequency distribution
1950	First cable systems
1952	First IBM computers
1952	Last London tram
1952	Universal Copyright Convention
1953	Press Council set up in Britain
1953	Mosaic
1954–75	Vietnam War
1954	Texas Instruments starts selling 'chips'
1954	Television Act in Britain establishes 'independent television'
1955	End of wartime newsprint controls
1955	First commercial television programme in England
1955	Ultrahigh frequency waves (UHF) generated at MIT (Massachusetts Institute of Technology)
1955	Beginnings of rock music
1955	First British subscriber trunk dialling exchange, Bristol
1956	First transatlantic telephone cable laid
1956	Television remote control invented

1956	Suez and Hungarian crises
1957	Russia launches Sputnik (first man-made satellite)
1958	Income from television advertising exceeds that of press advertising in Britain
1958	Stereophonic gramophone records
1958	First live television from Africa via Eurovision
1958	USA launches Explorer I
1958	USA establishes ARPA (Advanced Research Projects Agency)
1959	*Manchester Guardian* becomes *Guardian*, printed in London
1959	British hovercraft crosses Channel in two hours
1959	First stretch of motorway in Britain
1959	Sales of transistors exceed sales of valves
1959	Advent of the integrated circuit
1960	Pilkington Committee on Broadcasting in Britain
1961	Yuri Gagarin first man in space
1961	Breaking of genetic code
1961	*Sunday Times* colour supplement
1961	*Private Eye*
1962	First live television from the USA via Telstar satellite
1962	Anglo-French agreement to develop Concorde
1962	Packet-switching opens way to networking
1963	Assassination of President Kennedy
1963	William Olsen's mini-computer on sale
1964	Tokyo Olympic Games
1964	Japan introduces 'bullet' trains
1964	Start of pirate radio (Radio Caroline)
1964	First American space walk
1965	Early Bird commercial communications satellite
1965	First 'action replays' on American television
1965	Ban on television tobacco advertising in Britain
1966	*The Times* prints news on its front page
1966	Television of football World Cup (world audience c. 400 million)
1966	Optical fibre announced
1966	Roman Catholic World Communications Day
1967	Pirate radio banned in Britain
1967	BBC local radio
1967	USA creates Commission for Public Broadcasting
1968	Russian invasion of Czechoslovakia
1968	Assassination of Martin Luther King

1968	Student riots in Europe
1968	Demonstration of oNLine System (NLS) in San Francisco
1969	Neil Armstrong lands on moon
1969	BBC and ITV starts regular colour television
1969	Rupert Murdoch acquires *Sun*
1969	Sony launches videotape cassettes
1969	Woodstock rock festival
1970	OPEC threatens rise in oil prices
1971	Microprocessors launched
1971	First independent local radio in Britain
1972	Email developed within ARPA
1972	Home video-cassette recorders on sale
1973	Oil crisis
1973	Britain joins European Economic Community
1974	Resignation of President Nixon
1974	Annan Committee on Broadcasting in Britain (reported 1979)
1974	Two general elections in Britain
1974	Royal Commission on the Press in Britain (reported 1979)
1975	Fibre optics
1975	Prestel Viewdata system in Britain and teletext
1975	First computer shop (in Los Angeles)
1975	Liberalization of Radio Televisione Italiana (RAI)
1976	Apple Corporation founded; first portable computers
1976	United States Copyright Act
1977	Launch of Authors Lending and Copyright Society in London
1977	End of South African ban on television
1977	First optical fibre cable installed in California
1977	Cellular telephone
1978	Apple II personal computer
1979	European Space Agency set up
1979	Commercialization of Internet
1980	American Computer Software Act
1980	First mass-produced car with four-wheel drive (USA)
1980	*Voyager I*: first signals from Saturn
1981	Murdoch acquires *The Times*
1982	Falklands War
1982	*USA Today*

1983	Laser videodiscs marketed
1984	William Gibson, *Neuromancer*
1984	Compact discs marketed in the USA
1984	Camcorders
1984	First Congress statute deregulating cable TV
1984	Break-up of AT&T
1984	British Cable and Broadcasting Act
1985	British Copyright (Computer Software) Amendment Act
1986	*The Times* moves to Wapping
1986	Chernobyl disaster
1986	Microsoft becomes a public company
1987	Intifada
1988	International Services Digital Network (ISDN) launched in Japan
1988	British Copyright Act
1989	First mass-produced car with four-wheel steering (Japan)
1989	First transatlantic optical fibre cable
1989	Fall of Berlin Wall
1989	Tiananmen Square
1989	Fall of Ceauşescu in Bucharest
1989	Merger of Time Inc. and Warner Brothers
1989	European Union: Television Without Frontiers Directive
1990	New British Broadcasting Act
1990	Rise of Berlusconi Empire in Italy
1990	BSkyB formed by merger of BSB and Sky
1991	CAVE (Cave Automatic Virtual Environment)
1991	Unification of East and West Germany
1991	Gulf War
1991	Channel Tunnel completed (first railway train 1994)
1992	Clinton elected President of USA
1993	FCC authorized to auction unused portions of spectrum
1993	Separate listing of NASDAQ shares
1993	Proclamation of the 'super-highway'
1993	Privatization of British Rail
1994	Russian troops entered Chechnya
1994	Nelson Mandela elected president of South Africa
1994	Netscape
1994	CERN places World Wide Web in the public domain
1994	Amazon
1994	Yahoo!

1994	GATT Conference (Uruguay) removes audiovisual sector from agreement
1995	Merger of CNN and Time/Warner
1995	National Science Foundation hands over Internet to commercial interests
1995	Java programming language
1995	Dayton Peace accord for Bosnia-Herzegovina
1996	Russian Telecommunications Act
1996	United States Telecommunications Act
1996	European Year of Lifelong Learning
1996	British Broadcasting Act
1996	Al-Jazeera television station opened
1996	European Commission: Communication on Illegal and Harmful Information on the Internet
1997	The Kyoto Protocol on greenhouse gas emissions
1997	WARC Conference
1997	Netflix launched
1998	European Human Rights Act
1998	Google launched
1998	American Copyright Extension Act
1998	Internet Corporation for Assignment of Names and Numbers (ICANN)
1999	Disruption of World Trade Organization, Seattle
1999	Australian Online Services Act: Internet code of practice
2000	America Online merges with Time/Warner
2001	Merger of Disney and Fox
2001	Wikipedia launched
2001	Terrorist air attacks on New York and Washington (9/11)
2001	Introduction of the iPod
2003	War in Iraq
2004	Facebook launched
2005	*Fahrenheit 9/11*
2005	Tsunami in Asia
2005	YouTube launched
2005	Google Maps launched
2006	Google merges with YouTube
2006	Twitter launched
2007	Global financial crisis
2007	Launch of the iPhone
2008	Obama elected President of USA

2009	WeChat launched
2009	Iranian elections and 'green movement' protests
2010	Start of the 'Arab Spring'
2011	Start of the Syrian War
2012	Facebook merger with Instagram
2014	Facebook merger with WhatsApp
2014	'Gamergate'
2015	Charlie Hebdo attack in Paris
2016	Britain votes to leave the EU
2016	Trump elected President of USA
2016	The EU General Data Protection Regulation introduced
2017	The '#metoo' movement
2018	Cambridge Analytica scandal

Further Reading

General

J. W. Carey, *Communication as Culture: Essays on Media and Society* (Boston, MA, 1989)

L. Gitelman, *Always Already New: Media, History and the Data of Culture* (Cambridge, MA, 2006)

L. Gitelman and G. B. Pingree (eds), *New Media, 1740–1915* (Cambridge, MA, 2003)

D. R. Olson, *The World on Paper* (Cambridge, 1994)

J. D. Peters, *Speaking Into the Air: A History of the Idea of Communication* (Chicago, IL, 1999)

R. Williams, *Keywords: A Vocabulary of Culture and Society* (Oxford, 1976)

Chapter 1 Introduction

L. Abu-Lughod, *Dramas of Nationhood: The Politics of Television in Egypt* (Chicago, IL, 2005)

R. Barthes, *Mythologies* (London, 1972)

M. Castells, *The Rise of the Network Society* (Cambridge, MA, 1996)

J. Goody, *The Domestication of the Savage Mind* (Cambridge, 1977)

H. Innis, *Empire and Communications* (Oxford, 1950)

F. A. Kittler, *Gramophone, Film, Typewriter* (Stanford, CA, 1999)

A. Lord, *The Singer of Tales* (Cambridge, MA, 1960)

A. Mattelart, *The Invention of Communication* (Minneapolis, MN, 1996)

M. McLuhan, *Understanding Media* (New York, 1964)

D. Miller and D. Slater, *The Internet: An Ethnographic Approach* (Oxford, 2001)

W. Ong, *Orality and Literacy: The Technologizing of the Word* (New York, NY, 1982)

L. Parks and N. Starosielski, *Signal Traffic: Critical Studies of Media Infrastructures* (Champaign, IL, 2015)

J. D. Peters, *The Marvelous Clouds: Toward a Philosophy of Elemental Media* (Chicago, IL, 2015)

Chapter 2 Printing in Its Contexts

F. Barbier, *Gutenberg's Europe: The Book and the Invention of Western Modernity* (Cambridge, 2016)

M. E. Berry, *Japan in Print: Information and Nation in the Early Modern Period* (Berkeley, CA, 2006).

A. Blair, *Too Much to Know* (New Haven, CN, 2010)

R. Chartier, *The Cultural Uses of Print* (Princeton, NJ, 1987)

R. Darnton, *The Forbidden Best-Sellers of Pre-Revolutionary France* (New York, 1995)

E. Eisenstein, *The Printing Revolution in Early Modern Europe* (Cambridge, 1983)

A. Johns, *The Nature of the Book: Print and Knowledge in the Making* (Chicago, IL, 1998)

J. McDermott, *A Social History of the Chinese Book* (Hong Kong, 2006)

J. Raymond (ed.) *Cheap Print in Britain and Ireland to 1680* (Oxford, 2011)

F. Robinson, 'Technology and Religious Change: Islam and the Impact of Print', *Modern Asian Studies* 27 (1993): 229–251

R. W. Scribner, *For the Sake of Simple Folk: Popular Propaganda for the German Reformation*, 2nd edn (Oxford, 1994)

Chapter 3 The Media and the Public Sphere in Early Modern Europe

P. Burke, *The Fabrication of Louis XIV* (New Haven, CN, 1992)

J. Habermas, *The Structural Transformation of the Public Sphere* (1962; English translation, Cambridge, MA, 1989)

P. Lake and S. Pincus (eds), *The Politics of the Public Sphere in Early Modern England* (Manchester, 2007)

A. Lilti, *The Invention of Celebrity* (Cambridge, 2017)

A. Pettegree, *The Invention of News: How the World Came to Know about Itself* (New Haven, CN, 2014)

J. D. Popkin, *News and Politics in the Age of Revolution* (Ithaca, NY, 1989)

M. Rozpocher (ed.), *Beyond the Public Sphere: Opinions, Publics, Spaces in Early Modern Europe* (Bologna, 2010)

D. Zaret, *Origins of Democratic Culture: Printing, Petitions and the Public Sphere in Early Modern England* (Princeton, NJ, 2000)

Chapter 4 Technologies and Revolutions

A. Briggs, *From Ironbridge to Crystal Palace: Impact and Images of the Industrial Revolution* (London, 1979)

A. Briggs, *The Power of Steam* (London, 1982)

A. Fyfe, *Steam-Powered Knowledge* (Chicago, IL, 2012)

S. Giedion, *Mechanization Takes Command* (New York, 1948)

J. Hoppit and C. A. Wrigley (eds), *The Industrial Revolution in Britain* (Oxford, 1994)

T. P. Hughes, *Networks of Power: Electrification in Western Society, 1880–1930* (Baltimore, MD, 1983)

D. S. Landes, *The Unbound Prometheus* (Cambridge, 1969)

L. Mumford, *Technics and Civilization* (New York, 1934)

P. K. O'Brien (ed.), *The Industrial Revolution in Europe* (Oxford, 1994)

CHAPTER 5 NEW PROCESSES AND PATTERNS

A. Briggs, *The Birth of Broadcasting* (Oxford, 1961)

J. Brooks, *Telephone, the First Hundred Years* (New York, 1975)

B. Coe, *Camera from Daguerreotypes to Instant Pictures* (London, 1978)

M. J. Daunton, *Royal Mail, The Post Office since 1840* (London, 1985)

R. Gelatt, *The Fabulous Phonograph, 1877–1977*, rev. edn (New York, 1977)

R. R. John, *Spreading the News: The American Postal System from Franklin to Morse* (Cambridge, MA, 1995)

J. Kieve, *The Electric Telegraph: A Social and Economic History* (Newton Abbot, 1973)

P. O'Brien, *Railways and the Economic Development of Western Europe, 1830–1914* (London, 1983)

H. Perkin, *The Age of the Automobile* (London, 1976)

H. Powdermaker, *Hollywood, The Dream Factory* (Boston, MA, 1950)

E. Rhode, *A History of the Cinema from its Origins to 1970* (Harmondsworth, 1978)

T. Standage, *The Victorian Internet* (New York, 1998)

B. Winston, *Technologies of Seeing: Photography, Cinema and Television* (London, 1996)

CHAPTER 6 INFORMATION, EDUCATION, ENTERTAINMENT

T. W. Adorno, *The Culture Industry: Selected Essays on Mass Culture* (London, 1991)

R. C. Allen, *To Be Continued: Soap Opera Around the World* (New York, 1995)

D. Bell, *The Coming of Post-Industrial Society* (New York, 1976)

P. Bourdieu, *On Television* (English translation, New York, 1988)

L. Brake, A. Jones and L. Madden (eds), *Investigating Victorian Journalism* (Basingstoke, 1990)

A. Briggs, *The Golden Age of Wireless* (Oxford, 1995)

J. S. Brown and P. Duguid, *The Social Life of Information* (Boston, MA, 2000)

M. Castells, *The Information Age: Economics, Society and Culture*, 3 vols (Oxford, 1996, 1997, 1998).

D. Dayan and E. Katz, *Media Events: The Live Broadcasting of History* (Cambridge, MA, 1991)

R. Negrine and S. Papathanassopoulos, *The Internationalisation of Television* (New York, 1990)

D. Read, *The Power of News: The Story of Reuters* (Oxford, 1992)

M. Schudson, *The Power of News* (Cambridge, MA, 1995)
A. Smith (ed.), *Television, an International History* (Oxford, 1995)

CHAPTER 7 MEDIA CONVERGENCES

T. F. Baldwin, D. S. McVoy and C. Steinfeld, *Convergence: Integrating Media, Information and Communication* (Thousand Oaks, CA, 1996)
T. Berners-Lee, *Weaving the Web* (San Francisco, CA, 1999)
I. De Sola Pool, *Technologies Without Boundaries: On Telecommunications in a Global Age* (Cambridge, MA, 1990)
W. H. Dutton, *Society on the Line: Information Politics in the Digital Age* (Oxford, 1999)
K. Hafez, *The Myth of Media Globalization* (Cambridge, 2013)
K. Hafner and M. Lyon, *Where Wizards Stay Up Late: The Origins of the Internet* (New York, 1996)
S. Johnson, *Interface Culture: How New Technology Transforms the Way We Create and Communicate* (San Francisco, CA, 1999)
R. Negrine (ed.), *Cable Television and the Future of Broadcasting* (London, 1985)
E. M. Noam (ed.), *Technologies without Boundaries: On Telecommunication in a Global Age* (Cambridge, MA, 1990)

CHAPTER 8 THE RETURN OF THE SOCIAL

Y. Benkler, *The Wealth of Networks: How Social Production Transforms Markets and Freedom* (New Haven, CT, 2006)
A. Bruns, *Gatewatching and News Curation* (New York, 2018)
M. Bull, *Sounding Out the City: Personal Stereos and the Management of Everyday Life* (London, 2000)
M. D'Ancona, *Post-Truth* (London, 2017)
J. van Dijk, *The Culture of Connectivity: A Critical History of the Social Media* (Oxford, 2013)
B. E. Duffy, *(Not) Getting Paid to Do What you Love: Gender, Social Media, and Aspirational Work* (New Haven, CT, 2017)
A. Fagerjord, 'Reading-View(s)ing the Über-Box', in M. Eskelinen and R. Koskimaa (eds), *Cybertext Yearbook 2001* (Jyväskylä, 2002)
J. Juul, *A Casual Revolution: Reinventing Video Games and their Players* (MIT Press, 2010)
G. King, J. Pan and M. E. Roberts, 'How the Chinese Government Fabricates Social Media Posts for Strategic Distraction, Not Engaged Argument', *American Political Science Review* 111 (2017): 484–501
R. Ling and B. Yttri, 'Nobody Sits at Home and Waits for the Telephone to Ring: Micro and Hyper-Coordination through the Use of the Mobile Telephone,' in J. Katz and M. Aakhus (eds), *Perpetual Contact* (Cambridge, 2001)
S. Livingstone and L. Haddon, *EU Kids Online II: Final Report* (London, 2011)

A. Marwick and d. boyd, '"I Tweet Honestly, I Tweet Passionately": Twitter Users, Context Collapse, and Imagined Audience', *New Media & Society* 13 (2010): 114–133

E. Morozov, *The Net Delusion: How Not to Liberate the World* (London, 2011)

P. Napoli, 'Automated Media: An Institutional Theory Perspective on Algorithmic Media Consumption and Production,' *Communication Theory* 24 (2014): 340–360

J. W. Rettberg, *Seeing Ourselves Through Technology: How We Use Selfies, Blogs and Wearable Devices to See and Shape Ourselves* (Houndmills, 2014)

S. Turkle, *Alone Together: Why We Expect More from Technology and Less from Each Other* (New York, 2011)

S. Vaidhyanathan, *Anti-Social Media: How Facebook Disconnects Us and Undermines Democracy* (Oxford, 2018)

S. Wachter-Boettcher, *Technically Wrong: Sexist Apps, Biased Algorithms, and Other Threats of Toxic Tech* (New York, 2017)

S. P. Walz and S. Deterding (eds), *The Gameful World: Approaches, Issues, Applications* (Cambridge, MA, 2014)

Y. Zhao, *Communication in China: Political Economy, Power, and Conflict* (Lanham, MD, 2008)

Index